THE KINGS & QUEENS OF
ENGLAND

ABOUT THE AUTHOR

DAVID LOADES is Emeritus Professor of the University of Wales and an Honorary Member of the University of Oxford, History Faculty. He is also a Fellow of the Royal Historical Society, Fellow of the Society of Antiquaries and former President of the Ecclesiastical History Society. He is the author of over thirty books. He lives in Burford in Oxfordshire.

PRAISE FOR DAVID LOADES

Henry VIII
'The best place to send anyone seriously wanting to get to grips with alternative understandings of England's most mesmerising monarch… copious illustrations, imaginatively chosen'
BBC HISTORY MAGAZINE

'A triumph'
THE SPECTATOR

'David Loades Tudor biographies are both highly enjoyable and instructive, the perfect combination'
ANTONIA FRASER

The Six Wives of Henry VIII
'I warmly recommend this book'
ALISON WEIR

Mary Tudor: A Life
'An excellent and sensitive biography'
THE OBSERVER

Elizabeth I
'Succeeds in depicting her to us as a real woman'
LITERARY REVIEW

'Readable, searching and wise'
NEW STATESMAN

THE KINGS & QUEENS OF
ENGLAND
THE BIOGRAPHY

DAVID LOADES

AMBERLEY

First published 2013

This edition first published 2014

Amberley Publishing
The Hill, Stroud
Gloucestershire, GL5 4EP

www.amberleybooks.com

British Library Cataloguing in Publication Data.
A catalogue record for this book is available from the British Library.

ISBN 978 1 4456 3761 7 (paperback)
ISBN 978 1 4456 1972 9 (ebook)

Typeset in 10pt on 12pt Sabon.
Typesetting and Origination by Amberley Publishing.
Printed in the UK.

CONTENTS

Contents

INTRODUCTION

This is the story of a hereditary monarchy which has lasted for about twelve hundred years. It has survived depositions, usurpations and civil wars. For eleven years it actually ceased altogether, before returning in a modified form. It has evolved through several constitutional phases. Beginning as little more than war lords, kings have been the overlords of noble constituencies – divinely appointed rulers answerable only to God, and the heads of a gentry commonwealth. They have been responsible to Parliament, and more recently figureheads of a democratically constituted state, without power in any form which their predecessors would have recognised. Since the sixteenth century, six monarchs have been women, and have modified their style of rule to suit their gender. All these queens have led a state at war, but no woman could be a warrior, and that has affected their own perception of their roles profoundly. The last English king to lead an army into battle was George II at Dettingen in 1742, but earlier kings had expressed a marked aversion to physical violence, notably James I. It was in his reign that the war games which had been such a marked feature of the style of his predecessors Edward IV and Henry VIII finally came to an end. Tournaments had enabled Henry to project himself as a soldier without undergoing the hardships and dangers of actual campaigning. The shift of emphasis in that connection came during the second half of the sixteenth century, the reigns of Mary I and Elizabeth I. Mary showed no interest in war games – she left that aspect of monarchy to her husband, Philip – but Elizabeth exploited them in the female mode, presiding as the Queen of Faerie over the exploits of her knights. The Accession Day tilts were a celebration of the monarch's sex, but they bore little relation to real warfare, which had moved on from the hand-to-hand combats which Henry had vicariously enjoyed. By the seventeenth century a king was no longer expected to be a warrior, and a fundamental change had come about in the perception of royal authority.

Apart from the battlefield, another formative influence on the medieval and early modern monarchy was the Church. Irrespective of the personal piety (or morality) of individual kings, the ruler was expected to be a generous patron to ecclesiastical establishments, and he undertook in his coronation oath to uphold its privileges and authority. In return the Church supported the power of the Crown. Henry V, for instance, who had particular need of clerical endorsement in view of his father's disputed title, was a generous benefactor to religious houses. At the same time John and Richard II, who for different reasons fell out with the Church, had difficulty in maintaining themselves, and Richard was eventually deposed. Kings were the Lord's Anointed, and this conveyed a special relationship with God as well as the Church. Usually these obligations were compatible, but sometimes they were seen to be at odds. William I, for example, and Henry II, interpreted the Will of God rather differently from their clerical advisers. This could also cause problems, as Henry discovered to his cost. Eventually Henry VIII found himself locked in so serious a quarrel with Pope Clement VII that he broke with the Church altogether. The solution which he then found was to give himself the ecclesiastical franchise, in other words to create a national English Church. This enhanced rather than diminished his sense of direct dependence upon God, and enabled the mentors of his young son, Edward VI, to convert that Church to Protestantism. It was in this form, of a national Protestant establishment, that the English Church was settled during the long reign of Elizabeth I. Elizabeth, no less than her father, believed herself to be directly dependent upon God, but avoided the theory of the divine right of kings because her own title depended upon an Act of Parliament of 1544. It was left to James I, whose hereditary credentials were impeccable, to pick up that theory, and he was discreet enough not to emphasise it. His son, Charles I, ran headlong into the alternative theory of royal dependence on the law, and lost a civil war (and his head) in consequence. However, the alternative theory of direct popular responsibility to God quickly ran into fatal difficulties over the mode in which that dependence should be expressed, with the result that the monarchy was restored. Charles II and his successors never had the divine cachet claimed by Charles I, and when his brother and successor, James II, attempted to convert the realm to Roman Catholicism, the limitations of royal authority were ruthlessly exposed. After the Revolutionary settlement of 1689, the monarch was required to conform to the majority religion of the realm, that is Protestantism, and so it has remained ever since. No monarch since James has claimed to rule by divine right.

Instead the theory has prevailed that the King (or Queen) is bound by the laws of the land, and by the will of the realm as expressed through the legislative assembly – that is the parliament. The obligation to obey the law is of great antiquity, because the law was originally thought of as being of divine creation. It was only in the fifteenth century that Parliament was deemed to have a legislative voice, and the King, of course, was an essential element in Parliament. So the King was a party to the creation of that great body of enacted law which he was bound to observe, and that was a means of bringing the King's person and his office into line. A medieval king was bound to rule with the consent of the realm, which in practice meant the nobility, and a ruler who ignored that obligation, like Edward II, could also find himself in acute difficulties. Sometimes, like Edward IV, he used his nobles as prime agents of government. The Tudors, however, broadened the concept of consent to include the gentry as well as the nobility, and vested that consent in Parliament, which was the primary forum of gentry politics. It was a failure to heed the limitations imposed by Parliament which led Charles I into civil war. After 1660 the monarchy was confined to an executive role, both the legislative and the judicial having been taken over by the Parliament. Since then the executive function of the monarch has been progressively reduced. Since the late eighteenth century much of the function of the Privy Council, the monarch's principal agency of government, has been taken over by the cabinet. The cabinet now governs in the Queen's name, but is effectively dependent on the House of Commons, because since 1911 the House of Lords has played only an ancillary role in the functioning of Parliament. Since that date the House of Commons and its various agencies has been the governing institution of the state, although all its executive decisions are carried out in the Queen's name, and occasionally she has a discreet influence on their application.

It is also essentially an English story. In 1603 the Kingdom of England became linked to that of Scotland, and since 1707 they have been one state, called Great Britain. First the Lordship and then (from 1541) the Kingdom of Ireland also belonged to the English (and British) Crown until 1921, and the province of Ulster still does. Wales was joined to the Kingdom of England in 1284, and its government was unified with that of its neighbour in 1536. However, before 1284 Wales was never a single unit, and the Channel Islands, originally a dependency of the Duchy of Normandy, have never enjoyed a separate existence. So neither the Princes of Wales, nor the High Kings of Tara, nor the Kings of Scotland feature in this book. Each, and particularly the Scottish monarchy before 1603, would require a separate narrative. The Kingdom of Scotland evolved alongside that of England, although more slowly. Its nobility retained their importance longer, and its parliament never enjoyed the same power as its southern neighbour. From the thirteenth century to the sixteenth, English kings periodically claimed to be feudal overlords of the Kingdom of Scotland but that claim was always repudiated and never became effective. Latterly, it was used mainly for propaganda purposes. So the medieval and early modern kings and queens who appear here are the rulers of England, and King James VI only features when he appears as James I of the United Kingdom. Thereafter the monarchy should be understood as that of Great Britain, and neither Wales nor Ireland feature, because they were never ruled separately.

This is not a constitutional history, but essentially a narrative of the lives of men and women, because until comparatively recent times England was a personal monarchy. For about 800 years kings were war leaders, chief executives, and representatives of God on earth. Although circumscribed to some extent by the Church, by the law, and by the consent of the aristocracy, they ruled as well as reigned. Their personal predilections were therefore of great importance. Were they pious, and what form did their piety take? Did they rule through favourites, and if so how good was their judgement of such men? If a ruler followed his own will, and ignored the advice of his council, he was exposing himself to rebellion. If he decided to 'busy giddy minds with foreign wars', a lot depended upon the soundness of his information, and judgement, in respect of his potential opponent. His sexuality was similarly important. If he was (God forbid!) a homosexual, did this mean that his marriage was a sham, that he would remain childless, and the succession would be imperilled? In a hereditary monarchy which followed, roughly, the rules of primogeniture, it was crucial that a king should have a son, or sons, to follow him. His own sexual potency, and the fecundity of his consort, were therefore matters of acute public concern. This was particularly the case with Henry VIII, who struggled through more than twenty years to beget a legitimate son, and disposed of three wives in the process. On the other hand, a king like Edward III, who left a number of sons, could also confuse the succession, as was witnessed by the Wars of the Roses. The lives and deaths of individual princes could also be of great significance. Suppose Henry I's eldest son and designated successor, William, had not been drowned in the *White Ship* in 1120; Matilda would not have challenged for the throne and the disturbed reign of King Stephen would never have happened. If Prince Edward, Richard III's son, had not predeceased him in 1484, would Henry VII's victory at

Bosworth have been decisive? If Henry Stuart, Prince of Wales, had not died in 1612, would England have been spared a civil war and the temporary demise of the monarchy?

The sexuality of a ruling queen was, if anything, even more important, because the institution of monarchy was set up for men, and the identity of her husband would also identify the next king. There was no Salic Law in England, and a woman was perfectly entitled to inherit the throne, hence Henry VIII's concern with a legitimate son, but the nature of a woman's authority to rule was highly questionable, because her physical and mental inferiority were taken for granted. It was assumed that she would marry, if only to secure the succession, and the nature of her relationship with her husband was therefore a political issue. Should he take precedence over her? Would he inherit the kingdom if she should predecease him? These issues were tested during the reign of England's first ruling queen, Mary I, between 1553 and 1558, and resolved, significantly, by Parliament. It was enacted that the Queen's authority was equal to that of a king, and the limitations imposed on Philip by his marriage treaty were similarly enshrined in an Act of Parliament. Mary died childless, and Philip's role was aborted, but Elizabeth, who succeeded, faced the same problems. For more than twenty years she struggled with the question of marriage, eventually eschewing the idea, at great personal cost. Sexuality meant more to Elizabeth than marriage, however. Throughout her reign she use it as a weapon with which to manipulate the men with whom she had to deal, prevaricating and changing her mind in a way which no man could have done, because she needed to remain in control. It was a unique performance because by the time the next ruling queen came to the throne in 1689 the circumstances had changed. Mary reigned jointly with her husband, William III, playing little part in the government, and her sexuality was not a factor. The same was true of her sister Anne, who succeeded William in 1702. Her husband, Prince George of Denmark, was not even accorded the courtesy title of King, and the politics of her reign were run by her ministers. The monarchy had changed in the hundred years since Elizabeth's death, and Anne no longer ruled. The next sovereign queen, Victoria, was more a symbol than a ruler, and her sexuality was a private matter, except that she bore children who married into most of the royal families of Europe, earning her the title of the grandmother of kings. Elizabeth II is best known as an exemplar of married probity, and in spite of the waywardness of her children, her own sexuality has never been an issue, even in these days of intrusive media attention. It does not now matter whether the monarch is male or female, because the function is the same, but that was not always the case, and this needs to be borne in mind when assessing the personal factors in the reigns of the first two female sovereigns. Over the last three hundred years the sexuality of male monarchs, which is no longer of much political significance, has continued to fascinate the British public. George I with his fat German mistresses; George IV with his morganatic marriage and the scandal of Queen Caroline; and more recently Edward VIII and Wallis Simpson. In the absence of any scandal attaching to the present Queen, attention had shifted to the Prince of Wales, and Princess Diana became a media star of the first magnitude, especially in the circumstances of her death.

This is history from the top down, but it is not primarily a political or institutional narrative. The lives of kings and queens are important in their own right, originally because they bore the principal responsibility for government, and latterly because of their symbolic significance. George IV symbolised much that was wrong with the aristocratic society of his day; Victoria symbolised the Empire over which she presided; and the present Queen represents stability in a rapidly changing world. History is also largely determined by the nature of the surviving sources. Letters, both personal and official, are rare before the sixteenth century, and for the history of the medieval kings we are heavily dependent upon annals and chronicles, many of which were written by churchmen for their own purposes. This inevitably gives an ecclesiastical slant to what we know, which is not always helpful. Other documents available from the Middle Ages, such as the records of Chancery or the Exchequer, contain little that is relevant in this context, although valuable in other ways. Since the sixteenth century, however, diplomatic reports and business correspondence become increasingly common, until by the eighteenth century the sheer quantity of material is a problem in itself. The different agendas of the politicians and civil servants who wrote most of these letters also complicates the story, and often makes it difficult to discern the human beings inside the shell of political and social attitudes. The biographical approach to history is controversial, but it is legitimate and offers no short cuts. The biographical studies which follow are not either political or social history, but the story of a unique set of individuals whose special circumstances set them apart from the state which they aspired to rule, and from the society which made up that state.

From Warlords to Christian Princes, 500–927

The early history of the Saxon settlement has been rewritten in recent years. In place of the Germanic war-bands driving out the

British inhabitants, and gradually forcing them into the far west, we now have a more nuanced picture of intermarriage and social integration, resulting in composite political units, part Saxon and part British in nature and in culture. Without denying the existence of determined British resistance in some places, we now have a more peaceful perception of the process. However, the nature of those political units remains largely obscure. They were called kingdoms by chroniclers writing in the seventh century and later, but that was using a terminology with which they were familiar, and it is by no means certain that they would have so identified themselves in the sixth century. We do not know whether the leaders of the original warriors thought of themselves as kings or not. Probably some did, because a king was by definition a kinsman of the gods, and they brought their bogus genealogies with them. Equally the title may have been of Romano-British origin, a king being any ruler who recognised no superior authority, and the Imperial allegiance having disappeared with the withdrawal of the legions. The early kingdoms were small and flexible, and might equally have been termed *Provinciae*. They may have been defined by the settlement area of a particular tribe or extended family, or by the remnants of late Roman jurisdictional units. Contemporary evidence is almost entirely lacking, and what we have from later consists largely of the Lives of Christian saints who were supposed to have established bishoprics in the various kingdoms. The Latin terminology refers to *principes*, *reguli* and *subreguli*, which suggests that, in the early days at least, these jurisdictions were variously conceived, and may well have merged and divided in accordance with the inheritance pattern of the ruling families, which was what happened later to the great landed estates. It was natural in this indeterminate situation that some units should have emerged as stronger and more aggressive than others, and by the early seventh century these units were being generally described as kingdoms. Their kings were claiming the support and sanction of the Church, and beginning to assert a divine authority for their actions. It is not known what laws they enforced, but in most places it was probably a mixture of customary Germanic and Roman Law, which would have been reduced in status to the custom of the British population. Written codes from the period (if they ever existed) do not survive, the earliest being that of Eadric of Kent, dating from about 680. The first recorded king to have expanded his territories by military conquest was Penda of Mercia, who came to power in about 610. He was not styled King for about twenty years, so the nature of his original authority is not clear, but at the height of his power in the 630s his rule extended from the Humber to the Thames and from the Welsh marches to the Wash. Although his reign coincided with the rapid expansion of Christianity, Penda remained resolutely pagan, and consequently got a bad press from ecclesiastical chroniclers such as Bede.

In the seventh century almost every reign in the recorded kingdoms was marked by fratricidal bloodshed as kinsmen strove for the supremacy. This was partly the result of not sharing any clearly defined law of succession. The ancient custom which had prevailed among the Germanic tribes had been a species of election, whereby the successful candidate had been raised on the shields of his warriors. Any member of the royal kindred was eligible, and the theory was that the most suitable would be chosen. This ill-defined system of selection survived the period of settlement, and was modified only to the extent that the King's warriors were now defined as his thegns, that is to say those who held land directly of him in return for their military service. The result, inevitably, was disputed elections, disgruntled splinter groups and rebellions. It was very common for siblings to be killed or exiled in the course of this strife, and every court played host to one or more of these exiles. A typical example would be Oswiu of Bernicia, who sought refuge in one of the courts of southern Scotland when his brother Oswald succeeded in 634. Returning on Oswald's death in 642, he endeavoured to hold together the tenuous union of Bernicia and Deira, which Oswald had created, by marrying Eanflaed, the daughter of a previous Deiran king, Edwin. He then tried the experiment of appointing his wife's kinsman, Oswine, as Subregulus of Deira, but Oswine attempted to re-establish Deiran independence, and had to be dealt with by assassination in 651. He then put in his own nephew Athelwold, but Athelwold rebelled in alliance with Penda of Mercia in 655. The rebels were defeated and he was killed, which put an end to Deiran ambitions for the time being. Oswiu lived until 670, when he was succeeded (peacefully) by his son Ecgfrith. Such a mixture of battle, marriage and murder was typical of the expansion of Mercia at the expense of the Hwicce and East Angles, of Kent at the expense of the South Saxons, or of Wessex at the expense of the Dumnonians, the British kings who controlled Devon in the early seventh century. At the height of its power, under King Offa in the late eighth century, Mercia seems to have exercised overlordship over a number of minor units, which were sometimes called kingdoms and sometimes not. The Hwicce, for example, appear to have recognised Mercian lordship from the days of King Penda, but it is not until the late eighth century that we find their ruler, one Athelmund, being described as 'ealdorman' rather than as king. At the time of the Tribal Hidage, in the early tenth century, the heart of the Hwicce territory was known as Winchcombeshire, but by 1017 Winchcombeshire had been absorbed into Gloucestershire, and the former kingdom of the Hwicce was divided into the shires of Gloucester, Worcester, Oxford and Warwick. The tribal territory of the Stoppingas seems to have suffered a similar fate. Originally a kingdom, by the late eighth century it was known as a *regio*, and the only trace of its former status was the existence of a large Minster church at Wootton Warren, whose jurisdiction would originally have corresponded with that of the kingdom. Partible inheritance broke down the large estates which had originally existed, and enabled the kings to assert rights of taxation over these lesser units, which might have been resisted by greater lords. The Tribal Hidage is a taxation return, and an assertion of fiscal rights over subordinate units, which are not acknowledged as kingdoms.

In addition to providing moral and intellectual support to rulers, the Church also served in a number of practical ways. Many kings sought to atone for the sins committed in their rise to power by founding monasteries, and a number retired to foundations of their own making when age had removed their potency as warriors. Not a few went further and undertook the long and hazardous pilgrimage to Jerusalem. Having a kingdom divided into bishoprics was a symbol of power, and it was a sign of special influence when Offa succeeded in persuading Pope Adrian I to elevate his see of Lichfield into an archbishopric in 787, although the experiment only lasted as long as the incumbent bishop. Monasteries, or rather nunneries, often founded by royal ladies, also provided a safe refuge for those same ladies when they were widowed, either by the course of nature or by the endemic bloodshed which afflicted their families. Ironically, several of Penda's daughters became nuns. As we have seen in the case of Wootton Warren, Minster churches sometimes marked the boundaries of obsolete political units, and almost invariably served great estates. As these estates broke down, between the eighth century and the tenth, so the Minster jurisdictions broke down into parishes, as each of the successor lords wanted a church to serve his own lands. An excellent example of this is provided by the former *regio* of the Rodings in Essex, which produced no fewer than nine parishes, each of which still exists and bears the Roding name. The church also had disputes of its own, which sometimes impinged upon the political scene. The early impact of Christianity in the North came from Iona, via Lindisfarne, and followed the practices of the Celtic fathers. This led to rivalry with the practitioners of the Roman rite who were coming from the South, and disagreements over the date of Easter and the role of bishops. The latter had a firmly established jurisdictional function in the Roman Church, while the Celtic bishop was simply a superior rank of priest. This clearly had political implications, and it was therefore important that when King Oswy of Northumbria convened the Synod of Whitby in 663 he opted for the Roman rite. The succession to the Deiran see of York begins notionally with Paulinus in 626, but substantively with Wilfrid in 669, at which point a separate see was established for Bernicia at Hexham, dovetailing the political and ecclesiastical units in the Roman fashion. The influence of the Celtic Church remained strong, particularly in the Scottish kingdoms of Strathclyde and Dalriada, but the future in England belonged to the bishops of the Roman rite.

Throughout the seventh and eighth centuries, the struggle for supremacy among these kingdoms continued. Kent and East Anglia both enjoyed their Bretwaldeship (as Bede termed it) for short spells, but the leading contenders were Northumbria and Mercia, each of which held the superiority for several years.

Exactly what being a Bretwalde involved is not very clear, but it seems to have been some loosely conceived overlordship, which was acknowledged by other tribal kings. The West Saxons were not really contenders at this early stage, because in spite of its expansion into Dumnonia, Wessex seems to have been a federation of lesser kingdoms down to the time of Ine, who acceded in 688 and pulled the whole of the South West together into one unit. Cwichelm, who was a sub-king of the West Saxons, attempted to assassinate Edwin of Northumbria in 625. When Edwin took his revenge in the following year, he apparently killed no fewer than five similar sub-kings of Wessex in one battle, which may have helped to consolidate the regime of the over-king, who at that time was Cynegils. Cynegils was a pagan, who accepted baptism when his daughter married Edwin's successor Oswald in about 634. As a direct result the see of Dorchester-on-Thames was founded in the same year, and transferred to Winchester in 660. During the eighth century sporadic warfare between Wessex and Mercia resulted mainly in Mercian victories, as when Ethebald overran Berkshire or when Offa defeated Cynewulf at Bensington near Reading in 779. Offa even succeeded in imposing a puppet king, Beorhtric on the West Saxons in 786. However, the days of Mercian supremacy were numbered, and when Egbert returned from exile to take the Crown on Beorhtric's death in 802, he reasserted their independence and defeated Offa's successor, Beornwulf, at Wroughton near Swindon in 825. He also pushed the Britons of Dumnonia back into what later became Cornwall, and by the time of his death in 839 had made Wessex the dominant power in southern England.

It was thus Wessex which had to bear the main part in defending England against the Danes, whose incursions began on the North Kent coast in 835. Kent had by this time been annexed by the

West Saxons, and so it was Egbert who bore the brunt of the early attacks, both winning and losing battles in 836 and 838. These invasions were to redraw the political map of England between 865 and 878, as the kingdoms of East Anglia, Mercia and Northumbria were successively destroyed. The Church suffered severely at the hands of these pagan warriors, and the flowering of Christian culture associated particularly with the monasteries of Northumbria was brought to a bloodstained end. Having captured London and Reading, the Danes were briefly checked by Egbert's son Ethelred in a battle at Ridgeway in Berkshire, but Ethelred died young in 871, and his younger brother Alfred became king. While he was still attending his brother's obsequies, news arrived that the Danes in Reading had been reinforced by a great new army under Guthrum. Although delayed by a revolt in Northumbria, Guthrum's intention was clearly the subjugation of Wessex, and at the end of 877 he attacked by land and sea, assaulting Wareham and Exeter, and at the same time invading from West Mercia, taking Alfred unawares at Chippenham early in 878. The latter took refuge in the Somerset marshes, and it was there that the famous story of burning the cakes is alleged to have taken place. The Danes now looked set to overrun the whole of Wessex, but Alfred surprised them at Edington, some 12 miles from Chippenham, in June and won a resounding victory. This, and the victorious campaign which followed it, forced Guthrum out of Wessex, and resulted in him and his leading chieftains accepting Christian baptism, which effectively ended their activities as scourges of the Church. As a result of this settlement, by 880 there were only two powers left in England, Wessex and the Danelaw, although Mercia survived as a subject kingdom until 919. On Alfred's death in 899 the frontier between Wessex and the Danelaw was (roughly speaking) the line of Watling Street, with the latter being divided between kingdoms based in York and East Anglia. However, Alfred's son, Edward the Elder, had no intention of allowing this situation to continue, and attacked the Danish settlements in the East Midlands, which led to war with the Kingdom of York. When the men of York retaliated, they were routed at Tettenhall in Staffordshire in 909. This virtually incapacitated the Northern kingdom, and enabled Edward to assault the Southern state, with considerable success. By the time that Edward died in 924, his writ ran directly over the whole of England except the Kingdom of York, and the Mercians, who had been his allies as long as Queen Etheflaed was alive, were now subject to his direct rule. In January 926 his successor, Athelstan, reached an agreement with Sigtrygg, King of York, which was sealed by his marriage to one of Athelstan's sisters, but when Sigtrygg died in the following year, Athelstan drove out his brother and successor and seized control of the kingdom. This show of power led to the submission of Constantine II of Scotland, and that was followed later in 927 by the allegiance of the Welsh kings led by Hywel Dda, the King of Deheubarth, and in 928 of the West Welsh of Cornwall. Consequently by 928 the sovereignty of King Athelstan was recognised throughout the land from Glasgow to Exeter and from Anglesea to Norfolk. The dependence of Scotland and Wales did not last, but the Kingdom of England was now a single unit, owing allegiance to a single king.

PART 1
A UNITED KINGDOM,
927–959

I

ATHELSTAN (REIGNED 925–939)

Athelstan was born in about 895, the eldest of the fourteen children born to Edward the Elder by Egwina, who is thought to have been his first wife. There is some doubt about his legitimacy, as Egwina is not known to have been married to Edward at that time, but he is alleged to have been Alfred's favourite grandchild. He was largely brought up in Mercia by his aunt Ethelflaed, 'the Lady of the Mercians', who ran what was by then a sub-kingdom on Edward's behalf. So well was he thought of in Mercia that when Edward died in July 924 he was immediately proclaimed king. This could have caused a problem, because the Witan, or Council, of Wessex took some time to deliberate on his suitability before accepting him. His coronation took place at Kingston-on-Thames on 5 September 925, when he was proclaimed as 'King of the English, raised to the throne … by the hand of Almighty God', without any acknowledgement of the process of selection which he had clearly undergone. However, he was not yet King of England. That came only after his abortive agreement with Sigtrygg, King of York, in 926, because when Sigtrygg died in 927 his subjects elected his son Olaf to succeed him, which did not accord with Athelstan's plans at all. The result was a successful invasion of Northumbria in 927 which led not only to the seizure of York, but to the submission of the kings of Scotland and Strathclyde, and of the hitherto independent enclave of Bamburgh. This situation was consolidated ten years later by his victory at Brunanburh over a combined army of Danes and Scots, who were clearly having second thoughts about accepting Athelstan as King of England.

This invasion in 937, although it swept in disgruntled elements from Northumbria, consisted mainly of Scots from Strathclyde and Danes from the Viking settlement of Dublin and was not primarily a rebellion. By that time also he had thrown the Dumnonians back across the Bristol Channel, and accepted the homage of the Princes of Wales.

At home he was a notable administrator, consolidating the organisation of Wessex into shires, each of which was run by a shire reeve of the King's choosing. His ealdormen were more in the nature of regional magnates, and were responsible for the oversight of the shires only in a very general sense. He was also a lawmaker, at a time when the supplementation of existing law was in the hands of the King alone. He appears to have issued a number of codes, but the Anglo-Saxon Chronicle, which has so much to say about the Battle of Brunanburh, is largely silent on this subject. The evidence comes primarily from the large number of charters which he issued. He also continued his father's system of defending his realm by means of fortified burghs or small towns, as Edward had done at Hertford in 912 and Buckingham in 914. These burghs were intended to control access by river, which had been a favourite practice of the Viking raiders of previous generations, and also consolidated the King's hold over possibly dissident populations. The Burghal Hidage, which also dates from Edward's reign, describes the basis upon which these towns were maintained and manned. The additional security which they offered also meant that by Athelstan's reign they were becoming important trading centres, and adding to the King's wealth by way of taxation.

Athelstan never married, and died in 939 at the age of about forty-four, but the marriages which he arranged for his sisters made him a significant player in the European league of princes.

One married Otto, a German prince who subsequently became Holy Roman Emperor, while a second married Charles the Simple, the King of the Franks. Others were wed to Boleslav II of Bohemia and Louis of Aquitaine, making Athelstan the uncle of half the princely houses of France and the Empire. He died at Gloucester on 27 October 939, and was buried at Malmesbury Abbey, of which he had been a generous benefactor. He was succeeded by his younger brother Edmund I.

2

EDMUND I (REIGNED 939–946)

Edmund was Athelstan's half-brother, his mother having been Edward's third wife Eadgifu. He was also no more than eighteen at the time of his accession, having been born in about 921. He was crowned at Kingston-on-Thames on 16 November 939, the Witan apparently having accepted him at once. Although he had fought alongside his brother at Brunanburh, he had been no more than a youth, and lacked at first Athelstan's formidable reputation as a warrior. This led to an immediate challenge from Olaf Guthfrithson, who had been dispossessed of York, and had subsequently taken refuge in the Viking settlement of Dublin. At the head of a formidable army, Olaf invaded, and swept into the Midlands, aiming for Leicester in the summer of 940. He may have been taken by surprise by this sudden show of force, but Edmund was in no position to fight, and was forced to sue for peace. The price was high, because he conceded to Olaf a large tract of Northumbria, running as far south as Watling Street, and including the Five Boroughs. However, the loss was only temporary, and Edmund soon proved himself to be a warrior in the best family tradition. In 942 he defeated both Olaf's brother Raegnald and his cousin Olaf Sihtricson, and recovered the Five Boroughs. In 944 he marched into Northumbria and took York, regaining the rest of the province in the following year. Not satisfied with this, later in 945 he invaded and overran the Kingdom of Strathclyde, which marched with Northumbria on its western side, and handed it over to his ally, Malcolm I of Scotland. Ironically he was killed in 946 during the arrest of an outlaw.

In May of that year he went with his entourage to Pucklechurch in Gloucestershire to apprehend one Liofa, who was clearly an offender of some significance. In the skirmish which followed, Edmund, who was clearly not wearing any body armour, was stabbed and died on 6 May of his wound at the age of twenty-five. In spite of his youth, he had married twice, and his first wife Elgiva had presented him with two sons, Edwy and Edgar, before succumbing to puerperal fever. Because they were both infants at the time of their father's death, the Witan passed them over for the succession, giving the crown to his younger brother Eadred. Edmund is remembered as having been able and energetic, and but for his early death might have featured among the more remarkable Saxon kings. He was buried at nearby Glastonbury Abbey.

3

EADRED (REIGNED 946–955)

Aged about twenty-three at the time of his accession, he was the second son of Eadgifu and Edward the Elder. He was crowned at Kingston-on-Thames on 16 August 946, and stepped straight into the military situation which Edmund had bequeathed. In the

North he was challenged by Olaf Sihtricson, who seems to have been re-established at York, probably as sub-king with Edmund's permission. However, the situation was complicated by the fact that there were divisions within York, and in 949 Olaf was expelled by the party led by Archbishop Wulfstan, who promptly took the precaution of submitting to Eadred. However, within a year they had had second thoughts, and renounced their allegiance, accepting Eric Bloodaxe (a man whose name speaks eloquently of his reputation) as their king. Eadred responded with a punitive raid, but his forces were severely mauled by Eric at Castleford, and it was only when he threatened to return in full force that the City of York thought better of its defiance, and expelled Eric and his followers. This probably took place in 952, and Eric survived as a 'loose cannon' until 954 when he was ambushed and killed on Stainmore. The agent responsible for his death was Osulf, the Lord of Bamborough, who was an ally of Eadred, and was later chosen by the King as the first Earl of Northumbria. The expulsion of Eric marked the end of the pretensions of York to independent status. The 'kingdom' disappeared and the region was subsequently run directly by agents of the King of England.

Eadred was an able, even an energetic king, but he suffered from a debilitating illness which affected his digestive system. He was unable to swallow his food in the normal fashion and was consequently constrained to live mainly on liquids, a situation which his couriers found both puzzling and distasteful. Perhaps as a result of this illness he never married, and when he died on 23 November 955, his heir was his nephew Eadwig. He died at Frome in Somerset, and was interred at Winchester. Eadred was a man of exemplary piety, and a generous benefactor of religious foundations in the manner of his family. In his will he left £1,600 in silver 'for the redemption of his soul and the good of his people', particularly mentioning the need for succour if there should be another heathen invasion. How this might have worked is not apparent, and fortunately it was to be another twenty-five years before the pagan Danes struck again, by which time the provisions of Eadred's will had been long since forgotten.

4

EADWIG (REIGNED 955–959)

Eadwig was the son of Edmund I by his first wife Elfgifu, and can have been no more than about sixteen when he succeeded to the throne. This suggests that the hereditary principle was gaining ground over election by the Witan, as Eadwig seems to have had little to commend him as king. His relations with St Dunstan, Bishop of London and subsequently Archbishop of Canterbury, were poor, and it may be relevant that Dunstan's biography is one of our principal sources of knowledge about him. He was crowned at Kingston in January 956, and is alleged to absented himself from the coronation feast in order to go to bed with Elgifu, who was subsequently to be his wife, being discovered by Dunstan *in flagrante delicto* and returned to his place of duty. It was probably fortunate that there was no immediate military challenge to be confronted, and the politics of his short reign are confused. This is partly because 956 saw the issue of an unprecedented number of charters, suggesting that the King was buying support, and partly because of the ambiguous role played by Eadwig's younger brother Edgar. In 957, and again at the age of about sixteen, Edgar became King of the Mercians, and it is not quite clear whether this was in defiance of Eadwig or with his connivance. Dunstan's biographer makes it appear as a coup, claiming that Eadwig had been 'wholly deserted by the northern people' on account of his foolishness. However, a more sympathetic source says that the King 'dispersed his kingdom' by creating sub-kings, and that this did not impair the theoretical unity of the realm. Edgar issued charters as King of the Mercians in 958, but Eadwig continued to describe himself as King of the English, so it is quite possible that the division was by mutual consent. It may even have been Eadwig's way of recognising Edgar as his successor, because his marriage to Elgifu was dissolved in 958 on the grounds of consanguinity, and without having produced (as far as we know) any offspring. Elgifu died in September 959, and was followed to the grave just a few weeks later by her ex-husband, who died on 1 October. The circumstances of his death are unknown, but Edgar, having already been accepted by the Mercians and the Northumbrians, was duly endorsed by the Witan of Wessex, but the circumstances and the date of his coronation are alike unknown. It was presumably sometime early in 960.

PART 2
THE ENGLISH KINGS,
959–1016

5

EDGAR I (REIGNED 959-975)

The second son of Edmund I, Edgar succeeded his brother Eadwig in slightly mysterious circumstances, receiving full recognition after his brother's death in October 959. Nevertheless, his accession was peaceful, and he faced no military emergency for the duration of his reign. For this reason he is known as 'the peaceable', but it is important to realise that this immunity was based on strength, and particularly on naval strength which effectively deterred any possible incursions either from Scandinavia or across the Irish Sea. He was no more than sixteen at the time of his accession, but this obviously created no problem for his backers, who included Dunstan, at that time Bishop of London. The transition of power was smooth, which indicates that his relations with the Witan, and with other of Eadwig's advisers was good. Within a year Dunstan had been translated to Canterbury, and the King seems to have backed his reform programme enthusiastically, which earned him the golden opinion of Dunstan's biographer, who provides the principal source for our knowledge of his reign. His patronage of other Benedictine reformers was similarly well received, and both Ethelwold and Oswald benefited from his generosity.

The most outstanding and puzzling event of his reign is his second consecration, which took place at Bath on 11 May 973, when he and his queen Elfrida were anointed and crowned. Perhaps the original ceremony, which is not recorded, was felt to be in some way defective, or perhaps this was an event with a different significance. It may be that Edgar had not originally been anointed, and that this coronation was intended to cement his alliance with the church, giving a divine sanction to his rule, which had not been true of his predecessors. It has been described as an 'imperial' ceremony, intended to indicate his lordship over the other rulers of the British Isles, and that may have been the case. It was immediately followed by a meeting with the Kings of Scotland and Wales at Chester, where they rowed him on the Dee in what was clearly intended to be a gesture of submission. However, those taking part in it may not have seen it in that light, because Kenneth II of Scotland, who was one of the rowers, clearly saw himself as an ally of Edgar rather than as a subordinate. What may have been intended by the participants as an indication of solidarity was transformed by Edgar's ecclesiastical propaganda network into something altogether more significant.

Like his predecessors. Edgar issued law codes; three, or possibly four, are attributed to him, the last of which orders all ealdormen to copy and circulate it 'that it may be known both to the poor and to the rich', an unusual but significant provision. By this time the Wessex system of dividing the land into administrative districts called shires had also been spread to Northumbria and Mercia, and the original connection between ealdormen and shires had been broken. The latter were now under the control of shire reeves, who were directly appointed by the King, and each ealdorman had general oversight of several such units. At the same time shires were divided into areas known as hundreds for administrative and judicial purposes, except in the territories of the old Danelaw, where the Wapentake replaced the hundred. Hundreds and Wapentakes were also divided into tithings, so the impact of royal government was transmitted to the grass-roots level, the same concern as is reflected in the proviso attached to Edgar's law code.

Like most of his kindred, Edgar did not make old bones. He died on 8 July 975 at the age of thirty-two. In the course of his sixteen-year reign he had married three times, and was succeeded by Edward, his eldest son by his first marriage to Ethelflaed, who was about thirteen, having been born in 962. Again the hereditary principle seems to have taken precedence, and there is no reference to any deliberations by the Witan. Edgar was buried at Glastonbury Abbey, which had by this time acquired a reputation for especial holiness, and had been one of the numerous beneficiaries of his generosity.

6

EDWARD THE MARTYR
(REIGNED 975–978)

Edward's was one of the shortest of the pre-Conquest reigns, and is remarkable for nothing except the young king's capacity for making enemies. He was crowned at Kingston, probably in August 975 at the age of about thirteen, and seems to have suffered from all the problems which we now associate with that age, being both short-tempered and opinionated. He was assassinated on his way to Corfe Castle in Dorset on 18 March 978, where he was going to meet his younger half-brother Ethelred and his stepmother Elfrida. The context was one of tension, because although Edward was supported by Dunstan and by Ethelwine, the ealdorman of East Anglia, he was opposed by Bishop Ethelwold of Winchester and by Elfhere, the ealdorman of Mercia. Both sides were arming, and a civil war seemed likely, the issue being between Edward and Ethelred, who at that time was no more than twelve years old. The decision to dispose of Edward by murder rather than by war was apparently Elfrida's, and his body was buried secretly at Wareham. This created problems for the mentors of his successor Ethelred, because in the absence of a body Edward's death could not be proved. It was no doubt this consideration which led to the 'discovery' of the corpse in February 979, when it was decently transferred to Shaftesbury Abbey.

Edward's reputation for sanctity seems to have depended partly on his good relations with St Dunstan, whose reform programme he supported, and partly on the circumstances of his death. Although styled 'the Martyr', he was never so recognised by the Church.

7

ETHELRED 'THE UNREADY' (REIGNED 978–1016)

Following the somewhat messy circumstances of his accession, the boy Ethelred was crowned at Kingston on 14 April 979. Archbishop Dunstan, who performed the ceremony, and the remainder of the Witan who had supported Edward, had become reconciled to the inevitable. Since he was so young, his earliest days were dominated by those who had advised his father, King Edgar, notably the Bishop of Winchester and the ealdorman of Mercia, who had led his party against Edward. However, Elfhere died in 983 and Ethelwold in 984, and at about the same time Elfrida retired into a nunnery, leaving the King, now seventeen, in sole charge of the realm. The next ten years seem to have been dominated by faction, as ambitious magnates took advantage of his inexperience to further their own causes. These disputes left little trace in the records, but we know that Elfric, who had succeeded Elfhere as ealdorman of Mercia was exiled for some unspecified treason in 985, and in 986 the King 'laid waste the diocese of Rochester' as a result of a dispute between the Bishop and one of the King's men. In 993 Ethelred issued a charter in which he expressed repentance for these disorders, and particularly the plunder of various churches which had resulted, the purpose of the charter being to make amends for this sacrilege.

At the same time, the Viking fleets returned. Southampton was sacked in 980, and the coasts of Kent and Cheshire attacked. In 981 the church at Padstow was burned down and the coasts of Devon and Cornwall harried. In 982 it was the turn of Portland in Dorset, and in 988 of Watchet (Somerset). It seems likely that these raids were launched from Viking colonies in Ireland or the Isle of Man rather than Scandinavia and, being swift and relatively small-scale, were exceedingly difficult to defend against. Then in 991 a more serious threat appeared. According to the Anglo-Saxon Chronicle,

> Olaf [Tryggvason] came with 93 ships to Folkestone, and ravaged round about it, and then from there he went to Sandwich, and so from there to Ipswich, and overran it all, and so to Maldon. And Ealdorman Byrhtnoth came against him there with his army and fought against him; and they killed the ealdorman there and had control of the field.

The important thing about this attack was that it was launched directly from Norway, and led by the warlords who were competing for authority in their homeland. They were intent on securing substantial plunder which would give them the ascendancy, and England, which had been relatively peaceful for several years, offered the rich pickings necessary for that result. Olaf's fleet returned year after year: to East Anglia in 992, to Northumbria in 993, and in 994 to the South East coast from London to Southampton, where they camped for the winter. Unable to resist such incursions effectively (witness the defeat at Maldon), Ethelred sued for peace, and bought off Olaf with a Danegeld of £16,000. This was controversial at the time, and earned Ethelred his title of 'the ill counselled'. In return for this substantial payment Olaf accepted Christian baptism, and took himself back to Norway. The respite was brief, because another fleet under other leaders returned in 997 and 999. In the latter year it took itself off to Normandy, but it returned in 1001 and 1002, in which year another Danegeld was raised, this time of £24,000. This time there was a military response as well, but it did not extend further than a raid on the Norse colonies in Cumbria, plus a naval attack on the Isle of Man. No serious attempt was made to counter-attack against the source of these fleets, and such an effort would probably have been beyond Ethelred's resources. It was cheaper to pay the tribute. Marriage was also an option and in 1002 the King married (as his second wife) Emma, the daughter of Duke Richard II of Normandy, in an attempt to detach Richard, who was also a Northman, from his support for the Viking fleets. It did not work, and in November of the same year Ethelred plotted to massacre all the Danish merchants and mercenaries remaining in England in a demonstration of 'frightfulness'. That did not work either, and fatally poisoned relations with the Scandinavian kingdoms.

Partly in revenge, and partly just to seize an opportunity, Svein Forkbeard, King of Denmark, led the next raid in 1003. For the next four years Svein's campaigns wrought havoc in southern and eastern England, until he was bought off at the enormous cost of £36,000 in 1007. Ethelred then belatedly sought to reconstruct the English navy, working on the principle that such incursions were better prevented than remedied, and ordered all 300 hides to build a warship, or to pay for the building of such if they were distant from the coast. This appears to have been effective, because a great fleet was assembled at Sandwich in 1009. However, there was no immediate employment for such a navy, and it was dispersed, not without suspicions of dissension among the English commanders. No sooner had it broken up than 'Thorkell's army' arrived and began their own campaign of raiding and plunder. Perhaps this was one of the errors of judgement of which the King was later accused. Thorkell remained in England in various locations until 1012, sacking Canterbury and murdering its Archbishop in the process. He was eventually paid the even larger sum of £48,000 to go away, which he did, but only to the extent of entering Ethelred's service. This move had the effect of provoking King Svein, who was hostile to Thorkell, to renew his own attacks. His great fleet arrived off Sandwich in 1013, and proceeded up the east coast. Given the option on this occasion, the people of Northumbria and the former Danelaw submitted to Svein as king, and, landing with his forces, he swept into central England with the same agenda in mind. Oxford and Winchester submitted, and finally the south-western thegns submitted at Bath, and 'all the nation regarded him as full king'. London capitulated and Queen Emma fled to Normandy, to her brother. Thorkell did the only thing possible, and evacuated Ethelred, first to the Isle of Wight, where he spent Christmas, and then to join his family in Normandy. Neither he, nor anyone else, appears to have made any concerted attempt to defend his position.

Svein, however, died on 3 February 1014, and his son Canute, although acceptable to the Danish army, was not received by the English Witan. Instead they sent to Ethelred in Normandy, promising to reinstate him if he would agree 'to reform all the things which they hated'. He agreed and returned, we are told, to general rejoicing. His position thus greatly strengthened, he was able to lead a great army against Canute, and to expel him from the country. For the last two years of his life, he was able to hold his realm in peace. He was now fifty years old, and had reigned 'with great toil and difficulty' for thirty-six – far longer than any of his predecessors. He died on 23 April 1016, peacefully as far as we know, and was succeeded by his twenty-three-year-old son, Edmund II.

8

EDMUND II, 'IRONSIDE' (REIGNED 1016)

Ethelred enjoyed the longest reign of any of his kindred, and Edmund the shortest, just seven months in 1016. He was crowned in St Paul's Cathedral in London at some time in May, and died on 30 November. Virtually the whole of this brief period was taken up with his struggle with Canute, who had been proclaimed King of the English by the Danish host on Svein's death. Although unable to withstand Ethelred, he took advantage of the latter's death to renew his claim, and reappeared with a large fleet in 1016. Although about the same age as Edmund, he was a man of proven competence, and quickly found allies in England, particularly among his wife's kindred in Northumbria and in the person of

Eadric, the ealdorman of Mercia. Edmund called out the general levy no less than four times, and he and Canute fought five battles in rapid succession, at Penselwood (Somerset), Sherston (Wilts), Brentford (Middlesex), Otford (Kent) and at Ashingdon (Essex). At this last, Canute was victorious, and in a position to dictate terms. By an agreement signed at Olney, in Gloucestershire, England was divided: Edmund retained Wessex, while Northumbria and Mercia were ceded to Canute. However, Edmund survived this agreement by barely a month, dying at the end of November, and on his death Canute succeeded without dispute to the whole kingdom. The brief division of England into two parts can safely be ignored, as Edmund had no time to make his rule over Wessex effective.

PART 3
THE DANISH INTRUDERS,
1013–1042

9

SVEIN FORKBEARD
(REIGNED 1013–14)

Although he reigned for less than two months, Svein, like Edmund, nevertheless occupies a place in the English succession. He was the son of Harald III, known as 'Bluetooth', King of Denmark, and had succeeded his father in that kingdom by 988. As the ally of Olaf Tryggvason of Norway, he had taken part in the great attack on England in 994, but his objective on that occasion had been money, and he retired satisfied with his share of the £16,000 which Ethelred was constrained to pay. In 1003 he returned, again raiding, allegedly in revenge for the death of his sister Gunhild in the St Brice's Day massacre of 1002. He returned in the following year, sacking and setting fire to Norwich, and each year thereafter until he was again bought off in 1007. Svein, however, had a great reputation as a warrior, and had no opinion of the defences which Ethelred had been able to mount against him. In 1013 he came back again, with conquest in mind, and rapidly won the support of the Northumbrians and Mercians, many of whom were of Danish ancestry. Having secured a base in the old Danelaw, in the autumn of 1013 Svein moved rapidly to secure the submission of the midland and western regions, and when London surrendered in December he was accepted as king. Ethelred, as we have seen, fled to Normandy. However, Svein died at Gainsborough on 3 February 1014, and the English chose Edmund to succeed him in place of his own son Canute. He was buried at Roskilde in Denmark.

Svein married twice. His first wife was a Polish woman named Gunhild, who gave him two sons, Harald and Canute, and after her death he married Sigrid, known as 'the Haughty', who bore him a daughter. That daughter eventually married (as her second husband) Duke Richard II of Normandy, who was the grandfather of William I, called the Conqueror.

10

CANUTE (REIGNED 1016–1035)

The second son of Svein Forkbeard, Canute was selected as King of the English by his Danish army on his father's death. However, the English Witan opted for the return of Ethelred, and Canute was obliged to return to Denmark, where his elder brother Harald was then installed as king. He was about twenty years old at this point. When Ethelred died in April 1016, Canute returned to contest the monarchy with Edmund Ironside, and partitioned the kingdom with him after his victory at Ashingdon. He was to rule the country north of the Thames, while Edmund took the South; however, this arrangement hardly had time to become established when Edmund died on 30 November, leaving Canute in undisputed control. He was crowned in January 1017, in St Paul's Cathedral, and in the circumstances it is not surprising that he at once took steps to rid himself of potential challengers. In the summer he married Ethelred's widow Emma, probably to forestall any claim on behalf of the infants Alfred and Edward, who were swiftly smuggled out of the country. Edmund's younger brother Eadwig was also exiled – and probably killed, since he disappears from the records at this point. In 1019 Harald of Denmark died, and Canute succeeded to a throne which not only embraced the overlordship of Norway, but also of some parts of southern Sweden. It was probably to emphasise his importance in Northern Europe that he visited Rome in 1027 to attend the coronation of the Holy Roman Emperor, Conrad II, and later married his daughter by Emma to Conrad's son Henry, the future Emperor Henry III.

Meanwhile Canute had been working on his credentials as an English king, possibly because he was sensitive to the military basis of his rule. In 1018 he reached an agreement with the Witan, which was sealed at Oxford whereby he agreed to observe the laws of King Edgar, a code which was clearly accepted as normative. His own codes built on that foundation, and stand as the last great statement of English custom before the Norman Conquest. At the same time he administered the realm by a modified version of the traditional system rather than introducing Scandinavian practices. Ealdormen were replaced by earls, but their function remained much the same, and the country was divided into four earldoms – of Northumbria, Mercia, East Anglia and Wessex – only the appointment of an Earl of Wessex indicating a lack of sensitivity to traditional ways. At first one or two Danes were appointed to these responsible positions, but by the 1030s such men had disappeared, and by the time of Canute's death all the four were held by Englishmen, notably Leofric of Mercia and Godwine of Wessex. The much-discussed Housecarls, who have been presented as a kind of military guild, not unlike the later Ottoman Janissaries, seem in fact to have married into the local Saxon aristocracy and to have become indistinguishable from thegns. They also received lands on an early version of feudal tenure, and swiftly lost their original function as the King's bodyguard, or military companions.

Canute's ecclesiastical patronage similarly continued that of Ethelred. He patronised the cults of the West Saxon royal saints, Edward the Martyr and Eadgyth of Wilton, and was generally a generous benefactor of the Church. His desire to reconcile Englishmen and Danes was well demonstrated by his patronage of St Edmund's Abbey at Bury, which regarded him as a second founder. Edmund had been that king of East Anglia shot to death with arrows by the soldiers of Canute's ancestor, Ivar the Boneless. He even authorised the translation of the relics of St Elfheah, that Archbishop of Canterbury who had been murdered by Thorkell in 1012, from London, where he had been buried, to Canterbury, even supplying a royal guard for the occasion. Although best known as that king who rebuked his flattering courtiers by attempting to turn back the tide, Canute should really be remembered as the ruler who reconciled the English and Danish elements in his kingdom, a fact reflected in the high reputation which he left behind, particularly in the old realm of Mercia, where by the twelfth century he occupied a place alongside Edgar the Peaceable. Canute died at Shaftesbury, Dorset, on 12 November 1035, and was interred at Winchester Cathedral, thus symbolising his attachment to England. His father had been buried in Denmark. He had married twice – first to Elfgifu of Northampton and secondly to Emma – and was succeeded (more or less) by his son by his first marriage, Harold I, known as Harefoot, who was probably about eighteen at the time.

11

HAROLD I, 'HAREFOOT' (REIGNED 1035–1040)

Although he was the elder, Harold was at first recognised only as regent for his brother Harthacanute, who had, by his father's express intention, succeeded to the throne of Denmark. It was only when Harthacanute continued to be absent, and to show no sign of coming to England, that Harold was proclaimed king in his own right in 1037. As part of the original regency provision, it was agreed that his stepmother Emma would control Wessex, but that arrangement lasted less than two years. In 1036 Alfred, the younger of her two sons by Ethelred, arrived accompanied by a considerable force, intending to link up with his mother and assert a claim to the throne. Instead he was waylaid by Earl Godwine and handed over to Harold, by whom he was brutally murdered. This crime, and the threat which it implied, caused Emma to withdraw to Flanders before the end of the year, and meant that when Harold was proclaimed king in 1037, he was unencumbered by any power-sharing agreements. However, as the Anglo-Saxon Chronicle makes clear, he did not enjoy real power, which was divided between Leofric of Mercia and Godwine of Wessex. It was probably Godwine, who seems to have deserted the cause of Harthacanute early in 1037, who was responsible for the proclamation of Harold, a young man whom he clearly thought he could control. He did not get much chance because the twenty-one-year-old king died at Oxford on 17 March 1040, without having made any distinctive impression upon the realm. Harthacanute meanwhile in late 1039 had gone with his fleet to Bruges to visit his mother, and although he made no move to claim the English throne while Harold lived, he was immediately available upon his death to respond to the call which then came from England. Harold may have married, but left no known offspring, and even the identity of his wife is uncertain.

12

HARTHACANUTE
(REIGNED 1040–1042)

He seems to have been recognised as King of Denmark from 1028, although he did not succeed to full authority until Canute's death in 1035. He remained in Denmark thereafter in order to defend the kingdom against the Nowegians, who had expelled his half-brother Svein at some time after 1030, and were threatening to move south. Consequently his status in England was indeterminate until his brother Harold's death in March 1040. It is possible that he was planning an invasion to enforce his right when that was rendered unnecessary because he was then summoned to the English throne, and was crowned at Canterbury on 18 June. He proved deeply unpopular as king, largely because he raised the rate of the *heregild*, the tax which was imposed for the maintenance of the navy. He seems to have thought it necessary to keep a much larger fleet than either Canute or Harold had done, possibly a sign of his insecurity, or possibly to protect Denmark.

So low was his stock by 1041 that when Edward, Emma's son by Ethelred, came to England in that year, he felt constrained to accept him as his heir. It is possible that this was a mere gesture to appease his English subjects, because Edward was over forty, while the King himself was no more than twenty-four, but it is also possible that the powerful Earl Godwine was behind it. Harthacanute may have suffered from some congenital defect, because he died on 8 June 1042, while celebrating a wedding in Lambeth. In spite of his attachment to Denmark, he was buried at Winchester. He seems never to have married, and certainly left no children, so he was succeeded as he had planned by his kinsman Edward. The Witan, insofar as that still had any voice in such matters, acquiesced in his choice.

PART 4
THE LAST OF OLD ENGLAND,
1042–1066

13

EDWARD 'THE CONFESSOR'
(REIGNED 1042–1066)

Edward was born at Islip in Oxfordshire in about 1005, his father being King Ethelred and his mother Queen Emma. He was thus the half-brother of King Edmund II, and the stepson of Canute. Nothing is known of his early childhood, but on the accession of Canute in 1016 it was deemed prudent for him and his younger brother Alfred to take refuge with his mother's kindred in Normandy. He was then about eleven, and his brother nine. Very little information about his education has survived, but he was clearly brought up to be a knight, and one of his early heroes is alleged to have been Olaf Tryggvason. He could have found kindred in most of the courts of Northern Europe, but he (or his mentors) decided to remain in Normandy. At a time when the royal families of England, Scandinavia, France and the Empire were all closely related to each other, his mother's marriage to Canute gave him a second family of half-siblings with whom his relations seem to have been amicable. One of his mentors, and later a friend, was Robert of Jumieges, but the idea that Edward entered the novitiate with the intention of becoming a monk is a later fabrication. During these years he may have been a welcome visitor at the French court, but little is known of how he spent his adolescence and early manhood. When Canute died in 1035, Edward appears to have made an unsuccessful bid to challenge Harold for the throne when he invaded via Southampton Water in 1036. However, he retreated when resistance was offered, and thus escaped the fate of his brother Alfred, who, landing at

Dover, was captured and murdered. Faced with this evidence of hostility on Harold's part, Emma joined him in Normandy.

However, Harold died in March 1040, and Edward's relations with Harthacanute were very different. When he came back to England in 1041 it was by invitation of the King, and he was recognised as the heir to the throne. He may even have been associated with Harthacanute in the kingship. Not surprisingly for one who had lived in the Duchy for more than twenty years, his household was more than 50 per cent Norman, and this was to cause problems when he took over the reins of power. When Harthacanute died in June 1542, Edward was thus in a very strong position. He was eligible for the throne by birth (indeed he was the only plausible candidate), thirty-six years old, and enjoyed the endorsement of the last king. He still needed, however, recognition by the magnates and consecration by the Church. There may have been some opposition from the former, although none is recorded, because his coronation was delayed until Easter 1043, which was unusual. Easter Day, on the other hand, was a day of unique significance in the Christian year, and may have been selected in order to demonstrate that the *potestas* which he already possessed had now been converted into *auctoritas* by the rite of coronation. His crowning was a solemn event, attended by the ambassadors of the Emperor and the King of France, and seems to have ascended to a new level of symbolic significance. It would be interesting to know whether he was consulted about the royal style, which described him as king 'by the Grace of God'. His years in exile had left him flexible, tenacious and resilient, just the qualities which he needed to deal with the challenges which now faced him. He was also unmarried, and the sources speak fulsomely of his chastity, meaning that he had begotten no known bastards. The ecclesiastical chroniclers attributed this to a vow of celibacy, but suspicious modern minds will wonder about his sexual orientation. There is no overt evidence of this, and no contemporary would have wished to admit to anything so terrible as homosexuality, but the fact remains that Edward appears to have shown no interest in women.

Edward had to struggle from the moment of his accession, not against external threats, but against the power brokers at home. His estates were worth about £5,000 a year, compared with Earl Godwine's £4,000, the Earl of Mercia's £1,300 and the Queen's £900. So whereas he had an advantage over Godwine in terms of resources, it was a narrow one, and would have been overturned if the earls had combined against him. It may have been for that reason that he broke his mother's power base in 1043, and although they were subsequently reconciled she played no further part in the politics of the reign before her death in 1052. Edward has a reputation for being unwarlike, but in 1044 he assembled a fleet of thirty-five warships at Sandwich, not in response to any threatened invasion, but simply to demonstrate his capacity to do so. The navy seems to have been paraded in a similar fashion every year thereafter, and the message was well received by potential aggressors, who steered well clear of England. At the end of that year, and perhaps as a result of these martial displays, Edward and Earl Godwine came to an agreement, and the King married Godwine's daughter Edith in January 1045. The concord did not last, because although Edward later acquired the reputation of being a Church reformer, that was not much in evidence in his deployment of ecclesiastical patronage, over which he fell out seriously with the Earl. Broadly speaking, Godwine favoured local candidates for abbacies and other senior benefices, whereas

Edward favoured courtiers, some of whom were among his French friends. It would be an exaggeration to say that the King was endeavouring to flood the Church with French clerics, but the friction was considerable. This was exacerbated by disagreement over foreign policy, where Edward (understandably) favoured a Norman alliance, while Godwine preferred Scandinavia. These various quarrels came to a head in 1049, when, after a protracted row, in which Edward consistently backed Robert of Jumieges and his French friends against Godwine, Robert was promoted in the spring of 1051 to the vacant see of Canterbury. It may have been as a consequence of this that Edward signed a treaty of friendship with William of Normandy in the summer of that year. This was too much for Godwine, who staged a revolt in the winter of 1051/52, but, miscalculating the King's strength, was driven into exile in Flanders as a result, and the offices of his entire family were forfeited.

This, however, was far from being the end of Earl Godwine. In the summer of 1052 he returned, and a large number of his former thegns rallied to him. In order to avoid civil war, the King negotiated, and in a council held at Westminster agreed to restore him to his possessions and to rehabilitate his family. This was undoubtedly a defeat for Edward, but it was neither final nor decisive, because Earl Godwine died at Easter 1053, and his surviving sons, Harold, Tostvig, Gyrth and Leofwine, were not disposed to continue his feud. The realm settled down to a period of internal calm, during which the warlike energies of the earls were channelled into campaigns against Gruffydd ap Llewellyn and Malcolm of Scotland. The King's main domestic problem after 1053 was to satisfy the ambition of the Queen and her brothers without antagonising the other leading families. Fortunately they turned out to be reasonable men, so that it was possible to shuffle the existing family holding of shires to make provision for the younger siblings as they came of age. Typical of the King's strategy at this point was the replacement of Earl Siward of Northumbria, who died in 1055, with Tostvig Godwinson, the second son of Earl Godwine, and the displacement of Earl Eflgar of East Anglia on the ground of treason. It is not clear quite what treason Elfgar was supposed to have committed, but he had probably advanced his own claim to Northumbria. In the event a part of East Anglia was entrusted to Gyrth Godwinson, but the rest was distributed to third parties. Elfgar's sons were firmly excluded. Edward could control this situation because the sons of Godwine were not united, there being particular rivalry between Harold and Tostvig, the latter being a (relatively) clean-living young man who disapproved of his brother's lifestyle. After making sundry attempts to regain his position in alliance with Gruffydd ap Llewellyn, Elfgar appears to have died in 1062. It was during these years that ecclesiastical writers began to refer to Edward as 'Soloman', meaning the peaceable rather than the wise, but intended as a tribute to his political skills.

Meanwhile he remained childless, and the problem of the succession was unresolved. In the autumn of 1051 William of Normandy visited the court, and there is some reason to suppose that Edward recognised him as his heir at that point. This might explain the favour showed to Normans over the next few years, but there is no proof that it ever happened. In 1057 Another Edward, known as 'the Exile', who was Edmund Ironside's son, visited England with official encouragement, and there may have been some question of recognising him. However, he died within a few months without the question ever being resolved. Edward, who had lived abroad since he was about six months old, and could have spoken virtually no English, arrived accompanied by his family and a substantial treasure. He was therefore contemplating a lengthy stay, and such expectations as he may have had were inherited by his five-year-old son Edgar, but there was no question of recognising Edgar, at least for the time being. Then in 1065 Earl Harold Godwinson was sent on a confidential mission by Edward to William, Duke of Normandy. Later Norman sources allege that this was for the purpose of confirming the King's intention to make William his heir, and the story is embroidered by accounts of the oath which Harold is alleged to have taken. It is possible that this is true, although no contemporary source confirms it, and the real purpose of his mission may have been a good deal less focussed. Meanwhile Edward was struggling against failing health to complete the great rebuilding of Westminster Abbey which he had undertaken several years earlier. It was consecrated on 28 December, and just over a week later Edward died at the advanced age of sixty-one. His piety was much exaggerated by interested monastic chroniclers, and they attributed his childlessness to an oath of chastity, whereas it is more likely to have been due to poor relations with his wife. Edith outlived him by a decade, dying in 1075. The King was buried at Westminster on 6 January 1066. Owing to pressure from King Henry II, who was anxious to secure a national saint for England, he was canonised in 1161, and in 1169 his remains were transferred to a magnificent new shrine, where miracles soon began to be reported. Unfortunately he had further confused the issue of the succession on his deathbed by recognising Harold Godwinson as his heir – at least that was Harold's story.

14

HAROLD II (REIGNED 1066)

Harold was not a blood relation of Edward's, but was his brother-in-law. This was presumably close enough to bring him within the eligibility of kinship, but, more importantly, as Earl of Wessex he was by far the most powerful man in the kingdom. Whether or not he was designated by Edward on his deathbed, he was immediately accepted by the magnates, who had been brought together by the news of the King's impending death, and crowned in a hastily arranged ceremony the very next day, 7 January. It is clear that he expected to have to fight for his throne, and that William of Normandy would not be his only rival. The first to show was his younger brother Tostvig. Relations between the brothers had been bad for a long while, and Tostvig had been dismissed as Earl of Northumbria the previous year, a setback which he blamed on Harold's influence. Tostvig began raiding along the south coast in April, and in May actually landed near Sandwich, but without sufficient force to make a major incursion. He then sailed off up the east coast, his attacks diminishing in severity as he went. However, if Harold thought that he had seen off his brother, then he was to be disappointed, because in early in September Harald Hardrada of Norway (another member of Edward's ramifying kindred) decided to stake his own claim, and Tostvig quickly made common cause with him. Hardrada landed on the Yorkshire coast near Scarborough, and was immediately joined by the quondam earl. Their combined army then laid siege to York, which quickly capitulated, signing a peace treaty in which the citizens recognised Hardrada as king. Harold, however, was quickly on the scene and, bringing his army up by forced marches from the South, confronted the invaders at Stamford Bridge on 25 September. The result was a decisive victory, which left Hardrada and Tostvig among the dead, and forced the remainder of the Norwegian troops to retreat to their ships.

However, no sooner had this been won than news arrived from the South that Duke William of Normandy had landed near Pevensey with a large army of Normans and Bretons. It had taken all the summer for William to assemble this host, and obtain the papal blessing which he deemed essential to his success, but he came at an opportune time, while Harold was occupied far away. The King, however, allowed his men only the briefest time to recuperate from their exertions, and reached London again by 7 October, a remarkable feat considering that they had had to walk every step of the way. There he recruited fresh troops, and confronted William near Hastings on 13 October. The following day a great battle ensued, which was eventually decided by William's mounted men at arms. All the three remaining Godwinson brothers, King Harold, Leofwine and Gyrth, died on the field of battle, and that may have been as decisive as the victory itself in determining the fate of England. When news of Harold's defeat and death reached London, Archbishop Aldred and Earls Edwin and Morcar proclaimed the fourteen-year-old Edgar, son of Edward the Exile, as king, but he seems to have had little support outside of London, and submitted to William's superior military force before Christmas. William was thus left without a rival, and the Witan bowed to the inevitable, accepting him in time for a coronation on Christmas Day. Harold's body was allegedly identified by his mistress Edith 'swan neck', and interred eventually at Waltham Abbey, where his grave was subsequently lost. He left a number of children by her, and a son, Harold, by his wife, Ealdgyth, but their fates are unknown. According to William of Malmesbury, Edgar the Atheling was still alive in 1125, but whether he married or had offspring is not known. The future of England remained with William, 'the Conqueror'.

15

EDGAR, 'THE ATHELING' (DID NOT RULE)

Edgar was born, probably in Hungary, around about 1052, the son of Edward the Exile, and grandson of Edmund II, Ironside. He came to England with his father and the rest of his family in 1057, and was presumably brought up in England after his father died later in that year. Being the only surviving prince of Edward's line, he was accepted as king after Harold's death, but he enjoyed little support outside London, and submitted to William after a fierce campaign by the latter in Hampshire and Berkshire in November 1066. For some years a resistance movement was carried on in his name, but he withdrew to Scotland and appears to have given the rebels no encouragement. He was expelled from Scotland following a military campaign by William in 1072, and appears to have taken refuge in France, where he died in about 1126.

He was never crowned, and his reign extends to only a few weeks in 1066.

PART 5
THE ANGLO-NORMANS,
1066–1154

16

WILLIAM I, THE CONQUEROR
(REIGNED 1066–1087)

William's successful invasion of England in 1066 came as the culmination of a long history of mutual involvement, going back even before the marriage of Ethelred to Emma in 1002. When Svein was involved in England in 1013, his allies Olaf and Lacman were received with honour by Duke Richard II, and Olaf was baptised by the Archbishop of Rouen. When Emma married Canute, Svein's successor in 1017, the connections became even closer, and this was associated with changing relations between Normandy and the Kingdom of France. Born in 1027 or 1028, William was the illegitimate (but only) son of Duke Robert I, who ruled from 1027 to 1035, and when Robert died the seven-year-old boy was accepted by the nobles of Normandy as their lawful Duke. During his boyhood the English Athelings, Edward and Alfred, resided at his court, and Edward may even have been permitted to use the title King of England. However, during the years of William's minority he was troubled with opposition at home, and had no settled policy towards England during the reigns of Harold and Harthacanute. This situation was changed when Edward returned to England in 1041, and even more when he succeeded Harthacanute in the following year. The opening years of Edward's reign were threatened by the schemes of Magnus, King of Norway, to stake his claim to the throne, and it was only his death in October 1047 which finally resolved that issue. During these years the King of England was preoccupied with building his own party among the English earls, and in this connection his friendship with William was important. As the power of Earl Godwine and his sons increased between 1047 and 1050, Edward became increasing reliant on the Norman friends which he had made during his exile, and this was consolidated by the treaty of friendship between the King and the Duke, which was signed in 1051. Nevertheless, the infiltration of Normans into the power structure of England is easy to exaggerate. Only in the Church was it particularly noticeable, where, early in 1051 Robert of Jumieges, already Bishop of London, was translated to the metropolitan see of Canterbury. It is likely that Edward recognised William as his successor in the autumn of 1051, but not likely that William came in person to receive the nomination because he was much preoccupied with affairs at home. For the same reason, in spite of his friendly contacts with the Duchy, Edward cannot have expected much positive support from the Duke himself.

This was important because in 1052 the Godwines established an ascendancy in England which resulted in the expulsion of Archbishop Robert. Also from 1052 to 1054 William faced a crisis in Normandy which was only resolved in the latter year by his victory at Mortemer. Although in 1053 the English power structure was modified by the death of Earl Godwine, that did not lead to the recall of Archbishop Robert, and a plan was conceived to place Edward the Exile as heir to the throne instead of William, a scheme of which the King was probably aware but was helpless to prevent. This was aborted by Edward's death in 1057 and the schemers then turned their attention to Earl Harold of Wessex, who was sufficiently 'kinworthy' and was the most powerful man in the country. Relations between the Earl and the Duke therefore became problematic, and the reasons for Harold's visit to Normandy in the autumn of 1064 are something of a mystery. It was later claimed by William that it was for the purpose of acknowledging his right to the succession, a mission which it was alleged he accompanied by solemn oaths. But in the light of subsequent events, this seems unlikely. No sooner had Edward expired on 5 January 1066 than the assembled magnates accepted Harold as king, and he was crowned at Westminster the next day. William, who was free from the attentions of rivals at home by this time, began to assemble a great war fleet to invade in defence of his claim. He had to build a great many ships for this purpose, and recruited men not only from Normandy but from various other parts of northern France. It was advertised as a great venture, with a kingdom at stake, and William succeeded in persuading Pope Alexander II to bless his enterprise on the pretext that he was punishing an oathbreaker. He took the whole summer of 1066 in making his preparations, and when further delayed by adverse winds it was 28 September before this armada finally landed at Pevensey. Preoccupied in the North, Harold took until 14 October to confront the invaders near Hastings, where the decisive battle was fought on the following day. Although he had defeated and killed Harold, William was not at once accepted as king. It was only after he had marched through Hampshire and Berkshire, and isolated London, that the adherents of Edgar the Atheling came to terms. Archbishop Aldred, Earls Edwin and Morcar and Edgar himself met him at Berkhampstead and submitted to him as king, which enabled him to be crowned at Westminster on Christmas Day. By March he had installed his own supporters in a number of key positions, and felt able to return to Normandy, taking with him a number of his former opponents as hostages.

For the next year or two, William divided his time between England and Normandy, spending the summers of 1066 and

1067 on the Continent. Nevertheless, opposition in England was not over, and in the autumn of 1067 required a campaign in the South West to establish his authority. This he successfully did, and kept the Easter of 1068 at Winchester, supported by many English notables. There also he arranged for his wife Matilda to be crowned as queen. He was still not, however, able to regard his position in England as secure, and in the summer of 1069 Harold and Canute, the sons of Svein Estrithson of Denmark, launched a powerful attack upon the Yorkshire coast, which provoked a general rising in the old earldom of Northumbria. William's garrisons and agents were at first swept aside, but in a campaign of exceptional vigour and ruthlessness the King regained control, and, after harrying the countryside, burnt the city of York just before Christmas. Even his own supporters were dismayed by the ravaging of the North, but it ensured Norman domination of the region for the foreseeable future. This campaign also enabled him to extend into what was now clearly conquered territory the system of castle building which he had already initiated elsewhere as a means of overawing the population. Much land was confiscated, and Norman lords installed in place of the rebels. The same thing happened in East Anglia when the Danish fleet returned in the summer of 1070. The Danes entrenched themselves in the Isle of Ely, where they were joined by local dissidents led by Hereward, known as 'the Wake'. After assaulting Peterborough and sacking the abbey, the Danes were persuaded to withdraw, leaving Hereward and Earl Morcar, who had come to his assistance, to the mercies of William. The King led the campaign against Ely in person, and the rebels surrendered unconditionally. By the end of 1070 William's ascendancy was more or less secure, and he was able to turn his attentions again to Normandy, where relative peace had prevailed since 1068, enabling the King to concentrate on England.

Problems, however, had now arisen in relations with both Maine and Flanders, which demanded his urgent attention. Norman rule in the former province had collapsed, leaving the way open for other hostile powers to intervene, and regime change in Flanders meant increased intervention by Philip I of France, which threatened the stability of relations in that quarter also. William was in Normandy, seeking to resolve these problems, from late 1071 to Easter 1072, when a crisis in relations with Scotland recalled him to the North. In a remarkable campaign he subdued King Malcolm, who did homage to him and expelled Edgar the Atheling from his court. Edgar immediately took refuge in Flanders, demonstrating the links which bound the anti-Norman interest together, and had William scurrying back to Normandy, where another campaign re-established his authority over Maine. For the next few years only his extraordinary military energy and efficiency kept this grumbling situation under some sort of control. In 1074 Edgar returned from Flanders to Scotland, and relations with Brittany also deteriorated alarmingly, so that in 1075, when another rebellion broke out in England, the rebels had significant Breton support. A Danish fleet sought to take advantage of this situation, but in yet another successful campaign William defeated them and subdued the rebellion, executing its leader Earl Waltheof in May 1076. Hardly had this been accomplished than he was called back to Brittany by yet another military crisis. This time he was defeated at Dol and his relations with France were further impaired. To make the situation still more confused, his son Robert was making life difficult for his father within the Duchy of Normandy, and this also required time and energy to resolve. In the circumstances the efficiency with which England was governed was extraordinary, and arose largely from the King's good sense in utilising the administrative institutions which he had inherited. It was this structure of shires and hundreds which enabled his officials to compile that great survey of English landholding known as Domesday Book, which was completed in 1085. He was also careful to use, and observe, the sophisticated structure of Old English law which he found in place, and which enhanced the strength of his political position. This did not prevent him from dividing the country into great fiefs, and granting these to his Norman followers, but it did mean that he was careful not to give them consolidated estates, and he encouraged them to include Englishmen among their knights. He was also careful to take a direct oath of allegiance from these sub-vassals at the great assembly at Salisbury in 1086, thus binding the country more closely to the Crown than was possible in Normandy, which had a different tradition.

As England grew quieter after 1080, the situation between Normandy, Maine and Anjou continued to be turbulent. His son Robert was constantly on the verge of rebellion, and their periodic reconciliations never lasted. Hardly a summer passed without requiring a military campaign of more or less seriousness, and it was in the course of one such that William met his end. Riding into battle at Mantes, he was thrown from his horse and suffered severe internal injuries. He died at a priory near Rouen on 9 September 1087, aged about sixty. His wife, Matilda had predeceased him in 1083, but he was survived by several of the ten children which she had borne him. In spite of their difficult relationship, he was succeeded in Normandy by his eldest son, Robert. However, and rather surprisingly in view of the tenacity with which he had defended their union, he bequeathed the Kingdom of England separately to his second son, William Rufus. Perhaps he intended Robert to do homage to his brother for his duchy, but this was never made clear and for the time being at least the two states were distinct. Meanwhile Archbishop Lanfranc, who had succeeded the disgraced Stigand in 1070, held the fort in England and made sure that the late king's wishes were obeyed.

17

WILLIAM II, 'RUFUS' (REIGNED 1087–1100)

Circumstances favoured William at the time of his father's death, because Robert, who would have been a more natural choice for the succession, was occupied at Abbeville at the time. It may have been an awareness of this fact, or possibly the thought that his eldest son was too mild a person to control the factions of England, which prompted the old king's last decision, but he drew up a bequest in due form. William Rufus was on the spot, and his brother was not. He wasted no time in crossing to England and presenting his letters to Lanfranc, who immediately recognised his title and, in return for an undertaking to rule with the Archbishop's advice, took his oath and duly consecrated him at Westminster on 26 September. The English barons appear to have raised no objection at the time, but the thought that Robert had been dispossessed grew on them over the next few months, and by early 1088 several of the leading nobles would have been willing to transfer their allegiance to him, if only he could come and claim it. However, Robert, who had been accepted as Duke of Normandy by the assembled barons at Rouen, failed to take advantage of his opportunity and the dissidents operated at a disadvantage. Odo of Bayeux, who had been released from prison shortly before the Conqueror's death, and had returned to his earldom of Kent, appears to have been the ringleader, but the issue never really came to a head. The Church remained loyal to William. He secured London and raised an army, but apart from the Siege of Rochester there was no fighting. After the siege he demonstrated the ruthlessness of his grip on the situation, and rebellion elsewhere never came to a head. By the autumn of 1088 England appeared to have settled down under its new regime. There was never any intention to separate England from Normandy, but by 1089 Robert had been accepted as duke, and William as king. The relationship between them continued to be confused.

The latter's evil reputation derives largely from the fact that the churchmen who wrote the histories were prejudiced against him. He was not pious, had a fierce temper, and was probably homosexual; at any rate he never married, and begot no bastards. Nevertheless, he had a clear conception of the majesty of his office, and did his duty as he saw it scrupulously. He kept a firm grip on law and order, and was less devious than his father, qualities which were acclaimed by his knights. Only the monks appear to have despised him, because he taxed them hard, and did not give them the traditional endowments which they expected. He exploited his feudal rights rigorously, and his numerous wars were largely (and unwillingly) financed by the Church. His brother Robert, by contrast, although a good soldier, was a weak character, and the Norman barons reasserted their independence once the Conqueror's firm grip was relaxed. The confusion which then followed represented a return to the status quo rather than a new situation. Robert was indolent, and failed to prevent the breakaway movement in Maine, a movement which was supported by Philip I of France, because it was in his interest to weaken Normandy. Dismayed by this situation, in 1090 William endeavoured to get a grip on the Duchy, and civil war broke out. Henry, Robert's younger brother, appears to have supported William in this crisis, and allegiance became divided. Then in February 1091 William crossed to Normandy, and the brothers came to terms. The King retained the allegiance of those who had sworn to him, but agreed to give Robert money and support in maintaining his authority over those barons who remained loyal to him. The relationship between William and his brother was never spelled out, and when the barons of the Duchy assembled at Caen in July 1091 their main concern was the preservation of law and order rather than of feudal lordship. In the autumn of 1091 William returned to England to deal with problems which had arisen with the Welsh princes and with the King of Scots. He raised an army and confronted the Scots between the Tweed and the Forth, but Malcolm backed down and no battle resulted.

The Scots came back in 1093 but accomplished nothing and their king was killed on his retreat in November. This opened the way to a Gaelic resurgence in Scotland, and English troops were kept busy in the North until Edgar was established as King of Scots in 1097. This ought to have led to the reassertion of English overlordship, but in fact the relationship between England and Scotland continued to be ambiguous. Meanwhile, dissatisfied with the way in which his agreement with William was working out, Duke Robert denounced the treaty between them in December 1093, and this caused the King to lead an army to France in March 1094. Desultory fighting followed, in which Robert had the advantage because Philip I was supporting him, but the conflict was inconclusive, and William was summoned back to England by rebellion in the North in 1095. This was led by Roger Mowbray, and was caused by general discontent rather than by any particular rival bid for the throne. The King recaptured Newcastle and Bamborough and imprisoned Mowbray to bring the revolt to an end. Meanwhile warfare which did not require the King's presence was more or less endemic in Wales, where the Earl of Montgomery broke through to the coast, capturing Ceredigion in July 1093. This led to the division of Wales into North and South, and the overrunning of the latter by the English. By 1099 most of Pembroke and Glamorgan was under English control, but in the North Powys and Gwynedd remained independent. In one way or another, William, in spite of his firm rule, was constantly at war for the security of his dominion, and this struggle frequently involved his brother. However, in 1096 Robert decided to take the cross, and reached a new agreement with William at Easter. By the terms of this treaty the King was to supply his brother with 10,000 marks (£6,666 13s 4d) in return for which he would receive the whole Duchy of Normandy in pledge. The money was duly paid in September, and Robert set off for Jerusalem. While the latter was distinguishing himself in the capture of the Holy City and at the Battle of Ascalon, William remained in Normady from the autumn of 1096 to Easter 1097, where his authority was generally accepted. In November of the same year he returned at the head of a large army in an effort to recover Norman supremacy over Maine, and in February cut a deal with Count Fulk which gave him the essence of what he wanted, recognition of his overlordship. He also signed a truce with King Philip, and by 1099 had restored the authority of the Duke to the position which William I had left, which was a considerable achievement. At Whitsun 1099 he returned to

England in order to celebrate the season at Westminster, which he made the occasion for a demonstration of sovereignty. He was the ruler of Normandy and Maine as well as King of England, and Edgar of Scotland bore his sword before him. By that time Robert was on his way back from the crusade, and a question was about to arise: what would happen in Normandy if his debt was not paid? However, all such doubts were put on hold on 2 August 1100 when the forty-four-year-old king was shot with a stray arrow during a hunting expedition in the New Forest, and died immediately.

At the time of his death, William was secure in his secular rule, but his relations with the Church continued to be bad. He had just raised Ranulf Flambard to the see of Durham, and this move was badly received in orthodox circles. Flambard, who was a brilliant administrator, was a priest by convenience rather than conviction. As a royal servant he had helped the King to fleece the Church, and he had fathered numerous children by different women. The fact that he provided decently for all these mistresses and their offspring was largely ignored by his detractors, and his evil repute reflected badly on the King. The see of Canterbury had been vacant since 1089, until William, in an unusual spirit of generosity, had persuaded Anselm of Bec to accept the office in 1093. This inevitably led to friction between the King and the Primate, who was nothing if not puritanical in his ideas. In 1097 he persuaded William to allow him to go to Rome to receive his pallium, which also involved the recognition of Pope Urban II. England had not acknowledged any Pope since 1084, so this was a considerable concession. Having discharged his mission, Anselm deemed it prudent to remain in Rome, and was still out of the country when William was killed. William was hastily interred at Winchester, without the elaborate rites which should have accompanied such a burial. The Church was not slow to take its revenge on one who had been regarded as a 'godless' ruler, and when a tower at the cathedral collapsed soon afterward, the clergy were only too ready to draw the obvious conclusion.

18

HENRY I, 'BEAUCLERC' (REIGNED 1100–1135)

Henry was the youngest of William I's sons, and was born somewhere in England in the latter part of 1068. He seems to have spent most of his youth in England, probably under the care of Bishop Osmund of Salisbury, and was given sufficient education to make him literate. This was unusual among royal princes and may indicate that as the youngest he was originally intended for a career in the Church. This rare accomplishment set an example for later kings to follow, and although it seems to have been no more than basic, it earned him the later title of 'Beauclerc', or fine scholar. He was knighted by his father on 24 May 1086, a few months short of his eighteenth birthday, and at that stage left his childhood behind him and entered upon the normal career of a royal prince. He seems to have been a rather wild young man, and acquired numerous mistresses by whom he began fathering bastards at an alarming rate (more than twenty over his whole career), which may have been connected with the difficulties of finding a suitable wife. His mother, Matilda, had died in 1083, leaving him lands worth about £300 a year. This would have been nowhere near enough to support the lifestyle to which he aspired, and where the rest of his income came from is something of a mystery. When his father died in 1087 he was left a lot of money, but no land or title.

At that time he was in Normandy, where his brother Robert immediately made him Count of Cotentin, a position which carried wide authority. However, within a few months Robert suspected Henry of conspiring with Rufus against him, and had him arrested. He was imprisoned at Bayeux and not released until April 1089. Thereafter he understandably kept aloof from both his brothers, and was excluded and disendowed when they came to terms in February 1091. However, the agreement did not last, and thereafter he appears to have recovered his authority by coming to terms with William. This benefited him considerably when Robert went on crusade in 1096, because during his absence he governed the Cotentin effectively with William's consent. Between 1096 and 1100 Henry seems to have spent most of his time and energy in Normandy, but he appears from time to time at the English court, and was, most fortunately for him, in England at the time of William's death – a circumstance which increases the probability of his complicity. Ignoring the claims of Robert, who was still on his way back from the crusade, he made straight for Winchester and seized control of the royal treasury. In spite of those who endeavoured to maintain their oaths to the Duke of Normandy, he received sufficient backing from the assembled magnates to be proclaimed as king, and was immediately crowned at Westminster. As the younger brother of the late king, who had died childless, he was well within the bounds of eligibility, and election by the barons made him an authentic king, so there was no question of usurpation. At the same time he issued a charter making lavish promises of good government, returning to the good old laws of Edward the Confessor, and 'making free the church of God', undertakings which he subsequently honoured in substance but largely ignored in detail. This was partly because the laws of the Confessor did not consist of a coherent code, but rather a corpus of usages which survived in a variety of judicial decisions.

In these circumstances, Robert was not the man to pursue a claim which he would probably have lost anyway, and in a peace treaty between the brothers signed in August 1101 he renounced it altogether. Henry adjusted William's council rather than replacing it. The most significant casualty was Ranulf Flambard, who was imprisoned in the Tower as a signal that the new king intended to follow different fiscal priorities. Anselm returned, invited by the King immediately after his coronation, as a sign of improved relations with the Church. The friendship between the King and the Archbishop thereafter continued at a personal level, which eased the political quarrel which developed between them over the question of lay investiture. Anselm was determined to uphold Pope Urban II's ban on such investiture, which the King insisted on maintaining as one of his prerogative rights. The Archbishop, who was an administrator of genius, and invaluable to Henry as the head of his 'civil service', was not personally committed to the papal ban. He would have been quite happy to concede, but only with the Pope's consent, and this informed the negotiations which continued for best part of a decade. Henry was constantly on the brink of excommunication over this issue, but the Pope was as regularly dissuaded from issuing the sentence, realising that the King 'relies entirely on the advice of men of religion', and that that gave him an advantage not lightly to be sacrificed. A compromise formula was eventually found at the Westminster Council in 1107, and the political breach between Henry and Anselm was at last healed. This enabled the numerous vacancies which had arisen in the English Church to be canonically filled and lasted until Anselm's death at Bec two years later. The appointments made were respectable ones out of the Bec–Caen–Canterbury school of reformers; the bishops were men of administrative ability and the abbots men of sanctity.

Meanwhile Henry had been forced to maintain the order of his kingdom against the ambitions of one of his leading Welsh marcher lords, Robert of Belleme. Earl Robert held lands all over England, but his principal base was at Bridgenorth in Shropshire, and it required a vigorous campaign in 1102 to dislodge him. Earl Robert was a man of unsavoury reputation, and the King's ecclesiastical allies rejoiced at his downfall. His lands in England were confiscated, and he crossed to Normandy, where he proceeded to make an even bigger nuisance of himself. The situation in the Duchy was chaotic, thanks to the Duke's slack rule, and Robert was able to carve a large niche for himself in what passed for government. Only western Normandy was more or less quiet under lords who were sworn to William, and it was in response to their pleas that Henry invaded in 1105, with the express intention of restoring order. Duke Robert naturally objected, but was defeated and captured at the Battle of Tenchbrai in 1106, along with numerous other lords including Edgar the Atheling. Earl Robert was dispossessed of his Norman lands, and Duke Robert disappeared into Cardiff Castle, remaining in prison until his death in 1134. Thereafter peace descended on the Duchy, now ruled directly by Henry, and the only two periods of trouble which ensued during his reign, in 1118–19 and 1122–23, were caused by the ambitions of Louis VI of France. Both intrusions were defeated.

At home the King followed up his reforming Church appointments with various changes to the legal structure, which masqueraded as restorations. Hundred courts were to meet regularly 'as in king Edward's time', when in fact meetings had not been regular at all. The death penalty was decreed for burglary and theft, which were further innovations, applauded by churchmen as salutary discipline. Reforms were also introduced in the running of the royal household, so that certain requisitions were required at fixed prices, in place of the casual browsing which had characterised the court hitherto. The Exchequer was revamped to make it more like an institution of government and less like an aspect of the household, an objective which had been achieved by about 1110. This last reform was made necessary by the fact that Henry had negotiated a marriage for his daughter Maud with the Emperor Henry V, a coup for which he was forced to find 10,000 marks (about £6,600) in dowry. This required a special tax which was collected in time for Maud to be formally wedded to the Emperor when she reached the canonical age of twelve in 1114. Although known thereafter as 'the Empress', a childless Maud in fact returned to her father's court when Henry V died in 1125, and was subsequently (and more importantly) married to Geoffrey of Anjou in 1127. After Anselm's death in 1109, the King depended mainly on Bishop Roger of Salisbury for the administration of England and on Robert of Meulan for general policy, until the latter's death in 1118. Meanwhile Louis VI of France was probing Henry's Continental defences. He demanded homage for the Duchy of Normandy in 1109, but a bloodless confrontation resulted in a truce, which, although it resolved none of the issues, amounted to a retreat by the French king. Duke Robert's son, William Clito, was also making a bid for the Duchy, an attempt in which he was backed by Robert of Belleme, and which made him a natural focus for all the anti-English lords in the region. Clito's betrothal to a daughter of Fulk V of Anjou was in fact less significant than it seemed, because Fulk proceeded to do homage to Henry for his county, by an agreement of May 1119, and promptly departed on crusade, handing over his lands to Henry to manage. His son Geoffrey subsequently married Henry's daughter, as we have seen. Nevertheless for a while it seemed that Louis, Fulk and William Clito would form a formidable alliance against Henry, and did in fact force him into a major campaign in 1118–19, which culminated in the defeat of Louis at the Battle of Bremule in September 1119. When it came to the point, Henry was just too good a soldier to be confronted, and after this victory was the most powerful prince in Western Europe. In mid-1120, he signed a peace treaty with France which virtually sealed that supremacy, and gave him the peace which he had been seeking.

Meanwhile Henry had recognised his son William as his heir by June 1119. This was mainly for security reasons, because William did not exercise any real authority, and was certainly not a joint king. It was mainly an occasion for oath taking by the English magnates, which were as much gestures of loyalty to Henry as to William. Then on 25 November 1120 came the disaster of the *White Ship*, when William and a number of his young compatriots were drowned, leaving the King without a legitimate heir. Although Henry promptly remarried Adeliza, the daughter of Godfrey VII of Louvain, the Duke of Lower Lorraine, there was no guarantee of further offspring, and the foundation of Reading Abbey in 1123 was probably intended as a peace offering to God for that purpose. The death of Earl Robert of Chester in the *White Ship* also caused disturbances in North Wales, which Henry dealt with simply by going to the region with a force, whereupon the Welsh princes submitted. Meanwhile the King had fallen out with

Fulk of Anjou over the dowry which the latter had been due to pay for the marriage of his daughter to William – a union which had been aborted by William's death, and this led to renewed trouble in Normandy. A number of lords renounced their allegiance to Henry, transferring their loyalty to Louis as their overlord, but a brief campaign by the former, culminating in the Siege of Pont Audemar in October 1123 and the Battle of Rougemontier in December, effectively ended their resistance. This last, a small but decisive victory, put an end to trouble in the Duchy for the remainder of Henry's reign. From 1125 onward the King was preoccupied with the question of the succession. He was by then nearly sixty, an advanced age by the standards of the time, and he had no lawful son. In that year his daughter Maud's marriage to the Emperor Henry V was ended by his death, and he began to consider her as a candidate. The other possibilities were his nephew Stephen of Blois (who was married to Matilda of Boulogne, a member of the royal kindred); his illegitimate son Robert of Gloucester; and William Clito, the son of the imprisoned Robert Curthose. However, to have recognised the latter would have been to undo all that Henry had been striving for, and he was not seriously considered. In any case he died at the age of twenty-four in 1128. Neither Stephen nor Robert appear to have been regarded as serious contenders, and it was to Maud, who married Geoffrey of Anjou on 17 June 1127, that Henry was increasingly looking. Somehow he won over a reluctant baronage, and she was recognised as heir to the throne, to whom the appropriate oaths were taken. Meanwhile the King had finally settled his dispute with Louis VI by a treaty which was signed in 1129, and the last five years of his reign saw an unaccustomed peace on all fronts. He died unexpectedly at the age of sixty-seven, on 1 December 1135.

19

THE TROUBLED REIGN OF KING STEPHEN

Stephen ought not to have been king. Born in 1096 or 1097, he was the son of Stephen, Count of Blois and Chartres, and of Adela, the sister of Henry I. He was thus a grandson of the Conqueror, and benefited from the reluctance of the English barons to have a woman on the throne. He was at Boulogne when the news of Henry's death reached him, and crossed at once to England, taking advantage of reports that the late king on his deathbed had named him as heir. He was refused admission to Dover Castle, but made his way at once to London, where he was supported by the citizens, and enough magnates to make a formal show of acclamation. William of Corbeil, the Archbishop of Canterbury, crowned him at Westminster on 22 December, and he issued his first charter of liberties, aiming initially to secure the allegiance of the secular lords. He then went on to Winchester to secure the treasury, and there the support of his brother, Henry of Blois, who was the bishop, was crucial in securing the recognition of the ecclesiastical magnates. Aware of the precariousness of his title, he appealed to the Pope for confirmation, and Innocent II recognised the validity of his coronation. Meanwhile King David of Scotland, who was one of those who had sworn to recognise Matilda, invaded the north of England and had to be bought off with the grant of Cumbria, a concession which alienated Ranulf, Earl of Chester, who also had ambitions in the area. At his Easter court, held at Oxford in early April 1136, the King put in writing his commitment to the liberties of the Church, spelling out the rights and duties of bishops and abbots, particularly over elections and jurisdiction. He renounced his own right to the revenues of vacant sees, but confirmed that episcopal baronies were held of the King. These courts, in the spring of 1136, which were well attended, represented Stephen's acceptance by the great majority of the baronage of England. Although Matilda had launched an attack on Normandy from her base in Anjou, even her brother Robert of Gloucester did homage to Stephen at this point.

The King's troubles thereafter derived mainly from his own character. He was open-handed, chivalrous and brave, but capricious and unreliable. Above all, he was unable to rule men. The first king since the Conquest to succeed simultaneously in both Normandy and England, he found the task beyond him. He did not get to Normandy until the spring of 1137, and by then the situation was virtually out of control as local barons played off one allegiance against another. Lords like Baldwin de Redvers, with lands on both sides of the Channel, having been unsuccessful in raising rebellion in England, retired to their French estates to try their luck there. Geoffrey of Anjou, with the aid of these rebellious lords, conquered the Duchy between 1141 and 1144, and there did not seem to be much that Stephen could do about it. One of his troubles was that he tended to buy off opponents with concessions which then alienated those who had been his friends. Another was that he created far too many earls, some eight or nine in all, which resulted in gifts of jurisdiction which were detrimental to his authority. Above all, he upset the Church in a dispute over the election of Theodore of Bec to succeed William of Corbeil as Archbishop in December 1138, a dispute which temporarily alienated his brother and spread dissension among the bishops. Feudally, the crunch came in May 1138, when Robert of Gloucester formally renounced his allegiance. Robert was in Normandy at the time, and the King moved to confiscate his English estates, an attempt which provoked widespread rebellion. This time, however, the King was victorious and with the assistance of Alberic, the papal legate, succeeded in the late summer of 1138 in imposing an uneasy peace. However, in the summer of 1139 Matilda opened her campaign for the English succession with an appeal to the Pope to overturn Innocent's decision. He refused to be moved, but several of his cardinals supported the Angevin cause, and that sowed further dissension among the English prelates. This had an effect when it was claimed on Matilda's behalf that Stephen was not keeping the promises which he had made to the Church in 1136, and some bishops supported her when she came to England early in 1141 to claim her inheritance, a move which stirred Robert of Gloucester's growing following to renewed efforts, and caused various other magnates to join them. In a pitched battle at Lincoln on 2 February 1141, Stephen was defeated and captured, leaving the way open for Matilda to be proclaimed 'Lady of the English'.

Unfortunately for her followers, she swiftly proved arbitrary and tyrannical in power, and her support soon began to ebb away. The opposition of the Londoners was particularly crucial in frustrating her attempts to secure a coronation. Meanwhile Henry of Blois, forgetting his disagreements with his brother, rallied Stephen's followers, and in the fighting around Winchester towards the end of 1141 Robert of Gloucester was captured. He was soon exchanged for the imprisoned king, and by the beginning of 1142 the status quo had been restored. The one thing that Matilda's brief ascendancy had demonstrated was that she was not fit to be queen. In laying siege to Oxford Castle early in 1142, Stephen almost had revenge for his captivity, because the Empress was trapped inside. She made good her escape allegedly dressed all in white to blend with the snowy landscape, and the great opportunity was missed. By this time, however, Normandy had been lost, and when he achieved the age of fourteen in 1147, Matilda's son Henry was proclaimed duke. Meanwhile the war in England ground on, and it was of these years that a later chronicler wrote that 'God and his angels slept'. In 1149 Henry of Anjou was formally invested with the Duchy of Normandy, and in the same year made an unsuccessful bid to secure his position in England with an invasion of the North, in the course of which he was knighted by his kinsman, David of Scotland. It was during these years also that Stephen attempted to improve his precarious position by securing the acceptance of his son Eustace as his heir. In this, however, he failed, partly because the English magnates saw the need for a resolution of the Angevin claim, and partly out of a desire to reunite England and Normandy. When Eustace died in 1153, the way was therefore open for a reconciliation. Henry of Anjou returned to England, and at Winchester in November of the same year signed a peace treaty with the King whereby he was recognised as the heir, passing over the claims of Stephen's second son, William. This was the agreement in which he took pains to promise the restitution of the deprived and disinherited. As Robert of Torigny later observed, 'it was sworn that the land which had fallen to intruders should be restored to their former and legitimate possessors'. Although this might make the reign of Stephen appear to be a legal nullity, it was necessary to secure peace. Stephen's queen, another strong-minded Matilda, had died in 1152, and he did not remarry, which was no doubt one reason why he was prepared to settle the succession on Henry. The latter did not have long to wait for his inheritance, because Stephen died at Dover on 25 October 1154, and was buried at Faversham. He was about fifty-eight years old, and his successor was twenty-one.

PART 6
THE ANGEVINS,
1154–1272

20

HENRY II (REIGNED 1154–1189)

Henry had about a year in which to accustom himself to the idea of being King of England, and he made good use of the time. William was satisfied with the County of Blois, and did not attempt to mount a counterclaim, so the new king's accession was undisputed. He was already Duke of Normandy and Count of Anjou in his own right since the death of his father, and Duke of Aquitaine in the right of his wife, Eleanor, whom he had married in 1152, but the Kingdom of England provided him with his greatest challenge. He and his queen were crowned together on 19 December 1154, and he immediately issued a brief charter of liberties in which he confirmed his commitment to the rule of law, and all grants and concessions made by his grandfather, Henry I. However, by implication it annulled similar grants and concessions made by Stephen, which he reserved the right to confirm or not as he thought fit. He also appointed two men jointly to the newly identified position of Justiciar, to control the administration of the kingdom: Richard de Lucy, who had been one of Stephen's most skilful and experienced administrators, and Robert Earl of Leicester, who had been a peacemaker in the latter part of Stephen's reign, and had given his allegiance to Henry in 1153. A third senior post, that of Chancellor, was conferred by Archbishop Theobald's advice on Thomas Becket, the Archdeacon of Canterbury, with whom (in spite of their later falling out) his relations were at first amicable. The task of this new team was a formidable one, because the country was in no more than a watchful peace, where rival barons eyed each other warily, and fortified their castles against sudden attack. So the King set out 'to root out all causes for renewal of warfare and to clear away all inducements to distrust'. He got rid of Stephen's Flemish mercenaries and set a time limit for the demolition of all unauthorised castles, at the same time demanding the return to royal control of all those official fortifications which had been granted out. This was a gamble, but Henry took advantage of the mutual suspicions of the barons to enforce it, and the effect on public confidence in his government was transforming. He had mastered his aristocracy, and by the end of 1155 his authority in England was probably more secure than it was in Normandy. He was what his predecessor had not been, a skilled manager of men, with a restless energy and intelligence, which kept him constantly on the move. He was stocky, freckled, and unkempt, with a force of personality which was unmistakable. He was also careless of the niceties of courtly behaviour, on one occasion riding his horse into the hall at dinner time, and sitting down to eat in his hunting clothes – to the horror of his well-bred young courtiers.

At the beginning of February 1156 Henry crossed to France, and, meeting King Louis VII on the borders of Normandy on the 6th, did homage to him for Normandy, Anjou and Aquitaine, thereby defusing a potentially hostile situation. In the autumn Queen Eleanor joined him and together they made a tour of Aquitaine, receiving the homage of the barons there, and making a few adjustments to the power structure. By 1157 his power was secure in all his dominions, and he was able to turn his attention to the Scots and the Welsh. King Malcolm journeyed south at Henry's invitation in May 1157, and prudently surrendered Northumbria, bearing in mind 'that the king of England had the better of the argument by reason of his greater power'. He received in return the Earldom of Huntingdon, for which he did homage. The Welsh princes were less tractable, and it took an intelligent and well-organised campaign in the summer of 1157 to persuade Owain of Gwynedd to do homage for his principality, whereupon Rhys of Deheubarth followed suit. Henry's task in pacifying England had undoubtedly been helped by the death of several potential troublemakers between 1154 and 1157, most notably Ranulf, Earl of Chester. At the same time Hugh Mortimer was subdued by negotiation in 1155, and Henry of Blois, Stephen's brother, retired to Cluny, where he was to die in 1171. This helped to seal Henry's alliance with the Church, which was of great assistance when it came to the piecemeal resumption of regalian rights which had been granted away, and bringing the country under the sway of a uniform code of law. The consolidation of royal control over the administration of the law was one of Henry's great achievements. This involved the separation of pleas of the crown, that is offences against the King's peace, from other kind of pleas – over land use, for example. The former offences, which came to be known as felonies, were to be tried in the King's courts of hundred and shire, which were presided over by royal officers, while the latter were to be adjudicated in the feudal courts of honour and manor, presided over by the Lord's Steward. This distinction between the Common Law, which was uniform throughout England, and the Customary Law, which might vary from place to place, was fundamental to the later development of the judicial system. At the same time, Normandy, Anjou and Aquitaine were each governed in accordance with their own codes of law, which were similarly customary, but different from those of England. The Common Law was customary in origin, but had become the King's law through his monopoly of enforcement, and could only be modified either by royal decree or by judicial interpretation. To ensure uniformity of administration the King took to sending his judges out on Eyre, which was slow and cumbersome, but effective. These judges in turn were answerable to the Curia Regis, which became known in due course as the Court of King's Bench. This system of control which was developed over the whole reign undoubtedly had the effect of improving confidence in the central government, reducing the temptation for barons to take the law into their own hands, and generally improving the discipline of a hitherto unruly country.

After the pacification of England, which had been achieved by 1169, the politics of Henry's reign centred largely on the succession. Impressed by the achievement of Richard de Clare, Earl of Pembroke, in Ireland, he went there in 1171–72 to secure his control, and took the homage of de Clare and of the Irish chieftains, but the establishment of control there was never a priority. There was also rebellion in South Wales, provoked by the introduction of direct royal rule, but that was suppressed without great difficulty. Much more problematic was his relationship with his sons – and with his wife. He made his first disposition in 1170, when he decided that England and Normandy should go to his eldest son, Henry, Aquitaine to Richard, Anjou to Geoffrey, and Ireland (what there was of it) to John. He clearly had no sense of preserving the integrity of anything which could be called an 'Angevin Empire'. His daughter Eleanor was to be married to Alfonso VIII of Castile, and was to take Gascony to her husband as her dowry. Young Henry was duly (and most unusually) crowned later in 1170, but given no real share in the government, while Richard was created Duke of Aquitaine on similar terms in 1172. Apparently dissatisfied with this arrangement, Eleanor and all her four sons fled to the court of Louis VII in 1173, and Henry was faced with a major rebellion in his Continental lands. With his customary energy and efficiency, the King raised an army and campaigned in France, capturing Queen Eleanor and imprisoning her. His sons submitted and were reconciled, being restored to their lands and titles. By 1180 Henry was heartily sick of warfare, but the death of his eldest son, the young Henry, in 1183 raised the whole question of the succession again, and led to quarrels among the remaining siblings which necessitated their father undertaking further campaigns in 1184 and 1185. Another reconciliation followed, but Henry did not make any fresh apportionment of titles, and his bad relations with his sons were only squabbles which marred years of comparative peace and stability. His attitude towards his wife continued to be problematic. He had considered divorcing her as early as 1175, but had been deterred by the likely political consequences. He had also kept a mistress, Rosamund Clifford, known as 'Fair Rosamund', of whom he had been very fond, and who had exercised considerable influence over him. However, Rosmund died in 1176, and no one took her place in the King's affections – certainly not his wife. He took her to Normandy in 1185, but her restoration to queenly dignity was precarious and after Richard quarrelled with his father (again) in 1186 she seems to have been returned to captivity. She outlived Henry by a number of years, dying in 1204. The last months of Henry's life were spent in negotiations with Philip II of France, who had taken over the throne on Louis' death in 1180. Philip was a determined opponent of the Angevins, and seems to have entertained the ambition of expelling them from France. Acting in alliance with a dissident Richard, he had overrun Maine in 1189, but Richard had then departed to prepare for his crusade, and Philip was willing to come to terms. On 4 July the two kings met at Ballan, near Tours, and agreed a treaty, but Henry was already mortally sick and died at Chinon on the 6th. He was buried at Fontevrault, his son Richard arriving while his body still lay in state. He was not particularly old at fifty-six, but was worn out by a life of incessant toil, movement and emotional stress. Above all, his need to impose his will on those around him had taken its toll on his constitution.

One of those who resisted that will, and paid the price, was Thomas Becket. Archbishop Theobald died in 1161, and Henry, who was determined to exercise his grandfather's prerogatives in respect of the Church, nominated his Chancellor and friend Thomas Becket to succeed him. However, the Church had moved on since 1135, and when the King convened a council of clergy at Westminster in October 1163 for the purpose of resolving the problem of clerks who committed offences against the King's laws, the stage was set for a confrontation. The King's proposals were set out in the Constitutions of Clarendon in January 1164, and appeared to the clergy to involve a direct assault on ecclesiastical self-government – the *libertas ecclesiae*. That was not Henry's intention, and had Archbishop Theobald still been alive he might well have smoothed things over, but Becket was man of inflexible conscience. He had already demonstrated that in his pursuance of the King's rights as Chancellor, and now he proved equally tenacious in defence of the Church. It soon appeared that Henry had been mistaken in his choice of archbishop if he had wanted a compliant primate, and the King, not surprisingly felt betrayed. Typical of Becket's attitude was his demand that Roger de Clare, Earl of Hertford, do homage to him for the castle and bailiwick of Tonbridge in Kent. He had a clear duty to assert the rights of the barony of Canterbury, to which Tonbridge belonged, but it would have been more tactful to have sued for the same in the King's court, which was what Henry expected. He made other similar claims, and the King became alerted to fact that he had a problem.

The situation came to a head in September 1164 when a marshal of the royal household laid a claim before the Archbishop's honorial court, which was dismissed. The marshal then appealed to the King, and the Archbishop was summoned before the King's court. He sent excuses, and was then summoned to Northampton in October to answer charges of contempt. He was found guilty and sentenced to forfeit his goods at the King's pleasure. This led to a confrontation, in which the King began to level additional charges of embezzlement, and the Archbishop appealed to the Pope. Before the end of the month, Becket had fled the country, taking refuge with the King's antagonist, Louis of France. From there he went on to Rome, to lodge his appeal in person, and Henry refrained from touching his goods until the appeal should be held. Becket offered to resign his see, but was reinstated by the Pope with words of comfort and encouragement. Henry took it out on the Archbishop's friends and dependants, and began a futile six-year campaign to get the papal decision overturned. Meanwhile negotiations continued, sometimes through the mediation of Louis and sometimes directly, but both sides showed themselves obstinate and intractable. Then the coronation of Henry the Young King brought matters to a head. This had been carried out by the Archbishop of York, but Henry was prepared to have him reconsecrated by Becket, if the latter would submit. At a meeting between the two at Freteval on the borders of Touraine an agreement was ostensibly reached. Ostensibly, because controversies continued to disrupt relations. When Becket returned to England on 1 December, he met with a hostile reception and Henry the Young King refused to receive him. To this combustible situation, Becket himself provided the fire, because on the eve of his crossing he excommunicated the Archbishop of York and those other bishops who had assisted at the coronation of young Henry, in the name of the apostolic see. Why he did this is not clear, but it was a deliberately provocative action. The offended bishops sought out the King, who was keeping his Christmas at Bures, and appealed for his intervention. Angered by what appeared to him to be the Archbishop's betrayal of trust, Henry is alleged to have made the remark which led to Becket's murder at Canterbury a few days later – 'Will no one rid me of this turbulent priest?' The four knights who carried out the deed were not intelligent men, nor given to reflection on the likely consequences of their deed; they only knew that Becket must be made to submit to the King's will, or be destroyed. It seems likely that their victim was expecting them, and that the prospect of martyrdom was not unwelcome to him. At any rate, he proved more potent dead than alive, and a cult quickly developed. Although Henry had secured the substance of what he wanted, he was compelled to yield to the supposed sanctity of his victim, and in 1176 did solemn penance on the spot where Becket had been killed. Although humiliating, this may have been a small price to pay for having got rid of so formidable an opponent.

Although in this context Henry is King of England, it is important to remember that he spent only about 25 per cent of his time in the country, as opposed to 45 per cent in Normandy, 22 per cent in Anjou and 8 per cent in Aquitaine (176 months in Normandy, 154 months in England). Nevertheless, it was England which paid for this itinerant monarchy, because for the last ten years of his reign his English revenues averaged about £22,000 a year, whereas Normandy brought in only £6,750. Records do not survive for Anjou or Aquitaine, but the Angevin Empire was an economic as well as a political unit, and the towns both in England and in France were conspicuously loyal to the dynasty. The wine trade from La Rochelle and Bordeaux to England was one of the mainstays of the prosperity of both communities, and the money derived from it helped to make Henry's reign, for all its troubles, one of the most successful in English history.

21

RICHARD I, THE CRUSADER (REIGNED 1189-1199)

Outside the Houses of Parliament in Westminster stands an equestrian statue of Richard I, with his sword aloft, and it is as a warrior and crusader that we chiefly remember him. This is fair enough in terms of his own priorities as he spent only a few months in England in a reign which lasted for ten years. Towards the end of his life, Henry had fallen out seriously with Richard, who was always more inclined to his mother's point of view, and Richard had done homage to Philip Augustus for the Duchy of Aquitaine. There was a radical lack of trust between them, but shortly before Henry's death they met during an armed truce and agreed terms. Richard was to marry Alice, Philip's sister, and Henry acknowledged Richard as his heir. There was also an understanding that the troublesome John, Richard's younger brother, would take the cross. Richard was entirely French, he spoke no word of English, and at the time of his accession was deeply engaged with King Philip over the future of the Church of Tours, which was within the Angevin dominions, but had strong links with France. Having reached an agreement on this sensitive issue, Richard then went to Rouen, where he was installed as Duke of Normandy. John, who did not after all take the cross, was vested with the County of Mortmain in Normandy and with various lands in England. Richard confirmed his agreement to marry Alice, and turned his attention to the affairs of England, where he instructed the clergy to elect his stepbrother Geoffrey as Archbishop of York and made sensible arrangements for the keeping of the peace in Wales. He then went to England, and was crowned at Westminster on 3 September 1189, having received absolution from the Archbishop of Canterbury for his rebellion against his father, a point over which his conscience was obviously troubling him. This was also reflected in his disposition of offices, because he confirmed those who had been loyal to his father, and replaced those who had not, even if their defection had been in his own interest. For example, he dismissed Ranulf Glanville, the Justiciar, and replaced him with William de Mandeville and Hugh de Puiset. His coronation banquet was marred by the appearance of a group of Jews, who came bearing gifts, but were excluded from the royal presence. Anti-semitic riots followed, during which several were killed. Richard subsequently hanged a number of the rioters, and sent letters to the sheriffs to say that the Jews were to be left in peace. However, further riots followed and defied all attempts at pacification. In July 1190, the King left for Normandy, and thence on crusade. He would not return for four years.

To Richard, the recovery of Jerusalem was a solemn religious duty, and he gave it priority over any purely domestic concerns. One result of this was his very indulgent treatment of his brother John, who was given the regency of Normandy, extensive lands in England and Ireland and the hand of Isobel of Gloucester in marriage. John was now a prince in reality as well as in title, and many saw him as a threat to his brother's rule. Another result was the levying of heavy taxes in England to pay for the army and the navy which the King had taken with him. For all this William Longchamp, the King's Chancellor, was largely responsible. Since William de Mandeville had died within a few weeks of his appointment, Longchamps effectively took over his role as co-Justiciar as well as Chancellor, and this gave him a controlling say in public policy. He was particularly concerned to keep the right side of John, and many regarded that as a questionable tactic. Meanwhile Richard had reached Cyprus, where he abandoned his undertaking to Alice and married Berengeria of Navarre, the daughter of King Sancho VI, thus aligning himself with Navarre and Aragon against France in the matter of Aquitaine. King Philip, needless to say, was not pleased and began to threaten Richard's French lands. However, he did not take any action on that threat, partly because the lands of crusaders were supposed to be protected during their absence, and partly because he joined the crusade himself. As a military operation, this was a partial success. The crusaders took the city of Acre in 1191, and Richard defeated Saladin at Asurf near Jaffa, but he failed to take Jerusalem. Then in September 1192 a truce was signed, and the crusading princes headed for home. Philip went straight back to France, and Berengaria headed for Italy, but Richard was shipwrecked and decided to return overland. In the course of his journey he was taken prisoner by Duke Leopold of Austria, thus frustrating his intention to be back in Normandy by early 1193. The Duke and his overlord, the Emperor Henry VI, had every intention of exploiting their good fortune, and began to hold out for an enormous ransom. Richard's captivity temporarily changed the political landscape. John crossed to France and did homage to Philip for Normandy, but the majority of the English barons, and the King of Scots, remained loyal to Richard. Eleanor in fact raised an army against John, and prevented him from taking advantage of the situation. He tried to claim that his brother was dead, but the ongoing negotiations proved the contrary. Meanwhile Richard's location had been identified, allegedly thanks to the initiative of a minstrel called Blondel, who sang a song which they had composed together in happier days beneath the window of his prison.

Philip meanwhile sought in various ways to turn events to his advantage. His forces harried Normandy, reaching the gates of Rouen before being turned back, and he entered into an alliance with John, encouraging that irresponsible young man to stir up as much trouble for his brother as he could. He also tried to do a deal with the Emperor, to transfer Richard to his own custody, but that failed because by December 1193 enough money had been raised in England to pay the first instalment of the ransom demanded. Frustrated in their first attempt, Philip and John then tried offering the Emperor a monthly subsidy to keep Richard under lock and key. That also failed because the German princes, when appealed to, advised its rejection. Consequently a deal was done with the Council in England, and Richard's release was scheduled for 17 January 1194. On 13 March he landed at Sandwich, and immediately confirmed the confiscation John's English lands, and the sentence of excommunication passed upon him as a rebel against one who had taken the cross. The Pope also obligingly excommunicated Leopold of Austria for the same reason. Richard's return was marked by a public crown wearing, lest it should be forgotten who was really the king, and the collection of the balance of his ransom money continued to be a burden on the country for several years. By the end of May, the

King had gone back to Normandy, and spent the majority of his time there until his death five years later.

This did not mean, however, that English affairs were neglected. Before his release was even negotiated he had named Hubert Walter, the Bishop of Salisbury, as the new Archbishop of Canterbury, and as Chief Justiciar in succession to Walter of Coutances. It had been in that capacity, and as head of the regency council that Hubert had been responsible for the suppression of John's rebellion in 1193, personally conducting the siege of Marlborough Castle, and ordering the capture of all the other strongholds held by John's supporters. He also called the council of nobles which disseised John of his possessions, and the assembly of bishops which excommunicated him. After Richard's brief return, he took a number of initiatives with the King's approval to improve the administration of England, issuing comprehensive articles to the justices in Eyre for the keeping of the peace in 1194, and in the following year ordering that all men over fifteen should take an oath to uphold that order. Most significantly for the historian, however, were the improvements which he made in record keeping. He decided that all final accords in judicial cases should be preserved in triplicate: one copy for the litigant, one for the court and the third for the Exchequer. He also began the enrolment of all Chancery letters and other documents for future reference by the office. Although there is (rather surprisingly) plenty of evidence that the King took a personal interest in these administrative matters, he was far away and it fell to Hubert Walter to maintain and improve the government of the kingdom. There were those among the barons who resented this efficiency, and called it tyranny, particularly because it was associated with the Justiciar rather than with Richard personally. A new system of customs collection was instituted to improve the revenue, and to help fund Richard's ransom, which did not please the mercantile community of London, and the customers who collected these dues were given a management function in the control of the ports, which were organised into groups. All this was carried out in the King's name, but it is difficult to be sure exactly how much he knew of the reforms which were being instituted.

In France, Richard faced an uphill task, partly because of John's activities, but more because of the advantage which Philip had been able to take of his absence. In Normandy he advanced quickly and effectively when he was on campaign, but was constantly distracted by developments further south. By the end of 1195 he had secured control of Anjou, but was still struggling to establish himself in Aquitaine in spite of the support of his mother, who lived until 1204. This was partly because of the opposition of the counts of Toulouse, which continued despite his alliance with Navarre. Richard's campaigns in the north were intense, if sporadic, and set a pace which Philip found hard to match. On one occasion he narrowly avoided capture by Richard's forces, and lost most of his archive, as well as the booty which his army was carrying. This sustained pace, however, was broken by a sequence of truces. The first, negotiated by William Longchamps, was made at Tillieres in 1195, and was supposed to last for a year. It broke down in a series of skirmishes, and was renegotiated at Christmas 1196. This time it lasted rather better, but needed to be extended late in 1197. By the end of that year, he had made great progress in re-establishing his control, taking advantage of his truces with the French to besiege and take the fortresses of individual dissidents, mainly a legacy from John's rebellion. At the same time he spent much time, and money, building his great fortress at Chateau Gaillard, where he based his own household. It was in attacking one of these 'rogue' castles that Richard met his end. At Chalus Chabrol on 26 March 1199, he was shot by a crossbowman from the walls. The injury was not thought to be serious, but gangrene set in, and on 6 April the King died. His body was interred at Fontrevault, but his heart, on his own special orders, was conveyed to Rouen, in a fitting tribute to where his priorities had always lain.

22

JOHN (REIGNED 1199–1216)

It took eleven days for the news of Richard's death to be received in England, and John's succession was by no means assured. Quite apart from the fact that he had been expelled from the kingdom in 1194, there was another claimant in the person of Arthur, Geoffrey's son. Geoffrey had been John's elder brother, and there were many in England, including the Archbishop Hubert Walter, who preferred his claim. Arthur's position was strengthened by the way in which John had behaved towards Richard, but he was a child of eleven years old, and custom worked in favour of the adult. John, for all his selfishness and deceitfulness, was thirty-two years old and of proven competence. He also moved fast, going at once to Rouen, where he was immediately received as duke. The Norman barons generally supported him, and the customary law of the duchy also worked in his favour. Hardly had he taken the homage of his Norman vassals than he was on his way to England, where the promptness of his action in Normandy made a good impression. Hubert Walter (for all his misgivings) and William Marshall had acted immediately to put loyal garrisons in all the royal castles from Lancaster to Dover and throughout the marches of Wales, and John faced no serious rival. He was crowned at Westminster in May 1199, and within a month was back in France again. There he faced serious problems, because although Normandy was secure, the barons of Anjou and Brittany favoured Arthur, and Philip Augustus of France, with an eye to the main chance, took the same line. Ostensibly Philip was angry with John because he had not done homage to him as overlord for his Norman and Angevin lands, but in fact he saw his chances of manipulating a minority government snatched away, and there followed a military confrontation between these two erstwhile allies. However, there was no serious fighting, and the two kings met at Le Goulet in May 1200, to sort out the problems between them. The resultant treaty favoured Philip in one crucial respect, in that John agreed to recognise his overlordship with regard to all his Continental possessions. However, there were good precedents in favour of that, and Philip in return recognised John not only as King of England, but as the heir of his father and his brother in respect of all the other titles which he claimed. Arthur was to hold Brittany of John, and a marriage was arranged between the Dauphin, Louis, and John's niece, Blanche.

John's own marriage to Isabella, which went back ten years, but which had been childless, was at the same time belatedly annulled on the grounds of consanguinity. This move was not altogether unconnected with the King's desire for a political marriage to another Isabella, the twelve-year-old daughter of Ademar of Angouleme. In so doing he disappointed the expectations of Hugh of Lusignan, and took over the government of La Marche, a region in dispute between Ademar and Hugh. Hugh appealed to John's overlord, Philip of France, and that brought to an end the uneasy two-year peace between them. John was summoned to Philip's feudal court, but declined to go and his lands were declared forfeit. Normandy was to become part of France, and the remainder were to go to Arthur. This was to declare an open house for rebellion by John's erstwhile vassals, and Arthur, backed by the rebel Lusignans, besieged Queen Eleanor at Mirabeau. In his only striking military success, John then advanced on Mirabeau from Le Mans, defeated the besiegers and captured Arthur. The fate of Arthur has long been a subject of controversy, but it appears that he was murdered at Rouen in 1203, perhaps by John personally in a drunken rage. At any rate, the King was summoned to another feudal court by Philip to answer for his supposed crime in 1204, and that resulted in a second sentence against him. Meanwhile Normandy and Anjou were slowly slipping from his grasp. This was not the result of any major defeat in battle, but rather of an 'erosion of allegiance', not helped by the fact that his mother Eleanor died in 1204. Philip was advancing in Poitou, and a number of Norman lords had declared for him, particularly those who held no lands in England. By the beginning of 1205, John was back in England, preparing a major assault to recover what he had lost, and these preparations continued throughout the year. In April the Bishop of Norwich was ordered to send ships to Portsmouth on the King's business, and in the West Country 100 marks was spent on the hiring of other vessels. Food was gathered for the fleet, and in May a muster of land forces was held at Northampton. Other preparations were no doubt made, but these are the ones of which we have a record. The nature of John's problem is demonstrated by the behaviour of William Marshal, one of the greatest barons in England, who declined to support the King's campaign because he had rendered liege homage to Philip for his lands in Normandy. Other lords faced a similar dilemma, and Philip exploited this for all that it was worth. Consequently, when John eventually set sail on 20 May 1206, the great majority of his support came from England. He went originally to Poitou, partly because he knew that Philip was having great difficulty in controlling the Poitevin nobles, partly because he judged it easier to strike north into Normandy from a base there, and partly because he faced a challenge in Gascony from Alfonso VIII of Castile. The marriage clause of the treaty of Le Goulet had been observed better than the rest of that agreement, and the Dauphin, Louis, had married Blanche, the daughter of Alfonso and of John's sister Eleanor. Since he was also a son-in-law of Henry I, this encouraged Alfonso to claim Gascony in his own right, and this was a claim welcomed by those Poitevin nobles who did not fancy the close attentions of either Philip or John. Having captured Mons Alba, near the Norman border in August 1206, and taken with it a number of Spanish prisoners, John crossed the Loire into Normandy on 6 September and captured Angers. Since Philip declined to engage, this resulted in a two-year truce, signed on 13 October, but that settled none of the issues. John's base in Poitou was now stronger, but he had failed to make any impression on Normandy, and that was a failure for which many, both at the time and since, have condemned him.

To make any further headway, he needed Continental allies, and his attention now began to turn to his nephew Otto, the son of his elder sister Matilda and Henry the Lion, the head of the House of Welf. Henry had died in 1199, and the result had been a conflict for control of the Rhineland between Otto and Philip of Swabia. Since Philip was allied to his namesake of France, it was natural for John to look to Otto, and the latter came to England in 1207. This prompted the King to look for other allies, and in 1208 he recruited Henry, the Count Palatine, Otto's brother, who also came to England in 1209. As a direct result of this growing association, and of John's alleged failure to observe the oaths which he had taken to Philip Augustus, in 1209 Pope Innocent III, who was Philip's ally, excommunicated both John and Otto, and placed the Kingdom of England under an interdict. This stirred up rebellion in Ireland and in Wales, and conspiracy in the north of England, all of which required time and application to deal with. In addition there were rumours that Innocent had deposed John, and was encouraging Philip to invade in order to enforce the sentence against him. At the same time the Pope was supporting the claims of the Emperor Frederick II against Otto, so that the latter's position was also precarious. The English Church was divided, many of the bishops supporting the Pope, and withdrawing their cooperation from the government, which greatly increased the King's difficulties. Eventually, in May 1213, John submitted, and agreed to accept his kingdom as a fief from the Church. This was a largely notional concession, but it reconciled him to the Church, and removed any possibility that any of the bishops would support a French invasion. Meanwhile John had added Renaud d'Ammartin, the Count of Boulogne, to his Continental allies. Renaud had been a vassal of the King of France, but he had deserted him and forfeited his castles in consequence. In 1212 he came to England and did homage to John. The Duke of Limburg and the Count of Bar did the same, in return for promises of reinstatement, and money fiefs, so that by the beginning of 1213 the English position in France was looking fairly strong again. This was confirmed when John mobilised his navy at Portsmouth in May 1213, and carried out several lightning raids on the Seine and Dieppe. He also mustered an army and sent it across to Flanders to support Count Ferrand against Philip Augustus, and while the King of France was occupied in besieging Ghent, an English fleet routed its French equivalent at the Battle of Damme. Consequently things were looking a good deal more promising when John sailed again for Poitou in February 1214.

The allegiance of the Poitevin nobles this time seemed assured, while Otto and his allies were advancing on France from the north-east. John reached La Rochelle, and at first encountered little resistance. However, having taken a number of castles, he failed to advance any further, possibly because of fears of disloyalty within his army, which may also be why he wrote home in July asking for reinforcements. There is no doubt that militarily Philip was the superior strategist, and having defeated Otto at Bouvines, he then turned his attention to John, beating him also in what passed for a battle, but in which only the Earl of Salisbury earned any credit. On 18 September 1214 the two kings signed another truce, this time to last until 1220, and John's credit was further lowered. His incompetence had been demonstrated, his treasury emptied, and his Continental allies lost. This had its repercussions in England, where resentment against the financial and military exactions required by his French wars was mounting. Much of the power base which he had enjoyed at the beginning of his reign had been lost, as dissatisfaction with his government began to undermine the loyalty of those barons who had at first accepted him willingly. On 1 June 1212 he compounded this dissent by issuing writs of enquiry into feudal tenures by hundreds and counties rather than via the tenants in chief as had been done hitherto. These writs do not seem to have been enforced, and the matter did not immediately come to a head, but in 1213 the Northern barons in general declined to support the King's expedition to Poitou, on the ground that their military service was due only against the Scots. In this equivocal situation, John made concessions, making a general promise of reforms, which was focussed by Archbishop Stephen Langton on the charter of Henry I. Although this implied that the whole Angevin regime since 1154 had been corrupt, it was apparently accepted by John in July 1213, when clauses were added about not selling justice or making false imprisonments. Because no text of this of this submission survives it is called the 'unknown charter of liberties'; perhaps it was no more than a draft for discussion. In the event, some of the Northern lords did go on the expedition of 1214, and the barons of the South and of East Anglia remained loyal to the King.

One of the first things that John did on his return from Poitou was to demand a scutage, which immediately reactivated baronial opposition. Many refused to pay, and by the end of 1214 there was a concerted movement against the King in which numerous barons swore an oath that they would break their fealty unless he granted them their liberties 'in a charter under his seal'. In December he agreed to meet the dissidents in London at Epiphany 1215, meanwhile depending increasingly on his reconciliation with the Church to mobilise clerical support. He even wrote to Pope Innocent, asking him to send letters to the dissidents, urging their loyalty, and relied heavily upon the intercessory efforts of Archbishop Langton. The Great Charter which was famously sealed at Runnymead in June 1215 was the result of months of intensive negotiations. It was in essence a peace treaty between the King and his barons, in which they pledged their loyalty in return for certain specific liberties and privileges., and was probably drawn up jointly by Stephen Langton and William Marshal. Its first clause, which was not included in the Articles of the Barons, dealt with the liberties of the Church, and included the principle that 'the king was below the law, and that peace and justice were the objects of civil government'. Interpretations of the Charter have varied, some seeing it as a mere attempt by a feudal nobility to recover their jurisdictions from the intrusion of royal officers, but others arguing that it was a genuine attempt to guarantee the liberties of all free men, *nulli liberi homines* being used in no less than six clauses. Most important was a clause empowering a council of twenty-five barons to distrain upon the King should he fail to observe the concessions which he had made, a clause which, it has been observed, 'deprived him of his sovereign power', or at any rate made it impossible for him to claim that he was answerable to God alone. The Charter was vague precisely where it needed to be precise, and it is not surprising that it did not end the confrontation, in spite of the assurances which were given by John on 18 June, the day on which the document was sealed. A further meeting at Oxford in July failed to resolve these difficulties, and the situation deteriorated into civil war. In this the King enjoyed the advantage, partly because he held about 150 castles as opposed to the barons' 60, and partly because the rebels were excommunicated by the Pope as a part of his deal with John. It was only control of London which sustained the barons' cause at the end of 1215. Then in 1216 the Dauphin Louis invaded in their support, and although welcomed by the hard core of the rebels, his presence had the opposite of the intended effect, as the English barons rallied to the King against the foreigner. When John died suddenly at Newark in October 1216, Louis controlled London and most of East Anglia, but he was defeated by William Marshal in battles at Lincoln and Dover and forced to sign a peace treaty in 1217 whereby he withdrew from the scene. The Great Charter was also modified in small but significant ways. It soon became apparent that much of the opposition to John, although cast in legal terms, had in fact been personal in its nature. He had been neither a good man nor a good king. However, he had at least been a man; his son Henry was no more than nine years old and a protracted minority was in prospect.

23

THE LONG REIGN OF HENRY III
(1216–1272)

Young Henry succeeded in the midst of a civil war, in which each side was held together as much by its concept of honour as by more material advantages. Louis in particular was a pious young man, and conspicuously loyal to his followers. So at the end of the truce which had been negotiated before Christmas, he returned to England in April 1217 to continue the struggle. On the other side the regency government was controlled by William Marshal, and by the papal legate Bicchieri Guala, whose main mission was to bring peace, but who supported Marshal because Louis was technically excommunicate. Henry was crowned at Gloucester on 28 October 1216, in a somewhat hasty and scrappy ceremony, because London was controlled by Louis, and the new king's support was in any case mainly in the West Country. In early November a Great Council of these supporters was held, which resolved the matter of the regency and, on 12 November, reissued the Great Charter. The original version had been condemned by the papacy at John's insistence, but the papal legate was instrumental in this reissue, which was made in the name of the young king in spite of his minority. Guala realised the importance of this document for the process of pacification, and presumably claimed that it was a new charter, and unaffected by the Pope's earlier decision. Meanwhile the war continued, a truce over Christmas being secured by Marshal's surrendering of Berkhampstead on 20 December, and this was extended in January to 23 April, Louis' party not being willing to concede a peace settlement. Louis himself departed to France for the duration of this truce, to raise reinforcements, and during his absence Henry's position improved markedly as various English lords who had been alienated from John returned to their allegiance.

On his return to England, both Louis' own forces and those of the regent were divided. The Dauphin felt it necessary to leave a substantial contingent in Kent to cope with the fact that he had failed to take Dover Castle, while sending his main army north to take Lincoln. Realising the advantage which this gave him, Marshal reunited his own his own forces at Newark on 18 May, and advanced to the relief of Lincoln. There on the 20th he won a resounding victory and took a large number of important prisoners. It would be no exaggeration to say that this battle ripped the heart out of Louis' party, and determined the future of the English monarchy. The Dauphin was ready to give up, and peace negotiations were opened on the initiative of Guala, on 13 June. They did not immediately succeed, but the regent held a number of councils during July and August, which received the submission of more of Louis' erstwhile followers, and diminished his party to a hard core. It may be that the French were holding on, awaiting the reinforcements which Louis' energetic wife had been raising, because on 24 August a large French fleet arrived off Sandwich bearing additional troops. The English navy, however, was waiting for them and, gaining the weather gauge, pulverised them, inflicting a large number of casualties. This second disaster was more than enough for Louis, who on 28 August reactivated the peace negotiations. They were completed by 12 September when the Dauphin met Henry, his mother and the regent near Kingston on Thames, and formally agreed the terms. He himself was to return to France, and not to lay any further claim to lands or offices in England. His lay followers were to be reinstated in their fiefs as at the outbreak of war, and ecclesiastics were to be dealt with by the legate as he thought fit. In the event Simon Langton and three of his colleagues were forced to resort to Rome for absolution from the Pope himself. The evil practices which were alleged to have caused the war were to be abolished, and the good 'liberties and customs of the Kingdom of England' were to be restored. This last point was re-emphasised when another new version of the Great Charter was issued in November. Counsels of moderation had prevailed, no doubt to the disappointment of those who were looking for the spoils of victory. In the event the winners had to satisfy themselves with the ransoms of those who had been taken prisoner. The divisions created by the war were to be ignored in the working of the regency government thereafter.

From the autumn of 1217 until his death in May 1219, William Marshal strove to impose order on what was a fundamentally anarchic society. Power was vested in the aristocracy, and where they were cooperative, government worked well enough. Where they were recalcitrant, however, their coercion depended upon the politics of the area rather than upon the simple rights and wrongs of the case. This was particularly so when it came to collecting revenue, because the sheriffs were great men in their own right, and persuading them to account as their office required was often an uphill task. The invaluable Guala retired, at his own request, in September 1218, and although he was replaced by Pandulf, his statesmanship was sorely missed. A Great Council was held in November 1218, and it was decided that the King should have his own seal, which remained in the custody of the Chancery Clerk Ralph de Neville, and that the General Eyre should be reinstated. This last was a major step, because it was some years since the last Eyre, and the royal justices were suffering from a lack of oversight and support. It also went some way towards meeting the promise of good justice embodied in all versions of the Great Charter. Its justices oversaw all pleas, both civil and criminal, and carried out a detailed investigation into royal rights, many of which had been allowed to lapse during the war. The country was divided into eight regions for the purposes of this visitation, and although it ran into a number of difficulties, there is no doubt but that it was great success. It outlasted the regent himself, continuing until the end of 1219, and brought a vital injection of cash into the Exchequer from the fines and amercements which were not merely assessed, but actually paid. This was very important because in 1220 the income from the royal demesne was no more than £5,000 a year. It also helped in the general process of reconciliation, because the justices showed no favouritism to those who had fought for the King, and this inspired confidence in those who might have been fearful of their welcome in the royal confidence.

Meanwhile, young Henry was growing up. We know very little about this process, other than that he was under the care of a tutor called Henry of Avranches, who prepared an elaborate Latin grammar for the boy, running to some 2,000 lines. What use he made of it is not clear. He was certainly literate, and was given a basic training in theology, but otherwise it is not certain what he may have read. Presumably he received the usual instruction in the knightly arts of warfare, although he showed no aptitude as a soldier in later life. His political education, on the other hand, was practical and advanced. By the time that he was twelve or thirteen he was presiding at his own court under the guidance of Peter des Roches, the Bishop of Winchester, who was his official guardian, and he was personally receiving letters on sensitive political issues, such as the iniquities of Llewellyn of Gwynedd. By the time of his fourteenth birthday he was already being treated by the magnates as a separate entity from Peter des Roches, and there are some signs that he was responding positively to this treatment. Fourteen was, or could be, a very significant age, and there were certainly some among the English magnates who wanted him declared of age, presumably to free themselves from the government of the 'triumvirate' which had succeeded that of the regent in the summer of 1219. In particular they wanted to free him from dependence on the Bishop of Winchester, because the three who made up this new regime were the Justiciar, Hubert de Burgh, the Legate Pandulf, and des Roches himself. The disadvantages of this type of government were clear enough. Even when they were in agreement with each other, communications were far from perfect, and they did not always agree, conflicts over patronage being particularly apparent. So anxious were they to be conciliatory that it was said that those who had won the war were losing the peace, and the struggle to prevent powerful men from taking the law into their own hands was never-ending. Apart from this, the most pressing matter facing the triumvirate in the early months of its existence was the renewal of the truce with France, which was due to expire in March 1220. Philip delayed for reasons of his own, and the citizens of La Rochelle became anxious, but the negotiation was eventually successful and the truce was renewed for four years from Easter 1220.

In spite of a year of frustration, Pandulf and de Burgh enjoyed one huge success in the spring of 1220, and that was to arrange a second coronation for Henry III. In spite of the multitude of threats to the King's peace which arose in all parts of the country, this resounding endorsement of the King's personal position was highly significant. The King swore to preserve his rights and prerogatives, and the barons swore that they would surrender the royal castles which they held, and render faithful account of their stewardships at the Exchequer. This baronial oath, taken on 18 May 1220, was part of a wider programme, in which both Pandulf and the Pope were engaged, to remedy the King's poverty, because a lack of money lay behind much of the government's weakness. The barons also swore that they would aid the King in the recovering of his rights, and since that oath was taken by erstwhile opponents of the regime as well as its supporters, it marked an important step in the reconciliation of the quarrels which were now over. It also made government action against refractory castellans a more realistic proposition. Henry at this stage is described as being intelligent, almost precocious, but innocent and trusting by nature, warm in his affections, but poor in judgement. He was perceptive rather than imaginative, and devout rather than spiritual. Altogether he was a decent young man, caught up in a situation over which he could exercise only a limited control. When he was sixteen in 1223 he was given a limited use of his own seal, and declared himself to be of full age on reaching his twentieth birthday in 1227. Meanwhile it was often hard to determine whether the magnates were acting on his behalf, or merely in their own interests. Earl Ranulf of Chester was a good example of this as he conducted his own policy in the Welsh marches. Then there was the Earl of Salisbury, who dreamed of establishing a palatinate in Somerset and Devon. Sometimes, as in the case of William de Fortz in the North, such activities shaded over into rebellion, which happened at the end of 1220. A show of force was sufficient. William fled to Flanders, submitted and was subsequently pardoned – not for the first or the last time! The papal legate departed in 1221, leaving Hubert de Burgh as the Justiciar in virtual control. He was supported by an able group of bishops, but was often at odds with the Bishop of Winchester, who also remained influential and commanded the allegiance of a number of members of the Council. Only the Archbishop Stephen Langton (who had returned from Italy) remained independent of this division and consequently acted as arbiter between them.

On 11 February 1225 the King granted a new Charter of Liberties. This confirmed the earlier charters of 1216 and 1217, and emphasised the mutual responsibilities of Henry and his subjects, particularly for the maintenance of the peace. In return the Council granted him a fifteenth of all moveable goods, a special non-feudal tax which was to be paid by all and was to be assessed by lordships and hundreds. This raised the large sum of £58,000, which was none too much given that Louis of France made a rather half-hearted attack on Poitou in 1225, which was terminated by a truce after a few months, but which nevertheless cost a lot of money to resist. During this period England was lightly taxed, the scutage being the main feudal tax, which was levied on all vassals but only for emergencies. It was not supposed to pay for the regular government, and all such taxes together raised only about £112,000 between 1217 and 1257. The tallage of the towns was separate, but even that was light; for example, the tallages of 1223 and 1235 brought in a total of about £22,000. In short, Henry was living from hand to mouth, and the continuing peace had to depend not on mercenary troops but upon leadership and trust. The ineffectiveness of the feudal host was demonstrated when Llewellyn of Wales sprang into action in 1231. His incursion was ended by a truce in November, but failure to deal with that situation, together with similar failures to make any impression on Normandy or Poitou, spelt the end for the Justiciar. Hubert fell from favour in the summer of 1232, and was replaced by Stephen Seagrave, but the real beneficiary of these changes was Peter des Roches, the Bishop of Winchester, who now reigned supreme in the King's councils. Under his guidance the household became very much the centre of government, and a small group of councillors controlled events. This was not altogether compatible with the 'community of the realm' which had been sponsored by Archbishop Langton before his death in 1228, and which was a necessary underpinning for the continuance of the peace. By the end of May 1233 the grumbling, with Earl Richard to the fore, had turned into sporadic violence, and by the end of August the country was back into a state of civil war. Henry having failed to resolve this situation, the bishops combined to get rid of Peter des Roches, and his influence was replaced by that of the new Archbishop of Canterbury, Edmund of Abingdon, a saintly man who was trusted by all parties. The April Council in 1234 confirmed this new disposition of power, and another truce was negotiated in the marches of Wales. A conference was set up to resolve the troubled affairs of Ireland, and Peter des Roches took himself off to a monastery, where he died in June 1238. This general reconciliation was confirmed at the Council of Gloucester in May 1234, and the way was cleared for a stronger central administration to emerge.

This was symbolised by the fact that while the Curia Regis (or Court of King's Bench) continued to travel with the King, a new court for civil pleas (the Common Bench) was established to remain at Westminster. Beneath the superficial turbulence of high politics, English life continued to be fairly coherent, and the prosperity of the realm increased. In August 1234 the new General Eyre resulted in many useful decisions, and a Great Council held at Merton in January 1238 produced the first beneficial legislation since the Great Charter in the so-called Statute of Merton, which clarified many points of law on the basis of years of judicial experience.

Meanwhile in 1235 Henry's sister Isabella had married the Emperor Frederick, and in 1236 the King himself married Eleanor of Provence, the daughter of Raymond V, whose sister Margaret had recently wedded the King of France, Louis VII. She was to exercise a profound and on the whole beneficial influence over him for the rest of his life. Controversial issues continued to beset the Council, not least a dispute in 1238 over the Church's right to control matters of matrimony, triggered by the inheritance implications of bastardy. The barons were very concerned that the undertakings made in the charters should be observed, and in 1242 a request for taxation was turned down on the grounds that the King had not accounted for the money raised in 1237, an accountability which he was concerned to resist. From 1237 onward these Great Councils came to be known as Parliaments, to which all magnates and prelates were summoned. It was not until 1265 that knights were also summoned, but these meetings were held at least once a year for the rest of the reign, and the consultative function of the assemblies was much emphasised. Household government meant the rise of the Wardrobe, which was its financial aspect, and of another Poitevan, Peter des Rivaux, who was its head. Peter became treasurer, and sheriff of most of the counties, while fellow Frenchmen took over many of the offices of the court. The Queen's kindred were well endowed, notably her uncle Peter, who later became Count of Savoy, and who received the Earldom of Richmond. The king's Luisignan half-brothers also settled in England. Henry behaved in this respect without either foresight or judgement, and laid up a store of trouble for himself. His foreign policy was equally ill-considered, and resulted in his eventually being forced to concede (in 1259) not only the loss of Normandy, which had long since gone, but also of Poitou, which he had been doing his best to retain. This left only Aquitaine of the once extensive Angevin Empire in France. Equally mistaken was his acceptance in 1255 of the Pope's suggestion that his second son, Edmund, might like to be King of Sicily, a commitment which involved him in expensive and unsustainable wars.

Eventually his favour to the Poitevins, and his expensive tastes, caught up with him. The government of the country was being conducted by hard-working knights serving on juries and activating the numerous writs which were emerging from the royal chancery; and by mayors and aldermen in the towns. This constituency became increasingly resentful of the dominance of foreigners in the upper reaches of the administration, and of the King's regular demands for financial assistance. Such discontents communicated themselves to the barons and came to a head in the Easter Parliament of 1258. The King could only obtain a grant to rescue him from bankruptcy if he agreed to banish the Poitevins and accept the appointment of a committee of reform consisting of twelve royal and twelve baronial nominees. These reforms were decreed in the Provisions of Oxford, later in the same year, which placed Henry under the tutelage of a Council of Fifteen, and appointed a new Justiciar, Chancellor and Treasurer. An inquest was also decreed into the widespread abuses alleged against the erstwhile officers. Somewhat ironically, this inquest produced a rift within the ranks of the barons as some of their own misdeeds were also exposed, and a new political constituency emerged in the form of the lesser landowners, 'the community of the bachelry of England', who found a leader in the person of one of the greatest magnates of all, Simon de Montfort, Earl of Leicester. De Montfort was a most improbable leader for a grass-roots English movement, being a Frenchman, the son of an Albigensian crusader, and an erstwhile Governor of Gascony, but he was aggrieved with Henry and his private resentment was blended with a genuine desire to bring about reforms. He was appreciative of the English fabric of local self-administration, and saw in it the best way to assert both royal duties and subjects rights, which was in tune with the best political thought of the day. In spite of apprehensions about his private interests, several other magnates joined him in this quest. Henry meanwhile, freed from his futile war in France by the peace of Paris in 1259, and of his oath to the Provisions of Oxford by an obliging Pope in 1261, went on the offensive against the dissidents. The result was Earl Simon's victory at the Battle of Lewes on 14 May 1264, when the King, his son Edward and his brother Richard of Cornwall were all captured.

Earl Simon was now the master of the kingdom, and his policy was expressed in the re-enactment of the Provisions of Oxford, and in the establishment of a controlling council – albeit of nine rather than fifteen. It was also reflected in the nature of the parliament which the Council called in January 1265, because not only were all the barons and prelates summoned by individual writ (which had been done before) but two knights were called from every shire and two burgesses from selected towns, via writs directed to the sheriffs. Thus was created the precedent for what was in future to be a parliament, as distinct from a summons to the barons and prelates alone, which was henceforth to be known as the Great Council. It was a development of enormous constitutional significance, and marked the emergence of the middle (gentry) class onto the political scene. Simon de Montfort, however, bore himself with a high hand, and he alienated the marcher lords such as Gilbert of Gloucester, by forcing Prince Edward to hand the Earldom of Chester over to him. Edward escaped, and by linking up with the marcher lords, and with Llewellyn ap Gruffydd, whom he recognised as Prince of Wales, was soon able to confront the Earl again. This time the fortunes of war were reversed, and Edward was victorious at Evesham on 4 August 1265. Earl Simon died on the field, and that, in a sense, put an end to the movement which he had led. It did not put an end to the strife, however, because Edward, with a young man's lack of moderation, confiscated and re-granted the lands of his opponents with a lavish hand, thus provoking bitter resistance. Reconciliation came, not through his efforts but those of the new papal legate, Cardinal Ottobono, who in 1266 negotiated the Dictum of Kenilworth, laying down a policy of financial penalties in place of confiscation. By this dictum those being penalised were allowed to repurchase their properties, thus alleviating the sense of grievance and filling the royal coffers at the same time. However, this was too harsh for some and it needed a rebellion by Gilbert of Gloucester to bring about a genuine peace settlement, mediated this time by Richard of Cornwall, the King's brother and notional King of the Romans. A fresh treaty was negotiated at Shrewsbury with the Prince of Wales, who had been Gilbert's ally, making large concessions which Edward was later to regret. Finally the Statute of Marlborough in 1267 re-enacted most of the Provisions of Oxford, removing the restraints upon the King, but not the administrative reforms which curbed the officials of both king and barons. In many ways this marked the end of feudalism, and it brought peace to a country which was sadly in need of it. Edward departed on crusade in 1270, leaving Henry little more than an amiable cipher in the hands of competent but undistinguished officials. He was able to attend the consecration of his beloved Westminster Abbey – upon which he had spent far more money than he could afford – just a week or two before his death on 16 November 1272. He was sixty-five years old, and had reigned for fifty-six years. Edward's succession was unchallenged, which was just as well as he was in the Holy Land at the time and did not return until the summer of 1274.

PART 7
THE PLANTAGENETS,
1272–1377

24

EDWARD I, THE HAMMER OF THE SCOTS (REIGNED 1272–1307)

Edward I was a mature man of forty-three when his father's long reign came to an end. He was married since 1254 to Eleanor of Castile and had been the father of four children, two of whom were already dead. Edward had considerable experience of leadership, and had been the power behind the throne for nearly a decade when Henry III died. Although Henry was an old man, his death was unexpected, and his son was in the Holy Land when the news reached him. However, his accession was undisputed, and he was proclaimed on 17 November 1272, the barons swearing fealty to him on the 20th – the day of Henry's funeral. Consequently he did not hurry back, reaching London only in July 1274, when he and his queen were crowed at Westminster on 19 August. Edward was not only experienced, he had all the qualities which his father had lacked, including industry and shrewdness in his choice of advisers. He was a natural leader, and had an instinctive grasp of order and system which was to make his reign a landmark in the development of law and organisation. He began his work of reorganisation shortly after his return with the aid of his friend and Chancellor Robert Burnell, the Bishop of Bath and Wells. Commissioners were sent out to obtain sworn information on royal possessions and rights, infringements, usurpations and administrative misconduct of all kinds. This was registered in the Hundred Rolls, and was the most comprehensive survey of its kind since the Domesday Book. Armed with the returns of this visitation, Edward started his reform programme at the right point, and in his first parliament in 1275 enacted the First Statute of Westminster, which dealt largely with administrative abuses. He followed this up in 1278 with the Statute of Gloucester, which decreed the issue of writs *Quo Warranto*, demanding to know by what authority the multitudinous feudal rights claimed were actually held. Usurpations were usually condoned on the payment of a fine, but the King reserved his right of entry on any franchise if his commands were not observed. The object of this exercise was not to discontinue such franchises, but to overhaul them and bring them under effective royal control. The Statute of Mortmain of 1279 had a similar purpose. The intention was not to prevent grants of lands to the 'dead hand' of the Church, but to impose a system of licences by which adequate compensation could be secured for any loss of feudal obligations. In 1285 the Statute of Winchester attempted to repress the small-scale local disorders which continued to be the bane of rural society; a second Statute of Westminster in the same year prevented donees alienating at will land granted to them in entail; and a third Statute of Westminster in 1290 introduced the process of *Quia Emptores*, which laid down that the purchaser of land in fee simple became the direct vassal of the superior lord, not of the seller. The great advantage of all these statutes was that they brought the system of feudal landholding under the control of the King's courts, and thus made it both more workable and more transparent.

Edward was very earnest in maintaining the rights of the Crown, and as early as 1275 extended this to the collection of customs dues. These had existed in an undefined form for many years, but the parliament of that year decreed that the Great Custom on wool was to be fixed at *6s 8d* per sack, with a corresponding 'prise' on imported wine; and this gave formal recognition to the King's interest, which was acknowledged by the burgesses who had helped to vote it through. By this time there were three royal courts in operation, each with its own chief justice and staff: the King's Bench, the Common Pleas, and the Exchequer in its judicial capacity. The jurisdiction of these courts overlapped, and they competed with each other to some extent, each of them administering the Common Law, which was customary rather than Roman in its origin, and could only be extended by judicial interpretation. However, above all, and controlling all their operations, was the King and his council. These courts thus operated within the court, but other institutions, such as Chancery and the financial aspects of the Exchequer, were moving out of court, and becoming departments of state. The Wardrobe, like the law courts, remained within the court, and became increasingly flexible, dealing with business of every conceivable kind from kitchen supplies to the administration of war. Edward remained the centre of everything, and he was the determined opponent of corruption and of the petty oppressions regularly carried out by the swarms of officials who operated in his name. However, everything depended upon the personal efficiency and conscientiousness of the King, and while he was absent in France from 1286 to 1289, there was a general breakdown of honesty, which he was compelled to deal with rigorously on his return. The parliament also became more defined, the term gradually becoming confined to those assemblies where the King summoned knights and burgesses because he wanted money. Otherwise the composition of the assembly depended upon the business to be transacted – selected magnates, all magnates, magnates and prelates, and so on. At this time a full parliament also included representatives of the Lower Clergy because they were also to be taxed. Only later was their representation confined to the Convocations.

Edward's need for money was largely determined by the demands of war, and his first war was fought in Wales. Llewellyn ap Gryffudd had signed an advantageous peace with Henry III at Montgomery in 1267, whereby he had been recognised as the Prince of all Wales, but this success seems to have gone to his head. He refused homage to the new king, and thus provoked an invasion which revealed Edward's best qualities of generalship. Well supported by the marcher lords, he used his fleet to secure control of Anglesey, and thus confined Llewellyn to Snowdonia, where he starved him out, forcing his submission in 1277. The Welshman, however, had not learned his lesson, and when his people became exasperated by the alien government of Edward's officials, he renewed the war in 1282. This time Edward was seriously cross, and he mobilised his full resources, using the same strategy as before. Llewellyn escaped, but he was killed in South Wales while trying to open a second front, and his brother David, who continued the resistance for a few months, was captured and executed. Welsh independence was brought to an end by the Statute of Rhuddlan in 1284, and a fresh principality was created, vested in the English Crown. This consisted of the new counties of Caernarfon, Merionydd and Anglesey, the old principality of Gwynedd in the north, and of Cardigan and Carmarthen in the south. The remainder of Wales was divided among the existing marcher lordships. Although the English common law was introduced for criminal proceedings, there was no cultural imperialism and Welsh custom continued to be used for civil cases – and the Welsh language flourished. Castles were built at strategic spots, and English settlements grew up around them. These provoked a serious rebellion in 1294, but that did not seriously deter the English settlers, who knew a good opportunity for profit when they saw it. The story that Edward offered his young son to the Welsh at Caernarfon, as 'a Prince who spoke no English', is probably apocryphal, because although the child was born at Caernarfon at about the right time, his first language would have been Norman French. It was not until 1301 that the young Edward was formally created Prince of Wales, and the long tradition of the title of the heir to the throne was established.

In spite of the success of his policy in Wales, Edward is most remembered for his exploits in Scotland, where the troubled history of that kingdom had left him with a vaguely defined right of feudal suzerainty. In 1286 King Alexander III died, leaving only a daughter as his heir. Edward suggested, and the Scots council accepted, that the young Margaret should marry Edward of Caernarfon, but she also died in September 1290, leaving the succession highly uncertain. There were many claimants, and they appealed to Edward to arbitrate between them. After a long and complex investigation he decided that the best right belonged to John Balliol, a great grandson of David I (1125–1153) through the female line, and he was duly invested as king at Newcastle on 26 December 1292. He did homage to Edward, and accepted his overlordship – for the time being. The crisis was not long in coming, because by 1295 Edward was at war with Philip the Fair of France, and summoned King John to attend him in the field. He refused and instead made a defensive alliance with France, which was the origin of that association which was to last for over three centuries. Such defiance could not be tolerated, and once his French campaign was over, and the rebellion in Wales suppressed, Edward turned his attention to Scotland. Descending in force, he defeated Balliol and forced him to abdicate at Brechin in July 1296. He treated Scotland as a forfeited fief and removed the Stone of Destiny from Scone to Westminster, leaving English officials and garrisons to run the country. The result was the famous popular uprising of William Wallace, which by the autumn of 1297 had swept the whole of Scotland in short-lived triumph. Edward freed his hands by a truce with Philip the Fair, and bent all his energies to the subjection of Scotland. In 1298 he led north a large force, which encountered the full field army of the Scots under Wallace at Falkirk. The result was a decisive victory for the English, but not the end of the war. Wallace escaped, and continued guerrilla operations until 1305, when he was captured and executed, thus confirming his status as a popular hero in Scottish legend. His place was taken by the duplicitous Robert Bruce, Earl of Carrick, who had fought for both sides since the Battle of Falkirk. In 1306 he was high in Edward's confidence, but was already plotting a fresh revolt. His father had died in 1304, leaving him with a remote claim to the throne, and he improved his chances in January 1306 by arranging the murder of Red Comyn at Dumfries, a crime for which he was forced to seek absolution. He was crowned at Scone later in the year, and, after three months as a hunted fugitive, mustered sufficient force to win a battle at Loudon Hill in Lanarkshire against Edward's representatives in May 1307. How he would have fared against Edward himself we do not know because the English king, hurrying north with a large army to contain the situation, died at Burgh-on-Sands in Cumbria on 7 July, and his son abandoned the campaign.

Wars, as we have seen, meant money, and the conflicts in France, Wales and Scotland after 1294 put a disastrous strain on Edward's finances. The parliament of 1295 gave him only reluctant grants, and in February 1296 the Pope forbade subsidies from the clergy without papal consent. When the clerical convocation in January 1297 withdrew their consent to the grant of 1295, the King responded by outlawing them and seizing their temporal fiefs. In the face of this challenge, the Pope backed down in July 1297, and subsequent convocations did vote grants. However, between 1294 and 1297 the King also imposed a *maletolt*, which was an additional tax on exported wool in addition to the agreed custom. The merchants were not worried by this, because they could simply pass on the enhanced price to their customers, but it also affected the wool producers, and hence the aristocracy. They considered that the administration was becoming arbitrary and tyrannical, and started working 'to rule' in respect of their feudal obligations. When Edward was about to leave for his abortive campaign in Flanders in 1297, two earls presented him with a petition asking for redress against arbitrary taxation. He rejected it, but while he was away the regency council agreed that such taxes should not be repeated without common consent – which meant the parliament. The earls were pardoned for their disobedience. Part of the problem was that the King himself was becoming more autocratic and less adaptable. He missed his queen, Eleanor, who died in 1290, his mother, who died at about the same time, and his friend and Chancellor the Bishop of Bath and Wells, who departed in October 1292. He had already tried to divert the Jews from usury, and when that failed he expelled them from the country in 1290 in another outburst of autocratic rage. Eventually in 1300 Edward accepted twenty articles for the redress of grievances, and in a full parliament at Lincoln in 1301 solemnly confirmed the old charters. He was, of course, driven to these concessions by the need for money, but that did not make them any less real. Above all he had agreed that the common consent was necessary for new taxation, and that Parliament was the natural vehicle for that consent. This was a constitutional development of the greatest significance for the future.

Having been a widower for nine years, Edward eventually sealed his agreement with Philip III of France by marrying his daughter Margaret in 1299. She was forty years his junior, but in spite of his sixty years the King was still sufficiently vigorous to beget two sons and a daughter upon her, bringing the total number of his legitimate offspring to eighteen, seven of whom survived him. It must be supposed that he was uxorious, because he left only one recorded bastard, who took the name of John Botetourt, and who features regularly in the annals over the next few years. Henry had already renounced his titles to Normandy and Anjou in 1259, and Edward did not attempt to revive them. However, he did abandon his claim to Poitou in 1297, after several fruitless attempts to realise it, and his territorial possessions on the Continent were reduced to the Duchy of Aquitaine. He was succeeded without dispute by his oldest surviving son, Edward of Caernarfon, Prince of Wales.

25

EDWARD II
(REIGNED 1307–1327)

Even from an early age, Edward had not been a very satisfactory young man. He had showed no taste or aptitude for the war games which were the traditional pastime of his class, preferring manual labour and such plebeian feats as wrestling. Although he was twenty-three, he had not been entrusted with any military command, and his title had meant nothing. Politically his experience had been confined to quarrelling with his father, and with members of his father's council. He had also entered into a questionable relationship with the young Gascon Piers Gaveston, an association which had caused King Edward to banish Gaveston just a few months before his death. In short, the new king lacked credibility for the role he was now called upon to assume, and diminished his credit still further by recalling Gaveston immediately after his accession, and creating him Earl of Cornwall on 6 August. The new earl was a light-headed, showy man, and his relationship with the King became a political issue of the first importance as the English magnates clamoured for his exclusion, and the King resisted. They presented Edward with a warning document before the end of the year, and the convocation in February 1308 added to the general disquiet. In January Edward had crossed to France to marry the twelve-year-old Isabella, and thereby added to his own difficulties because Philip IV, Isabella's father, hated Gaveston, apparently suspecting that their friendship was of a homosexual nature and would impede Edward's affection for his wife. In fact that seems not to have been the case, and the King eventually fathered four children by Isabella before they fell out for other reasons. Meanwhile Edward had yielded to the pressure applied by the Easter parliament of 1308, which had reminded the King of his coronation oath and renewed the pressure for Gaveston's exile. He sent him to be Chief Governor of Ireland. In response, the Statute of Stamford in July granted the King a tax of one-fifteenth, which was considerable relief, because the magnates' campaign against foreign influences had also extended to his bankers, the Fresobaldi, who had also been exiled. Even so, by 1310 the King owed over £21,000.

In May 1309 Gaveston returned from Ireland, and his first action was to quarrel with Thomas, Earl of Lancaster, one of the leaders of the baronial opposition. This made a bad situation worse and in March 1310 Edward was constrained to accept the 'guidance' of a committee of Ordainers, who were established with full powers to reform the household and the administration. They at once insisted that no grants in future were to be made without their consent, and demanded (again) the exile of the hated favourite. Edward tried to distract attention from his problems with a Scottish campaign in the summer of 1311, and had he been victorious he might well have succeeded. However, like most of his campaigns, this one was a failure, and in August 1311 he was constrained to receive forty-one ordinances for the reform of the government. These included provision for the reduction of the role of the household, the payment of all revenues into the Exchequer, the appointment of sheriffs by the Chancellor, the control of royal officials, and a number of legal issues. Consent was to be vested henceforth in Parliament alone, and grants of taxation required the presence of the knights and burgesses. In normal circumstances the King should 'live of his own'. These ordinances, important as they were for the development of Parliament, were unacceptable to the King, who withdrew to the north of England, making an armed conflict more likely. Under pressure from the Ordainers, Gaveston had briefly gone into exile again, probably in Flanders, from whence he was recalled by Edward, and joined him at York in January 1312. By this time a full-scale baronial revolt was in progress, led by John, Earl of Lincoln, and their forces set out in pursuit of the King. They did not catch him, but they did take Queen Isabella, and Piers Gaveston, who surrendered at Scarborough under a guarantee of safe conduct. The guarantee was not honoured, and Gaveston was summarily executed – in effect lynched. Those responsible were the earls of Warwick, Lancaster and Hereford, and the result was a split in the baronial ranks, because the Earl of Pembroke, who had issued the safe conduct, promptly joined the King. These events turned the situation Edward's way, as did the birth of the future Edward III on 13 November 1312, which restored good relations with the French court. He was extremely reluctant to accept the baronial reforms, and the stupid aggressiveness of Thomas of Lancaster further weakened the latter's cause. By 1313 powerful voices of moderation could be heard. Unfortunately this hopeful development was ruined by the disaster of the Bannockburn campaign in the summer of 1314, the Scots' invasion which followed, and the death of the principal mediator, the Earl of Gloucester. Consequently when Parliament met at York in September, there was virtually no resistance to the demand that the Ordainers' ordinances be implemented and observed. Officials were reshuffled, and virtually all the sheriffs were replaced. In spite of the economic hardships caused at this time by bad weather and failed harvests, Parliament granted taxes of a fifteenth and a tenth in 1316, and relations with the Church were regularised by the *Articuli Cleri*, largely in the King's favour. Edward was not disposed to make further concessions, and since the papacy was concerned to stabilise the situation in England, this raised no further problems.

The Earl of Lancaster became head of the Council in January 1316, but withdrew from government altogether in August in the face of the King's uncooperative attitude. At about this time the Earl's wife was apparently abducted by one of the King's followers, and although the affair is obscure both sides began to mobilise and civil war again seemed likely. However, complex negotiations followed instead, and agreement was reached at Leake in August 1318. The ordinances were to be observed, and

Lancaster pardoned for his defection. A council of seventeen was appointed, of whom four were to be always with the King; there was a general reshuffling of offices (again) and the younger Hugh Despenser became Chamberlain. Some grants were also cancelled. This agreement was subsequently endorsed by a parliament held at York in October, and in 1319 Edward reached an accommodation with Philip IV over his fiefs of Aquitiane and Ponthieu. A moderate group, led by the Earl of Pembroke, and consisting of both reformers and royalists, now held the reins of power. However, it was a fragile agreement, because the King was incurably wilful, and because he needed a favourite, never having really forgiven the barons for Gaveston's death. The new occupant of that position was Hugh Despenser, who used his office to undermine all other influences on the King, and to lead him as the saying was 'like a cat after a straw'. Despenser's ambition was to enlarge his lordship of Glamorgan into a great fief and to create an earldom for himself in South Wales, which resulted in a private war between himself and the other marcher lords, led by none other than Thomas of Lancaster. This reunited the opposition, and a further parliament held in 1320, which was attended by the barons in arms, forced Edward to exile both Despenser and his father. Meanwhile Earl Thomas was engaging in unsuccessful negotiations with the Scots, and rallying to himself those marcher lords, like the Earl of Hereford, who had been driven out of the borders by a surprisingly swift and effective royal campaign in 1321. Edward, meanwhile, had recalled the Despensers and, with unwonted energy and purpose, mustered an army in the North towards the end of February 1322 and confronted and utterly defeated his opponents at Boroughbridge on 16 March. It was his one unequivocal victory, and for the time being it was decisive. The Earl of Hereford had fallen in the battle, and Thomas of Lancaster was executed a few days later at Pontefract. A number of his associates died with him, and the Ordainers were broken. Those who were pardoned were mulcted of substantial fines, over £17,000 being collected in consequence, and a full parliament held at York in the summer annulled the Ordinances, declaring that in future only a parliament including the knights and burgesses should deal with the affairs of the King or of the realm.

There then followed a period of remarkable efficiency, considering that the king had not changed his nature. The Despensers were greedy and amoral, but they were no sponsors of incompetence or muddle. The Exchequer and the Chancery were reorganised; the Privy Seal became a department of state, and the Wardrobe receded into insignificance. Inevitably the younger Despenser's chief office became paramount, and the Chamber became the instrument of the King's personal actions. Bureaucratic competence did not, however, settle the woes of the realm, nor did efficiency translate into political support. The Northern shires were ravaged by the Scots until a thirteen-year truce was negotiated in June 1323, at a considerable cost to Edward's pride, and in 1324 war was resumed with France over the status of Aquitaine. Under Despenser influence Edward seized the Queen's dower lands, and then had the folly to send her to France to negotiate with her brother Charles IV, a mission in which she was later joined by his twelve-year-old heir. Isabella made a peace, but she also formed a friendship, ripening into adultery, with Roger Mortimer, who had escaped from imprisonment after Boroughbridge and taken refuge in Paris. On hearing this news, Edward denounced the treaty which she had negotiated, leaving him with few friends on either side of the Channel. Only the Despensers and their allies could be counted upon. Meanwhile Isabella had been dismissed from the French court on account of her liaison with Mortimer, and had taken refuge with him in Hainault, where she succeeded in doing a deal with the Count, William I. Aware of the feelings prevailing in England, she bargained money and military support for the hand of her young son, who became betrothed to Philippa, the Count's daughter. In September 1326 she and Mortimer landed at Orwell in Suffolk, meeting with almost universal approbation. The Londoners, in particular, rioted in her favour. Part of the explanation for this unanimity lies in the fact that royal taxation had succeeded in raising £40,000 in 1322 and another £60,000 in 1324. The people were unaccustomed to exactions on this scale, especially when they were collected with brutal effectiveness. The royal treasurer, Bishop Walter Stapledon of Exeter, was murdered during the London riots, which tells its own story. Money was no help to the King in this crisis, because the Despenser ascendancy simply collapsed like a house of cards. Edward and his favourites fled to Wales, perhaps looking for support in the marcher lordships, but finding none. The elder Hugh was taken before he ever got to Wales, and summarily executed on 26 October; the younger Hugh made it to the principality, but was caught there and dealt with in the same fashion on 24 November. Edward was taken at the same time, and imprisoned at Kenilworth. At first he refused to cooperate with his captors, and there was no precedent for the royal deposition which it was now agreed would have to take place. However, a parliament was called in his name and met at Westminster on 7 January 1327, and when only a few bishops supported his cause he accepted the inevitable and abdicated. His fourteen-year-old son was proclaimed as King Edward III on 25 January. On 21 September the deposed king was brutally murdered at Berkeley Castle, allegedly by having a red-hot poker thrust up his rectum, although this may be an embellishment alluding to his supposed sexual preferences. In fact there is no evidence for homosexuality in the contemporary sources, and it is intrinsically improbable, but it is easy to see why the closeness of his relationships with male friends, and his apparent need for emotional support should have bred that misapprehension.

In the aftermath of the coup, Roger Mortimer was created Earl of March, but the government which he conducted jointly with Isabella in the name of the boy king was no improvement on its predecessor either in method or success. It was the rule of a greedy faction. Its feebleness was reflected in a losing peace with France, signed later in 1327, and in the Treaty of Northampton with the Scots in May 1328, which accepted the full independence of the Northern kingdom. The union which had brought about Edward II's downfall soon dissolved, as Mortimer attempted to engross power and land, dealing brutally with any opposition. Meanwhile Edward III had married Philippa in 1328, and was growing up rapidly. Perhaps the birth of his oldest son on 15 June 1330 encouraged him, but in October, just before his eighteenth birthday, he carried out a daring strike. Mortimer was now as generally hated as the Despensers had been, and the young king with a few followers surprised him at Nottingham Castle on 19 October and consigned him to prison, the King's presence paralysing any possible resistance. Edward III dated his personal rule from the following day. In November, Parliament, meeting at Westminster, condemned Mortimer to death, and he was duly executed soon after. Isabella was reduced to her dower lands in November 1330 by the same parliament. She died in 1357.

26

THE VICTORIOUS KING: EDWARD III (REIGNED 1327–1377)

Few mourned the passing of Roger Mortimer, but the ineptitude of Edward II's government had left deep discords among the ruling elite. It was all very well for Edward III to proclaim that 'the king's affairs and the affairs of his realm have been directed until now to the damage and dishonour of him and his realm', but it was something else to do anything about it. The economy had been weakened by the fiscal demands of the 1320s, and there had been famine in the early part of that decade, leaving the lower levels of society materially weakened. The King's laws were openly flouted by protection rackets and other similar abuses. So the young king needed to re-establish some respect for himself and his crown, and some order in the society which he now ruled. He promptly replaced some of the senior administrators, John Stratford, Bishop of Winchester, taking over as Chancellor from Henry Burghesh, Bishop of London. Stratford and his family were to dominate the civil service for the next decade, bringing purpose and coherence to the government, but Edward's main asset was his own personality. Unlike his father he was able, adroit and strong-willed. He also had a tendency to concentrate on the short term, which made his long-term promises unreliable, but which served him well in dealing with the constantly shifting patterns of magnate alliances. He was also warlike, and whether by accident or design succeeded in rallying the aristocracy behind him in his foreign adventures. Scotland was first on his list, being a more manageable proposition than the larger issue of France. Robert Bruce had died in 1329, leaving his crown to his young son, David II. However, David was not acceptable to everyone, and Edward Balliol, the son of John, raised a counterclaim. This was supported by a group of Northern English lords, led by Henry Beaumont, who had been alienated from the regime of Mortimer and Isabella by the humiliating peace of 1328, which had cost them dear. When these Northern lords defeated the Scots at Dupplin Moor in 1332, the King decided to give his official backing to Balliol. He won control of Berwick and embarked upon a long campaign which culminated in victory at Halidon Hill on 19 July 1333. David Bruce was forced into exile, and Balliol installed in his place. Edward in return gained full control over eight border and lowland counties, and secured the new king's homage at Newcastle in June 1334. However, Philip VI of France had taken David into his protection, and insisted upon Scotland forming a part of any future Anglo-French negotiations. Warned of the possible implications of further intervention, the English backed off, rumours of a massive French invasion in 1335 effectively diverting Edward's attentions to the South, while the Scottish conflict degenerated into an exchange of border raids. Although his pride would not allow him to desist entirely, the King had won his principal battle in recovering the loyalty of his own Northern lords. A truce was patched up with Scotland in 1328.

With France the main issue was Gascony, or rather the Agenais, the land between the Dordogne and the Garonne, which had been ceded to France in 1325 but was now being claimed as a part of the Duchy of Gascony by Edward's negotiators. In 1336 Philip moved his war fleet into the Norman ports, and the threat of war was clear enough. In spite of papal attempts to mediate, talks between the two powers had broken down and on 24 May 1337 Philip VI formally confiscated both the Duchy of Aquitaine and the County of Ponthieu on the pretext that Edward owed liege homage for those lands, which had not been performed. Previously such gestures had been followed by a display of strength on either side, followed by a compromise settlement in which the English king would acknowledge his duty of homage, and be restored to his fiefs. However, on this occasion Edward upped the stakes by claiming the crown of France itself in 1340 on the grounds that he was the grandson of Philip IV and the nephew, through his mother, of Charles IV, the last Capetian king. It was this claim which forced the French to invent the so-called Salic Law, which banned any claims to the throne by or through a woman, which was given a spurious antiquity by being attributed to the Salian Franks. Edward probably had no intention of trying to enforce his claim, but it was a useful device to assert full sovereignty over the English lands in France, and a publicity trick designed to attract allies of whom the most prominent were the Flemish cloth towns and the Emperor Louis IV. The early stages of the French war were marked by the naval victory at Sluys in 1340, but more relevant to contemporaries was the extreme financial pressure which was exerted to support them. In 1337 the Great Council was induced to grant over £100,000 in tenths and fifteenths, while the clergy conceded to demands for over £50,000, and in 1338 the same council awarded him 17,500 sacks of wool as an additional impost. A further grant in 1340 brought the King's income from taxes and forced loans to well over £500,000, which was quite unprecedented. Most controversial of all was purveyance, in origin a feudal entitlement which enabled the King to purchase foodstuffs for his troops at his own valuation – if they were ever paid for at all. At a time of economic recession these exactions were particularly hard to bear, and caused considerable resentment. This discontent was aggravated by the lack of any adequate achievement to justify such extravagant expenditure, and most of the English population became thoroughly disillusioned with the war effort. The King was blamed for pursuing unreal dreams abroad and neglecting the hardships of his people at home. Outright condemnation was voiced of Edward's foreign and domestic policies, and according to both official and unofficial sources the country was ripe for revolt by the end of 1340.

In spite of the general relief at the deposition of Edward II in 1327, his son had in fact done little to resolve the political problems which that regime had bequeathed to him. Even the apparent stability of the administration was temporary, and another reshuffle preceded his departure for France in 1338. Preoccupied with warfare, Edward was inclined to leave the government of the country to others, but then apparently did not trust those to whom the work had been allocated. A similar lack of positive direction characterised his treatment of the nobility during the early 1330s. In spite of his generosity to adherents of the old regime, he tended to create factions by favouring small groups of personal friends. When he created six earldoms in March 1337, one or two were scions of old noble families, but the majority were relatively humble men promoted because of their relationships with the King. It would be an exaggeration to say that relations had broken down, but they were highly uncertain, and much would depend on his ability to unite the baronage for a great offensive against France. In the event, the opening exchanges of that war were disappointing, and when Edward tried to resolve his differences with the regency council by sending Archbishop Stratford back to take charge of the administration, that only served to emphasise the priority which he was giving to fighting. The problems which he was encountering in raising money for that purpose prompted him to return and face up to Parliament in March and April 1340. He managed to obtain a tax of a ninth, but was forced to concede that his collectors would be accountable to Parliament, and that the new levy would be spent only on the war. In the event this tax, which was supposed to raise £100,000, had realised only £15,000 by January 1341, and Edward was effectively bankrupt. The Siege of Tournai failed and he was forced into an ignominious truce at Esplechin in September 1340. Irrationally indignant with the supposed failures of his government at home, on 1 December he suddenly returned and carried out a purge. The Chancellor and Treasurer were dismissed, and five judges together with several members of the regency council arrested, thus provoking a major political crisis. This manifested itself in the form of a bitter quarrel with the Archbishop of Canterbury, who was refused admission to Parliament for over a week, until the nobles rallied to Stratford's support and forced the King to make peace with him. Alarmed by what they took to be manifestations of arbitrary rule, the Lords then went on to insist that none of their rank should be arrested, tried or imprisoned except in a full parliament and before his peers. The Commons also combined with the Lords to demand a detailed public audit of the King's finances, and the appointment of great officers of state in Parliament, where they should swear to uphold the law. Edward had no choice but to assent to these demands, which were solemnly written into the Statute Roll. Stratford had inflicted a serious defeat on the King, and left him dangerously isolated. Moreover, unlike previous defeats which had been inflicted on the Crown, this was not only the work of a baronial faction, but of the Commons and clergy as well. Edward's disregard for the welfare and rights of his subjects had produced a powerful coalition of disaffected parties drawing strength and inspiration from their support in the country.

From this low point, the King began to recover. During the summer of 1341 he exercised his charm on the baronial opposition, and began to break it up. On 1 October he dispensed with the statutes of the previous parliament on the grounds that these had been exacted under duress, and no one was in a position to challenge his legal right to do so. By rallying his baronial support, Edward neatly turned the tables on Archbishop Stratford, isolating him in his turn, and bringing him to a reconciliation which lasted until Stratford death in 1348. Parliament met again in April 1343, and the Commons were sufficiently indignant about the king's repudiation of their earlier statutes, but they could do little without the magnate support which was no longer forthcoming. Instead they were also won over, as Edward made a serious attempt to improve the law and order situation, and the military fortunes of the war turned in his favour. These were also recovering from a low point. The King's Low Countries allies deserted him, and David Bruce returned to Scotland in 1341, necessitating a Northern campaign in the winter of 1341/42 which achieved little as David became re-established. However, at the same time he developed a so-called 'provincial strategy' for dealing with France, which involved supporting those vassals of the King who were in dispute with him, and to whom he could offer an alternative allegiance on account of his claim to the throne. This was tried out in the 'war of the Breton succession' in 1341–42 when he supported John de Montfort against the French-backed Charles of Blois. The campaign of 1342 was inconclusive, but Edward was sufficiently encouraged to launch a number of simultaneous attacks on different fronts. In 1345 the Earl of Northampton was sent with an expeditionary force to Brittany and Aquitaine, while the King himself went to Flanders, and then in 1346 a Norman baron appealed for his assistance against his Valois overlord. Edward decided to make this the pretext for a major campaign, and sailed to Normandy with 15,000 men, marching into the Isle de France before turning north to Ponthieu. He met the French in a pitched battle at Crecy on 26 August, and was totally and memorably victorious, this being the occasion on which his sixteen-year-old son, Edward, Prince of Wales, 'won his spurs'. Meanwhile David Bruce, encouraged by his French ally, had invaded the north of England, only to be defeated and taken prisoner at the Battle of Neville's Cross. Suitably encouraged by these successes, Edward led another large army to France in 1347 and laid siege to the town of Calais, which eventually fell in the summer. It could no longer be argued that the King's heavy military expenditure was producing no results; doubts about his abilities as a war leader were dispelled, and the nobility were encouraged to lend their support to a series of great adventures.

The magnates were quick to respond to this upturn in martial achievement. Not only did they produce the men and money necessary for these multiple campaigns, they offered their advice in the council of war and served as commanders of those armies which the King was unable to lead in person. His cousin Henry of Grosmont was not only the greatest lord in England, he was also the busiest of all Edward's lieutenants, serving throughout the 1340s and 1350s in Brittany, Normandy and Aquitaine. Others who had sat at home and criticised the campaigns of 1338–40, were now challenged to prove their worth in the field, and quickly established their loyalty to the King. Within five years of the great crisis of confidence Edward had redeemed his reputation with the magnates and made them his companions in arms. As the older generation of nobles died out, younger men came to the fore who were temperamentally more inclined to support the King's policies, and Edward also began to make more sensible use of his patronage. Members of his own family continued to be ennobled, but beyond that far fewer 'new men' came to the fore. Old titles were revived for the descendants of former holders, and lapsed earldoms passed to existing members of the baronage. Thus Roger Mortimer, the grandson of Isabella's paramour, was created Earl of March in 1354, and Henry of Grosmont was promoted to the Dukedom of Lancaster in 1351. It was in the interest of this new solidarity that Edward created the Order of the Garter in 1348, the only criterion for election being military honour, and the prestige of election taking the place of more substantial gestures of recognition. Administratively these were also new days. Instead of the uncertainties of the 1330s men were now in place who had served their apprenticeship in Aquitaine between 1338 and 1340 – William Cusance, John Offord and John Thoreseby in particular – men who had also supported the King in the crisis of 1340–41. The most influential of all these ministers was William Edington, who had been a receiver for the unpopular ninth in 1340, and had then progressed to being Keeper of the Wardrobe (1341–44), Treasurer of the Exchequer (1344–56) and Chancellor (1356–63). The long and uninterrupted careers of these officials suggest that Edward had at last found men congenial to him and supportive of his policies. The most conspicuous of their achievements was in finance. Edington inherited a huge debt from his predecessors in the Exchequer, and the King's demands continued to make him nervous in the late 1340s but the later campaigns were less expensive, being partly self-supporting, and the yield from taxation increased as the economy recovered. Consequently by 1356, when he handed over his office, he had transformed Edward from an embarrassed bankrupt into a wealthy man, which was not the least of the government's successes. Some of the older generation of political bishops also died in the 1340s, and Edward had little trouble in filling the bench with amenable and obedient men. Many of the new bishops indeed were established servants of the Crown, and although there were squabbles between the King and the Bench in the 1350s, they were nothing by comparison with the quarrel with Archbishop Stratford in 1340. Indeed the King's victories at Crecy, Neville's Cross and Poitiers convinced many of the higher clergy that Edward was fighting a just war, which turned them into enthusiastic supporters of royal policy. Rarely has the King enjoyed such unanimous support as that which the Church accorded to Edward III after about 1345.

This general popularity was much needed, because the taxes needed to pay for these military enterprises were no more welcome than they had been before. There were angry responses from the Commons both in 1346 and in 1348, but they could do little in the way of obstructing policies without the backing of the Lords, which for reasons we have seen was not forthcoming. At the same time the taxpayers' woes were increased by the first visitation of that lethal affliction known as the Black Death. This was a form of bubonic plague, and in the year 1348/49 it killed about 30 per cent of the population, severely disrupting all forms of economic activity. There was an acute shortage of tenants and manpower on estates all across the country, and some lands were left almost entirely uncultivated. Overseas trade slumped, partly because of the drop in wool production and partly through the collapse of the foreign markets, all parts of Europe being equally afflicted.

The revenues of the Duchy of Cornwall, for example, fell by 40 per cent between 1347 and 1351; food prices slumped and wages soared. However, the sociological effects were more lasting than the economic ones. The labour market never returned to its old equilibrium; manumitted serfs became free labourers, and sold their work on an open market, with the result that the old feudal control collapsed to the bitter chagrin of old-fashioned landlords. Some lords began to lease out their demesne lands in the hope that rents would provide a more stable source of income. On the other hand changes in the customs regulations after 1353 were rewarded with a boom in the wool trade and a rapid increase in the production of woollen cloth for foreign markets. While the great estates struggled to maintain or restore their lords' proprietary rights, the merchants were enjoying a great increase in their activities – once the first shock was passed. There was little that the government could do, but it did issue an Ordinance of Labourers in 1349 in an endeavour to cap the rising wage rate. In the circumstances this was bound to be futile, but it did indicate that the King was aware of the problems which affected his most prominent supporters, and this solidarity had political implications.

The plague also led to a general scaling down of military activity. Edward won a victory at sea over the Castilians in 1350, but elsewhere little was achieved, and by 1352 peace was in the air. This optimism was shared by Parliament, which in that year granted a three-year subsidy in return for the redress of a long list of grievances. The King agreed that in future feudal aids would only be raised with parliamentary consent, and that his purveyors would abide by existing legal controls on their activities. He also conceded that no one except his own feudal tenants should be required to provide soldiers without the consent of Parliament.

The resulting statutes symbolised the emergence of Parliament as an effective political force, willing to work in cooperation with the Crown, and the years after the plague therefore witnessed an effective alliance between the King and the political community. Another result of this spirit of cooperation was the changes brought about in the long vexed question of law enforcement. The General Eyre had been seen as a threat to the self-government of the shires, and had been too irregular for the task of maintaining the peace. The last General Eyre had been an incomplete affair in 1330. Since then Assizes and Gaol Delivery sessions had in theory taken its place. These were presided over by royal judges and were supposed to take place three times a year, but they proved inadequate to cope with the upsurge of lawlessness which accompanied Edward's military campaigns in the late 1330s, and a new system was urgently needed. This came about when the King entrusted the enforcement of the Ordinance of Labourers to the local landowners, who had, of course, a vested interest. In 1351 these were constituted into commissions of the peace, which included a nucleus of trained lawyers, and were gradually given first-instance jurisdiction over all criminal cases arsing within their counties. This meant that the King and the country had at last come to a satisfactory compromise, which both enhanced the initiative of Edward's natural supporters, and considerably improved the popularity of the Crown. Meanwhile there were many arguments after 1353 for the renewal of hostilities with France, not least the eagerness and ambition of the King's sons, Edward, the Prince of Wales, Lionel, John and Edmund, who were not only keen to indulge their chivalric fantasies, but were also on the lookout for foreign titles and lands. However, in the end it was Charles of Navarre who took the initiative, attacking John II of

France and appealing for English assistance. Unable to resist the temptation, Edward unleashed his son on a series of plundering expeditions from Aquitaine and began to prepare a great campaign for 1355. However, he was diverted to Scotland in the winter of 1355–56, for the recovery of Berwick, and did not lead his army in person. Instead two separate forces set out in the summer of 1356, the Duke of Lancaster and the Prince of Wales failing to meet in Normandy as they should have done. Consequently the Prince had only about 6,000 men when he met the army of King John II at Poitiers on 19 September. The result was a hard-fought English victory in the course of which King John was captured.

Edward now enjoyed an extremely strong bargaining position, holding two kings as prisoners. He first came to terms with the Scots at Berwick in October 1357, agreeing a ransom of 100,000 marks (£66,666 13s 4d) for King David, but by passing the English claims to the Lowlands. He then turned his attentions to France, proposing a ransom of £700,000 for King John, and full sovereignty over a huge stretch of land from Calais to the Pyrenees, in return for which he would renounce his claim to what was left of France. These terms were put forward in May 1359, and understandably rejected. Edward then undertook a fresh campaign, which was frustrated at the Siege of Rheims early in 1360, and he responded positively to the Dauphin's suggestion for a negotiated settlement. This was agreed at Bretigny in May 1360. Edward was to give up his claims to the throne of France in return for Aquitaine and Calais in full sovereignty, and John's ransom was settled at £500,000. Bretigny was supposed to provide a secure basis for future peace, but in fact all that it achieved was a nine-year truce, during which both sides ignored its terms. It also gave France an opportunity to recover. John II died in 1364 and was succeeded by his son Charles V, who was man of much greater vision and talent. He improved the revenues of the French Crown, and used Bertrand du Guesclin to transform his army into a formidable and up-to-date war machine, no longer prone to the mistakes of Crecy and Poitiers. Edward III, by contrast, marked time, merely indulging in protracted and tense negotiations over their mutual failure to observe the terms of the peace. He continued to attempt intervention in the French provinces, but his earlier success had deserted him and he failed to obtain any meaningful leverage. This relative inactivity was compounded by events in Aquitaine, where in 1362 he conferred the title of Prince upon his eldest son. With extraordinary lack of sensitivity, the Prince then tried to impose an English-style administration upon the province, thereby stirring up the independent-minded lords of the region to anger and resentment, and causing some of them to enter into intrigues with Charles V. In 1367 the Prince of Aquitaine also intervened in neighbouring Castile, an involvement which failed two years later, but involved his taxpayers in heavy expense, and added to the resentment against his rule.

At home, similarly, Edward achieved comparatively little. In Ireland he had originally been content to leave the government in the hands of the Anglo-Irish lords, but in 1361 he sent his son Lionel in an attempt to reduce the island to better obedience. The only result was to increase the animosity which the Irish lords felt towards any representative of the English Crown. Meanwhile the older generation of service peers was dying out, and not being adequately replaced. The only new creations of the 1360s were in favour of his children and their spouses, most particularly of his son John, who was raised to the Dukedom of Lancaster when he married Henry of Grosmont's daughter in 1362. The same was true of the administration, where power became increasingly engrossed by William Wykeham, the King's new favourite, who became Keeper of the Privy Seal in 1363 and Chancellor in 1367. Unfortunately Wykeham had no time for bureaucratic detail, the accounts were not properly overseen, and charges of corruption and inefficiency grew loud and persistent by 1370. This situation was aggravated by a fresh outbreak of plague in 1361–62, not as virulent as the previous one, but reinforcing the tendencies which had begun then. By 1369 all labour services on the royal manor of Windsor had been abandoned, which was an increasingly prevalent tendency. This helps to explain the 'feudal reaction' of the 1370s as the landholders used the commission of the peace to try and enforce the now unworkable traditional conditions, which was to be an important driver of the Peasants' Revolt in 1381. One result of this was that the Crown grew closer to the political community, which may now be described as consisting of the peers and the gentry, and the Commissions of the Peace had won almost complete control over the maintenance of order in the shires – a situation which suited them admirably. Both sides were well satisfied with the politics of peace; direct taxation was no longer required, and the parliaments of the 1360s were among the most peaceful of the century.

However by 1369 the King's subjects in Aquitaine had had enough of their Prince, and rose in revolt. This situation was complicated by the fact that Blanche of Lancaster, John of Gaunt's much-loved wife, had died in 1369, and in 1371 he married the daughter of Edward's old ally, Peter I of Castile. This gave him a claim to the Castilian throne, which proved to be an unnecessary military distraction, and left Aquitaine open to the forces of Charles V. Caught between the French and the Aquitainian rebels, the English armies faltered. The Black Prince's sack of Limoges was a terrible mistake which alienated what sympathy remained in the duchy, and when he returned to England to nurse his health soon after, the commanders whom he left behind proved inadequate to the task. Even Gascony was disrupted by defections, and in 1372 the French took over the north of Aquitaine, leaving the English confined to a narrow coastal strip between Bordeaux and Bayonne. A truce, which effectively conceded defeat, was concluded with the French at Bruges in 1375. Just about everything which Edward had gained at Bretigny had vanished in the space of fifteen years. Nor was the King in any position to redeem this failure. Queen Philppa had died in 1369, and Edward was so adversely affected by her death that he called off the military expedition which he had been planning for that year. Age had caught up with him, and after 1370 he increasingly withdrew from public life, access to him being effectively controlled by Lord Neville, William Latimer and Alice Perrers, the King's ambitious and forceful mistress. The court therefore ceased to epitomise the political unity of the realm, and became dominated by a narrow and unpopular clique. This situation was aggravated by renewed demands for direct taxation. Between 1369 and 1375 Edward had spent about £670,000 on the war, and these bills had to be met somehow. Parliament inevitably flexed its muscles and in 1371 demanded (and obtained) the dismissal of Chancellor Wykeham and Treasurer Brantlingham in return for grants. The government refused to call parliaments in 1374 and 1375, so that when that assembly met again in April 1376, its backlog of grievances was considerable. Although its positive achievements were short-lived, this was one of the most important sessions of the century, because it saw the first election of a regular Speaker by the House of Commons and the creation of the process of impeachment. Apart from its determination to resist demands for taxation, the principal concern of this parliament was the King's 'evil counsellors'. John of Gaunt, representing the King, dealt with a joint committee of both houses on this issue, and eventually conceded the need for a new (and named) council. The Commons then pursued both Latimer and Neville in a suit adjudicated by the Lords, presided over by Gaunt, which resulted in a defeat for the court and the dismissal of both officers. At the same time Alice Perrers was banished from the household. The initiative taken by the Commons in all these matters was altogether unprecedented. Having made so many concessions, the government hung on to the session in the hope of some financial reward, and was eventually granted a wool subsidy for three years. Meanwhile the role played by John of Gaunt in these proceedings gave rise to rumours that he was planning to seize the throne when his father (who was obviously ill) should die. When the Black Prince died on 8 June, during the session, these rumours multiplied, and the parliament insisted that his young son be immediately created Prince of Wales as a guarantee of his succession. When the session ended on 10 July it had passed a massive vote of no confidence in the regime, and the court was in disarray.

In spite of these humiliating reversals, it was not slow to strike back. By October 1376 the displaced courtiers had been restored to their titles, lands, and influences. The Speaker of the Commons was arrested, and various opposition peers were deprived of their offices. At the same time John of Gaunt fell foul of the governing elite of London, and a mob attacked his palace of the Savoy. It must have seemed that the bad days of the 1320s had come again. However, when Parliament assembled again in January 1377, it proved surprisingly amenable, and granted a direct subsidy in the form of a poll tax. It also accepted the reversal of its earlier impeachments, because this was within the King's prerogative rights. The absence of several peers who had been prominent in opposition in the earlier session probably accounts for this change of attitude. It even staged an elaborate reconciliation between Gaunt and the Londoners. By the late spring of 1377 it seemed that the policies which Gaunt had been pursuing were paying off, and a degree of normality was restored to political life. This came not a moment too soon because anxiety about the King's health was mounting, and he died at Sheen on 21 June. In the last months, indeed years, of his life, Edward had become a rather pathetic figure, and there is more than a suspicion that he became senile, but the epitaphs which followed his death remembered only his glory days. 'He departed this life,' wrote the chronicler Froissart, 'to the deep distress of the whole realm of England, for he had been a good king for them. His like had not been seen since the days of King Arthur ...' His reign had indeed been long, and full of achievement, some of which had been the King's, so it is scarcely fair to remember him as an old man under the thumb of his pushy mistress, Alice Perrers.

PART 8
A TROUBLED THRONE,
1377–1413

27

RICHARD II (REIGNED 1377–1399)

Richard was only ten years old at his accession, because his father, who should have succeeded his grandfather, had died the previous June at the age of forty-six, having contracted some lethal disease on campaign in Castile. There should therefore have been a regent, but the obvious candidate, Richard's uncle John of Gaunt, was too unpopular both with the magnates and the Commons in Parliament to be considered. At the same time, he was too important to be bypassed in favour of anyone else. In the circumstances the system of councils which had already been evolved provided a workable solution, and for the first three years of the reign formed what was in effect a collective regency. John was probably influential behind the scenes, as was the King's mother, the Princess Joan, but the councils were not bound to take their advice, and in fact seem to have consulted widely. The continual councils were wound up in 1380, following a petition from the House of Commons and the King, then aged thirteen, became theoretically responsible for his own government. This was not real, but neither the magnates nor the officers of state exercised much leadership over the next few years. The most important of the latter was probably the Chancellor, Archbishop Simon Sudbury, although the Chamberlain Aubrey de Vere was also influential, and the favour which Richard showed to his family undoubtedly aroused hostility within the court.

Richard was crowned on 16 July 1377 at Westminster, but almost immediately the rejoicings were cut short by news of French raids on Winchelsea and Rye – a swift reminder of the on-going war. Attempts to counter-attack were unsuccessful, but at least the King's first parliament was in a generous mood as a result, granting no less than two-fifteenths and two-tenths. The mood did not last, and in the next parliament in 1378 there was criticism of how this tax had been spent. Assertions were made that taxation was only for the purposes of defence, and that otherwise the King should 'live of his own'; as a result the new grant made was a small one. In the spring of 1379 a further parliament showed similar discontent, granting a graduated poll tax, but asking for a committee of lords to investigate the King's finances. It was partly in response to this poll tax that there occurred in 1381 that great uprising which is known as the Peasants' Revolt. This revolt, which broke out in a number of different places in south and south-east England, appears to have arisen spontaneously, provoked largely by local grievances connected with the 'feudal reaction' against the emancipation which had resulted from the Black Death. It was not entirely rural, because there was serious trouble in the City of London as well, complicated by factions within the City government. It started in Essex in the second week of May with resistance to the poll tax, spread to Kent by early June, and then swept through East Anglia by the middle of that month. In mid-June also the Kentish men, supported by those of Essex, marched on London, where they were welcomed by discontented elements in the city, and for several days there was a virtual collapse of government. During that time the rebels seized and put to death the Chancellor, Archbishop Sudbury, and the Treasurer, Sir Robert Hales, giving a fair expression to their prevailing grievances. Lawyers also were particularly targeted and large quantities of manorial records went up in flames, as the peasants strove to eliminate the evidences of their servile status. On the 15th the King, well guarded, met the rebels at Smithfield, and there in a skirmish the leader Wat Tyler was killed. The result could have been an all-out battle, but the fourteen-year-old Richard, seizing an opportunity, proclaimed himself the peasants' leader, and thereby exploited that aspect of the rebels' propaganda which had declared their loyalty to the Crown and their discontent with 'evil counsellors'. Various concessions and pardons were promised, and the rebels dispersed. Within a week the authorities were back in control of the South East.

In East Anglia the climax came slightly later. There the rebels had gone on a rampage through Norfolk, Suffolk and Cambridgeshire, and had killed the Chief Justice of King's Bench and the Prior of Bury St Edmunds in the process. They had also divided their forces, and Bishop Despenser of Norwich, leading the royalist troops, caught and defeated them in detail between 18 and 25 June. The clearing-up operations took some time, and the concessions extracted at Smithfield were not honoured, but only 287 out of the thousands who had been involved were excluded from the general amnesty, so the government's revenge was distinctly limited. The motives of the rebels had been to some extent political, as was demonstrated by the murders of Sudbury and Hales. John of Gaunt's palace of the Savoy was burned down, and the Duke himself would probably have been lynched if the mob could have caught him. There had also been a xenophobic aspect to their actions, especially in London, where a number of Flemings fell victim and their premises were destroyed. The so-called confession of John Rackstrawe, one of the leaders, appears to reveal a truly radical agenda which involved killing the King, the Lords and the prelates, and establishing a 'king' in every county. However, the actual actions of the rebels do not reveal any such purposes, and it is probably a figment of the chronicler's imagination. The only genuine radical among the leaders appears to have been the preacher John Ball, whose egalitarian sermons deeply shocked the political nation at the time, and were subsequently used to attack John Wycliffe, with whom he was associated. The seriousness of the rebellion seems to have arisen as much from its sudden and unexpected explosion as from the actual size of the bands which were raised. Those supporting Wat Tyler at Smithfield were actually outnumbered by the loyal householders of London who had turned out for the King. It is also an open question what effect it had, once the initial shock of the murders had been absorbed. Politically, it seems to have made little difference, and socially the most that can be said is that it served to alert the aristocracy to the strength of feeling which their attempts to re-impose feudal services had aroused. Certainly the process of emancipation went on, but that may have been due to the economics of the rural situation rather than to the politics of the Peasants' Revolt. Its high-profile encounters served mainly to reveal the King to be a young man of initiative and strong will.

Who was running the country over the next few years is, however, a difficult question to answer. Richard had his favourites, of whom Michael de la Pole, who became Chancellor in 1383, was probably the most important, and he continued to rely heavily on the advice of John of Gaunt. However, it is often hard to determine which members of the council should be associated with which pieces of advice in a regime which was in theory being led by the King himself. In 1378 the papacy had gone into schism; Urban VI in Rome and Clement VII in Avignon squared up to each other and issued mutual anathemas. The French inevitably supported Clement, which led the English to recognise Urban, and in 1383 to launch a campaign in Flanders in his support. Flanders was an important market for English wool, and the French had been campaigning successfully there in 1382, so an expedition was sent over under the command of Bishop Despenser. The result was a fiasco because no magnates supported it, and Parliament made only a small grant. The operation fizzled out in a truce in October, in spite of the bellicose noises being made (in the background) by the Earl of Arundel and others. By 1385 two opposed groups had emerged in the Council: the Courtiers, led by de la Pole, and their critics led by the Earl of Arundel. The critical attacks were fierce, and ranged over a wide variety of grievances, of which the failure in Flanders was only one. Moderates were not lacking; indeed the opposing groups probably represented only a minority of the nobility; but their attempts to mediate proved futile. Richard's uncle the Duke of York was among them, as was the Earl of Northumberland, but their task became increasingly impossible as the King became more closely identified with his courtiers, and their opponents turned from criticising their enemies to attacking Richard himself. The gentry who made up the House of Commons tended to take the middle way, because they had little to hope for from the victory of either of the opposed parties, but their concern to protect their own interests led them, on issues such as taxation, to side with the critics of the regime. In 1387–88 these quarrels boiled up into the most dangerous political crisis of the reign so far. In December 1387 five of the court's opponents, led (in terms of status) by Richard's youngest uncle, the Duke of Gloucester, laid charges of treason against the courtiers, on the basis of their failure in Flanders. The remaining four, the Earl of Arundel, the Earl of Warwick, the Earl of Nottingham, and John of Gaunt's son the Earl of Derby, all had particular grievances to work off, and there seems to have been a degree of personal dislike between the King and the Earl of Derby, but the crisis had not come on suddenly. It had been brewing up since the parliament of October 1385, when the Commons had restricted Richard's power to make grants, imposed a commission of Lords to oversee the Exchequer, and compelled him to abandon attempts to levy a scutage. In 1386 the dismissal of the Chancellor and the Treasurer was demanded, and conceded under threat of deposition. De la Pole, the ex-Chancellor was impeached and imprisoned, and a second commission established to oversee the government in general, particularly the royal household. The new officers of state, headed by the Earl of Arundel as Chancellor, were not likely to be sympathetic to the King, and over the following twelve months he did his best to undermine the work of the commissions. Consequently, when the Appellants (as they were known) laid their charges of treason, they added the names of four of Richard's more recent servants: Robert de Vere, Chief Justice Tresilian, Nicholas Brembre (a former Lord Mayor of London), and Archbishop Neville of York. De Vere had been raised to the title of Duke of Ireland and had tried to raise forces for the King in Cheshire, while Tresilian had in 1387 declared the commissions derogatory to the royal prerogative. The Merciless Parliament of 1388 was therefore followed by a bloodbath. Sir Simon Burley (the King's former tutor), Sir John Beauchamp (the Steward of the Household), Brembre and Tresilian were all executed, and four puisne judges were exiled to Ireland for their share in Tresilian's decision. However, having secured their objectives, the Appellants' alliance then gradually fell apart, and the second parliament of 1388 was markedly critical of the new regime which they had instituted. Sympathy for the King's position began to replace suspicion, particularly among the Lords, and Gloucester and Arundel drifted into a position of isolation over the next few months. On 3 May 1389 the King reasserted his authority. Gloucester and Arundel were removed from the Council, and veteran administrators returned to office. Old courtiers were again about Richard's person, and the commissions were emasculated.

The remarkable thing about the King's recovery was the ease with which it was accomplished. Richard was sensible. He did not attempt to recall de la Pole or de Vere from exile, and appointed some members of the commissions to high office. Above all John of Gaunt returned from his Castilian adventure in October 1389. He had gone there in 1386 in an attempt to win the crown, and his advice had been much missed in the crisis which was just past. Although he had played no part in the events of May, his steadying counsel over the next decade was to be one of Richard's main political assets. The other asset, which is hard to quantify, was the propensity of the magnate class as a whole to accept royal government, save in the most exceptional circumstances, and to seek a return to normality as soon as those circumstances disappeared. Gloucester and Arundel were restored to the Council by the end of 1389, and Richard agreed in 1390 to submit any future grants to a committee of senior councillors for approval. In this respect the King had taken the lesson of 1388 to heart, and the rewards given to his new generation of Chamber knights were nothing like as lavish as those of their predecessors had been. The Council as a whole was balanced between courtiers and magnates, and the early 1390s were a period of relative political tranquillity. The main development was in the peace negotiations with France because the Appellants for all their bellicosity could not make war without money, and Parliament was very reluctant to supply it. Consequently by the time of the King's coup, discussions were already well advanced, and on 18 June a three-year truce was sealed at Leulingham, between Calais and Boulogne. This was to be extended for two further spells of two years; however, definitive peace eluded both sides, because the issue of Aquitaine could not be resolved. In 1390 John of Gaunt was created Duke of Aquitaine, to hold of Richard as King of France. This was a bargaining position, because the English were in fact willing to concede French sovereignty over the duchy, but still peace proved elusive. The Gascons in particular did not like the terms offered. They did not want a resident duke, and especially not one whose position was hereditary, which were the terms of Gaunt's grant in 1394. His arrival in person in the following year did nothing to quieten these fears, and as a result the truce with France was merely extended. Nor was everyone in England in favour of peace. There was an element among the knights in Parliament which favoured a continuation of the war in the hope of ransoms and profit, and the Earl of Arundel continued making bellicose noises. However, when Richard's much-loved wife, Anne of Bohemia, died in 1394, Arundel alienated the King by his behaviour at her funeral, which earned him a spell in the Tower, and greatly reduced his influence thereafter. Another group which was hostile to the peace was the Northern marcher lords, who did not want to see Scotland included in any agreement, which was the King's intention. So Richard's best efforts were frustrated, and the result in 1396 was a twenty-eight-year truce, which did not resolve the issues, but at least suspended hostilities for the foreseeable future. As a result, Richard married Isabella, the seven-year-old daughter of Charles VI on 1 November 1396, a marriage which postponed the prospect of an heir to the throne for about eight or nine years. Meanwhile, and while these negotiations were still ongoing, Richard had been to Ireland, where a winter campaign in 1394/95 forced the submission of Leinster, but left an ongoing dispute in Ulster between the Anglo-Irish Earl of March and the native chieftain Niall Og O'Neill. In the event, the quarrel proved more enduring than the settlement, and the death in battle of the Earl of March in 1398 prompted Richard to go a second time in 1399 – an expedition which was to contribute to his downfall.

With hindsight it can be seen that that downfall began in the parliament of 1397 when a certain Thomas Haxey presented a bill to the Commons, which was highly critical of the costs of the royal household. There are a number of unanswered questions about the provenance of this bill, to which the King reacted badly. He persuaded the Lords to declare such complaints treasonable, and Haxey needed a subsequent pardon, but the general atmosphere of the parliament was hostile, and when Gloucester and Arundel refused to attend council meetings about a month later, the prospects for continued peace were not good. Another source of trouble was money. Richard had improved his relations with Parliament in the early 1390s by not asking for subsidies, but this was only because he was using alternative methods. Some he raised in the principality of Wales, and some from the City of London. In 1392 he suspended the City's privileges on the pretext of disorder, and extracted a series of loans from the citizens before granting a new charter in 1397 through the agency of his new ally in the city, Mayor Richard Whittington. The King did not repay the loans which he had been granted, and although no reference was made to such matters in the deposition articles of 1399, his treatment of London contributed significantly to his reputation as an aspiring tyrant.

Richard managed this parliament largely by threats, arresting the three senior Appellants, Gloucester, Warwick and Arundel, withdrawing pardons, and banishing Archbishop Arundel. The Earl of Arundel was eventually executed, Warwick submitted and Gloucester was murdered at Calais. The King immediately opened negotiations with Rome to have the Archbishop replaced, a move which was not ultimately successful. The lands of the disgraced Appellants were used to reward the King's loyal followers, who by this time included the two younger Appellants, Derby and Nottingham, who were raised to the dukedoms of Hereford and Norfolk respectively.

When Parliament reassembled in January 1398 it was at Shrewsbury, close to Richard's power base in Cheshire, and the King again used threats to keep the Commons subservient. He was granted the customs dues for life, an unprecedented concession which was to become the norm over the next century, and he issued almost 600 pardons – probably in return for money – but, since these were revocable at will, too much significance should not be attached to that. The issue which eventually led to Richard's downfall, however, was unconnected to Parliament. It took the form of a quarrel between the dukes of Hereford and Norfolk, those former friends who had now fallen out bitterly. This had got to the point of a trial by battle, when the King stepped in and put a stop to it in September 1398. He banished Norfolk for life and Hereford for ten years, thereby alienating Hereford's father, John of Gaunt, who had hitherto been Richard's most effective supporter. When John died in May 1399, the King confiscated his entire domain, thereby depriving Hereford of his expectation, and alienating the inheritance-conscious nobility altogether. Made overconfident by these apparent successes, Richard departed for Ireland in the summer of 1399 to deal with the unsatisfactory situation there, leaving the Duke of York in command in England. While he was away, the Duke of Hereford invaded with support from Louis of Orleans, ostensibly to claim his inheritance, and the Duke of York did not move against him. Richard had miscalculated disastrously, and when he returned in haste from Ireland to confront this new threat, he found himself virtually without support. He was forced to concede defeat at Conway in North Wales, and became the prisoner of Henry Bolingbroke, Duke of Hereford (and Lancaster). Richard was only thirty-two, and Bolingbroke knew perfectly well that there was only one way to protect himself and his allies from the King's future revenge. Taking advantage of his universal, if temporary, unpopularity, he deposed him on 29 September 1399. Richard was consigned to Pontefract Castle, where he died on 6 January 1400, probably murdered on Henry's orders. Because his first marriage had been childless, and his second wife was a child herself, he left no heir to succeed him, and Henry was able to claim the throne on the strength of his descent from Edward III through the male line. For the time being his position was a strong one, but his claim was not beyond challenge, as we shall see.

28

HENRY IV AND THE HOUSE OF LANCASTER (REIGNED 1399–1413)

Henry had been born about 3 April 1366 and was the eldest child of John of Gaunt, Duke of Lancaster, by his first wife, Blanche. John was the third son of King Edward III, younger than Edward, the Black Prince, and Lionel, Duke of Clarence. Lionel had died in 1368, leaving a daughter, Philippa, who had married Edmund Mortimer, Earl of March. Edmund had died in 1381, leaving a son, Roger, to inherit his claim. However, Roger had also died in 1398 and in 1399 the Mortimer line was represented by his son, another Edmund, who was only eight years old and in no position to bid for the throne, although others made motions on his behalf. Henry was crowned at Westminster on 13 October 1399. It was plausible, therefore, once Richard was safely dead, for him also to claim that he was the heir male to the throne, and had succeeded as much by hereditary right as by coup d'etat. However, the events of 1399 had demonstrated how vulnerable the King could be to a determined magnate assault, and Henry spent much of the first few months of his reign buying support. He was extravagant with gifts and pensions, and that inevitably began to attract the same kind of criticism which had been levelled against his predecessor. The deposition articles which had been drawn up against Richard had implied that he had overstepped the limits of the royal prerogative, but no one knew exactly where those limits were supposed to lie, so Henry was defending an undefined position. The King, for instance, had the undoubted right to choose his advisers and ministers, but Parliament seemed to have developed a similar right to examine and to criticise their actions, as well as to exercise some control over royal spending. Consequently relations between the King and Parliament were not constitutionally defined, and much depended upon the monarch's ability to control the steps of an increasingly complicated dance. Henry's chief asset in the opening months of his reign was Richard's unpopularity, as was demonstrated by the fate of a group of aristocratic plotters on his behalf at the end of 1399, who were lynched by mobs in various places. As a result this plot was a non-event, but it probably sealed the ex-king's fate. Next time the rebels might have better fortune, if Richard had still been alive.

Meanwhile Henry had strengthened his position by appointing experienced Lancastrian supporters to key positions in government. The new Chancellor, for example, was John Scarle, who had been a Chancery clerk and had served in the administration of the Duchy of Lancaster. Such appointments preserved continuity and inspired confidence. At the same time magnate families which had suffered under Richard rallied to the new regime. The heirs of Warwick and Arundel were minors, but the great Northern families of Neville and Percy come into this category. Ralph Neville, Earl of Westmorland, was to remain one of Henry's most loyal supporters throughout his reign, but the allegiance of the Percies proved to be short-lived. The Earl of Northumberland, his brother the Earl of Worcester and his son Henry 'Hotspur' all initially received substantial offices from the King, but apparently they were not satisfied and they rose in revolt in 1403, or at least Worcester and Hotspur did. Their aims are unclear, but they seem to have been demanding more power than Henry was prepared to concede them. Hotspur was defeated and killed at Shrewsbury in the same year and Worcester taken and executed soon after. Northumberland had not been directly involved, and he was pardoned in 1404 on the intercession of Parliament. He repaid this generosity by rebelling on his own account in 1405, this time in alliance with Archbishop Scrope of York and the young Earl of Nottingham. It was in this connection that he signed the tripartite agreement with Owain Glyn Dwr, who was leading a parallel revolt in Wales to carve up England between them. This never had much substance, and prompt action by the Earl of Westmorland secured the persons of the Archbishop and Nottingham before they could make any headway. Both were executed as traitors. Northumberland escaped into Scotland, where he continued to plot against Henry, invading again in January 1408 only to be defeated and killed by the sheriff of Yorkshire at Bramham Moor on 19 February. This not only marked the end of Percy ambitions, but the end of any serious attempt to unseat Henry, who had by this time secured his position against any possible rivals.

Glyn Dwr, whose revolt continued for some years, had no such exalted ambition. His aim was to establish an autonomous principality in his homeland. Although he had some claims to princely ancestry, he had fought for the English crown in France, and had not hitherto shown any animosity towards the marcher lords. However, in 1400 he failed in a private suit against Lord Grey, and took out his frustration with a raid on Oswestry. As a result he quickly found himself leading an ethnic Welsh uprising against the English. This was sporadic but effective in places, and Aberystwyth and Harlech castles fell to his forces. Although he was too late to assist Henry Hotspur at Shrewsbury in 1403, by 1404 most of north-west and central Wales was under his control, and he felt strong enough to call a parliament in his own name to meet at Machynlleth. The seriousness of his intention was demonstrated in the same year when he wrote to the French king as 'Owynus dei gratia princeps Wallie', asking for military support. He was by this time something of a national leader, and although not all the Welsh supported him, he had won a number of engagements against the marcher lords in both North and South Wales. In 1405 he signed the tripartite agreement already referred to with the Earl of Northumberland and Archbishop Scrope, which would have given him control, not only over the whole of Wales, but of the marcher lordships and some western English counties as well. This was the zenith of his pretensions. Within a year Northumberland and Scrope had been defeated and the campaigns against him in

Wales were being conducted by Prince Henry, the King's nineteen-year-old son. Young Henry proved himself to be a commander of ability, and in a series of small campaigns drove Glyn Dwr back to his heartlands in North Wales. When French assistance arrived in the south in 1406, it proved totally ineffective and was soon withdrawn. Glyn Dwr was defeated, but he was neither killed nor captured. And his legend survived until at least 1412, when the last report of his appearance proved mistaken.

As the French intervention in Wales demonstrated, relations with the court of Charles VI were still unsettled. In spite of the rapprochement represented by Richard's marriage to Isabella, peace between the two realms still depended upon the long truce, a permanent settlement not having proved possible. Part of the problem was caused by the fact that from 1392 onward Charles suffered from periodic bouts of insanity, during which he was incapable of conducting affairs, and as a result the court became torn with faction. The two protagonists were Charles's brother Louis of Orleans and his uncle Philip of Burgundy, and they were divided over policy towards England; indeed if it had not been so, Henry might have been unable to launch his invasion. The King was therefore to some extent indebted to Louis, and extended the truce between the two countries in November 1399. Henry may have considered improving his popularity by renewing the war, but decided against it, partly because of the unresolved problem of what to do with Isabella. There were suggestions that she might marry the Prince of Wales, then aged thirteen, but these were abandoned, possibly on the Prince's insistence, and instead she was returned to France in 1401, at which point the truce was renewed. In spite of this, there continued to be sporadic fighting in Gascony, which had shown no affection for the House of Lancaster in the 1390s, and showed no signs of changing. The Earl of Rutland went out as governor and did something to establish the credibility of the new regime, but the French invaded Guienne in 1403 and blockaded Bordeaux, without officially repudiating the truce. Gascon lords continued to be disaffected, and periodically handed over border castles to the French. This uneasy tension provoked occasional small-scale expeditions from England, which needed financial support. However, in the winter of 1407/08 a further truce was agreed locally, and this seems to have held – more or less.

Both politically and strategically the French held the initiative, but were inhibited from taking advantage of this fact by the continuing hostility between the houses of Orleans and Burgundy. The death of Duke Philip and the succession of John in 1404 only made matters worse, because John was even more hostile to Louis than his father had been. The aim of both sides was power in France, but the Burgundians, through their Flemish connections, were more likely to look to England, and this inclination was enhanced when the Duke of Orleans was murdered by Burgundian agents in November 1407. The feud became even more bitter, and degenerated into open civil war by 1410. The Armagnacs, as they were known from the father-in-law of the new Duke of Orleans, Bernard of Armagnac, drove the Duke of Burgundy out of Paris, and he turned to England for help. This was conceded because the English council was at that time under the control of the Prince of Wales, who stood to gain a bride from the negotiations, and troops were sent who contributed to the Duke's victory. The marriage negotiations failed, and the King, having recovered control of his council, came to terms with the Armagnacs. However, they repudiated the agreement within two months, and instead patched up a reconciliation with their opponents, which left the Duke of Clarence's expeditionary force with nowhere to go. Instead it was bought off, and retreated into Gascony. The Prince of Wales remained pro-Burgundian throughout, but he was not in power after 1411, and it had to wait until he became king in 1413 before that alliance came to fruition.

Meanwhile patchy campaigns in Gascony, the cost of suppressing the early magnate unrest and of encountering the Welsh revolt of Owain Glyn Dwr left the King with financial problems. Because there was no official war, the Commons were reluctant to grant taxation, and a slump in the woollen industry left the customs revenues over 16 per cent down by about 1405. This slump also affected the wool growers, and there was a general decline in estate income at the same time, which reduced the revenues from the royal demesne. Equally important were the controls which the Commons sought to impose. In 1406, for example, they insisted on making a new grant conditional on a proper audit of the 1404 grant, a concession which they won after a protracted political battle. At the same time they attempted to impose fresh controls on household expenditure, and tried to insist on the recall of grants. This also came to a head in 1406, when the Speaker of the Commons, Sir John Tiptoft, was appointed Treasurer of the household As such he was remarkably successful, not merely in curbing household extravagance, but also in winning the King's confidence, because he was appointed Treasurer of the realm in 1408. By about 1409 the King's financial problems were under control, and the loans which he was still raising could be serviced out of income. By that time the issues in government were political rather than financial. The trouble, as usual, was noble faction, but this time exacerbated by the fact that the Prince of Wales had emerged as a leading opponent of his father. He was twenty by this time, and his following tended to be among the younger generation of magnates. Apart from the fact that he was pro-Burgundian, while the King was inclined to support the Armagnacs, the differences between the parties seem to have been as much personal as political. The Prince's motivation is not easy to understand, unless he was attempting to build a power base ahead of his accession, which the King's declining health indicated might not be far off. He had a certain affection for the memory of Richard II, whom he had served as a child, but that is unlikely to have been a main cause of his behaviour. By the end of 1409 his friends were in the ascendancy, and secured the dismissal of Tiptoft as Treasurer and Archbishop Arundel as Chancellor; their replacements, Lord Scrope and Sir Thomas Beaufort, were certainly of the Prince's party, and they retained their ascendancy for nearly two years. However, they also ran into trouble with Parliament, which seems to have resulted in something of a crisis. The King, perhaps stirred up by suggestions that he might abdicate, reasserted himself at the end of 1411. Arundel returned to the Chancellorship and John Pelham was appointed Treasurer on 23 December. The Prince was certainly out of favour during 1412, but there was no witch hunt against his friends. Thomas of Lancaster, the King's second son, was created Duke of Clarence, possibly as a counterpoise to the younger Henry, but Thomas Beaufort was also created Earl of Dorset. There seems to have been a lot of court intrigue going on in the summer of 1412, but it is not well documented, and may have been simply the result of jockeying for position as Henry IV's health continued to decline. The Prince declared that malicious rumours were being spread about him, particularly relating to monies he was alleged to have received as Captain of Calais, and produced documents to defend himself. A reconciliation was patched up in October 1412 which lasted until Henry died on 20 March following. He had allegedly been told by a 'soothsayer' that he would die in Jerusalem, which was proved true as he collapsed on a visit to Westminster Abbey, and expired in the Jerusalem Chamber. This was not the only apocryphal story perpetuated by William Shakespeare; the tale is also told that during one of his father's bouts of sickness, towards the end, the Prince of Wales was caught at his bedside, trying on the crown. In spite of the fact that he had three surviving brothers, twenty-five-year-old Thomas, twenty-four-year-old John, and twenty-three-year-old Humphrey, there was no challenge to the twenty-six-year-old Prince and he was crowned a few days later.

PART 9
THE LANCASTRIANS,
1413–1461

29

HENRY V, A VICTORIOUS INTERLUDE (REIGNED 1413–1422)

Henry was born at Monmouth in South Wales, probably on 11 September 1386. The date is not quite certain because nobody expected at that time that he would become king. His mother, Mary Bohun, Henry's first wife, died in childbirth in June 1394, and very little is known about his upbringing. He had a nurse, Joan Waryn, who was generously rewarded once he came to the throne, and he appears to have been regarded as a puny child. However, his education was that of any normal aristocratic boy, consisting largely of riding, hunting and the courtly and martial arts. He was later literate in English, French and Latin, and someone taught him to play the harp, but the names of his tutors are not known. As king he was to patronise artists, scholars and musicians, as did his brothers John and Humphrey, but we do not know how he acquired these tastes. After his mother's death he was placed with his maternal grandmother, Joan, Countess of Hereford, and it may well have been she, rather than his father, who made this provision for him. During the latter's exile his son lived at court, possibly as some kind of hostage, and went with Richard to Ireland in 1399. As soon as Richard was deposed, he was sent for and created Prince of Wales on 15 October 1399, this status being a recognition of Henry IV's de facto kingship. He was thus acknowledged as heir to the throne. Thereafter until 1406 he was largely occupied in Wales, where he was taken on campaign by his governor Hugh le Despenser. He took part in the siege of Conwy Castle in April 1401, and after Despenser's death in October accompanied his replacement, the Earl of Worcester, until the latter defected to the rebels at Shrewsbury. Thereafter the Prince was appointed Lieutenant for the whole of Wales, and took part in a number of small but successful campaigns, as we have seen. He began his service as a royal councillor in 1406, and came to the fore during the King's illness in the winter of 1408/09, becoming the effective head of the new council which was appointed in 1410. This council, which was entirely noble and clerical in its composition, was courteously dismissed in 1411, possibly because it was serving the Prince's interests too well. For the last fifteen months of the reign the Prince of Wales was excluded from power – by the King – although they were ostensibly reconciled in October 1412. One of the main reasons for his exclusion was a difference of opinion over French policy, and as King Henry V continued to favour the Burgundian alliance. His brother John followed their father in favouring the Armagnacs.

Henry was crowned on 9 April 1413 in a specially splendid ceremony using the sacred oil of St Thomas Becket. His nobles swore their oaths of allegiance ahead of the coronation, which was an unprecedented move, but optimism was in the air. Henry swiftly made clear his personal interest in the Duchy of Aquitaine, and his desire to return to the favourable terms of the Treaty of Bretigny of 1360, an intention which the French were bound to frustrate to the best of their ability. There was early talk of a marriage between Henry and Catherine, Charles VI's daughter, but the restoration of order in the border areas of Gascony was top priority for both sides, and negotiations continued. Towards the end of 1413 an agreement was signed with the Duke of Burgundy, but both made it clear that their quarrel was with the Armagnacs and not with

Charles VI. Henry spent 1414 testing the waters and forming alliances with the Emperor and the King of Aragon, but by the end of the year it seems that he was determined upon war, and began to assemble a large army. The story of the tennis balls is probably apocryphal, but what is clear is that early in 1415 Henry made a series of demands relating to Normandy, Aquitaine, Anjou, Maine, Poitou, and various other territories that were clearly unacceptable, and were refused. This gave Henry the pretext for which he was looking, and in August 1415 an armada sailed for France.

Meanwhile his security had been challenged nearer home by a plot favouring the Mortimer claim to the throne. There are a number of mysterious features about this conspiracy, which featured Richard, Earl of Cambridge, Lord Scrope, Sir John Oldcastle, and a number of other prominent men, not the least of which seems to have been the promotion of a rumour that Richard II was still alive. It may have been a Lollard plot, but was in any case too complicated to be really dangerous, added to which it was betrayed to the King by its ostensible beneficiary, Edmund Mortimer, Earl of March. The principals were rounded up on 31 July, and the Earl of Cambridge, with one or two others, was executed a week later. Before the end of August Henry had brushed aside the threat, such as it was, and sailed to Harfleur. His fleet on this occasion consisted of some 1,500 vessels, mostly small transports hired in the Low Countries, but including some thirty fighting ships of his own, led by the *Trinity Royal* of 540 tons. Harfleur was a French naval base, and the siege lasted some five weeks. However, since no relieving army appeared on the scene, the keys were handed over on 22 September. Henry treated the citizens well, established a garrison there and encouraged English merchants to set up business. This was clearly an initial step in a 'hearts and minds' campaign to reconcile the French to English lordship, and in the short term it worked well enough. Then in the first week of October the King set out with 6,000 fighting men to march through Normandy to Calais, in what was essentially an act of bravado. On 25 October he was intercepted near the village of Agincourt by a French army of 20,000. Exploiting the ground, and displaying the finest qualities of generalship, Henry won a striking victory against the odds in a battle which quickly entered into English folklore. In the course of this unexpected triumph he took a large number of prisoners who may (or may not) have been killed at the climax of the battle – it depends on which account you read. In spite of this possible blot on his escutcheon, Henry promptly returned to England and gave thanks at Canterbury on 15 November, moving on to a triumphant reception in London on the 23rd. If the English were reluctant to finance his wars, it did not appear on this occasion. The King spent 1416 trying to exploit his success. Early in the year he was forced to revisit Harfleur, by this time under siege, which he relieved in a naval operation, culminating in another victory at Valmont. However, this time the French did not give up easily and by the summer the port was again besieged, by sea as well as by land. Henry's navy won a striking victory outside Harfleur on 15 August 1416, capturing several Genoese carracks (large fighting ships) in the process, after which half the navy remained based at Harfleur to deter any similar operations in the future. By September the news of this victory had spread as far as Venice. His diplomacy was equally successful. In the spring the Emperor Sigismund offered his good offices as a mediator in the conflict, but by the autumn had become convinced that right was on the English side, and that the French were being unreasonable. Henry persuaded him to sign the Treaty of Canterbury, committing the parties to a 'perpetual alliance' – which somewhat undermined his credibility as a mediator! At the same time, on 13 October, he signed an agreement with Burgundy, indicating a new approach to the problems of France. However, this bore no fruit in the short term, and in the meantime it was business as usual, as Henry prepared another expedition for the summer of 1417.

He sailed in July with 10,000 men, and this time there was no pretence that his quarrel was not with the government of Charles VI. He sent the French king a formal defiance, and moved into Normandy, reducing its towns one at a time. Most offered little resistance, and the French army was nowhere to be seen. By the time that he captured Falaise in February 1418 Henry had driven a wedge through Normandy, and he was able to spend his Easter at Caen. By midsummer the whole province apart from Rouen was in his hands. Meanwhile in May John of Burgundy had seized control of Paris, and with it the government of France. This meant that determined resistance was not to be looked for, and when in July the English laid siege to Rouen no army was sent to its relief. Nevertheless the siege lasted until January 1419, by which time the besiegers' control of river access to the town forced a negotiated surrender. A large fine and the giving of hostages was the only sign of the frustration which the siege had caused Henry. In Paris the news of the surrender was greeted with relief because it reopened the trade routes to the north, which had been blocked for months by the siege operations. To the English Rouen was valuable acquisition, because not only did it complete the conquest of Normandy, but it also assured control of a sizeable base which had been used for the deployment of war galleys against English shipping. Southern Normandy was also important because the unreconciled French – the supporters of the Dauphin – were based in the Loire valley, and the war against them seemed set to continue. By this time Henry was master of the situation because John of Burgundy, accompanied by the King and his court, remained aloof at Pontieu, largely it would seem because John simply did not know what to do and Charles was in no fit state to make decisions. Negotiations were resumed, and Henry actually visited the French court at Veron at the end of May 1419. A further meeting followed at Meulan, at which Henry is supposed to have met Catherine, Charles's daughter for whom he had been angling, for the first time. However, neither the King nor the Duke were present at this encounter and no political progress was made. Meanwhile the latest truce between the two sides was due to expire on 29 July. It was not renewed and Henry moved to secure control of the Vexin, a process in which neither the King nor the Duke intervened. At the same time war weariness and complaints about the cost from England were putting pressure on Henry to find a settlement and his own inclination was moving in the same direction.

If France was to survive, some kind of an understanding between the Duke of Burgundy and the Dauphin was imperative, and a meeting between them was arranged at Montereau on 10 September. However, far from reaching an agreement the meeting terminated when agents of the Dauphin set upon Duke John and killed him, an incident which raised the feud between the two parties to a new level of intensity and virtually drove Duke Philip, who succeeded his father, into the arms of the English. Negotiations between Henry and the representatives of Charles continued, and on 2 December 1419 the Duke wrote letters in which he agreed to support the treaty which was by then impending. The two courts eventually met at Troyes on 20 May 1420, and the treaty was ratified in St Peter's

Cathedral on the following day. By its terms Henry was to marry Catherine without a dowry, and their children were to inherit both crowns. At the same time Henry's possessions in France were recognised in full sovereignty, and he was accepted at Charles's heir when the latter should die. Meanwhile he was to be regent of France. The whole of both courts and all the nobles present then swore to uphold these terms, which were clearly dictated by the English. The Dauphin, who had been disinherited, was not included in the settlement, which he at once repudiated, so the war seemed likely to continue, although on different terms. Henry was committed to reconquer those lands which still adhered to him, but he would now do that as regent on behalf of Charles VI. Having achieved most of his aims, Henry decided to take some time out, and early in 1421 returned with his bride to England, where he introduced Catherine to the rest of the nobility and had her crowned. He also succeeded in getting her pregnant because after he had returned to France on 6 December 1421 she gave birth to a son at Windsor Castle. The child was named Henry, and his prospects seemed infinite. During his absence the Dauphin gave proof of his fighting qualities when his army defeated and killed Henry's brother, the Duke of Clarence, at Bauge in Maine. Although the main English force was extracted from this battle without undue loss, it was a victory which greatly improved morale in the Dauphin's camp, and persuaded the Duke of Brittany to sign a truce with him. Consequently when Henry returned to the action he found the going a good deal tougher, and the Siege of Meaux in the winter of 1421/22 took longer than that of Rouen, as well as causing heavy casualties in the English camp. It also introduced the deadly infection of dysentery into the army, and by the time that Meaux fell in May, the King had become infected, so that he could no longer take an active part in the war.

He was carried in a litter to his last siege in July, and on 22 August he expired at Vincennes, aged thirty-six. The English crown and his claim to France thus passed to a nine-month-old child, and Henry's achievements were about to be put to the test.

It is as a warrior in France that Henry is chiefly remembered, but his government at home also had its successes. Because of the uncertain nature of his title, he needed the support of the Church, and he encouraged Archbishop Arundel to proceed against the Lollards immediately after he came to the throne. It was for that reason that Sir John Oldcastle landed in the Tower in September 1413. He escaped after a few months and a conspiracy grew up around him, which was supposed to come to a head with a rally at Eltham on 9–10 January 1414. The authorities broke this up, and Oldcastle became a fugitive. It was nearly four years before he was captured. He was then proceeded against for both treason and heresy, although he does not seem to have been guilty of any treasonable action. The same was true of his followers, of whom some 300 were arrested and 38 executed. Altogether the Oldcastle revolt seems to have existed mainly in the imagination of the council, providing an excuse to associate sedition with heresy and a justification for the fierce persecution of Lollards which followed. In other words, like the King's famous support for the religious orders, it was part of a bargain with the Church, which recognised and upheld him as king. Victory in France also exercised its magic upon Parliament, which voted a double subsidy in November 1414, and in 1415 (after Agincourt) granted the wool custom for life and another subsidy. In 1416 they approved another double payment, which so enhanced his credit rating that he was able to borrow £34,000 in 1417. After the Treaty of Troyes, only one more grant was made in 1421, but by that time the King had established a right to borrow money without paying interest on his loans, which he exploited on a number of occasions in his borrowings from Richard Whittington of London. The King's finances were probably hit by a decline in the wool trade after about 1419, which affected both the customs revenues and also the resources of the wool growers, but he still managed to pay for a major war without the kind of clashes with Parliament which had characterised the reigns of his immediate predecessors. This is as much a tribute to the efficiency of his administration as of his charismatic personality. All sources speak of his personal charm, and his direct manner of speaking, which disarmed suspicion. We are told that he was above medium height, with a strong, well-coordinated body, and that he was fast runner. He was stately in his bearing and had fine manners, perhaps the flattering opinion of a courtier, and he was strict in his religious observances. We know approximately what he looked like from two contemporary illustrations, both in illuminated manuscripts: the one in Corpus Christi College, Cambridge (MS 213) and the other in the British Library (Arundel MS 38). The well-known portraits are late sixteenth- or early seventeenth-century in date, and appear to have been taken from a common original, now lost. Whether that was contemporary or not in unknown.

30

HENRY VI, AN INEPT KING (REIGNED 1422–1461)

Henry was not merely a child, but an infant, and for the time being remained under the charge of his mother at Windsor. There was no doubt that he was the King, but it would be a long time before he would be in a position to do anything about it. Within about seven weeks his maternal grandfather, Charles VI, also died, and in accordance with the terms of the Treaty of Troyes he became King of France as well. The treaty had stipulated that the two realms were to be kept separate politically, and this therefore required two distinct regencies. The Council, guided by the Chancellor Bishop Langley of Durham, swiftly appointed the King's two surviving uncles to these positions. In his will Henry V had declared that Duke Philip of Burgundy should be regent of France, if he wished, but Duke Philip declined the honour, and John, Duke of Bedford, was appointed. John was the older and the abler of the two brothers, and decided that his first priority must be to pursue the late king's campaign against the Dauphin to a successful conclusion. He set off well enough, winning battles at Cravant in 1423 and at Verneuil in 1424. He also married Duke Philip's sister in 1423, and that created a bond of kinship between them which endured until her death ten years later. Meanwhile in England a similar regency had been conferred on Humphrey, Duke of Gloucester. Humphrey, however, was more self-centred and less astute than John, and quickly became embroiled in disputes with the Council. He also became involved with Jacqueline of Hainault, who had fled to England in 1421 to escape from her husband, John of Brabant. Humphrey took up her cause, secured an annulment of her marriage, and married her himself in 1423. He then attempted to secure her inheritance in Hainault, in the process disrupting relations with both Duke Philip and his brother. Having failed in his quest, he then abandoned his wife and returned to England with Eleanor Cobham in 1425. After securing yet another annulment, he married her in 1428, a circumstance which did nothing to improve his relations with his fellow magnates. When Parliament met in 1428 he made an effort to reassert his authority, but this was unsuccessful, the Lords of the Council putting forward a formal document requiring him to adhere to the declaration of authority to which he and Bedford had set their seals at the beginning of their regencies. The Commons also, which had hitherto been sympathetic to him, would grant taxation only on condition that proper provision was made for his deserted wife Jacqueline. He also found himself at odds with Henry Beaufort, the powerful Bishop of Winchester, who returned to England at this point bearing a commission as papal legate. This was a feud which was to continue with debilitating effect for a number of years.

The eight-year-old Henry was crowned at Westminster on 5 November 1429, and Gloucester's formal protectorate ended at that point. This, however, made little difference to the situation, because Humphrey was still recognised as the chief councillor, and the Council itself provided the overriding collective authority. When the Commons made a special grant of taxation in that same year, they went out of their way to commend the good services of the Bishop of Winchester, which was an ominous sign for the future of Gloucester's authority. Meanwhile the situation in France had deteriorated sharply. The Earl of Salisbury was killed at the Siege of Orleans in 1428, and the French, led in principle by the Dauphin but in fact by Joan of Arc, successfully raised the siege, as a result of which the Dauphin was crowned as King Charles VII at Rheims in July 1429. There were now two kings in France, and these events had tipped the military balance against the English. However, this was not yet decisive. Joan was captured by the Burgundians in 1430 and handed over to the English, who burned her as a witch in 1431. Although it did not have the mystique of Rheims, Bedford was able to arrange the coronation of Henry as King of France in Paris in December 1431. In spite of Philip's periodic negotiations with the French court, the Anglo-Burgundian alliance was still holding at this point. It was only following the death of the Duchess of Bedford in 1433 that it began to unravel. In 1434 the Duke of Bedford returned to England to nurse his failing health; in January 1435 Philip came to terms with Charles VII by the Treaty of Arras. On 15 September the Duke died, and although the English still arguably held the upper hand, no one of similar ability could be found to take his place, and that advantage was slowly lost over the next few years.

As a youth, Henry appears to have shown a taste for piety and the things of the spirit rather than for the martial arts in which he was expected to excel. Little is known of his upbringing, or the identity of his tutors, although the Earl of Warwick was officially his guardian. In about 1429 his mother remarried, and ceased to play any part in his care, and although he remembered her with affection, she had no further influence over his development, except in one important respect. She seems to have transmitted to her son elements of that mental weakness which had afflicted her own father, Charles VI. Although she showed no sign of that weakness herself, her son soon acquired a reputation for feebleness, mixed with a kind of petulant obstinacy, which became increasingly noticeable after he took up the reins of government himself. This took place in 1437, although the King was only sixteen, probably as a means of resolving the continuing feud between the Duke of Gloucester and the Beauforts. When a new council was named in November 1437, the majority were men who were, or had been, associated with the Cardinal Bishop. The most prominent among these was William de la Pole, the Earl of Suffolk, whose wife was a Beaufort. He had earlier been associated with the Duke of Bedford, and had been appointed Steward of the Household in 1433. This position had brought him much in contact with the young king, whose confidence he seems to have gained. Suffolk's position was enhanced by the apparently spontaneous decline in the influence of the Duke of Gloucester. He was fifty years old in 1440, and may have been feeling the advance of time. His appearances at the Council became less frequent, and the impression is that he was being edged out of power. He suffered a further blow in 1441 when his duchess, Eleanor Cobham, was convicted of sorcery and consigned to prison. He was divorced from her before the final sentence was passed, and there was no suggestion that he was involved, but the setback was both personal and political. With Gloucester's eclipse, there was no obvious magnate leader to stand up to Suffolk, because the Duke of York, who was later to fulfil that role was at this stage still friendly with him. Meanwhile the Earl continued to build his position, the Beaufort brothers (the Cardinal's nephews) being his main supporters. John, the elder, was Earl of Somerset and created duke in 1443. He died in 1444 and was succeeded by Edmund, who after de la Pole's death in 1450 was to take over his role as chief favourite. There is no doubt that Suffolk abused his position, maintaining the interests of his clients and dependants, and interfering in the processes of justice. He controlled the courts when it mattered to him to do so, for example protecting William Tailboys of Kyme, who was conducting a virtual reign of terror in Lincolnshire. He became Marquis of Suffolk in 1444, and Duke in 1448. Clearly in the eyes of the King he could do no wrong, but his actions provoked violence among those magnates who were opposed to him, and who could find no redress except by taking the law into their own hands. Meanwhile the Commons became increasingly disgruntled by a breakdown of law and order, for which they justifiably blamed the Duke of Suffolk and his retainers.

Meanwhile the English position in France continued to deteriorate. Charles gained control of Paris in 1436, and although the Duke of York, who had been appointed Lieutenant of the English lands, threatened the city in the following year, and won small victories as late as 1441, lack of resources deprived him of the initiative. Although Charles was also afflicted by plots and revolts in 1437, 1440 and 1442, the English were not astute enough to take advantage of his difficulties. The main reason for this was not obtuseness but the vacillation in the King's attitude between peace and war. Negotiations began as early as 1439, but each side found the other's terms unacceptable, and the release of the Duke of Orleans to act as a mediator found no favour in the French court. In 1443 the Earl of Somerset was sent across to establish a presence in Aquitaine, but his relations with York were never clarified and the two failed to cooperate. Indeed it seems that Somerset's principal objective was to secure lands for himself in Maine and Anjou. He succeeded only in stirring up the hostility of the Duke of Brittany, and falling out bitterly with the Duke of York, whose campaign expenses remained unpaid in London while Somerset appears to have enjoyed the free run of the Exchequer. Even while these expeditions were still ongoing, negotiations for a truce were in hand, and these succeeded at Tours in 1444. Both sides were glad of a breather, but nothing was resolved, the only positive outcome being a marriage agreement between Henry and Margaret, the daughter of the Duke of Anjou, which offered the prospect at least of a permanent settlement. The Marquis of Suffolk, who had negotiated the truce, enjoyed one of his few moments of public approval as a result. The couple were duly married in April 1445, and in December the King, without apparently consulting his council, offered to cede the province of Maine to Charles as a gesture of goodwill. His ministers were furious, but had no option but to obey the royal will. The blame was (most unfairly) divided between Margaret and Suffolk.

While this was going on, the situation in England was going from bad to worse as magnates who were opposed to the court struggled to maintain themselves and their clients against the Marquis of Suffolk and his followers. Private wars broke out between the Bonvilles and the Courtenays in Devon and between the Percies and the Nevilles in Northumberland. In January 1447 the Duke of Gloucester was arrested and died in custody, probably of a heart attack, although Suffolk was inevitably blamed for his murder. In these circumstances the parliament of January 1449 declined to support the war effort, and an ill-considered attack on the border town of Fougeres in October provoked an all-out French assault on Normandy. In spite of a feeble attempt to send reinforcements the whole province was overrun in the course of the next few months, Caen fell in July 1450 and Cherbourg in August. With that the whole of Normandy was lost. That disaster had already had its repercussions in England because, seeing what was happening across the Channel, the second parliament of 1449 impeached the Duke (as he had become in 1448) of Suffolk. In January 1450 Bishop Adam Moleyns, the Lord Privy Seal and a close associate of Suffolk, was murdered at Portsmouth by unpaid soldiers, and in order to save his favourite from a similar fate Henry agreed to exile him for five years. As he attempted to leave the country, his ship was intercepted, and he was summarily beheaded.

In June the men of Kent rose in rebellion under the leadership of Jack Cade, proclaiming that 'the law serveth for nought else in these days but to do wrong'. Thanks to Henry's failure to get a grip on the situation it appeared that the whole civic order was in meltdown. The government of the country was shaken, and the immediate outcome was rivalry for influence at court between the dukes of York and Somerset – the latter being the heir of his brother and of the Duke of Suffolk and the former the putative heir to the throne. Neither was present in London in the immediate aftermath of the Cade rising; Somerset was coming from defeat in France and York from Ireland, whither he had been sent after being withdrawn from Normandy. York took the obvious line, and set himself up as the champion of law and order, circulating bills calling for the reform of the judiciary, and declining at first to act in any extrajudicial way. However, as the court party recovered its nerve he rethought his strategy, and began to resort to self-help in his efforts to remove Somerset from the royal presence. In 1452 he marched into Kent at the head of an armed following, demanding his rival's arrest and punishment. Confronted by a royal army, he negotiated, and dismissed his soldiers in return for assurances as to his personal safety. It seems that he was tricked, because he was then imprisoned and attempts were made to exclude him from the Council. However, in August 1453 the King went out of his mind, and it became obvious that the driving will behind the court faction was not Somerset but Henry. In these new circumstances York was released and in January 1454 made Protector of the realm for the duration of the King's infirmity. Meanwhile he was no longer heir to the throne, because in September Queen Margaret had given birth to a son, who was named Edward, and recognised as Earl of Chester. The Duke of Somerset was committed to prison.

While these disturbing events were happening in England, the last of England's possessions in France was falling. In July 1453 the French were victorious at the Battle of Castillon, and in spite of reinforcements being rushed out, Bordeaux fell shortly after. The English response had been too little and too late, and over 200 years of English rule came to a messy end. Some Gascon lords had remained loyal to Henry almost to the end, but the majority were only too glad to see the back of what they had always regarded as an intrusive presence. Because of its timing, the fall of Gascony added to the disrepute of the Duke of Somerset rather than York, and gave the latter another stick with which to beat him. As Protector, York was neither better nor worse than Somerset had been, except that the advantage in the localities now went the other way. In May 1454 he put down a rising in Yorkshire by Henry Holland, Duke of Exeter, and committed the Duke and his associate Lord Egremont to prison. However, later in the year Henry recovered, and as if to emphasise his importance to the government of the realm, the whole political situation was reversed. York's protectorship was terminated, and Exeter and Somerset emerged from prison, the latter to resume his control of affairs, in spite of the loss of Gascony and all that had happened over the previous twelve months. In 1455 he summoned a Great Council to meet at Leicester, well away from London, where he was bitterly unpopular, and may have been contemplating some action against York. However, supported by the Nevilles, the latter raised an army which encountered the royal party at St Albans in May. The outcome was more a skirmish than a battle, but it resulted in the death of the Duke of Somerset and the capture of the king by the victorious Yorkists. The Duke of York professed his loyalty to the King, and an effort was made to resume the normal course of business, but the most significant result of the battle was the emergence of the twenty-five-year-old Queen as the real leader of the court party, because there was no way in which she could be removed from the scene except by the deposition of her husband. In the immediate future, York resumed his protectorship on the (probably spurious) ground that Henry had relapsed, but this lasted only until February 1456 when the Queen intervened to have it brought to an end. In January 1458 Henry was sufficiently sane to attempt a reconciliation between the factions that were destroying the country. This appeared to work, but the appearance was deceptive and within months the agreement had broken down into renewed civil war. In the autumn of 1458 the Earl of Warwick, a committed Yorkist, was forced to flee to Calais to escape from his enemies in London, and by the summer of 1459 it was clear that the Queen was out to destroy her opponents. There was no longer any room for a middle ground. In September the Yorkists won a skirmish at Blore Heath, but lost a rather more important engagement at Ludford Bridge, after which York and his second son were compelled to take refuge in Ireland, while his eldest son, the Earl of March, went with the Earl of Warwick to Calais.

It was by this time clear also that Margaret intended to give her supporters the benefit of their victory and in a parliament which met at Coventry a month after Ludford she had York, his two eldest sons, Neville, Salisbury and Warwick attainted. Their lands were immediately redistributed, to the consternation of the propertied class as a whole. Exploiting this alarm, the Yorkist lords issued a manifesto, claiming that the Coventry parliament was fixed for their own benefit by the court peers, particularly Shrewsbury and Wiltshire, and when they returned with an armed force in the summer of 1460, many of the hitherto uncommitted rallied to them. The Earl of Warwick was the first to arrive from Calais. And he attracted considerable support from Kent and London, as he advanced to confront the royal army at Northampton. In the ensuing battle the royal captains Buckingham and Shrewsbury were killed and the King was captured. There was an immediate reshuffling of the officers of state, and the Duke of York belatedly arrived from Ireland. Parliament was reconvened for 7 October 1460, and the Duke stunned his followers by claiming the crown himself as the heir general of Edward III. The Lords were reluctant to accept such a claim, even from the victor in a civil war, and the result was negotiated settlement with Henry, whereby he would occupy the throne for the rest of his life, and that after his death it would pass to York rather than to his own son. It was not unlike the agreement reached with the French at Troyes in 1420, but there was no way in which Margaret was going to accept the disinheritance of her son. In spite of the King's captivity, she resolved to continue the fight. She raised an army in the North, and when York and Salisbury advanced to confront her, her army won a startling victory at Wakefield on 30 December. The Queen was not actually present, because she was in Scotland trying to raise support, so the story of her ordering the execution of York after the battle is an invention, but he nevertheless died in the battle. Margaret then advanced south, beating Warwick at St Albans, but coming up against the resistance of London, which refused to open its gates to her, thus forcing her to retreat. Meanwhile Edward, York's eldest son, had defeated the Lancastrians in the west, and similarly advanced to London, joining up with what was left of Warwick's force on the way. His reception in the capital was very different. He was proclaimed king as Edward IV and duly installed at Westminster. However, his kingdom was still to be fought for and Henry was with his wife in the North, having been rescued after the Second Battle of St Albans. Three weeks later, in a blinding snowstorm Edward defeated the Queen at Towton, and that was the decisive victory of the war. Henry, Margaret and their son escaped the field, but became fugitives, and effective power now rested with Edward. He was crowned at Westminster on 28 June 1461.

Henry is remembered for his feebleness, and that is legitimate, but there was also another side to his personality. He was obstinate, and loyal to those who served him to his satisfaction, as was demonstrated when he recovered from his illness in 1454. Until the last few months of his reign he could never be ignored. He was also a man of generosity, particularly to the Church, and founded the twin educational establishments at Eton and King's College, Cambridge, in the 1440s. He was a gentle, Christian man, unfitted for the tough times in which he had to rule, and years later attempts were made to have him canonised. He provoked the loyalty of many lords, who remained faithful to him through thick and thin, despite his disastrous failure in France and his inability to grapple with the forces of opposition in England. In many ways the most remarkable thing about Henry is not that he was deposed, but that he managed to survive as king for nearly forty years. The monarchy was clearly tougher than any individual king!

PART 10
THE YORKISTS,
1461–1485

31

EDWARD IV (REIGNED 1461–1483)

Edward was just nineteen when his victory at Towton secured him in possession of the throne. His father, Richard, Duke of York, had claimed the crown in November 1460 as the descendant of John of Gaunt via his daughter Philippa, who had married Edmund Mortimer, and of Edmund's granddaughter Anne, who had married his father Richard, Earl of Cambridge. The Earl had been the son of Edmund, Duke of York, John of Gaunt's younger brother, so he had a claim to the throne in his own right, and their son Richard of York united their two lines. Not everyone was convinced, and although Towton gave Edward the reality of power, it did not end the war. Henry, Margaret and Prince Edward had escaped into Scotland, and for three more years Margaret was to try, with inadequate French and Scottish help, to regain control of the north of England from the remote castle of Bamburgh. Late in 1463 there were revolts in Lancashire and Cheshire, and the Duke of Somerset renounced his pardon by joining the rebels. However, the revolts were suppressed, and the Duke was taken and executed. It was not until May 1464 that the last Lancastrian army was defeated at Hexham and Bamburgh was taken by assault. By that time Margaret and Edward were in France, but Henry was with the army at Hexham. He escaped and went into hiding, but was captured in the following year and lodged in the Tower. Only in North Wales did a few pockets of resistance remain until the end of the decade.

Meanwhile the new king was endeavouring to build a government of reconciliation. Henry's Chancellor and Treasurer were retained in post, and pardons were distributed with a free hand. This inevitably disappointed those like the Pastons of Norfolk, who claimed to be seeking royal justice against the depredations of the Duke of Norfolk, but were probably after a bit of revenge. Norfolk was one of those counties which continued in a disturbed state through 1461, in spite of the new regime. It would have been unreasonable to expect an overnight transformation in a situation which had been deteriorating for nearly forty years, and Edward did his best by energetic progresses and personal involvement in difficult cases, particularly those involving members of the nobility. He made extensive use of his justices in commissions of oyer and terminer, and appointed household knights to be sheriffs of particularly difficult counties – such as Norfolk. Attempts were made in Dorset and in Gloucestershire to exploit the supposed weakness of Edward's government, but these were swiftly dealt with and their leaders were before the royal commissioners within days of their capture. The King even dealt with cases of maintenance, where duly convicted offenders had escaped punishment because of the support of noble patrons. In acting so, he was discharging his royal duty as that was traditionally understood, but it did not always make him loved. When Parliament met in November 1461, Edward took a number of steps to strengthen his position. First he registered a long defence of his title, claiming that the injustices and oppressions from which the country had been suffering were induced by the wrath of God in punishment for the sin of Richard II's deposition; a myth which was intended to indicate that wrongdoers could not expect similar indulgence now that a legitimate government was in place. Secondly he withdrew the hearing of indictments from the sheriff's jurisdiction on the grounds of abuse, and transferred them to the Justices of the Peace in Quarter Sessions, the thinking being that a group would be less liable to corruption than a single official. Thirdly he drew up a series of articles designed to limit the practice of retaining to household servants, and thus to withdraw permission from the private armies which had done so much damage over the previous decade. It remained to be seen whether these articles would be obeyed, but their formal proclamation was a start. Finally, and less wisely, he attainted 113 men, including thirteen peers for their adherence to the defeated party. Unless pardons were quickly implemented, this ran the risk of creating irreconcilables, ripe to the hand of any enemy who might chance to invade, and a few of those did in fact appear, notably Jasper Tudor and the Earl of Oxford. Nevertheless, Edward was a nobleman by upbringing and by instinct, educated in the traditional values of that class. He was tall, well built and athletic, expert in those war games which Henry had so conspicuously ignored. He was literate and not without intellectual interests, but the library which he later assembled consisted mostly of French romances, chronicles and works of conventional piety. The budding world of scholarly humanism was a closed book to him, and he made no effort to educate his sons in that discipline. Noblemen dominated his court and social circle, and no doubt more than one of them hoped to match him with one of their daughters in marriage. The marriage of a prince was, however, a matter of international significance, as both his Lancastrian predecessors had demonstrated, and Louis XI of France was anxious to seal a full peace between the realms by marrying him to his sister-in-law Bona of Savoy. Edward's self-appointed mentor, the Earl of Warwick, was much in favour of this match, and in the summer of 1464 the King sent him on a diplomatic mission to France which included some discussion of this proposal. The negotiation was close to success, but then in September Edward disclosed that he was already married. On 1 May he had secretly wed Elizabeth, the daughter of Richard Woodville, Lord Rivers, and widow of Sir John Grey, who had died fighting for the Lancastrians. Such an unsuitable marriage could only have been the result of love – or lust – and the news was badly taken by his peers, especially by the Council, which by tradition had a right to be consulted in such matters. Rumours quickly spread of a quarrel between the King and the Earl of Warwick, especially in France, where it was felt that Warwick had been made a fool of. There was for the time being no open estrangement between them, but the Earl was clearly offended, and with reason. Quite apart from being of relatively humble origins, the new queen had a large family to be provided for – not only her children by her first marriage but also numerous brothers and sisters, the latter looking for profitable marriages among the aristocracy. It would probably not be true to say that Edward deliberately raised his wife's kindred to be a counter-balance to the Earl of Warwick and his affinity, but that is how it looked at the time, which gave a sharper edge to Warwick's resentment. By the summer of 1467 relations were definitely bad, but this was not entirely on account of the King's marriage. There were also disagreements over foreign policy. Warwick favoured a French alliance, and was allowed to pursue a number of negotiations tending to that end, while Edward was inclined towards Burgundy, a preference which he kept to himself. In March 1468 he signed a treaty with the new Duke Charles, committing his sister Margaret in marriage with a substantial dowry, and Warwick was confronted with a *fait accompli*. He was not pleased, and it may have been at this time that he first entered into an intrigue with Edward's disaffected brother George, Duke of Clarence.

The reason for George's discontent is obscure, but probably arose from the fact that he had not been given as much power as he expected. The action of the conspirators was a pure coup d'etat, unsupported by any significant military action. They took the King completely by surprise, capturing him in Buckinghamshire before any adequate defence could be put in place. Their demands were straightforward and old-fashioned: the King was to stop listening to evil councillors (the Woodvilles), and to heed the advice of his true lords (Clarence and Warwick). They made their point by executing Lord Rivers, Sir John Woodville and a few others. Disorders broke out all over the country, and the plan to hold a parliament at York had to be abandoned. It soon became apparent that the rebels did not know what to do next, and in October Warwick was forced to release the King, who immediately returned to London, where the majority of the magnates rallied to him. In spite of the executions, Edward appears to have regarded the whole episode as a bad joke, and by the end of the year was apparently reconciled to his brother. However, this turned out to be a mistake, and in the following year an insurrection in Lincolnshire seems to have been designed to trap the King away from London, while Clarence and Warwick, professing their loyalty, would move to cut him off from his base. The King moved too fast, and defeated the Lincoln rebels before his brother could get in position. This time he was undeceived, and proclaimed both Clarence and Warwick as traitors. Unable to respond, they fled, landing in Normandy at the beginning of May 1470. Louis was quick to seize his opportunity, and swiftly brokered a deal between Warwick and Queen Margaret, whereby the former would proclaim his loyalty to Henry VI and seek to place him back on the throne. Clarence's pretentions, based on charges that Edward was illegitimate, were quietly forgotten, and the Duke's role thereafter is obscure. In early September Warwick landed near Exeter with an Anglo-French force of about 2,000, and the earls of Pembroke and Shrewsbury swiftly joined him along with other Lancastrian peers. As he was a professed adherent of Henry VI, his position was much stronger than it had been in the previous year, and Edward again seems to have been taken by surprise. He was in Yorkshire with only a small force, and when Lord Montague, who was powerful in the North, turned against him, he had no choice but to flee. He went first to Lynn and then overseas to Burgundy. Henry VI was released from the Tower, dusted down, and replaced on the throne.

However, the government of the 'readeption' had little substance, and the French alliance was unpopular. Margaret and Edward remained in France, not apparently believing their good fortune, and there is no reason to suppose that Warwick's reconstituted government would have worked any better than before. In any case, it did not get much chance. King Edward was not a particularly welcome guest as far as his brother-in-law was concerned, and he was only too glad to give him a few ships and men in order to get rid of him. Consequently he landed at Ravenspur on the Yorkshire coast on 14 March 1471 and was immediately joined by his Chamberlain, Lord Hastings, with a substantial force. Incredibly, the Lancastrian peers declined to come to Warwick's assistance, because they were waiting for Margaret to arrive from France. On 11 April Edward was able to enter London unchallenged and three days later annihilated the Earl's inadequate forces at Barnet, when Warwick was killed in the rout. On the very day that happened,

Margaret and her son belatedly arrived in the South West, and the old Lancastrians began to rally to her. However, they lacked both speed and resolution, and before she could join forces with the Welsh supporters of Jasper Tudor, the King had caught up with her at Tewkesbury. The decisive battle was fought on 4 May, when Prince Edward, the Earl of Devon and many other leaders died on the field, and Margaret herself was captured. A few days later the last Lancastrian force in Kent surrendered to the King's brother, Richard of Gloucester, and on 21 May Henry VI died in the Tower, to which he had been returned, probably on Edward's orders. Louis XI, disgruntled by his failure to bring England into his war against Burgundy, came to terms with Duke Charles, and made no further attempt to help his erstwhile protégés. Later he ransomed Margaret, who no longer had a cause to fight for after the deaths of her husband and son, and who had become something of an embarrassment to the English government. The acts of the readeption were formally repudiated and the parliament which had met in November 1470 was not even recorded in the rolls. Tewkesbury and Barnet had eliminated the principal challenges to Edward's rule, because the only surviving male of the house of Lancaster was the fifteen-year-old fugitive, Henry Tudor. The Duke of Clarence had played no part in Henry VI's brief restoration, and was reconciled to his brother before either of the battles had been fought.

Edward was a man without originality or imagination. His ideas on government were summed up by his Chancellor Robert Stillington in the parliament of 1468, when he said that 'justice is every person to do his office that he is put in according to his degree or estate'. In other words he intended that the three estates, the Lords Spiritual and Temporal and the Commons should serve him in their traditional capacities. In order to bring that about he did two things. In the words of the Croyland chronicler he

> took care to distribute the most trustworthy of his servants though out all parts of the kingdom, as keepers of castles, manors, forests and parks, so that no attempt could be made in any part of the kingdom by any person … but that he was immediately charged with the same to his face.

The price of security was constant vigilance, as had been demonstrated by the fact that he had twice been taken unawares by noble conspiracies. The other thing that he did was to govern through trustworthy nobles, particularly Lord Hastings in the Midlands and his brother Richard of Gloucester in the North. Far from being suspicious of their armies of retainers, he gave permission for them, and was repaid with conspicuous loyalty. They in turn knew that part of their function was to enforce the King's laws without fear or favour, and that on the whole they did. Even the greatest magnate was not permitted to take the law into his own hands, as was demonstrated in the case of his troublesome brother George. George's wife, the Duchess Isabel, had died at Warwick on 22 December 1476, almost certainly of natural causes. The Duke, however, got it into his head that she had been poisoned by a servant, one Ankarette Twynho. Pretending an authority which he did not possess, he ordered Ankarette's arrest, and intimidated a jury into convicting her. On 15 April 1477 she was hanged at Warwick. So great an abuse of the King's justice could not be ignored, and towards the end of June Clarence was arrested. He was consigned to the Tower, and was convicted on the King's personal testimony in the parliament which met in January

1478. His subsequent fate provides one of the more colourful stories of the reign. It is highly unlikely that he was drowned in a butt of Malmsey, but he was probably murdered quietly on Edward's orders, to remove the painful necessity for his public execution. The attribution of this murder to Richard of Gloucester is pure fiction, although Richard would probably have approved of Clarence's conviction, and the lesson was not wasted upon other independent-minded noblemen.

Edward IV's foreign policy was based on an optimistic desire to recover the ground which Henry VI had lost, in order to emphasise the contrast between the misfortunes of a usurper and the blessings attendant upon a legitimate government. For this purpose the Burgundian alliance initiated in 1468 was essential, and a new treaty was signed in London on 25 July 1474. Duke Charles recognised Edward as King of France, and in return was promised a share of the dismembered kingdom. To achieve this aim the King of England was to invade France not later than 1 July 1475. In order to clear the way for this adventure, Edward had signed a disadvantageous peace with the Hanseatic League in September 1473, conceding virtually all the League's demands in terms of commercial privileges. This was deeply unpopular in London, but the King could not afford the risk of having to fight on two fronts. For the same reason he locked his back door by signing a marriage treaty on 26 October 1473 between his young daughter Cecily and the infant Prince James, and concluded a truce with Scotland which was to last (in theory) until 1519. At the beginning of July 1475, therefore, two years of elaborate diplomatic, financial and military preparations came to fruition when Edward landed at Calais for his great expedition. Unfortunately it turned out not to be so great, largely because the Duke of Burgundy emerged as a very reluctant ally. He turned up at Calais poorly supported, and showed no sign of increased enthusiasm as the army advanced into France. Louis shadowed them, and when Charles left on 12 August, ostensibly to join his own troops at Bar, he wisely offered negotiations. The English, strong militarily but in a weak strategic position, accepted willingly, and on 29 August the campaign fizzled out in the Treaty of Picquigny. By the terms of this agreement a marriage was to be concluded between the Dauphin and Elizabeth of York, Edward's eldest daughter, and Louis agreed to pay the King of England 50,000 gold crowns every year in perpetuity. The marriage never took place, and the subsidy was paid only as long as Louis felt inclined, but the peace which was thus agreed lasted for the remainder of the reign. Edward went on styling himself King of France, but no one now took that very seriously – certainly not the King himself.

Perhaps the most important event to have occurred during the readeption of Henry VI had been the birth on 2 November 1470 of Edward IV's son and heir. This event took place in the sanctuary at Westminster, whither Queen Elizabeth had fled when her husband departed overseas, and the boy was named Edward, for his father. Within a matter of months she had emerged to retake her place at the centre of affairs, and her position was greatly strengthened as the mother of the heir to the throne. She was also the leader of a considerable affinity. Not only had her brother become Earl Rivers, but no fewer than seven of her close kinswomen had married into noble families, including the Staffords, the Fitzalans, the Mowbrays and the Greys of Ruthin. It would be an exaggeration to describe these men as a political party, but their blood relationship to the royal family certainly counted for something in determining their allegiance. It was later alleged that the Woodvilles formed a coherent political faction which was opposed to Richard of Gloucester, but there is little sign of that before Edward's death; perhaps his own conciliatory temperament kept the lid on that situation, or perhaps it was a later invention to justify Richard's actions.

Edward died unexpectedly on 9 April 1483, aged forty-one. His achievement had been considerable. By tirelessly moving around the country, hearing petitions, adjudicating quarrels and overseeing the administration of his nobles, he restored confidence in royal justice; and by strict impartiality earned respect. He was also the first king since Henry II to die solvent, thanks partly to a revival in the wool trade, partly to efficient estate management, and partly to the cooperative attitude of Parliament, which was due to his efforts to provide good justice. As a gesture towards his chivalric following, he provided the Order of the Garter with a sumptuous chapel at Windsor, and virtually refounded the order, to bring it into line with the Golden Fleece, the Burgundian Order founded in 1435. Edward was a great admirer of the Burgundian court, and modelled his own on its example – even after he fell out with Duke Charles in 1475. The one thing that he did not do, however, was to live long enough to be succeeded by an adult son. The Prince of Wales was only twelve, and a regency of some kind was inevitable. Unfortunately the King left no clear instructions for this. During his absence in France the Queen had stood in for him, and there was a natural assumption that she would do so again. However, on his deathbed he indicated clearly enough that he wished his faithful brother Richard to take charge of the realm as Protector until his son should come of age. He did not put this instruction into writing, and consequently Richard's position was, or could be seen to be, vulnerable.

32

THE BRIEF REIGN OF EDWARD V
(APRIL–JUNE 1483)

A royal minority always tested the resources of government, and on this occasion the problems were aggravated by the uncertainty of Edward IV's intentions. The Queen's claim was not pressed, but the Council remained divided over just what kind of a regency had been envisaged. Those most sympathetic to Richard argued for the full powers of a protectorate until the King achieved his majority, that is until 1489. Those least sympathetic alleged that the protectorate should finish with Edward's coronation, and that would have been in a matter of a few weeks. The majority would probably have preferred a more limited authority, amounting to little more than the presidency of the Council, which would have extended for the full term. Richard, for all his power and record of loyal service, was a nervous and imaginative man, who tended to see conspirators behind every bush, and he saw the minimal position as part of a Woodville plot to leave the Queen in effective charge, with benefit to themselves. These suspicions were heightened by the actual deployment of power at the time of Edward IV's death, because the Prince of Wales was at Ludlow under the care of his maternal uncle, Earl Rivers. Another uncle, Sir Edward Woodville, commanded the fleet, and the Queen's son by her first marriage, Thomas Grey, Marquis of Dorset, was Constable of the Tower of London. Arms, men and money were available in the capital, whereas Richard was far off at Middleham in Yorkshire, and had no great force ready to hand. He did, however, have the support of two of the greatest magnates of the former regime, Lord Hastings and the Duke of Buckingham, both of whom were regional satraps with great power at their disposal. Most significant of all, however, was the fact that Edward was known to be close to Rivers, who had been his guardian for several years, and if he expressed himself forcibly in favour of the Woodvilles, he would be hard to ignore, despite his youth.

There is no reason to suppose that at this stage Richard had any designs on the crown himself. He had served his brother with conspicuous loyalty, and throughout the 1470s had ruled the North with a strong and judicious hand. This had made him popular with the Commons and respected by the magnates. That interpretation of his life which sees it as a sequence of bloody crimes, designed to eliminate all who stood between himself and the throne is a creation of Tudor propaganda, and has no foundation either in fact or in contemporary opinion. However, when he heard towards the end of April that his opponents in the Council were pressing for a very early coronation, and intended to represent that as the end of his protectorate, he decided to strike at once. Lord Hastings aided his plans, perhaps unintentionally, when he persuaded Elizabeth to limit the royal escort from Ludlow to London to 2,000 men, arguing that to use more would be provocative. As a result Richard and Buckingham were able to intercept the King's party at Stony Stratford on 30 April, and Rivers, who seems to have been taken completely by surprise, did not have the power to resist. He was arrested, the royal escort was dismissed and Edward proceeded to London under the conduct of another uncle, only this time one that he scarcely knew. Now it was the turn of the Woodvilles to fear that their interests and perhaps their very lives were threatened. Richard was the lawful Protector and there was no question of an appeal to arms, but the Queen, with her younger son Richard of York and the Marquis of Dorset, took refuge in sanctuary, while Sir Edward Woodville, abandoning his command, escaped to Brittany. The King and the Duke of Gloucester reached London on 4 May, and the latter's authority was immediately confirmed in its fullest form. Within a few days he had remodelled the administration to his own liking, and conferred upon his ally the Duke of Buckingham immense power and jurisdiction in the West Country and the Welsh marches. By the end of May suspicions began to appear that this was not the limit of Gloucester's ambition, but nevertheless he pressed ahead with plans for a coronation on 22 June, to be followed at once by a parliament which would confirm him as Protector with full powers until the King came of age.

However, some of the Council were beginning to turn against the idea. He probably had not consulted them as he should have done over his reorganisation, and some undoubtedly found his hostility to the Woodvilles unreasonable. The highest placed defector was Lord Hastings, who seems to have used his mistress Jane Shore as an intermediary for negotiations with the Queen. At a Council meeting on 12 June Richard suddenly confronted him with his knowledge of these negotiations, and charged him with treason. Unwise they may have been, but there was no way in which these contacts were treasonable, and Gloucester's reaction was completely disproportionate. There was no attempt at judicial process – even the law of arms was not invoked. Hastings was simply executed out of hand on the Protector's orders, and a shiver ran through the law-abiding community. Before this happened, by a mixture of cajolery and threats, Richard had managed to prise Edward's younger brother from the sanctuary at Westminster. He now had both the royal princes under his control, and appears to have decided on his next step. When the Lords and Commons arrived in London for the coronation, and the parliament which was to follow it, they found the capital awash with rumours. Richard had summoned forces from the North, whose loyalty to himself could not be doubted, on the grounds that 'the queen, her blood adherents and affinity ... have intended and daily doth intend to murder and destroy us and our Cousin the Duke of Buckingham'. This was nothing short of paranoia, because there is not, and was not, any evidence of such an intent; indeed the fear was all the other way round. However, the object of the exercise soon became apparent when Richard set up preachers in the city to declare that Edward V was illegitimate. His father had been contracted to marry a certain Eleanor Butler when he had actually married Elizabeth. Eleanor had died before Edward was born, and this was a hoary old scandal that no one in authority had ever believed before, but now it served the Duke of Gloucester's purpose admirably. Pretending to be outraged by this discovery, on 22 June, the day which should have witnessed Edward's coronation, instead the Duke of Buckingham, speaking as though on behalf of the assembled Lords, offered the crown to Richard. There was no arguing with his overwhelming physical force, and on the 25th the Lords assembled for the parliament endorsed his request. Edward was deposed and disappeared into the Tower of London. A few days later, on 6 July Richard III was crowned with great splendour.

The subsequent fate of Edward and his brother Richard is one of the great mysteries of English history. For a little while they were seen around, but the last reported sighting was in September, and after that nothing. It is reasonable to suppose that they were killed soon after on Richard's orders, but there is no conclusive evidence, and whole books have been written using the conflicting stories which circulated until well into the sixteenth century. When the Duke of Buckingham rebelled against Richard in the autumn of 1483, he did so at first in the name of Edward V; but he soon switched his allegiance to Henry of Richmond, which is a fair indication that he at least believed that by then Edward was dead. The other possibility is that Henry Tudor himself was responsible. He would have had at least as good a reason as Richard had for wishing the princes out of the way, but it is intrinsically unlikely that they would have survived that long. Perkin Warbeck later claimed to be Richard of York, who had somehow or other escaped, but he was an imposter and there is no real likelihood that either of the princes emerged from the Tower. Because Edward remained a minor, the appointments which were made during his brief reign can be attributed to Richard of Gloucester, and in fact both the Chancellor and the Treasurer appointed in May 1483 continued in office under Richard III. His Council, however, was that of Edward IV, and considerable changes were made under the new king.

33

RICHARD III, THE USURPER (REIGNED 1483–1485)

Richard's action split the Yorkist party right down the middle, and many of those who had been most loyal to Edward IV were alienated from the new regime. That did not appear at once, however, and immediately following his coronation, the King set out on a progress, intending to show himself to his people and to win their love by declining offers of money, which he received at London, Gloucester and Worcester, saying he would sooner have their obedience than their treasure. His route was carefully chosen to pass through the lands over which his adherents enjoyed control, moving from the Thames valley through the West Midlands, where Clarence's son the young Earl of Warwick was powerful, and so to the Duchy of Lancaster lands in the north-east Midlands. He arrived at York on 29 August to a rapturous reception, marred only by the refusal of the Archbishop Thomas Rotherham, who was an Edwardian loyalist, to participate. Richard remained in York for over three weeks, milking the adulation, but in that time the news from the South became more and more ominous. Before the end of July a plot to rescue the princes from the Tower had been discovered and thwarted, and by late September a whole string of conspiracies existed for the same purpose, in which Margaret Beaufort, Henry Tudor's mother, was deeply involved. Richard, who seems to have been well aware of what was going on, waited at Pontefract for the rebels to declare themselves. On 10 October the risings finally broke surface, in Kent spreading thence westward into Wiltshire, and by November had reached the far south-west. However, they were ill coordinated and lacked competent leadership, being made to appear more formidable than they were by the participation of the Duke of Buckingham. He commanded enormous resources, but not the skill to bring them to bear on an issue of this kind. The Duke of Norfolk, with a large force, interposed himself between the East Anglian and Kentish rebels and defeated them in detail, while Buckingham, who had been proclaimed a traitor on 15 October, was delayed in the west by floods, and found his army melting away. By the end of the month he had taken refuge in flight, but was no more successful as a fugitive than he had been a commander. He was captured near Salisbury, and summarily executed on 2 November. The King's speed of action had enabled him to snuff out what could have been a dangerous rebellion with deceptive ease. Deceptive because he could not address the underlying cause of the discontent without giving up his throne, and he was never to enjoy the real security that an unchallengeable title would have given him. Sympathy for Henry of Richmond became widespread and several of the Woodvilles and their clients joined him in exile, notably the Marquis of Dorset. Henry's attempt to take advantage of Buckingham's rebellion came too late to be effective, but by the end of November he had extracted 10,000 gold crowns (about £3,250) from Duke Francis II of Brittany towards his next attempt, and at Christmas 1483 he contracted to marry Elizabeth, Edward IV's eldest daughter, 'when he had secured his inheritance'. It was entirely Richard's own fault that this improbable outsider had become by this time a realistic challenger for the throne.

In these circumstances it is quite difficult to assess the effectiveness of Richard's normal administration, but the evidence suggests that he intended to continue along the lines which his brother had laid down. The single parliament of the reign, which assembled in January 1484, was much concerned with the affirmation of the King's title and the attainder of Buckingham's supporters, but it did also enact property qualifications for jurors, very much along the lines of those specified for Justices of the Peace in 1461. The object was to ensure that all those involved in the administration of the King's justice were men of substance, who would be harder to influence than their less affluent neighbours. The spirit of the King's intentions is probably best reflected in two sets of instructions drawn up in 1484. The first was directed to Sir Marmaduke Constable, steward of the royal honour of Tutbury, and ordered him to ensure that the tenants of the honour were not retained by any lord other than the King. He was also to investigate complaints of extortion which had been levelled at the bailiffs under his jurisdiction. The second was prepared for the Council of the North. This had begun life as the Duke of Gloucester's private council, to administer his wide Northern estates, but it had also exercised the extensive jurisdiction with which Edward had entrusted him. As king, Richard intended to continue this as a royal council, on an independent footing, with power to hear all cases of 'riot, rout or forcible entry' contrary to the King's laws, and to punish the offenders without waiting for indictments under the common law. It was to meet at York four times a year and the King's nephew John de la Pole, Earl of Lincoln, was commissioned as president. The creation of this flexible and potentially powerful instrument of royal government reflects not only Richard's continuing interest in the affairs of the North, but also his awareness of the need to supplement the normal machinery of the law in order to bring casual and irresponsible violence under control.

Like Edward, Richard depended heavily upon the knights and esquires of his household to fill such key positions as keeperships of royal castles and stewardships of important estates, but there was little time for him to overcome the suspicions of many of his magnates, or to establish normal relations with them. His financial administration seems to have continued under the momentum which Edward had given it, although Richard explicitly renounced one of his predecessors favourite devices – the collection of interest-free loans or 'benevolences' – probably in the hope of gaining a little much-needed popularity. However much evidence the King might give of his intention to govern well and maintain his laws, the fact remained that confidence in the royal justice had been seriously undermined once more by his actions in acquiring the throne. There were justifiable doubts whether anyone who had acted as Richard had towards Lord Hastings could be trusted to uphold the rule of law, or whether anyone who had murdered his nephews could escape the judgement of God. Such doubts were reinforced when his young son Edward died in April 1484. When his wife Anne also died on 14 March 1485, this not only left him in the dynastic wilderness, but compelled him to make a public denunciation of rumours that he had had her poisoned. As 1484 advanced there were further defections to Henry, and although Richard managed to patch up relations with the Dowager Queen

Elizabeth, there were sporadic and abortive attempts to rise in Henry's favour. One of these, at Colchester at the beginning of November, resulted in the indictment of a number of leading Essex and Suffolk gentry, including Sir William Brandon, and demonstrated just how deep the divisions among the county elites had become. Meanwhile English diplomatic pressure had succeeded in squeezing Henry out of Brittany into France, where the regency council of Charles VIII at first hesitated whether to assist him. By the end of the year they had offered him grudging and limited support, and he had decided that the time was ripe for a further attempt. Richard, realising that an invasion of some kind was imminent, took up his position at Nottingham, and redoubled his defensive preparations, being certain that he would be attacked in the spring.

In the event it was August before Henry arrived. For several months his agents had been passing back and forth across the Channel, sounding out the attitudes and resources of the English magnates, and it was only when he was satisfied that a realistic amount of support would be forthcoming that he committed himself to the venture. On 7 August 1485 he landed near Milford Haven in Wales with about 2,000 men, including some 500 Lancastrian exiles. Richard had expected his landing to be resisted, but Henry already had a secret understanding with Sir John Savage and with Rhys ap Thomas, the two most powerful men in the region. Henry had been born at Pembroke in 1457, and his Welsh origins may well have dictated his point of entry, because he had for years been hailed by the bardic poets as the *mab darogan*, or son of prophecy – that champion long ago foretold by Merlin, who would re-establish the British race of kings. In fact there was little Welsh about Henry, apart from his surname, but that was apparently enough for the bards. He was three-quarters English and French by blood, and had spent most of his life in exile in Brittany and France. Nevertheless he landed unopposed, and as he advanced through what is now Powys, Rhys ap Thomas joined him with a substantial number of men, just about doubling the size of his army. As he advanced towards Shrewsbury he was also joined by another contingent of sympathisers under Sir Walter Herbert, and after he had taken the town against a nominal resistance on 15 August, Gilbert Talbot turned up with a substantial number of men from Staffordshire. As he advanced to Newport in Shropshire his army numbered about 5,000, about half the size of the host which Richard had assembled at Nottingham. However, appearances were deceptive because Henry was also in touch with his stepfather Lord Stanley, who had a large independent command, but who was being held neutral by Richard's retention of his son as a hostage. Stanley was powerful in Mid Wales and the King was suspicious of the fact that Henry had passed through his domain unfought. Nevertheless there were no signs of supportive risings elsewhere in the country, and Henry may well have been disappointed by the number of men who had actually joined his banner. He did not know, although he may have suspected, that Richard's imposing-looking army was actually riddled with disaffection, and when it came to the point parts of it would refuse to engage.

When the two armies encountered near Market Bosworth in Leicestershire on 22 August, Henry was ostensibly outnumbered by two to one. He was also a man of no military experience, up against one of the foremost soldiers of the kingdom, and the odds appeared to be heavily stacked against him. However, his deficiencies as a commander were largely made good by the presence of the Earl of Oxford, a resolute Lancastrian soldier who had shared much of his exile. The outcome of the battle was decided partly by treachery and partly by Richard's foolhardy courage, because as the armies came together, the Earl of Northumberland held back, and the King, suspecting his intentions, decided to end the battle at a blow by taking out his opponent. He led a charge against Henry's personal bodyguard, which if it had succeeded, would have guaranteed a quick victory. Unfortunately for him, the bodyguard offered a tough resistance, and Lord Stanley, seizing his opportunity, attacked the King's forces in the rear. The result was a rout, which encompassed the deaths of Richard himself, the Duke of Norfolk and several other loyalist leaders. The King's death made Henry's victory at Bosworth decisive. The story of Lord Stanley discovering the crown under a hawthorn bush on the battlefield and placing it on Henry's head is probably apocryphal, but it is symbolically true. The new king owed his triumph to success in battle, and to the prevailing feeling that Richard had courted the judgement of God. His body was stripped on the field, and later taken to Leicester Abbey, where he was interred. In 2012 human remains were uncovered in a public car park in Leicester. The park was the site of Leicester Abbey, which had been dissolved in 1539, and the remains were thought to be those of Richard III, who had been buried there. This was the reason for the dig, which was instigated by the Richard III Society. DNA tests have indicated that that is probably the case, and a fierce debate has ensued about how and where these remains should be reburied. The logical place would probably be Leicester Cathedral, but there are those who argue for York Minster, because York was the centre of his support while he was alive, or Middleham, which was his power base for a number of years. Others, particularly members of the Richard III Society, suggest Westminster Abbey as being more appropriate for a crowned monarch. At the moment of going to press, this debate is unresolved, but the general voice seems to favour Leicester. Being a childless widower, he left no direct heir, and his designated successor, the Earl of Lincoln, made no move to advance his claim. Legally the person with the best title in 1485, and better than Richard's own, although that had never been emphasised, was the ten-year-old Earl of Warwick, the Duke of Clarence's son, who had been shunted to one side in 1483 by Richard's determination. However, Warwick had won no victories and was still a child. It was generally assumed that it was the will of God that Henry Tudor, Earl of Richmond, should be king.

Richard had a 'bad press', largely due to the circumstances of his accession. He also became, inevitably, a victim of Tudor propaganda, which was anxious to justify Henry's action. He undoubtedly dispossessed his brother's legitimate heir, and may well have been responsible for the deaths of the two princes thereafter. Richard does appear to have been slightly deformed, but his hunchback and lopsidedness were deliberately exaggerated by Tudor propaganda, and were not mentioned in his lifetime, when he was described as handsome. The Tudor assumption seems to have been that one so warped in soul must have borne the marks on his body. There is no evidence that he had plotted his coup well in advance, nor that he was responsible for the fall of the Duke of Clarence. The indications are that his seizure of power was undertaken on the spur of the moment, provoked by an unreasonable, even paranoid, fear of the Woodvilles. Once he had taken his extreme course against Lord Hastings there was, in any case, no way back. He had acted illegally, and only as king would he not have to answer for it. Had the circumstances been different, he might well have been as effective a king as his brother, reigned for another twenty years and married again, in which case the Tudors might never have come to the throne. On the other hand, if the circumstances had been different, he might never have been king at all.

PART 11
THE EARLY TUDORS,
1485–1547

34

THE PRUDENT KING, HENRY VII
(REIGNED 1485–1509)

Henry was the only son of Edmund Tudor, the half-brother of King Henry VI, and of Margaret Beaufort, daughter of John Beaufort, Duke of Somerset. Edmund was the son of Owain Tudor, whom Queen Catherine de Valois had married around 1427 in defiance of the wishes of the Council. He was born about 1432, and was created Earl of Richmond in recognition of his royal kinship in 1452. In 1455 he married Margaret, with whose wardship he had been entrusted when her uncle Edmund had died in that year, and he had died while fighting for the Lancastrians in South Wales in December 1456. Henry was born posthumously in January 1457, when his mother was about fourteen. The premature nature of this experience may have affected her fertility, because although she married twice more, she bore no further children. Henry's only close kinsman was therefore his father's younger brother Jasper, who assumed responsibility for his upbringing. Henry was half Welsh and half French on his father's side, and had by that connection no claim at all to the English throne. If it had not been for the Salic Law, he might have had a better claim to the crown of France. Margaret on the other hand, who was purely English on both sides, was a great-granddaughter of John of Gaunt, through his third marriage to Catherine Swynford. Unfortunately at the time of her grandfather's birth Catherine had been John's mistress, not his wife, and although their subsequent marriage had legitimated him in the canon law, both Richard II and Henry IV had explicitly excluded any right to the succession. It was of course possible to argue that they had no right to do so, and that Margaret's claim, as far as it went, was good. That was the claim which she transmitted to her son, and constituted his sole hereditary entitlement. It was slender enough, but by 1471, after the death of Prince Edward at Tewkesbury, he was the last male standing on the Lancastrian side with any claim at all. Hence the importance which he had assumed by 1483.

After Henry VI's brief readeption, and the deaths of the King and his heir, Jasper had very wisely taken his fourteen-year-old nephew into exile with him in Brittany. There he had remained, with very little hope of any improvement in his circumstances until the death of Edward IV, and the usurpation of Richard III gave him his chance. Not very much is known about his upbringing. Before 1471 his education is likely to have been typical of aristocratic boys of that time, with a basic training in literacy, and much emphasis upon the courtly arts of conduct, of riding, jousting and feats of arms. If this continued after his withdrawal to Brittany, there is no record of it; as far as we know, for twelve years he eked out a penurious existence as a pensioner of the Duke, presiding over a small court of fellow exiles without much in the way of hope or expectation. However, the events of 1483 made him a person of importance. He was forced to flee from Brittany into France to escape the attentions of Richard III's agents, and at the end of the year undertook to marry Elizabeth of York when (not if) he had recovered his inheritance. Anne of Beaujeu, who was heading the French regency council at that point, was eventually persuaded to support him at a modest level, and in August 1485 he set sail to try his fortune, as we have seen. After his victory at Bosworth, Parliament somewhat wearily confirmed his title, and he set out to form a government. He was devoid of any experience more relevant than that of running a small exile household, but he took good advice – probably from John Morton, the Bishop of Ely, whom he translated to Canterbury in 1486 – and made wise appointments. Both his Chancellor and his Treasurer were former servants of Edward IV, and like Edward in 1461 he set out to create a council of reconciliation. Policy required the attainders of those who had fought for Richard at Bosworth, because the late king had now become 'Richard, late Duke of Gloucester' and a traitor against his sovereign lord King Henry. However, no executions followed, and those like Thomas Howard, the son of the Duke of Norfolk, who were prepared to work their way back into favour patiently, were eventually pardoned and restored. John de la Pole, the Earl of Lincoln, who could have caused problems, chose not to do so in the short term, and there was no hasty flight of the disaffected into exile. Instead Henry distributed rewards with a lavish hand to those who had materially assisted him. His uncle Jasper became Duke of Bedford, his stepfather Lord Stanley became Earl of Derby, Sir Peter Courtenay became Earl of Devon and the Earl of Oxford was restored to his title and estates. With the exception of Jasper, however, he did not entrust these new peers with high office, and in that respect he differed significantly from Edward. From the very start he preferred prelates and commoners to nobles as councillors, and showed no inclination to entrust noblemen with extensive powers in the localities.

On 27 October he was crowned at Westminster, and on 7 November presided at the opening of Parliament. When Parliament was prorogued on 10 December the members of the Commons presented the King with a petition that he should remember his promise to Elizabeth, and the wedding duly took place on 18 January. It would no doubt have been sooner, but the kinship between the couple made a dispensation necessary, and that took time. It was granted verbally on 16 January, just in time for the planned nuptials to go ahead, although the full document did not arrive until March. When it did arrive, it proved worth the wait, because the Pope not only dispensed the impediments of marriage, but recognised Henry's title to the throne and placed an anathema upon anyone who tried to refute it. In terms of the loyalty of his bishops, to say nothing of the clergy as a whole, this endorsement was priceless, and marked the beginning of an alliance between England and Rome which was to last for the rest of Henry's life – and well beyond. The King then, as Richard had done, set off on progress to York, but with the opposite expectation. York had been the centre of Richard's power and the prospects of a friendly reception for Henry were not good. In the event nothing untoward occurred, and the proprieties were correctly observed; although his welcome lacked the warmth of his predecessor's, there was no question of any resistance being offered. It was on his return journey, first in Yorkshire and then in the West Country that the first stirrings of disaffection appeared, in the form of small risings by Viscount Lovel and the Stafford brothers. These disturbances turned out not to be dangerous and were soon suppressed, but they justified Henry's preoccupation with security. He created a personal bodyguard of 100 archers, soon to be known as the Yeomen of the Guard. Much more serious, although not without its comic side, was the imposture in 1487 by the young son of an Oxford joiner, named Lambert Simnel. Simnel was groomed by a priest named Richard Simmonds to impersonate Edward, Earl of Warwick. Simmonds may well have believed the current rumours that the real Warwick had disappeared, and was probably prompted in his action by the Earl of Lincoln, who had in March taken refuge in

Flanders. Henry duly produced the authentic earl and paraded him in London, but this did not check the imposture, and in February Simnel was taken to the Netherlands, where he was 'recognised' by his putative aunt, Margaret of Burgundy, who was an inveterate enemy of Henry VII. At the beginning of May she dispatched him to Ireland with 2,000 German mercenaries, and the company of a few Yorkist exiles, of whom the most prominent were the Earl of Lincoln and Viscount Lovel. Once there, for reasons connected with the political history of the colony, he was received by Gerald Fitzgerald, the 8th Earl of Kildare, the King's Deputy Lieutenant, and duly crowned in Dublin as King Edward VI on 24 May. News of the defection of Kildare caused consternation in London, and the seriousness of the situation prompted Henry to raise an army with which he moved to the Midlands to counter any possible invasion. It was uneasily reminiscent of his own situation two years earlier, except that in this case his forces were solidly loyal, as Richard's had not been. Lincoln, commanding about 8,000 men, mostly Irish and German, landed at Furness on 4 June, meeting little opposition, and crossed the Pennines, heading south. Henry intercepted him at East Stoke near Newark on 16 June. The battle was hard fought, thanks largely to the Germans, but Lincoln was decisively defeated and died along with most of the other leaders on the field of battle. Simnel and Simmonds were captured, the latter to spend the rest of his days in an episcopal prison, and the former to be contemptuously dismissed to the role of scullion in the royal kitchens. The Battle of Stoke consolidated Henry's position, convincing the waverers that there was little future in armed insurrection, and everything to be gained from supporting the King. Meanwhile he had also been strengthened in another way, when on 16 September 1486 his queen had given birth to

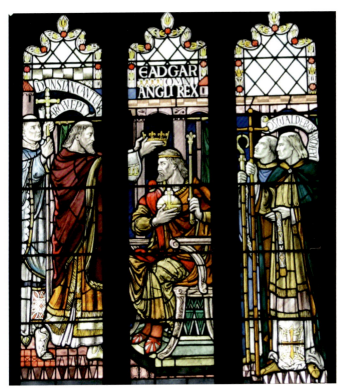

1. The coronation of King Edgar at Bath Abbey.

2. The final resting place in Winchester Cathedral of Harthacanute and his mother, Queen Emma (King Canute's second queen).

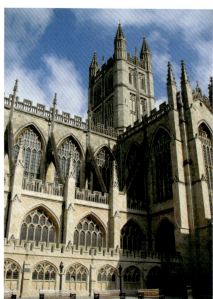

Above left: 3. Fourteenth-century painting of Edward the Confessor as a saint. *Above right*: 4. Winchester Cathedral.

5. Edward the Confessor conferring with Earl Harold (the future Harold II) from the Bayeux Tapestry.

Above left: 6. Harold II is enthroned as the King of England, from the Bayeux Tapestry.
Above right: 7. The White Tower at the Tower of London, built by William the Conqueror.

8. A manuscript page from *Itinerarium of King Richard Coeur-de-Lion*. The chronicler describes Richard as 'of noble bearing and was a fine figure of a man ... his arms somewhat elongated, which came in very handy for the drawing of his sword'.

9. Eleanor of Aquitaine. Henry II married her in 1152 and they were crowned together on 19 December 1154. Her sons included Richard I and King John.

Above left: 10. Eleanor of Castile, Edward I's queen. The couple were devoted to each other, and rarely apart and she accompanied him on military campaigns in Wales, famously giving birth to their son Edward (the future Edward II) on 25 April 1284 in a temporary dwelling erected for her amid the construction of Caernarfon Castle. *Above right*: 11. Isabella of Angouleme, King John's queen and mother of Henry III.

Above left: 12. Edward II. *Above right*: 13. Edward III. *Below*: 14. Richard II, kneeling in front of Edmund the Martyr, Edward the Confessor and St John the Baptist.

Above: 15. Edward, the Black Prince, Richard II's father. *Bottom left*: 16. Tomb of Henry IV Canterbury Cathedral. *Bottom right*: 17. Henry V.

Above left: 18. Henry VI. *Above right*: 19. Richard Neville, Earl of Warwick, better known as Warwick the Kingmaker. At first a supporter of Henry VI, he later supported the rebellion that led to the crowning of Edward IV. He fell out with Edward IV and helped to restore Henry VI to the throne. He died at the Battle of Barnet in 1471.

Above left: 20. Edward IV. *Above right*: 21. Elizabeth Woodville, Edward IV's wife.

22. Richard III with his queen, Anne Neville. *Richard, Duke of Gloucester, and the Lady Anne* by Edwin Austin Abbey.

23. Edward V.

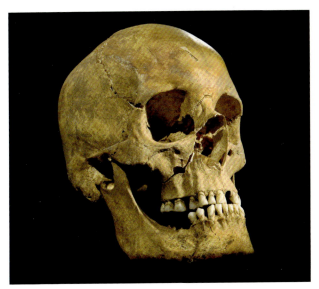

Above: 24. Richard III's skull from the recent archaelogical dig at the Franciscan friary in Leicester. A cut mark on the lower jaw is clearly visible. (UMOA1404) *Below*: 25. Richard's skeleton, displaying the severity of his scoliosis (curvature of the spine). Despite centuries of wrangling this discovery finally proves that Richard was a hunchback. (UMOA1608)

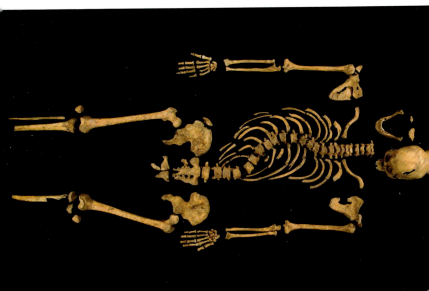

Above left: 26. Elizabeth of York, wife of Henry VII and mother of Henry VIII. *Above centre*: 27. Margaret Beaufort, Henry VII's mother. *Above right*: 28. Statue of Henry VIII's first wife Catherine of Aragon in front of the Archbishop's Palace in Alcalá de Henares, Spain, where she was born on 16 December 1485. *Below left*: 29. Prince Arthur, first son of Henry VII and Elizabeth of York, who died in 1502 leaving his younger brother next in line to the throne. Henry VIII would go on to marry his dead brother's widow, Catherine of Aragon. *Below right* 30. Henry VIII. A statue in the great gate at Trinity College, Cambridge (a royal foundation), showing a mature Henry, around 1541.

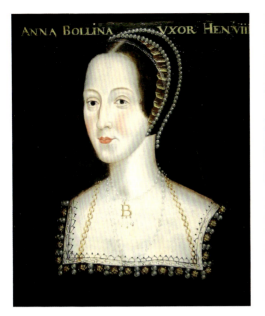

ANNA BOLLINA · VXOR · HEN · VII

Top left: 31. Anne Boleyn, Henry VIII's second wife. her feisty sexuality left her vulnerable to political attack by those she had offended in the course of her rise to power. *Right*: 32. Henry VIII's favourite wife (his third) Jane Seymour by Hans Holbein. She was not a great beauty, but carried little political baggage, and had no agenda of her own. She was greatly praised for her sweet disposition. *Top right*: 33. Anne of Cleves. Wife number four. Henry VIII's marriage to her following Jane Seymour's death was a mistake borne of the need for a German ally. Their marriage lasted six months. *Centre right*: 34. Catherine Howard, Henry VIII's fifth wife. From the stained-glass window representing her as the Queen of Sheba, and Henry VIII as King Solomon in King's College Chapel, Cambridge. *Bottom right*: 35. Henry VIII's last queen, Catherine Parr, from the window at Sudeley Castle. After Henry's death, Catherine married Thomas, Lord Seymour of Sudeley, and died there in childbirth in 1548.

Above: 36. *An Allegory of the Tudor Succession*, the family of Henry VIII. *Below*: 37. Edward VI by Hans Holbein. Edward was born on 12 October 1537, and this drawing was made some time before Holbein's death in 1543. *Left*: 38. Lady Jane Grey. Put up by Edward VI as an alternative to Mary for the succession, she was defeated in July 1553, and executed after the Wyatt rising in February 1554, at the age of seventeen.

Above left: 39. Elizabeth in old age. *Above right*: 40. James I, his wife Anne of Denmark and their son Prince Henry Stuart.

Above left: 41. Charles I. Charles was exceptionally short. *Above right*: 42. Charles I's queen, Henrietta Maria, by Sir Anthony van Dyck.

Above left: 43. Charles II miniature by Samuel Cooper. *Above right*: 44. Catherine of Braganza, wife of Charles II.

45. Queen Anne, statue outside St Paul's Cathedral.

Above: 46. George IV. *Right*: 47. Queen Charlotte, consort of George III. *Below left*: 48. The future George IV when Prince of Wales, with Caroline of Brunswick. *Below right*: 49. Queen Victoria, *c.* 1843. Studio of Franz Xaver Winterhalter.

INSTRUMENT OF ABDICATION

I, Edward the Eighth, of Great Britain, Ireland, and the British Dominions beyond the Seas, King, Emperor of India, do hereby declare My irrevocable determination to renounce the Throne for Myself and for My descendants, and My desire that effect should be given to this Instrument of Abdication immediately.

In token whereof I have hereunto set My hand this tenth day of December, nineteen hundred and thirty six, in the presence of the witnesses whose signatures are subscribed.

SIGNED AT
FORT BELVEDERE
IN THE PRESENCE
OF

Above left: 50. Abdication letter from Edward VIII. *Above*: 51. George VI's wife, Elizabeth Bowes-Lyon, with their daughter, the future Elizabeth II. *Below left*: 52. George VI and Queen Elizabeth, who became better known as the Queen Mother. The future Elizabeth II is next to her mother. *Below right*: 53. The procession through London of Princess Diana's funeral.

a son, alive and flourishing. The prince was named Arthur, and his advent convinced many that God really was on Henry's side, a sentiment not to be despised as he prepared his army to face the intrusive Simnel, and to add a further proof that the God of battles had not deserted him either. The Earl of Kildare submitted and, lacking the resources (or the inclination) to make a major expedition to Ireland, Henry accepted that and restored him to his position. The Irish bishops who had supported Simnel, on the other hand, were excommunicated by the Pope in fulfilment of his earlier undertaking.

However, Henry had not seen the last of the Yorkist threat. His commitment to Brittany led him into a somewhat notional war with France in 1492, and Charles VIII welcomed Perkin Warbeck as a prince. Warbeck was the son of a boatman from Tournai, who on a visit to Ireland in 1491 had been persuaded to impersonate Richard, Duke of York, the younger of the princes in the Tower, who was supposed somehow to have escaped. By the summer of 1492 about a hundred Yorkist exiles had joined him in Paris, and Charles clearly intended to use him against Henry. The treaty of Etaples on 3 November put an end to that phase of his activities, and he was expelled from France, only to receive a warm welcome in Flanders, where Margaret recognised him as the nephew whom she had not seen since his infancy. The Emperor Maximilian, who was aggrieved with Henry for making a separate peace with France, paraded him around Europe as the Duke of York, and promoted him diplomatically to Henry's intense annoyance. Meanwhile the King had good intelligence of what was going on. He purged the commissions of the peace of likely Warbeck supporters, and increased the proportion of councillors, appointing special commissions to investigate reports of sedition in the Midlands and North. By 1493 he had discovered the pretender's true identity, and knew a lot about his resources and contacts in England. As a result there was a series of treason trials in February and March, the most conspicuous of which was of Sir William Stanley, the Chamberlain of the Household and a man close to the King's person. Stanley's guilt was by association rather than direct, but he was executed nevertheless, an action which caused Henry acute distress. Some of those implicated managed to make good their escape, and Warbeck's following in Flanders grew. In 1494 he tried his fortunes in Ireland, but the Irish had learned their lesson with Lambert Simnel, and this new pretender was a damp squib. Sir Edward Poynings, sent across by Henry in October, had no difficulty in controlling the situation there. By 1495 Maximilian was becoming disillusioned with his protégé, and offered him a little help to try his fortunes in England, with the result that he appeared off Deal on 3 July with three ships and a motley collection of followers. He landed about 300 men, who were promptly cut to pieces by the local levies. Any Englishmen caught were hanged, and Warbeck, becoming increasingly desperate, moved on to Scotland, where in the closing months of 1495 he received his final taste of princely honours.

By that time the Archduke Philip, Maximilian's son, had decided that there was no future in supporting the imposter, and in February 1496 negotiated an agreement renouncing any further interest in him, and resuming the trade which had been interrupted by the stand-off. England was admitted to the Holy League which had been formed against France, although without any commitment to war, and negotiations were reopened for a marriage between Prince Arthur and the nine-year-old Catherine, daughter of another League member, Ferdinand of Aragon. This negotiation, which was fraught with the greatest significance for the future, was successfully concluded in October. By the end of 1496 Henry was thus internationally secure, having been recognised by all the leading rulers of the West, and the only spot of uncertainty remaining was Scotland. There James IV welcomed Warbeck as 'Prince Richard of England', and gave him his kinswoman Catherine Gordon in marriage. In return Perkin undertook to hand over the border fortress of Berwick and to reimburse his host £50,000 when he had won his kingdom. Unfortunately the great invasion which was to achieve this aim turned out to be little more than a border raid. The Scottish nobles were unenthusiastic and Warbeck's proclamations met with no response whatsoever in England. The only result was a rebellion in Cornwall, triggered off by the King's demand for taxation to meet the Northern threat. The Cornishmen did not see why they should pay for a conflict so far away and remote from their interests. In May they rose, and, sweeping aside the local defences, advanced on London, taking advantage of the fact that the King's army was in the North, confronting the Scots. However, by that time the threat from Scotland had evaporated, and the Earl of Surrey was able to turn his forces south. On 16 June he met and defeated the rebels at Blackheath, taking numerous prisoners, who were subsequently executed. James, disillusioned in his turn with Warbeck, dispatched him to Cornwall to take advantage of this new opportunity, but he arrived after the revolt had been quelled and aroused only a flicker of interest. He recruited a few countrymen, but failed to gain admission to Exeter on 17 September, and, warned of the approach of a royal army, gave up and fled into hiding. A few days later he threw himself on the King's mercy, and was lodged in the Tower. There he remained for the next two years, until he was executed in 1499 for a supposed attempt to escape from confinement, a fate which he shared with the Earl of Warwick, in what appears to have been a tidying-up operation of possible claimants to the throne ahead of Arthur's marriage to Catherine, which was confirmed in the same year. The Yorkist claim devolved on the Earl of Suffolk, the younger brother of the Earl of Lincoln who had fallen at Stoke, and in 1501 he fled to the court of Maximilian, where the tattered remnants of the Yorkist faction gathered around him. He posed no threat, and was eventually traded to Henry VII in 1506, when he disappeared into the Tower.

Henry husbanded his resources carefully. After a brief hesitancy caused by his inexperience, he continued Edward IV's practice of using his Chamber as the principal revenue department, which received taxation income, and windfalls like the French pension. This left the Exchequer with the traditional revenues paid in by the sheriffs, and with the responsibility for audit, a division of labour which enabled the King to control expenditure personally. Contrary to his popular image, he was not mean, and spent lavishly on his court to maintain his magnificence, a necessary commodity in that competitive age, but he was careful with grants, and improved the efficiency of his estate management. He also developed the system of taking bonds and recognisances, both from officials for the discharge of their duties, and of putative offenders for their good behaviour. Towards the end of his reign it was alleged that more than half the aristocracy was bound to him in that fashion. Of course this was only income if the bonds were forfeited, and in most cases that did not happen, but it was a tactic which was much resented. He avoided war to the best of his ability, and taxed sparingly to finance such campaigns as he could not escape. The reaction of the Cornishmen in 1497 demonstrates how wise that caution was, and after 1504 he met no further parliament, because by then his other fiscal policies had guaranteed his solvency. When he died there was about £300,000 in the coffers. As we have seen, he kept most of the nobility at an arm's length, relying mainly on gentlemen to run his numerous commissions, and by refraining from warfare deprived most of them of their traditional mode of service. He built up his own affinity in the counties, and avoided using the retinues of his nobles as far as possible, being particularly severe on any of his own men who took another lord's livery. Finally, in 1504 he introduced a system of licences to retain any men beyond household servants. He recognised the need for such retinues, particularly for military purposes, but was determined to keep a tight grip on their scale and nature. The prohibition was traditional, as we have seen, but the idea of licensing was new, and typical of Henry's attention to detail. It has been alleged with some justice that the King became more preoccupied with money in the last five years of his life, and that is the source of his miserly reputation, but it was never really justified – he was just being prudent. Henry was in most respects a thoroughly medieval king – it was just that he made the traditional system work better than his predecessors had done. Only in his preference for the service of the gentry could he be said to have introduced a 'new monarchy', but that was to be of considerable significance for the future.

Henry's marriage was a happy one. Elizabeth functioned modestly as a patron in her own right, and was exemplary in her piety, both of which were necessary assets in a consort. She produced four children who survived infancy, and several others who did not, and was influential in the lives of all of them. Arthur was conceived with admirable promptness in 1486, and was given a first-class humanist education by scholarly tutors – the first royal prince to be given the advantage of such an upbringing. He was created Prince of Wales in November 1489, and married to Catherine of Aragon in November 1501. Tragically he died in April 1502 at Ludlow in the Welsh marches, where he had been sent to 'bear the king's presence', and his parents were devastated. It was in attempting to make amends for this disaster that Elizabeth became pregnant again late in 1502 and died in childbirth early in 1503, depriving the King of her loving company and accounting partly for the morose image of his latter years. For political reasons he made as though he intended to marry again, but probably these were mere gestures, and in any case they came to nothing. Henry, his second son, succeeded his brother as Prince of Wales in February 1504, and became the sole hope of his father's declining years. He had shared the humanist education of Arthur, for which he showed considerable aptitude, and unlike Arthur was large-built and athletic of frame. He became a famous tennis player and jouster, thanks to the training which his father provided, but was given no political responsibility in Henry VII's lifetime. Margaret, who came between the two boys in age, was reared in the domestic virtues and married to James IV of Scotland in August 1503, sealing the treaty of peace which had been signed between the two counties at Ayton in 1501 – the first full peace for many years. She was later to be the mother of James V and the grandmother of Mary, Queen of Scots. The youngest of Elizabeth's children, Mary, was born in 1496, and was only thirteen when her father died. Henry's health had been declining for some time and on 21 April 1509 he died, leaving his throne to the magnificent specimen that his son had grown into, and a few weeks before his eighteenth birthday Henry VIII became king. His father had lived just long enough to ensure that no one dared to suggest a minority government, and the young king assumed the full authority of his office from the moment of his accession.

35

HENRY VIII (REIGNED 1509–1547)

Young Henry came on the scene like a breath of fresh air. He was not concerned with money, or with prudence, but with magnificence and glory – particularly his own. Seizing his opportunity he immediately married Catherine, his sister-in-law, who had been lurking unhappily in England since Arthur's death seven years before; he thereby gratified his own lust and her prayers. It was at first a happy union and she fell pregnant almost as quickly as her mother-in-law had done nearly quarter of a century earlier. This time the outcome was less fortunate and early in 1510 she was delivered of a stillborn girl, but these things happened and within months she was pregnant again. In addition to conveying his potency in the most obvious way, Henry had two other objectives at the outset of his reign. He wished to distance himself as far as possible from his father's drab image, and he wished to fight the French. The first was achieved by the rapid arrest and eventual execution of two of Henry VII's most unpopular financial enforcers, Sir Richard Empson and Edmund Dudley. Neither of these men had committed any offence at law, but they were as unpopular with the Council as they were with the public at large, and their sacrifice signalled the end of Henry VII's oppressive financial policies. Fighting the French was partly the instinct of the young man aspiring to be a warrior, partly a nod of recognition towards his hero, Henry V, and partly a shrewd move to give his younger aristocrats something congenial to do. As we have seen, the English nobility was disgruntled at the old king's policies of peace, and wanted the chance to show their mettle on the battlefield. The King, who shared their ambitions, thought it sensible to oblige, and joined the Holy League against Louis XII in 1511.

The resulting war was successful in a modest way. There was inconclusive fighting at sea in 1512, and a victorious campaign to capture Tournai in 1513. More importantly, James IV of Scotland decided to renounce the Treaty of Ayton by attacking him in the rear while he was preoccupied in France, and was comprehensively defeated and killed at the Battle of Flodden. Henry sent the keys of Tournai to Catherine in token of victory, but she replied with the bloodstained hauberk of the late King of Scots. The King's reaction is not recorded. War was hugely expensive and, in spite of not having achieved a tenth of his objectives in France, Henry was willing to be persuaded into peace by a new pontiff who had no time for Holy Leagues, but wanted a Christendom at peace in order to confront the Ottoman menace which was developing in the Levant. In the summer of 1514 Henry was reconciled to Louis, and gave him his sister Mary in marriage without apparently consulting her wishes. He also mothballed his navy instead of disposing of it, and created a rudimentary organisation to deal with it in peacetime – the beginnings of the Royal Navy. Equally important, he found a servant to suit his needs in the person of Thomas Wolsey. Wolsey was a court chaplain who had caught his eye as prince, and became his almoner soon after the beginning of the reign. Wolsey was diligent and efficient, and in organising the logistics of the Tournai campaign he made his mark on the royal administration. He was a man after Henry's own heart, and within a year he was his chief councillor, replacing those whom the King had prudently retained from his father's time, notably William Warham and Richard Fox. Like them, he was a prelate who could be rewarded without becoming a drain of the royal finances. In March 1514 he was appointed to the see of Lincoln, and translated to York in September. Meanwhile, having run through the money which his father had bequeathed him, the King was hard up. In January 1515 Louis XII had died at the age of fifty-two, casting his widow on the marriage market, and leaving his throne to his young kinsman Francis of Angouleme. With or without Henry's connivance, Mary was quickly snapped up by his friend the Duke of Suffolk, and Francis I (who was too like Henry for comfort) began to make bellicose noises. However, his attention was directed mainly to Italy, and Henry could not afford to take up the challenge; so instead he followed Wolsey's advice and began a 'peace offensive', which was brought to a successful and prestigious conclusion in the Treaty of London of 1518.

While his international presence was being thus enhanced, his domestic life had run into difficulties. Catherine's second pregnancy had ended in January 1511 with the triumphant delivery of a prince, who was named Henry and whose advent caused huge rejoicings. However, young Henry lived less than a month, and this time his parents were afflicted. The King took himself off to war and the Queen to her prayers. No one knew what had gone wrong, but God was clearly displeased. Two years later Catherine conceived again, and this time her pregnancy was ended by a miscarriage. The honeymoon was over, and Henry began to flirt with other ladies of the court. There was probably nothing in these escapades, but Catherine was also the symbol of her husband's alliance with her father, Ferdinand of Aragon, and Ferdinand had signed a separate peace with France in 1513, to Henry's intense annoyance. Relations between the royal couple became strained, and there was even talk of divorce. The storm passed and by 1515 the Queen was pregnant again. This time the outcome was successful, up to point, because in February 1516 she was delivered of a healthy child, but it was girl not the longed-for son. She was named Mary and the rejoicings were muted. Catherine conceived only once more, in 1518, and that time a second miscarriage was the result. The King did not give up on his wife, but he had by that time acquired a proper mistress, one Elizabeth Blount, and she was also pregnant in 1518. Her condition was better rewarded than the Queen's and in 1519 she was delivered of a healthy son, whom Henry immediately acknowledged and named Henry Fitzroy. Catherine was deeply chagrined, but there was nothing that she could do about it apart from redoubling her pious exercises, which she duly did to the admiration of everyone – except her husband.

The Treaty of London was a considerable achievement, bringing into line, temporarily at least, the kings of England and France, Charles of Spain, who had succeeded his grandfather Ferdinand in 1516, the Holy Roman Emperor and numerous secondary powers such as Portugal, Sweden and Venice. The Pope was delighted, but unfortunately it was too good to last, and the very next year, in spite of professions of eternal friendship, the death of the Emperor Maximilian opened the way to further conflict. The principal candidates to succeed him were Francis of France and Charles of Spain, and Charles, who was Maximilian's grandson and who had the deeper pockets, emerged triumphant. This placed the Empire and Spain under the same ruler, and sandwiched France between the two. It was only a matter of time before conflict would erupt between them, probably in that favourite Franco-Imperial battleground, northern Italy. Henry found himself strategically placed between the two, each of whom was bidding for his support, and in this congenial position held 'summit conferences' with the two rivals in 1520. The grandest, and by far the best known, was the Field of Cloth of Gold, with Francis on the edge of the Calais pale in July. This was an exercise in competitive magnificence on the grand scale, and was orchestrated down to the last detail by the immensely hard-working Wolsey, who was by this time Cardinal Archbishop of York and Lord Chancellor, having succeeded Warham in the latter office in December 1515. Not even Wolsey's efforts, nor his presence, however, could make this the friendly encounter that it was supposed to be. Peace was talked, but the competition was obsessive, and the two rulers heartily detested one another, with the result that no business was done. Henry's meetings with Charles, however, which were modest affairs on either side of the Anglo-French extravaganza, did real work and resulted in an alliance which committed England to join the Imperial side in the war which was clearly pending. The conflict duly erupted in 1522, and Henry found himself engaged in a war which he lacked the financial resources to fight. To the Emperor's displeasure he put off action until 1523 and set out (or rather Wolsey set out) to raise the necessary money. This took him inevitably to Parliament, and with characteristic self-confidence (or arrogance) the Cardinal demanded a subsidy which would have amounted to £800,000. The House of Commons refused, and there was no way past their obstructiveness except to resort to benevolences, which Richard III had renounced. Instead they offered the more modest sum of £400,000 spread over two years, and this Wolsey was constrained to accept, with the result that the King's war effort in 1523 was a good deal more modest than either he or the Emperor wanted.

It consisted of an invasion of northern France by the Duke of Suffolk, intended to take advantage of a rebellion by the Duke of Bourbon against Francis, and an invasion from the east by the Emperor. However, Bourbon did not show up, and the Emperor's invasion became distracted, with the result that Suffolk was left to do the best he could on his own; and stuck in the freezing mud of Normandy in November, he was able to achieve nothing. Even extracting what was left of his force after disease had done its worst was a considerable feat, and Henry did not blame him for his failure. He blamed Charles, and played virtually no part in the war as it ground on through 1524. However, in February 1525 the Emperor inflicted a shattering defeat on his rival at Pavia, and captured him, which aroused all Henry's predatory instincts, and reawakened his enthusiasm for the alliance. He put forward an ambitious plan for the dismemberment of the leaderless kingdom, which Charles comprehensively snubbed. If the King of England wanted part of France, then let him conquer it for himself. He already had Francis where he wanted him, but would release him on terms of his own devising, which would have everything to do with Burgundy and northern Italy and nothing at all to do with most of France. Henry was angry but helpless, because his attempt to raise an extra-parliamentary tax, known hopefully as the 'Amicable Grant', had run into difficulties. On the ground that they had only just voted the king a subsidy, those assessed for the grant simply refuse to pay, and, confronted with this taxpayers strike, the King was forced to back down. Wolsey took the blame, as he was expected to do, but the error of judgement was the King's. Not being able to afford a new campaign, Henry came to terms with the interim government of France and signed the Treaty of the More in August 1525.

Meanwhile a revolution had taken place in Henry's relations with his nobility. Early in his reign he had taken chivalric claims and the prestige of lineage seriously. In 1514 he had raised the Earl of Surrey to the Dukedom of Norfolk following his victory at Flodden, and elevated his friend Charles Brandon to the Dukedom of Suffolk. At about the same time he had recognised the claim of Clarence's daughter, Margaret Pole, to the Earldom of Salisbury, and given her that title in her own right. This was against the advice of Thomas Wolsey, who preferred Henry's father's sceptical attitude towards nobility, and in 1521 an event occurred which converted the King to his minister's opinion. The Duke of Buckingham was a man with a remote claim to the throne, and an inordinate pride in his own ancestry. He had been consulting 'wise men' who had forecast that one day he would be king, and he had made an enemy of Cardinal Wolsey with remarks about base birth, which he also seemed to apply to the King. In addition he was a great man, with vast estates and a large affinity in the marches of Wales. The King at this point had no legitimate son, and became increasingly worried by Buckingham's pretensions. Then in 1521 the Cardinal trapped him. Using the testimony of servants whom the Duke had dismissed, he put together an accusation of treasonable utterances, and had him arrested. Charged with treason, he was duly convicted by his peers and executed in a state of bewildered incomprehension. No one moved a finger to help him. Buckingham's downfall was his pride of ancestry, and this experience turned the King against the whole idea of a lineage-based nobility – one based upon the deeds of forebears – and in favour of one based upon service to himself. When Henry created new peers thereafter, as he did in 1525 and again in 1529, they were either members of his own family, like Henry Fitzroy, who became Duke of Richmond, or were raised for personal and political services in the immediate past, like Thomas Boleyn, created Earl of Wiltshire in 1529. Although there were still ancient peerages around, like Arundel and Oxford, by the end of the reign the majority of nobles were service peers, soldiers or administrators who had served Henry VIII.

By the time of Buckingham's fall, the succession was causing serious anxiety. It was clear that Catherine would have no more children, and the King had no legitimate son. What was to be done? Henry had taken another mistress in the person of Mary Boleyn, a daughter of his servant the diplomat Sir Thomas Boleyn, but that was no help, and in any case another bastard would have been no use. Then in about 1525 he fell in love with Mary's younger sister, Anne, who had just returned from a spell of conditioning at the French court. The chronology of their relationship is uncertain, but by 1527 he had decided to end his marriage with Catherine, and try again for a son with Anne. Catherine, he decided, had been forbidden to him by the law of God. Unfortunately she was the aunt of the Holy Roman Emperor, Charles V, with whom Henry was on bad terms, and Charles committed himself to obstructing the King's suit at Rome by all the means in his (very considerable) power. Faced with this impasse, which Wolsey was unable to break, Henry sacked his Chancellor and tried a process of blackmail to induce Clement VII to yield. Unsuccessful in this manoeuvre, and determined to have his own way, he then declared the English Church independent of Rome, and proclaimed himself its supreme head. This he did by statute, having persuaded and cajoled Parliament into supporting his cause in spite of determined resistance by Catherine's followers, who had a significant presence at court. At the beginning of 1533 his new Archbishop of Canterbury, Thomas Cranmer, who had replaced

William Warham, conveniently deceased in the previous August, declared his marriage to Catherine null and void. In anticipation of this decision, Henry had already married Anne, who was pregnant, and had her crowned as queen on 1 June 1533. Unfortunately the child she was carrying turned out to be a girl, Elizabeth, who was born in September, and their subsequent efforts to produce a son turned out to be futile. Catherine died in January 1536, and their daughter Mary, who had taken her mother's side throughout, was in deep disfavour, having been disinherited by the annulment of her mother's marriage, so that Henry now had no heir at all. In May 1536 Anne's feisty personality caught up with her, and Henry became convinced that she was indulging in adulterous affairs. He had her tried and executed, thus clearing the way for a third marriage.

This took place almost at once, his bride on this occasion being Jane Seymour, the daughter of Sir Thomas Seymour of Wolf Hall near Marlborough. Henry may have been attracted to her before Anne's fall, and he subsequently referred to her as his first 'true wife'. In September 1537 she bore him his longed-for son, who was named Edward, but died of puerperal fever a few days later, leaving the King genuinely grief-stricken. However, although now the succession was apparently secured, one child was never enough, and nearly three years later he married again, this time to Anne, the sister of William, Duke of Cleves, in a match designed to protect him from the diplomatic isolation which followed his unresolved quarrel with the papacy. This turned out to be a mistake from every point of view. Henry was so put off by her that he was unable to consummate the union, and in deep humiliation had the marriage annulled. On the rebound he fell for the nubile niece of the Duke of Norfolk, Catherine Howard, and married her in June 1540, but they produced no children either, and he had her executed for treasonable adultery about eighteen months later. By this time he was probably impotent, which was the cause of her misdemeanours, and in any case was humiliated again. By the time that he took his sixth and final wife, Catherine, Lady Latimer, in 1543, his fires were spent. Although correct noises were made in official documents about children born of the marriage, it was fairly clear that there would be none, and what Henry was looking for in his declining years was less a bedfellow than a companion, and a nurse, as circumstances required. He settled the succession in 1544 by Act of Parliament, leaving his crown to Edward, as everyone expected, but in default of heirs of his body, first to Mary and then to Elizabeth, neither of whom was legitimated. Henry Fitzroy had died in 1536, and these girls were Henry's only other surviving children, but it was altogether unprecedented to include bastards in the succession, and a reflection of the enhanced power of Parliament.

Those enhanced powers were Henry's major legacy to the realm. The medieval estates had had real but limited powers which did not touch the spiritual jurisdiction. So in using statute to declare the independence of the English Church, the King was breaking new ground. That he ventured to do this was almost certainly the result of the influence of his new chief minister, Thomas Cromwell, who had taken over that role three years after Wolsey's death, in 1533. Cromwell was a 'ways and means' man who identified statute as the best means of conveying the will of the whole realm, which he mobilised in the King's support. A quantity of legislation then followed from 1533 to 1536, establishing the royal supremacy and making it effective. This was highly controversial and there was much opposition, but Cromwell effectively enforced the new laws, and they were accepted by the nation as a whole. This made Parliament in principle omnicompetent, and enabled it to resolve such issues as the succession to the throne, which the Lords had declared in 1461 to be beyond their powers. It was by Parliament that the King was given the authority to introduce the English bible in 1536, to alter the calendar of the Church, and to dissolve the minor monasteries. Henry had been brought up in the humanist tradition which had no time for monks, and the *opus dei* had become an unfashionable piety by this time, so these measures were generally acceptable. The only serious opposition came in the Pilgrimage of Grace, which erupted in Lincolnshire and Yorkshire in the autumn of 1536. The King played for time and the leadership was divided, so the Pilgrimage, which had seemed formidable at one stage, had collapsed by the end of the year. By that time Mary had been reconciled to her father, and she lent the Pilgrims no countenance, which helped to end their protest. Having successfully dissolved those religious houses with incomes below £200 a year, Cromwell then went after the bigger fish, and by the spring of 1540 the great houses had all surrendered, adding significantly to the royal revenues and creating a great pool of patronage upon which Henry could draw in creating a vested interest in his supremacy.

Cromwell did not live to see this success. As early as 1521 Henry had written in defence of the papal authority against Luther, and had earned himself the title of 'Defensor Fidei', and although he had subsequently changed his mind about the Roman jurisdiction, he continued to see this dispute in ecclesiastical rather than doctrinal terms. In other words, he was a better Catholic than the Pope! This he tried to emphasise in the Act of Six Articles in 1539, which laid down an orthodox interpretation of the mass.

This orthodoxy was at variance with Cromwell's preferred policy of encouraging the reformers, and in 1540 he got caught by the conservative clerics in a trap, wherein they convinced the King that he was a scaramentary – that is one who denied the real presence in the mass. This was a heresy to which the King was dogmatically opposed and, becoming convinced that Cromwell was guilty, he had him arrested and condemned by Act of Attainder. He was executed in July 1540, just five years after Sir Thomas More and John Fisher had suffered for denying the supremacy which he had created.

From 1533 to 1542 Henry had been mainly concerned with domestic affairs, and his foreign policy had been largely confined to avoiding isolation in his quarrel with the Pope, a preoccupation which involved a certain dependence on France. However, after Catherine's death in 1536, the Emperor became less hostile, and the prospects improved for a new Imperial alliance. This had become serious policy by 1542, and a new treaty was signed, involving a commitment to support Charles in his everlasting war with Francis. In order to free his hands for this, Henry decided to take out the Scots first, bearing in mind what had happened in 1513. Consequently he successfully provoked James V to invade in November, and then destroyed his army at the Battle of Solway Moss, taking a large number of prisoners. When James died a few weeks later, he left his Crown to his infant daughter Mary, and Henry conceived the notion of uniting the two kingdoms by marrying her to his own five-year-old son, Edward. The Scots resisted the idea, and the diplomacy which resulted kept Henry out of the Continental war during 1543, much to Charles's annoyance. So in 1544, with his coffers full of monastic loot, Henry launched his army against Boulogne, which fell in September. This was not quite what the Emperor had meant by a joint offensive, and he signed a separate peace with France at the same time that Henry entered his conquest. This left the King to defend his acquisition as best he could, and Francis made clear his intention to recover it. A great invasion fleet was prepared and entered the Solent in July 1545. The result was more a confrontation than a battle, thanks to the fickle weather conditions, and the only notable event was the loss of the *Mary Rose*, which got caught with its gun ports open as it tried to turn against a sudden gust of wind. The French withdrew with nothing accomplished, and Francis signed the Treaty of Camp with Henry the following year. This left Henry in possession of Boulogne and about £200,000 in debt, having run through the proceeds of the Dissolution. In the last few weeks of his life, the politics of the court were taken up with the rivalry between the conservative and reforming religious factions, a legacy of the struggle which had gone on after Cromwell's fall. In December 1546 this finally resulted in the victory of the reformers, and the elimination of the Howards, which gave the former control of the King's will in the last days of his life. By Christmas he was obviously seriously ill, and he died at St James's on 27 January 1547. After all his struggles over the succession, he left his crown to the nine-year-old Edward, and no specific arrangements for a regency.

PART 12
THE LITTLE TUDORS,
1547–1558

36

EDWARD VI (REIGNED 1547–1553)

Edward did not live to achieve his majority, so the whole story of his reign is the story of his mentors: until October 1549 Edward Seymour, Duke of Somerset, and after Christmas of that year John Dudley, Earl of Warwick and Duke of Northumberland. For the first six years or so of his life the young prince had been brought up 'amongst the women' as was customary with noble infants. In spite of the fact that he had his own household, and succeeded to the title of Duke of Cornwall at birth, he was never created Prince of Wales. Such a creation was under consideration when Henry died, but the intention was never realised. From about 1543 onward his education was entrusted to tutors, particularly John Cheke and Richard Cox, and he was trained in the humanist tradition of biblical scholarship. His father placed great emphasis upon the importance of the Bible, and he would have read it both in Latin and in English. He seems to have been a bookish child, and somewhat priggish in his opinions, although it is hard to tell with one so young. It cannot be demonstrated that he was taught any explicitly Protestant theology before his father's death; but, given his rapid emergence as a convinced reformer after 1547, it is reasonable to suppose that these ideas had been implanted in him earlier. It would have been dangerous to have done this openly, as Henry never wavered in his hostility to heresy, but since both his tutors emerged as strong Protestants soon after his accession, some such instruction can be assumed. Apart from a precocious intellect, Edward seems to have been a normal enough boy. His health was reasonably robust and he threw off the usual childish ailments without difficulty. He was also deeply interested in war and in war games, although at this stage he was too young to have taken part in either.

He is alleged to have wept copiously when he learned of his father's death, but in truth he could hardly have known him. He was far closer to his stepmother Catherine and to his thirteen-year-old sibling Elizabeth. Mary he also knew, although the evidence suggests that he did not approve either of her lifestyle or her religious opinions, which were far too conservative for his taste. Henry had provided by his will for a body of executors to carry out his wishes in respect of the succession, but had left no precise instructions as to how they were supposed to do that. Consequently when they met on the day after his death, they had to take order for a regency, and this they did by creating two offices, Protector of the Realm and Governor of the King's Person, both of which were bestowed upon his maternal uncle, Edward Seymour, Earl of Hertford. They then constituted themselves into the Privy Council of King Edward VI, and the young king duly confirmed their actions. The only opposition came slightly later from the Chancellor, Thomas Wriothesley, Earl of Southampton, who was removed from office upon a technicality, and thereafter counts as an opponent of the regime. Edward was crowned on 13 February, the ceremony being somewhat curtailed on account of his tender years, and by that time various honours and rewards had been distributed, allegedly (and probably in fact) in accordance with Henry's last wishes. The Earl of Hertford became Duke of Somerset; John Dudley, Viscount Lisle, became Earl of Warwick; and William Parr, the Queen's brother, was raised from the Earldom of Essex to the Marquisate of Northampton. Various baronies were also conferred, including one on Thomas Seymour, the Protector's brother, who was seriously disgruntled at not having been made Governor of the King's Person.

The coronation was carried out in the traditional fashion, but a hint of things to come was given by the Archbishop, Thomas Cranmer, when he renewed the commissions of the bishops in the name of the new king. This was normal with secular offices, but is the only occasion on which bishops were similarly handled, and provoked an immediate protest from Stephen Gardiner, the conservative bishop of Winchester, on the ground that he owed his authority to his consecration and not to his appointment. His objection was overruled. In the summer a royal visitation was carried out on the lines of those of 1536 and 1538, and although that did not portend any innovation, the Archbishop issued a series of homilies at the same time, which in certain respects (as Bishop Gardiner pointed out) contravened the Act of Six Articles of 1539. His objections were answered in the most effective way in the first parliament of the reign, which met in November and repealed the Six Articles, leaving the Church of England for the time being without any standard of orthodoxy to appeal to. The same parliament also took another step in the direction of doctrinal reformation by dissolving the chantries – those foundations which had been set up to provide prayers for the souls of their donors, and which usually supported mass priests, and sometimes schools. Their property was taken over by the Crown, to a capital value of some £600,000, and the sale of this went some way towards discharging the debt bequeathed by Henry VIII. By the end of 1547 it was fairly clear that a Protestant reformation was in the making, and Princess Mary joined Stephen Gardiner in protesting. However, the young king was all in favour and that counted for much with those who hoped to serve him beyond the end of his minority. As a ten-year-old his views were scarcely articulated, but they were well enough known to, and approved by, his tutors.

Apart from easing gently in the direction of doctrinal reform, the other concern which the Protector had during the summer of 1547 related to Scotland. The Scots had signed a treaty at Greenwich in 1543, committing themselves to the marriage of Mary and Edward, but they had then repudiated the agreement, and in the last days of his life Henry had been anxious to punish this 'treachery' and get the treaty reinstated. He may even have charged the Earl of Hertford on his deathbed to see to this unfinished business. At all events, as Protector, Somerset took up the challenge, and spent the summer preparing an army royal to lead into Scotland. Alleging various fictitious provocations, he launched his attack on 1 September, his army going by way of Berwick and supported by a large fleet under Vice Admiral Lord Clinton. On 10 September he encountered the Scots field army at Pinkie Cleugh near Musselborough, and comprehensively defeated it. However, it soon transpired that victory was easier to achieve than to consolidate, and Scotland had no intention of submitting to his will. He established garrisons throughout the border regions, and as far north as Broughty Crag on the Firth of Tay, and then retreated. It soon transpired that he had given hostages to fortune, because his fortresses were not only harried by the Scots, they were subjected to regular sieges by the French troops which arrived to support them in the summer of 1548. Not being anxious to provoke war with France, Somerset was constrained to deal with this situation on the ground, but in spite of various relief expeditions, it continued to deteriorate until the summer of 1549 when his plans for a new army royal were overturned by events in the south of England. The Treaty of Greenwich was no nearer reinstatement than it had been before Pinkie, and Somerset simply did not have the resources to conquer Scotland.

The trouble in lowland England had been brewing for some years, and mostly concerned agrarian grievances. As the population recovered from the Black Death, and took off in the late fifteenth century, the pressure for arable holdings increased, and discontents mounted about the number of tenements which had been converted into sheep runs when the population was low. 'Enclosure' became a major issue, particularly in the Midlands. Added to which there were many discontents about the gentry misusing the common land, and taking more than their fair share when a manor was enclosed. Taking advantage of the perceived weakness of a minority government, and alleging the Protector's support, the leaders of the 'Commonwelth men' began a propaganda campaign against the gentry and nobility which resulted in the 'camping movement', a series of riots and disturbances which spread rapidly through East Anglia and into the Midlands. At the same time the South West erupted with discontents provoked by the introduction of the Protestant Book of Common Prayer at Whitsun 1549, and rebellion spread from Devon and Cornwall into Somerset. At first the government tried to deal with these revolts by negotiation, but it rapidly transpired that this would not work and that armed force was required. Consequently the troops mustered for a campaign in the North were diverted to the South in July 1549, and the attack on Scotland abandoned. The remaining garrisons mostly surrendered over the next few months. Once the troops, including contingents of German mercenaries, were deployed to deal with the rebellions, they did not take long to defeat, and Lord Russell in the South West and the Earl of Warwick in East Anglia soon had the situations under control. However, grievous doubts had been raised about the competence and resolution of the Protector, who had appeared only too willing to deal with the malcontents by negotiation on an issue which affected the economic interests of the gentry and nobility profoundly. He was suspected of being too favourable to the Commons. He had also become arrogant in his demeanour, treating the Council on which he depended with contempt, and making many decisions without consultation. He was ignoring the well-meant advice of his friends, and appeared to be forgetting that he was not the king. Having installed his brother-in-law, Sir Michael Stanhope, as Chief Gentleman of the Privy Chamber, he then left him to get on with it, neglecting to keep his personal relations with the court amicable, and virtually ignoring his young sovereign. In short he was showing signs of megalomania, and in September 1549 a majority of the Council decided that he would have to go. To make matters worse, in August the new King of France, Henry II, had decided to take advantage of the turmoil in England to recover Boulogne, and declared war. By the beginning of October the government was in a terminal mess, and those conservative bishops who had been imprisoned for resisting the Protestant reformation, notably Gardiner and Bonner of London, were anticipating their release and a return to religion as King Henry had left it. Unfortunately for such aspirations, the King had different ideas.

In the autumn of 1549, Somerset was vulnerable. In January the jealousy of his brother Thomas had erupted into a scheme to get the Protector's patent annulled by Parliament. At the same time he had plotted to marry Princess Elizabeth, and these two offences together had been construed as treason. Thomas had been executed in March, and although the Council had been fully supportive at the time, that was now remembered against him, and in addition to his other misdemeanours he was accused of fratricide. The Council gathered in London, while Somerset and the King remained at Hampton Court. Then on 7 October, becoming alarmed by their threatening demeanour, he whisked Edward off to Windsor, and summoned the Commons to defend their King. This turned out to be a big mistake, because it enabled the Lords in London to represent him as a traitor to the establishment – and in any case hardly any turned up. The 'Good Duke' may have been popular, but he was not worth fighting for. A few days later the crisis was resolved, largely by the mediation of Archbishop Cranmer. Somerset agreed to stand down as Protector on the understanding that his person and property would remain secure, and that the Protestant reformation would continue. In this last condition can be seen the influence not only of the Archbishop but also, possibly, of the King, who remained largely a frightened spectator of this drama. Somerset's men were removed from the royal presence, and the Privy Chamber was reconstructed – with his consent, as Edward noted. Those religious conservatives who had expected the Protector's fall to herald a return to 'the true religion' waited with diminishing hope for that to happen, while the Earl of Warwick consolidated his position as leader of the Council. Warwick, with one eye on the King, had committed himself to further reform, and in December frustrated a coup by the conservatives, aimed at his removal. In February 1550 he assumed the position of President of the Council, and set about the political education of the young king.

By that time England was a (mildly) Protestant country, or at least the establishment was. The repeal of the Act of Six Articles had been followed up in the spring of 1548 with an English version of the mass, which was urged but not enforced, and a year later by the Book of Common Prayer. This was imposed by the First Act of Uniformity in January 1549. It replaced the mass with a communion service, and modified the sacraments, so it was unequivocally Protestant, but it was modelled largely on the Sarum rite and retained many traditional features. For that reason it was not regarded with much favour by the more extreme reformers, who continued to press for further change. Their first success came with the issuing of a new ordinal in the spring of 1550, which recognised only the orders of bishop, priest and deacon. However, Martin Bucer and Peter Martyr, the leading Continental reformers then resident in England, had also been consulted about the necessary revisions to the Prayer Book, and Cranmer had started work on that, assisted by a commission of reformed divines. Gardiner and Bonner remained in prison, and Princess Mary witnessed these developments with growing alarm. The Emperor's reaction to this evidence of advancing Protestantism was one of increasing hostility, and since he had no intention of making concessions on this matter, Warwick became keen to end the war with France. Boulogne, he decided, was not strategically worth the cost of maintaining and defending it, and, being unsentimental about Henry's last conquest, he sold it back to the French for 400,000 crowns (£130,000) by a treaty signed in March 1550. Thereafter he exercised himself to bring about an alliance with the Old Enemy, as the best means of fending off the Emperor's hostility. This he succeeded in achieving in July 1551, in a marriage treaty between Edward and Elizabeth, the young daughter of Henry II. Edward was mildly interested in his intended bride, but, being only thirteen years old, was more taken with the Marshal St Andre, who came to seal the treaty. He was a consummate courtier, and the King was much impressed by him, all of which made friendship with France a more palatable prospect.

Meanwhile Mary's deeply rooted hostility to the Reformation was being backed by Charles V, who was anxious to secure a pressure point upon an unfriendly government. Every time that the Council attempted to impose conformity upon her, he instructed his ambassador in England to make representations on her behalf, threatening a breakdown of relations if her mass was not tolerated. Somerset had sidestepped this pressure by granting a verbal licence for private celebrations, but pointed out that to give her formal permission to break the law was out of the question. Warwick took a similar line, and mobilised the King to make his displeasure at her defiance clear. Edward's personal intervention was a blow to Mary, who had always claimed that he, 'sweet child', knew nothing of his Council's tactics of harassment. In the summer of 1550 she resolved to flee abroad, probably to Flanders, and the preparations were all in place, when she changed her mind – probably influenced by those in her entourage who pointed out that, once out of the country, her claims to the succession would be overlooked. So she stayed put, and the pressure continued until Charles, perhaps wearied by her persistence, encouraged her to accept a limited indulgence, which extended only to herself and her immediate servants. No more public displays. This she was constrained to do, and Warwick accepted it as the best solution available; so there was truce over the last eighteen months of the reign.

Edward turned fourteen in September 1551, and Warwick took his political education in hand. He had been writing a journal for about four years, which constitutes a principal source for our knowledge of the reign, but that was purely a schoolroom exercise, intended for the eyes of his tutors. Now, however, Warwick encouraged him to write position papers on current issues, such as the economy. This was in a dire mess, thanks to Henry's and Somerset's policies of debasing the coinage to make ends meet. Consequently the exchange rate had collapsed and the cloth trade had overheated, resulting in unsold stocks and unemployment. This had contributed to the troubles of 1549, and was an urgent subject for the young king to be tackling. Unsurprisingly he had no original contribution to make to the debate, but at least his essay demonstrated an awareness of the problems. The same is true of his Discourse of Abuses, his memorandum on ways and means, and his notes for the guidance of his Council. In no case can it be demonstrated that his input made any difference to the real world of decision making, but Warwick encouraged him to sit in on Council meetings, and he no doubt learned a lot that would be relevant to him when he took over the reins in person. His celebrated Device for the Succession belongs in this same category, being a theoretical response to the question of what would happen to the crown if he died without direct heirs – a contingency which was not looked for at the time when it was written.

After a decent interval, the Duke of Somerset was readmitted to the court and the Council, and was apparently reconciled to his supplanter, whose son married his daughter. However, appearances were deceptive. Somerset did not approve of many of Warwick's policies, least of all his friendship with France, and began surreptitiously to build a party in the country, aimed at his overthrow. This threatened to split the Council, which would have been a disaster for a minority regime, even if it had not succeeded, and Warwick decided that he must strike. In November 1551 he arranged for himself to be created Duke of Northumberland, and took advantage of Somerset's appearance on that occasion to have him arrested upon a variety of conspiracy charges, many of which were invented, as he later confessed. The former Protector was supposed to have conspired to murder Warwick, and to have raised the City of London against the government. He was charged with treason – and acquitted. He had, however, unlawfully raised men for his own protection, and that was a felony of which he was convicted. He was executed in January 1552, just before the reconvening of a parliament which might have asked awkward questions. There is no doubt that Northumberland acted in self-defence, but it was his power that he was defending, not his life, and the legend of the Good Duke, unlawfully done to death, continued to haunt him for the remainder of his time in office. Edward had long since lost any affection which he might have felt for his uncle, and noted his death dispassionately in his journal, as a matter of little interest.

In January 1552 he was more concerned with the passage of the Second Act of Uniformity, imposing the revised Prayer Book. Cranmer's commission had at last reported, and the book was attached as an appendix to the Act. It simplified the 1549 Prayer Book considerably, removing the last rites altogether, and making it clear that the communion was intended mainly as a commemorative meal. It was not due to come into force until the autumn, because adequate numbers had to be printed and also because there were still controversial details to be resolved. John Knox (who was a royal chaplain) objected to the rubric requiring kneeling at the communion, and in deference to his opinion the Council ordered the 'Black rubric' to be inserted, explaining that kneeling was simply a matter of order, and did not imply any reverence for the host. Cranmer was most annoyed at this intervention, which occurred after the press had been set up, but the King supported

Knox on this issue, and he was not to be gainsaid. At the same time the Archbishop lost his revision of the canon law, because the House of Commons thought that it gave too much jurisdiction to the clergy. So he wasted two years of work, and the Church courts still had no workable code to use. He was not pleased by this either, and his relations with the Duke of Northumberland became strained. More successfully, although outside Parliament, Cranmer had drawn up a set of Forty-Two Articles, setting out the faith of the Church of England, and this received the royal approval for implementation in the summer of 1553. In the event this occurred only weeks before the King's death changed the entire political landscape, and they hardly became operative at all.

Edward's health had never given cause for concern, and he had much enjoyed the robust shooting matches in which he had indulged with his guard, but at Christmas 1552 he caught a cold which did not go away. At first this was merely inconvenient. He was unable to open Parliament when it met on 1 March, but he was well enough to close it in the usual way at the end of the month, and no one at this stage thought that his condition was life-threatening. However, in April he became worse, and it seems clear that he had contracted pulmonary tuberculosis, a condition which the medical knowledge of the time could neither diagnose nor treat. He went through a cycle of rallies and relapses, each one a little worse than the last, and then at the beginning of June he collapsed completely. His physicians, who had been hopeful hitherto, were suddenly in despair. It was now a question of when, not whether, the King would die. The succession suddenly became an urgent concern, and the Device which he had written months before as a school exercise was brought out and examined. It was now virtually certain that he would die without direct heirs, and the question had arisen – what was to be done about it? By Henry's last Succession Act, confirmed later by his will, the heir was the Princess Mary, but Mary had been excluded by the Device on the grounds of her illegitimacy, and Elizabeth also. There was also the question of Mary's religious opinions, because if she came to the throne there was no doubt that she would turn back the tide of reformation, by which Edward set such great store. There would be no time to get Henry's Succession Act repealed, and the Device was all the guidance that existed. As it stood, however, it was useless, because it decreed the succession to unborn sons of the Duke and Duchess of Suffolk, or of their as yet unmarried daughters. However, Jane Grey, the eldest daughter, did marry in June, her bridegroom being Guildford, the son of the Duke of Northumberland, and that brought her into the frame. Someone, with the King's knowledge and consent, altered the provision of the Device from 'the heirs male of the Lady Jane' to 'Lady Jane and her heirs male', thus decreeing that Jane Grey should be the next monarch, not Mary. The Duke of Northumberland used to be blamed for this alteration, because of his vested interest in the Crown Matrimonial, but it now almost certain that it was the King's own wish. Consequently, when Edward died on 6 July at the age of fifteen, the unfortunate Jane was duly proclaimed.

37

JANE GREY
(REIGNED 7–19 JULY 1553)

Jane was probably born in October 1537, and was thus about a month younger than Edward. Her parents were Henry and Frances

Grey, at that stage Marquis and Marchioness of Dorset and later (October 1551) Duke and Duchess of Suffolk. Jane was not a Tudor, and her connection with the royal family was through her mother, who had been born Frances Brandon, the elder daughter of Charles Brandon, Duke of Suffolk, and Mary 'the French Queen', Henry VIII's younger sister. Her claim to the throne was thus inferior to Mary's in every respect save one – she was undoubtedly legitimate. Mary was legitimate by the canon law, but not by the law of England, and it could be argued that her inclusion in Henry's last Succession Act was *ultra vires*, that Parliament had no power to confer the throne upon a bastard. Elizabeth similarly should be barred because her parents' marriage had likewise been declared null and void, and that was the position adopted by Edward's Device. The King had been preoccupied by his search for a male heir, believing originally that no woman should succeed, a circumstance which also caused him to ignore the claim of his cousin Mary of Scotland, who was actually the next heir by blood if Mary and Elizabeth were excluded. However, the urgency of his situation in June 1553 caused the King to relent, and to bequeath his crown to Jane, of whose person and religion he approved. She had indeed been brought up in the reformed faith, and was a formidable bluestocking, fluent in Latin, well seen in Greek, and thoroughly familiar with the works of the fathers of the Church, the Bible, and the writings of the best-known Protestant theologians. She had even corresponded (in Latin) with Heinrich Bullinger, who formed a good opinion of her opinions in consequence. It was naturally supposed that Protestants would rally to her cause because of the threat which Mary posed to their ascendancy, but in fact that did not happen. Bishop Ridley of London preached on her behalf on 9 July, but his efforts were not well received, and the people of London, in spite of their reformed sympathies, were hostile to her from the start. From far-off Gloucester, the radical reformer John Hooper even sent a contingent of men to support Mary, and such backing as Jane had was political in its motivation, not religious.

In spite of her poor reception in London, and the news that Mary had proclaimed herself in Norfolk, most contemporary observers thought at first that Jane would prevail. That was certainly the opinion of the Imperial ambassadors, who had been sent specially by Charles to keep a watching brief. They were strictly instructed not to intervene, but naturally sympathised with Mary, and had at first little hope of her success. The Council was apparently united in Jane's support, and the Duke of Northumberland controlled the resources of the kingdom. Edward's death had been concealed for a few days, as was normal, and it was 10 July before Jane was brought by water to the Tower of London 'and there received as queen'. The same afternoon, about five o'clock, she was proclaimed in the city, to the sullen indifference of most of the citizens. One young man had his ears nailed to the pillory for questioning her title, although the King's letters patent appointing her were read at the same time. Meanwhile Mary's intelligence system had informed her of her brother's death, and as soon as this news was confirmed, on 9 July, she proclaimed herself queen and wrote to the Council commanding their obedience. She had obviously been preparing against such an eventuality, because her affinity immediately gathered upon hearing this news, and the local gentry rallied to her. Her proclamations, which must have taken many days to write, were dispatched to all parts of the country, and had the effect of swiftly augmenting her following. On 12 July she moved what was by then a substantial army from Kenninghall to the more defensible fortress of Framlingham in Suffolk, where she received the Council's response to her letter, bidding her to be a good subject of Queen Jane. Nothing was further from her thoughts, and a military confrontation seemed likely.

Meanwhile in London the first news of her movements was of her journey from Hunsdon to Kenninghall, and it was assumed that she was in flight for the coast. Ships were dispatched to the East Coast to frustrate any such intention, but this was soon followed by news of her proclamation, and by 12 July it had been decided that an armed intervention was called for. This was originally entrusted to the Duke of Suffolk, but Jane with tears begged him off, and the Duke of Northumberland set off in his stead. Northumberland was the best soldier in England, and if there was serious work to be done, then he was the best man to do it. He was accompanied by about 1,500 household troops and a small siege train, which should have been enough for his purpose as it was then perceived. On 12 July also the Imperial ambassadors were visited by members of the Council, who informed them that their mandate had expired with the King's death, and that they should not contemplate intervening on Mary's behalf. Simon Renard, who was the brains of the mission, expressed pained surprise. As he understood it, Mary was the lawful heir, and Jane Grey was merely a stool pigeon put up by the French to conceal their intentions in favour of their preferred candidate, who was Mary of Scotland. According to his own account this confused the councillors, who did not press their requests. The turning point came between 12 and 14 July, because on the 13th the ships which had been sent to prevent her flight, declared for Mary, and sent their men and guns to her camp, giving her the essential firepower which she had hitherto lacked. Meanwhile the Earl of Oxford, who had been expected to reinforce Northumberland instead turned up at Framlingham with a substantial number of men. The Council in London were wavering, as Mary's natural supporters, such as the earls of Arundel and Pembroke, began to sense a shift in the wind and on the 16th a group of the defectors met at Barnard's Castle to plan their next move. On the 18th the split became open, Mary's supporters emerged as the majority, and when the news of this defection reached Northumberland at Bury, he retreated to Cambridge, while many of his men slipped away. On the 19th the Duke of Suffolk gave up, and informed his daughter that she was no longer queen. The same morning Mary was proclaimed in London to universal rejoicings. Jane's twelve-day reign was over, and the reckoning began.

It had been too short to speak of any normal administration, and no appointments had been made. The only action which Jane is known to have taken as queen was to deny her husband, Guildford Dudley, the Crown Matrimonial. Her marriage, she alleged, had been forced on her by her parents, and her relations with her spouse were not good. In view of the powerful position of his father, the Duke of Northumberland, this refusal could have caused problems, but there was no time for them to develop. Those members of the Council who had declared for Mary hastened to Framlingham to make their peace with the new queen, and usually succeeded. The Duke of Northumberland had proclaimed Mary at Cambridge, and simply waited there. He was arrested a few days later by the Earl of Arundel and conveyed to the Tower, where the Duke of Suffolk and his family had already been confined. The principal defendants were tried on 18 August, and the Duke of Northumberland, having made a vain and grovelling attempt to save his life, was executed on the 22nd. In the course of his attempt, he had renounced his Protestant faith, and attended mass, the news of which when conveyed to his daughter-in-law evoked her withering contempt. 'Woe worth him,' she is alleged to have said. His sons, John, Ambrose, Henry, Robert and Guildford, were all condemned with him, but their execution was stayed and all but Guildford were eventually pardoned. Jane was tried and condemned at the same time, but was returned to prison, and her life would probably have been spared if it had not been for the events of the following January. Meanwhile the Queen ordered strenuous attempts to be made to convert her to the Catholic faith, and John Feckenham, the newly installed Dean of St Paul's, paid her a number of visits for that purpose. She responded with piety, and a learning remarkable for her years, and he made no progress.

Then at the end of January erupted the rebellion of Sir Thomas Wyatt, in which Jane's father, the Duke of Suffolk, was foolish enough to become involved. Suffolk's attempt to raise Leicestershire came to nothing, but Wyatt assembled 3,000 men in Kent, and advanced threateningly on London. He was eventually frustrated when the city refused to open its gates to him, and his rising collapsed on 7 February. The Duke of Suffolk was arrested, tried and executed on the 17th. Meanwhile his involvement and the politics of the Council dictated that this rebellion be represented as an attempt to replace Jane on the throne. Its real motivation was antipathy to Mary's proposed marriage to Philip of Spain, which had just been announced, but the Queen was understandably reluctant to admit that her choice of partner was so unpopular. Consequently Gardiner's theory that it was a Protestant plot to reverse the decision of the previous summer, found immediate acceptance at court, and this spelled the end for Jane. Having been warned for death, she spent her last hours in pious exercises, and was executed, along with her husband, at the Tower on the morning of 12 February. She made, according to John Foxe, a 'Godly end'. This was a logical but pointless sacrifice, which did Mary's reputation no good at all, because in truth Jane had been a pawn in the hands of others. There was no good reason why, after Edward's death, his eccentric but not legally binding wishes for the succession should not have been quietly abandoned. After all, no one was accused of any treason in connection with these events except after 6 July; until then they had been obeying the commands of their lawful sovereign. That this did not happen was due to the ambitions of the Duke of Northumberland and his associates (including Jane's father) who put the unfortunate sixteen-year-old in a position which she had neither expected nor desired.

38

MARY (REIGNED 1553–1558)

During her brother's reign, Mary had become the champion of the Old Faith. However, no one knew exactly what that faith involved. To most people it meant the mass, and 'religion as king Henry left it'. Mary had always acted publicly in the interests of her father's settlement. However, it could also mean the restoration of the papal allegiance, and that it soon transpired was the new queen's intention. Having settled her Council to her own satisfaction, released the Duke of Norfolk, and promoted Gardiner to the Chancellorship, she was duly crowned with traditional rites at Westminster on 1 October. Owing to the circumstances of her accession there were a number of attainders to be dealt with, and several positions to be filled in the administration. Sir William Petre, the senior secretary, and William Paulet, Marquis of Winchester, the Treasurer, retained their posts, but Stephen Gardiner became the new Chancellor and John Bourne replaced Sir William Cecil and Sir John Cheke as Secretary. Cranmer was arrested and tried for his part in the elevation of Jane Grey. After his conviction he remained in prison, and the primatial see was in effect vacant until Cardinal Pole was appointed in 1556. Most important of all, however, was the unofficial position accorded to the Imperial ambassador, Simon Renard. It was to Renard rather than to her Council that she confided her intention with regard to the ecclesiastical supremacy, and it was his voice of caution that she heeded about how to proceed. In the autumn of 1553 he became her most influential adviser, and it was to him that she turned to resolve the vexed and urgent question of her marriage. He referred so weighty a matter to his master, and Charles advised that she should try his only legitimate son, Philip of Spain, who was then a widower. Negotiations followed, largely with Charles and Renard, and agreement was reached in principle by the end of October. The matter was urgent because Mary was already thirty-seven, her time for childbearing was rapidly running out, and the securing of the succession was the main point of such a union. Her Council was imperfectly aware of her intention, and in November Parliament petitioned her to marry within the realm, which she had no intention of doing. She told Parliament to mind its own business, and informed her Council, which took her decision in good part and settled down to negotiate a marriage treaty. This they did with Charles's representatives, not Philip's, and came up with a good deal which gave Philip very little power in England, but declared that any offspring of the union should inherit the

Low Countries as well as England, Spain being reserved for Philip's existing son, Don Carlos. Philip was not pleased with these terms, but confined himself to making a protest. The attractions of the Crown Matrimonial of England were not to be denied.

It was this treaty which was proclaimed in London at the time of the Wyatt rising, and helped to turn opinion in the city in the Queen's favour, with the result that the Kentishmen were denied access, as we have seen. Nevertheless the marriage remained deeply unpopular in the country at large, and Renard was acutely anxious about the security arrangements put in place for Philip's visit. If he had had his way, Princess Elizabeth would have been executed for her supposed part in the uprising, but the evidence was so meagre that the Queen would not hear of it. At the same time the Catholic Philip would be coming to wed in a realm still technically in schism. Following the sensible advice which she had been given, Mary had set about rescinding her brother's religious settlement by repealing the relevant Acts of Parliament. By 20 December 1553, the Church had been returned to the position of 1547, and most of the Protestant bishops had either recanted or been put in prison. However, she had gone no further, there being difficult questions in the way over the alienated Church lands, and the backlog of other jurisdictional problems which had been piling up since 1533. Consequently Bishop Gardiner's attempt to get the Henrician Acts repealed, also before Philip's arrival, failed in the parliament of April 1554, to Mary's annoyance. However, she recognised the strength of the counter-arguments and decided to leave this difficult question for the King to resolve after their marriage. This duly took place at Winchester on 25 July 1554, the day having been chosen as a compliment to San Iago, the patron saint of Spain. He made an unexpectedly good impression on the assembled crowds, and Mary appeared to be radiantly happy. A few days later they were received in London, the bodies of the victims of the Wyatt rising having been thoughtfully removed shortly before.

For all his benign presence, Philip was not a happy man. His household and followers were causing problems, and their bad relations with their English hosts were resulting in violence. He got rid of most of them, but the problems did not entirely go away as long as he was in England. His personal relations with Mary were good, but he enjoyed no independent authority in her kingdom, and his main interest continued to be focussed on his father's situation in the Low Countries. He was, as it were, constantly looking over his shoulder. The only positive thing that he did immediately was to shut out the officious Renard, whom he did not trust. Fortunately, the Queen soon found a job for him, and one for which his Imperial contacts in Rome ideally suited him. He set out to renegotiate England's relations with the papacy, on the basis of the monastic settlement which was already in place. In this he was eventually successful. Julius III agreed to waive the Church's claim to the secularised lands, on the ground that they were too difficult an egg to unscramble, and Cardinal Pole, who had been in exile in Italy for almost twenty years, was able to return as papal legate. Parliament welcomed the returning exile, and in January 1555 repealed the Act of Supremacy, restoring the ecclesiastical jurisdiction to the pre-1533 position. It also resurrected the fifteenth-century heresy laws which had been repealed by Edward, opening the way for the persecution which was about to commence. Stephen Gardiner was of the opinion that the Protestants were time-servers, whose main concern had been to plunder the Church. He therefore did not expect them to stand up to the threat of burning for heresy, and was disconcerted to find his expectations disappointed. John Rogers, a celebrated preacher, went to the fire unflinchingly in early February, and he was rapidly followed by several others, including John Hooper, the former Bishop of Gloucester. For the time being Gardiner persisted, using Pole's legatine authority as his cover, but by the summer he had become disillusioned. As a policy designed to enforce conformity, persecution clearly was not working, and he began to advocate milder penalties. Unfortunately neither the Queen nor the Cardinal were listening. For them the burning of unrepentant heretics was not a policy but a duty, and the persecution continued beyond Gardiner's death in November 1555, moving down to the rank-and-file Protestants, who by 1557 were being burned in batches. The redemptive purpose of persecution had been forgotten and the punitive mechanism taken over. The reaction of the general public was not as hostile as John Foxe's *Book of Martys* makes out, but in London in particular the crowds which turned out to witness such punishments were often sympathetic to the victims, and Bishop Bonner started advocating burning in the very early morning, before the crowds were about. This defeated the exemplary purpose of the executions, and is a sign that the burnings were proving counter-productive.

While these events were taking place, Mary became convinced that she was pregnant, and began to put a nursery in place for the expected child. On 20 April she retreated into the customary female seclusion at Hampton Court, and waited. At the beginning of June she was still waiting. The scandalous tales began to multiply: she was not pregnant at all; it was a Spanish trick to intrude an heir to the throne; she was bewitched, or ill, or even dead. By the end of July it was clear that the supposed pregnancy had been a phantom, although whether induced by illness or by her own intense desire no one knew – or knows now. At the end of that month she emerged, shattered physically and depressed in mind, only to be confronted by the news that Philip was leaving. His father's health was deteriorating, and he had been anxious to go for some time; only a sense of duty had kept him at his post while awaiting the delivery of the Queen's child. If she had died in childbirth, he would have had business to attend to. Now that is was clear that there was no child, he made his preparations for departure, sure in his own mind that the dynastic purposes of his marriage had failed, and that Mary would never bear a healthy son. Towards the end of August he left, and Mary was by then strong enough to see him off, to the great relief of her people, who had feared the worst from her long seclusion. Philip stayed away for eighteen months, during which time Mary was left pretty much to her own devices. The parliament of November 1555 was difficult, refusing a bill to confiscate the property of those who had quitted the realm without licence, and the King began to press for a proper coronation. This had not taken place for the same reason that Philip had been given no property in England, so that he would not claim any interest in the realm in the event of Mary's death, but that could hardly be admitted publicly. The Queen refused his request, and relations between them deteriorated. He continued to be kept in touch by means of the Select Council which he had instituted, but did little with the information which he received. Having taken over the Low Countries from his father in September 1555, and the crowns of Spain in January 1556, he had quite enough to occupy himself without troubling about the problems of England, where he was not a proper king in any case.

1556 was a miserable year in England. It started with a conspiracy against the Queen, the so-called Dudley Plot for an invasion by English exiles with French support which was aimed at displacing the Queen in the interests of her sister Elizabeth. How much of a threat this presented is still mysterious, but it came to nothing, and Philip instructed that Elizabeth was not to be troubled about the way that her name had been taken in vain. The weather was wretched and the harvest failed for the second year in a row, producing food shortages and discontent, and Philip did not come. Instead he began to turn his attentions to Elizabeth, not in any improper way but in terms of her right to the succession. When his bid for a coronation was rejected, he began to think seriously about what would happen if his wife's suspect health should collapse. He would not bid for it himself, because he knew how unpopular he was, and that such an attempt would result in a civil war which he could not afford to fight. So he recognised Elizabeth as the next heir, greatly to Mary's anger, because her own relations with her sibling were hostile. She had, she had already made it clear, no desire for her throne to pass to Elizabeth – she was too much like her mother (Anne Boleyn). Philip knew about this, but did not allow it to deflect him, and he began a campaign to get her married to an acceptably Catholic Spanish acolyte, namely the Duke of Savoy. Elizabeth knew perfectly well what he was about, and would have nothing to do with it. If (or when) she came to the throne it would be as an independent woman and her own mistress. Meanwhile Philip's truce with France was breaking down, thanks to the aggressive behaviour of Pope Paul IV, who being a Neapolitan was fiercely hostile to Spain and all its works. By the autumn of 1556 war was raging again in central and northern Italy, and the question of England's involvement began to come onto the Council's agenda. The majority, led by Cardinal Pole, were opposed. England had no interest in the affairs of Italy, and in any case could not afford to go to war. The Queen had been struggling with some success to reduce the burden of debt which her brother had bequeathed to her, but a war would ruin all her efforts and set her back where she had started.

However in January 1557 the truce in the North also broke down, and this was a good deal nearer to home. The King decided that he needed English support to deal with this new menace, particularly her navy, and that he would have to come to London in order to solicit it. So he came in March, to Mary's intense personal joy, and tried to put pressure on the Council. This appeared to be failing until a somewhat mysterious raid on the Yorkshire coast, which could be represented as French provocation, tipped the balance of the debate in his favour and a majority of the Council were persuaded to support a declaration of war. This was duly made in June, and in July Philip returned to the Continent accompanied by an English expeditionary force commanded by the Earl of Pembroke, for which he was paying! In spite of some confusion over its deployment, this force fought well at the siege of St Quentin in August, and came back in October with battle honours. Unfortunately the Council then decided to economise and, thinking that the fighting season was over for that year, reduced the garrison of Calais, just when the French, smarting under their defeat at St Quentin, were looking for a soft target to redeem themselves. The Duke of Guise identified a weakened Calais as such a target, and struck suddenly and unexpectedly in January 1558. The defences were overrun in a matter of days, and a relief expedition had to be abandoned because the influenza epidemic which was then raging in England had reduced the available manpower to a level which was not viable. Mary agonised over the loss, and her subjects (most unreasonably) blamed Philip for not coming to the rescue, but it was setback with advantages. Calais had been expensive both to administer and to defend, and constituted a standing temptation to interfere in the affairs of France in a way which England could no longer afford. Its loss turned English eyes westward towards the Atlantic, where her future opportunities lay.

In the spring of 1558, Mary persuaded herself that she was pregnant again, but this time no preparations were made, and nobody took her very seriously. Her health did not appear to be any worse than usual, but then in October she took a fever, which did not respond to treatment. There was talk of a 'dropsy', and on 17 November she died. Philip did not come, partly because her deterioration was sudden, and partly because he did not want to be in England when she died, in case his honour should require him to bid for the succession, which, as we have seen, he had no desire to do. So he sent his trusted servant the Count of Feria, whose reports constitute our best information of her last days. She died surrounded by loyal familiars, but missing the man who meant most to her – her husband. She also died heavily in debt, because just as her Council had feared, the war which was still ongoing had cost well beyond her means, and had pushed her debt level back above where it had been in July 1553. She owed over £300,000, mostly in Antwerp. Thanks to the efforts of her agent there, Thomas Gresham, the exchange rate had been restored, and the servicing of this debt had been largely taken over by the Merchant Adventurers, but it still constituted a considerable burden – and all for 'King Philip's war' in which England had no direct interest. Mary was a tragic figure, because she never managed to come to terms with being both a sovereign and a wife. The crown had been 'ungendered' by Parliament in April 1554, when it was declared that the authority of the monarch was the same, whether male or female, but that had not solved her problem. As a monarch she was supposed to be decisive, and to make her own decisions, but as a wife she was supposed to be passive and dependent. She could not afford to be passive, and that preyed on her conscience. Mary's conscience was an affliction, because it not only pointed to irreconcilable courses of duty, it also made it impossible for her to compromise over things like religious persecution. She restored the Church in a remarkable way, making it both popular and effective, but she left it stained with the worst persecution in English history, and her sister was to make sure that she was remembered as 'Bloody Mary'.

PART 13
THE LAST TUDOR,
1558–1603

39

GLORIANA, ELIZABETH I
(REIGNED 1558–1603)

Elizabeth was a very different kind of woman from her half-sister. She had Henry VIII's intelligence, and his wilful obstinacy, as well as his colouring; but she also had her mother's wit and feisty sexuality. It was this latter which enabled her to devise a strategy of survival and control in the male-dominated world of late sixteenth-century politics – a strategy which Mary could not even have imagined let alone carried out. It was based upon the courtly love tradition, whereby the damsel was always desirable, but never attainable, and she acted the part of the damsel with consistency and success for more than forty years. The fact that it rapidly became a fiction, and the expressions of devotion which it engendered were bogus, did not matter. It became a courtly and political game in which all those who wished to do business with the Queen had to engage. She was, as the Count of Feria observed shortly before her accession, very clever and very vain. She intended to have her way absolutely as her father had, and seemed to have learned her practices of government from him. She acknowledged no obligation to Philip for his support, and put her trust entirely in the people, who were certainly (he went on) all on her side. She was also a heretic and surrounded herself with like-minded men and women.

At the outset of her reign she faced three issues. She had to determine the shape of her government, to settle the Church and to end the war with France. In the first place she decided to retain the services of Mary's aged Treasurer, the Marquis of Winchester, who had also served Edward in the same capacity, but not of her Chancellor, Nicholas Heath, the Archbishop of York. The Great Seal went to Nicholas Bacon as Lord Keeper. She retained most of the nobles from Mary's Council, but dismissed the rest, reducing the size of that body to about twenty – less than half the size of its predecessor. Her court she handled in a similar fashion, retaining most of the Chamber and Household servants, but replacing the Privy Chamber entirely, bringing back her former mentor Katherine Ashley as Chief Gentlewoman. Most important of all, she entrusted the key office of Secretary to Sir William Cecil, who had also occupied one of the secretarial posts under Edward, and entrusted him with a special role of advice and admonition. Elizabeth was greatly assisted in her religious settlement by the fact that Cardinal Pole, the Archbishop of Canterbury, died within hours of Mary, leaving the primatial see conveniently vacant. The persecution stopped immediately Mary's death was known, which was a sufficient indication of what was expected, but the Queen did not rush things. For the time being she inhibited controversy, and insisted on the existing laws being observed. However, the appearance of Protestant preachers at Paul's Cross, and the omission of the elevation of the host in the mass at her coronation on 15 January 1559 caused her bishops sleepless nights. Their anxieties were fully justified by the passage of the Acts of Supremacy and Uniformity in the first parliament of 1559. Together these acts restored the Edwardian Church in its fully reformed guise, and in spite of the most tenacious opposition the bishops were outvoted in the House of Lords. It is clear that the Queen's wishes were well enough known to the members, and that she got more or less what she wanted. Peace with France was secured at the end of March, in a treaty which Elizabeth reluctantly accepted because it left Calais in French hands. Philip was not prepared to sacrifice his peace for the sake of returning it to England, and the Queen was in no position to continue the war alone, so Calais was sacrificed, in spite of dire threats as to what would happen in that event.

Marriage was not high on Elizabeth's agenda, although it was on that of her parliament, and when they petitioned her to wed she put them off with comfortable words. Philip proposed almost immediately, more out of a sense of duty than from desire, and was probably relieved to be politely declined. One Tudor woman was enough for any man! As far as the Queen was concerned, marriage was an aspect of foreign policy, and a Habsburg match had its attractions, so she allowed a negotiation to be opened for the hand of the Archduke Charles, the second son of the Emperor Ferdinand I, and this continued inconclusively for the best part of a decade, until Elizabeth's religious position finally put an end to it. Meanwhile the Queen had been reluctantly persuaded to intervene in Scotland, and she had fallen in love. The Scottish adventure was wished on her by William Cecil, to take advantage of a rebellion by the Protestant lords against the Catholic and French-backed regime of the Queen Mother, Mary of Guise. Mary died in the summer of 1560, and her cause died with her, the French being in no position to intervene further thanks to their own domestic troubles. Elizabeth signed the Treaty of Edinburgh with the victorious lords, carefully omitting any claim to overlordship, and a new friendship was established with the Scots government which was to endure through various ups and downs until James VI finally became James I of England in 1603. This treaty was largely negotiated by William Cecil, because the Queen's mind was elsewhere at the time. She had known Robert Dudley since childhood, and had made him Master of the Horse at her accession, but quite suddenly in the winter of 1559/60 their relationship took on a new character. She began to flirt with him, to visit his chamber at unseasonable hours, and generally to behave as a woman infatuated. Her behaviour became the scandal of the court, and the laughing stock of Europe. Cecil became desperately worried and spoke of resigning his office. Then in September 1560 Robert's wife Amy died in suspicious circumstances, and it was not a question of adultery but of marriage. Her Council were horrified, and pointed out that to marry a man who was suspected of having his wife's blood on his hands would ruin her political credit, and might even cost her the throne. Faced with these compelling arguments, the queen overcame the woman, and Elizabeth painfully drew back. Attractive as he was, there could be no question of her marrying Robert Dudley, and after an anguished interlude he settled into the role of favourite and best friend, in which he was to continue until his death in 1588.

While this was going on, her Church settlement was slowly taking root. All but one of Mary's bishops refused the Oath of Supremacy and were deprived, making way for a new bench of Protestants, several of whom had been exiles under the previous regime. In December 1559 Matthew Parker was at last consecrated Archbishop of Canterbury, and the ecclesiastical commission decreed by the Act of Supremacy came into existence. Elizabeth was sympathetic to the argument that no woman could be Supreme Head of the Church, and therefore distanced herself from its daily government by styling herself Supreme Governor. This did not prevent her from believing that it was an office directly conferred by God, and uniquely responsible to Him, but it was a gesture towards conservative opinion. It was, however, this sense of special responsibility which made her so reluctant to take advice on ecclesiastical matters, or to allow others to interfere in the processes of decision making. She was to inhibit many parliamentary discussions on the need for further reform, and to adhere strictly to the terms of her settlement until they had become an acceptable orthodoxy for the great majority of her subjects. When sharp measures were required to enforce conformity, as was done in 1566 and 1583, she was quite happy for her Archbishops to shoulder the responsibility, provided that they did not intrude upon her prerogative. After 1563, Elizabeth, in spite of her religious position, was reluctant to appear as the Protestant champion of Europe, and this was largely because she had burned her fingers badly intervening on behalf of the Huguenots in the religious struggles of France. She had been persuaded to this action partly by Lord Robert Dudley and partly by the hope of recovering Calais, being always on the lookout for opportunities to diminish her sister's government which had lost it. She consequently responded positively to the Prince of Conde's appeal for assistance, and accepted Le Havre as a cautionary town for Calais, which was not under Huguenot control. The outcome was a disaster, because the Huguenots were defeated and came to terms with the Guises, leaving the garrison at Le Havre to face the combined forces of France. Plague broke out in the town, and it was surrendered. By the Treaty of Troyes in 1564 all claims to Calais had to be abandoned in return for peace, and this was a humiliation which Elizabeth would not soon forget.

The Queen preferred more subtle ways of advancing herself, and above all ways which did not cost so much money. She had promptly tackled the debt which Mary had left, and taking advantage of an upturn in trade, and of the indulgence of Parliament towards a new and popular regime, had significantly reduced it. More particularly she had shifted most of it back to London, where it could be more easily controlled, and Thomas Gresham, continuing his service in Antwerp, had the relatively straightforward task of servicing what was left. However, war, even on a small scale, was expensive and by 1563 Elizabeth was on the lookout for ways of augmenting her income which did not depend upon grants. Instead she began to invest in private commercial ventures to West Africa and the New World, most notably those of John Hawkins. Hawkins made three voyages between 1563 and 1568, picking up slaves on the Guinea coast of Africa and selling them – quite illegally – to the Spanish colonists in the West Indies. The Queen invested in each of these ventures, with money, provisions and ships, and took a share of the profits. This was all done unofficially, but Philip was not deceived, and relations between the two realms deteriorated as he blamed her openly for indulging in acts of piracy. The presence of her own ship the *Jesus of Lubeck* at San Juan d'Ulloa, when Hawkins was caught by the viceroy of the Indies in 1568, told its own story. However, Philip was not anxious to add England to his growing list of enemies, and was even prepared to swallow the insult when Elizabeth borrowed the money intended to pay his troops in the Low Countries in January 1569. The Genoese ships bearing this cash had been driven into Southampton by bad weather, and the Queen took advantage of the fact that it had not been handed over to the Duke of Alba to tell the bankers that she would take it up herself. Alba was furious and imposed an immediate trade embargo, but Philip would not allow him to go further, and when it proved more damaging to Antwerp than to London, it was lifted.

So far the King of Spain had restrained the Pope from taking any action against the heretical kingdom, on the grounds that the Queen was better disposed to the Old Faith than were her subjects, but that changed in 1570. In the autumn of 1569 the conservatively inclined earls of Northumberland and Westmorland rose in rebellion. There were a number of reasons for this, including personal grievances and dislike of William Cecil, but the main reason was discontent with the religious settlement. They had also been caught in the open by the failure of a scheme to marry the Duke of Norfolk to the fugitive Queen of Scots, who had been deposed in 1568 for suspected involvement in the murder of her husband, Henry, Lord Darnley, and who had taken refuge in England. Elizabeth did not know what to do with her, but refused to countenance any plan to marry her to Norfolk. Northumberland and Westmorland had been openly in favour of this scheme, and felt exposed to the royal wrath in consequence. They attempted to use their supposed strength as Northern lords to force the Queen to compromise over religion and to relax her hostility to Mary – perhaps even to recognise her as the heir to the throne. However, their supposed power turned out to be largely an illusion. After celebrating mass in Durham Cathedral, they set off to rescue the Queen of Scots, who was being held at Tutbury in Staffordshire. However, they failed to attract recruits, and their own men began to melt away. Having got to Bramham Moor near Leeds, they gave up and turned back. Meanwhile a royal army was advancing from the South under the command of the Queen's cousin Lord Hunsdon, and being in no state to risk a battle the rebel earls disbanded their force (or what was left of it) and fled into Scotland. The Rebellion of the Northern Earls was thus something of a non-event, but it had two important consequences. Confiscations broke up the earldoms, and enabled the Queen to redistribute their property to loyal Northern gentry.

This changed the political landscape of the north of England, bringing it more into line with the lowlands, and eliminated it as a threat to the government in London. Secondly the Pope responded to an appeal for assistance which had been directed to him when the rising was at its height. It had long since collapsed by the time that his response came, but it took the form of a bull, *Regnans in Excelsis*, which declared Elizabeth a heretic and deposed, releasing all her subjects from their oaths of allegiance to her. This was the long-delayed declaration of war, and it altered the position of the English Catholics fundamentally. Hitherto they had been non-conformists, a nuisance rather than a threat. Now if they continued to accept the Pope's authority, they were traitors in the service of a hostile foreign power. Faced with this dilemma, many conformed, and those that did not became identified as recusants, and subject to increasingly harsh penalties as the foreign Catholic threat developed.

Philip did not approve of Pius V's action, not least because he anticipated being called upon as the obvious prince to enforce such sanctions – a task which he was not prepared at this stage to undertake. Elizabeth, however, did not know that and, anticipating increased Spanish hostility, decided to get closer to France, which, in spite of the turmoil of its civil wars, was still an ally worth having. Apart from the Dutch, she was also the only ally available, so diplomatic advances were made. The French Crown, desperately trying to maintain its authority between the conflicting factions, was disposed to be friendly, and negotiations developed. At first these took the form of a marriage between the Queen and the French king's younger brother, the Duke of Anjou. Elizabeth was about thirty-eight by this time, and Anjou was rising seventeen, but that was not the main obstacle. He was a staunch Catholic, and that Elizabeth could not indulge, so the negotiations broke down. However, the desire for friendship remained on both sides, and resulted in the Treaty of Blois in 1572 whereby each side undertook to support the other in the event of attack by a third party. Spain was not named, but the implication was clear. This has been described as a diplomatic revolution, but it was not really such, because relations with Spain had been strained for a number of years. It was more in the nature of a common-sense precaution. At the time when the treaty was signed, Huguenot influence had been strong at the French court, but within a few months the thought of war with Spain had turned that situation around, with the result that Charles IX and the Queen Mother, Catherine de Medici, countenanced one of the worst atrocities perpetrated during the century – the massacre of St Bartholomew's Eve. On 23 August 1572, taking advantage of the presence in Paris of a large number of Protestant leaders for the marriage of Henry of Navarre to Catherine's daughter Margaret, the Guises staged a surprise attack. They killed Gaspar de Coligny, the Huguenots' principal commander, and hundreds of his followers in a campaign which soon spread outside Paris to all those other areas where the Catholics had control. The result was renewed civil war, and horror in London. Elizabeth was not to be derailed from her alliance, but relations between the two courts became understandably frosty. However, in 1574 Charles IX died, haunted it was said by Huguenot ghosts, and the wheel turned another circle. Elizabeth was soon negotiating optimistically for the hand of yet another Valois prince, the Duke of Alençon, who was even younger than Henry, the former Duke of Anjou, now King Henry III. Alençon was thought to be more flexible in his religion than Henry had been, and he certainly wanted the alliance, but the negotiations again dragged on inconclusively. In 1581, while he was in England trying to activate his suit, Elizabeth, with a sudden rush of blood, kissed him in public and announced that she would marry him. However, the next morning she had changed her mind, leaving him fuming about the inconstancy of women, and that, as it transpired, was her last fling in the marriage market. She was now forty-eight and even the most optimistic held out no hope of an heir of her body, so the main point of marriage was gone, and what was left was not attractive.

One of the reasons why the Alençon negotiation had gone on for so long was Elizabeth's desire to control the Duke's interest in the Low Countries. Since the 1560s there had been grumbling discontent in the Netherlands, provoked by Philip's centralising schemes and general insensitive handling of noble and urban privileges, which were the relics of a complex process of provincial evolution. In 1567 the King had dismissed his regent there, Margaret of Parma, on the grounds that she was making too many concessions, and replaced her with the Duke of Alba. Alba's instructions were to suppress all dissent, and in that he was largely successful, until he faced the threat of French intervention in 1572. While his forces were concentrated in the south a band of pirates known as the Sea Beggars (who had recently been based in England) sneaked in behind him and took the port of Brill. This reignited the revolt, and by the time that Alba had turned his troops around, the rebels were too strong to be dislodged. Alba was recalled, but his successor had no better fortune, and by the time that mutinous Spanish army sacked Antwerp in 1576, the revolt had spread far and wide.

Elizabeth was naturally sympathetic to a (largely) Protestant resistance movement, and concerned to prevent Philip from regaining control of the Dutch coast, but did not feel able to intervene, in spite of appeals from the rebel leaders. English volunteers, however, served in the rebel armies in considerable numbers. Then in 1578 the largely Catholic nobility of Flanders and Hainault came to terms with the King, leaving the explicitly Protestant northern provinces, particularly Holland and Zeeland, to continue the war alone. It was in this context that the Duke of Alençon's assistance was sought, and promised. However, Elizabeth was no keener on seeing French influence predominate in the Low Countries than she was Spanish, and tried for about two years to make his intervention serve her own purposes. In that she was unsuccessful, and it was Alençon who first accepted the title of Governor General, with a view to stabilising the anti-Spanish front. It was no thanks to her that he made a mess of it, trying to seize control of Antwerp in an attempted coup d'etat and, when he failed, withdrawing from the scene in disgrace. He died in 1584 without making any further impact on the situation. However, the Queen's relief was short-lived because in that same year William of Orange, the rebel leader, fell victim to a Catholic assassin, and she became the only possible resort of the remaining leaders in their desperate bid to keep their movement alive. Faced with this simple and unpalatable truth, she signed the Treaty of Nonsuch with the rebellious provinces, and thus committed herself to sending a substantial army to the Netherlands. War with Spain, so long delayed, had come at last.

By the time that this happened, the religious situation at home was giving renewed cause for anxiety. The Catholic recusants, although a small minority, were proving unusually obdurate, and from 1577 onward were being reinforced by missionary priests from the newly founded English College at Douai. For nearly twenty years the Catholic community had survived on the services of those priests who had refused the Elizabethan settlement: a few hundred, many of whom who had subsequently died. Now came a new wave of dedicated young men, committed to mission and prepared to take the risk of martyrdom. *Regnans in Excelsis* had been promptly countered by an Act of Parliament forbidding the importation of bulls from Rome (1571), but the danger now was of reconciliation with the Catholic Church, which was made a treasonable offence by an Act of 1581. In spite of their propaganda the seminary priests did not convert many Protestants. What they did was to confirm the wavering and redeem the conservative, which counted as conversions in their eyes, and in the eyes of the authorities. Convictions under this statute were not numerous, but it was undoubtedly useful in catching the seminarians, several of whom were executed under its provisions. From about 1580 these secular priests were reinforced by a Jesuit mission, and these learned and astute men were feared by the government much more than the seminary priests, who for all their dedication lacked the intellectual edge of the Society of Jesus, which had begun to attract English recruits several years before. Edmund Campion, the first of these new missionaries, was caught, tried and executed in 1581, and they were never numerous, but their impact was out of all proportion to their numbers. An Act specifically against them was passed by Parliament in 1585, but by that time they had fallen out with their secular colleagues, and the disputes between these two sets of priests undoubtedly weakened their mission in the 1590s. At the same time, the established Church was under attack from another angle, because those who were discontented that the Reformation had not gone far enough began to mount a series of attacks in Parliament. These had begun as early as 1569, and rapidly became Presbyterian in their aim. That is to say that they opposed the government of the Church by bishops, preferring the Scottish and Calvinist system of control by synods of clergy and laity. This the Queen interpreted as an attack upon the royal supremacy, which it was, and refused to countenance it in any shape or form. The battle continued until 1587 when the Puritans, as they were called, shot themselves in the foot with the so-called 'Marprelate Tracts'. These made such merciless fun of Episcopal authority that the lay magistracy took fright. Today the bishops, tomorrow the gentlemen? This debacle split the movement, the majority choosing to remain within the Episcopal Church, unsatisfactory though it was, rather than to venture into the uncharted waters of separatism. By 1593 these separatists were seen as almost as big a threat as the Catholics, and an Act against seditious sectaries was passed, under which several notorious dissidents were executed. The fact that such an Act could be passed in a forum traditionally sympathetic to Protestant dissent indicates that the government had won that battle by the end of the reign. Militant Puritanism was no longer an issue, and the Catholics were locked into their own disputes. Conservative religious opinion, which the majority shared, was now focussed on conformity to the Prayer Book, which was just where the Queen wanted it.

Meanwhile there was a war to be fought. In fact Philip had anticipated the Treaty of Nonsuch by impounding English ships in Spanish harbours in the summer of 1585. This was not an act of war in itself, but it was hostile, and both sides assumed a state of war to exist without any formal declaration on either side. Elizabeth promptly dispatched Sir Francis Drake, who had earned his knighthood by circumnavigating the globe in 1577–80, with instructions to demand the return of any English vessels that he could find, and then to proceed to raid the Spanish colonies in the New World, an occupation in which he was already adept. He succeeded in both parts of his mission, to Philip's intense annoyance, and this anger provoked the King into initiating a seaborne invasion of England. This armada began to take shape in the summer of 1586, under the command of the Marquis of Santa Cruz, the most skilful and experienced of Spanish admirals. It was not designed to conquer England, but to knock it out of the war, and hopefully to force a regime change in favour of Mary of Scotland. The armada from Spain was to link up with the Duke of Parma's army in the Low Countries and together these two forces would strike at the south-east of England, taking out London. However, these plans were disrupted in two ways by the events of 1587. In the first place Mary of Scotland was executed for her involvement in the Babington Plot against Elizabeth's life, and in the second place Drake raided Cadiz. The raid was immensely destructive of the supplies which had been painfully gathered, and effectively frustrated any attempt to launch the armada that year. Meanwhile the armada costs were running at the rate of about 2 million ducats (£700,000) a year, and bade fair to bankrupt the state. Then the Marquis of Santa Cruz died in February 1588 and was replaced by the Duke of Medina Sidonia. The Duke turned out to be an organiser of genius, and he turned the demoralised enterprise around, getting it to sea more or less ready for action in May 1588. After a long struggle with adverse weather, it turned up off the isles of Scilly at the end of July, and was shadowed up the Channel by the English fleet, commanded by Lord Howard of Effingham. Howard's gunfire inflicted only minimal damage, and the formation remained intact, but it soon transpired that the Duke's instructions were defective. He had no idea when or where he was supposed to rendezvous with the Duke of Parma, and their attempts at communication had been frustrated. Consequently he arrived at Calais a week too soon, and had nowhere to go to wait. Once his fleet was at anchor in the Calais roads, Howard sent in the fireships and broke up his formation. The following day he moved in on the disorganised armada, and put it to the sword, or rather the cannon. During the Battle of Gravelines which followed, the superior English gunnery inflicted terrible casualties and even sunk a few ships. It was only a change in the wind which enabled the battered remains of the great Spanish fleet to escape into the North Sea. The English pursued them as far as Scotland before returning to deal with their own problems of plague and lack of pay, and the armada went north about Cape Wrath. It liberally distributed its damaged ships along the Scottish and Irish coasts, and less than half those which had set off eventually limped back to Spain. It was a great English victory, and was celebrated as such for years after, the fate of those who died of the plague being quietly forgotten, except by those who had tried to succour them.

It was a great victory, but it was not decisive, and the war ground on. An attempt to destroy what was left of the armada foundered in 1589 in an abortive strike against Lisbon, the failure of which cost Drake his favour at court. The immensely rich Portuguese carrack the *Madre de Dios* was captured off the Azores by a privateering fleet in which the Queen had an interest in 1592, and 1595 saw a last hurrah for Drake and Hawkins in the West Indies. The colonial defences had been much improved and the venture cost both their lives. Meanwhile Philip had rebuilt the Atlantic fleet which had been so badly mauled in 1588, constructing galleons of the latest design. In spite of this the English and the Dutch successfully raided Cadiz in 1596, capturing the town and inflicting immense damage, both on Spanish pride and on Spanish resources. In many ways this was the most successful operation of the war, and provoked Philip into launching two further armadas in 1596 and 1597, both of which were frustrated by the weather rather than by the English. In 1590 the King of Spain had endeavoured to seize control of Brittany, for the purpose of making short-haul attacks on England, but after a messy Anglo-French campaign that intention was frustrated by the capture of the fort of Crozon in 1594. Crozon had been built by the Spaniards to control the harbour of Brest, and if that had succeeded then the coasts of Devon and Cornwall would have become exposed to attack. In 1595 long-rumbling discontent in Ireland flared up in the rebellion of the Earl of Tyrone, who immediately appealed for Spanish help, so that it was Ireland rather than England which had been the destination of the abortive armadas of 1596 and 1597. In the event it was only after Philip's death in 1598 that his successor eventually sent help to Tyrone, in the form of a small force which landed at Kinsale in 1601. This proved too little and too late, and was easily dealt with by Lord Mountjoy, the Queen's Governor at that point. Mountjoy gradually gained the upper hand of Tyrone, and the latter submitted in March 1603, just days before Elizabeth's death.

By that time the war with Spain was in stalemate, and the Dutch were managing very nicely without English help, so peace negotiations were in the offing, although they had not progressed very far.

In her latter years, the Queen became a tiresome old lady. This was partly because of the deaths of her old friends and servants. Robert

Dudley, who had been created Earl of Leicester in 1564, died in September 1588. He had been seriously out of favour in 1585 and 1586, owing to his mishandling of the Netherlands commission with which he had been entrusted, but he had been forgiven and Elizabeth felt his death keenly. Sir Francis Walsingham, her faithful 'spymaster', died in 1590, and her long-serving intimate Sir William Cecil, Lord Burghley, in 1598. Partly to compensate for these losses, the Queen had taken a new favourite, Leicester's stepson, the irrepressible and irresponsible Robert Devereux, Earl of Essex. The relationship between them was more that of an indulgent grandmother with her wayward grandson than that of lovers, but Essex's position was much resented. She gave him military commands, notably that at Cadiz in 1596, and bailed out his finances, but he always seemed on the brink of disaster. In 1599 he talked himself into the job of Governor of Ireland, and went across with a substantial force. However, he wasted his resources and carried out unauthorised discussions with Tyrone, with the result that his critics went to work at home. Dismayed by this news, he quitted his post without licence, and turned up at court to argue his case with Elizabeth. This time he had gone too far, and he was disgraced. With his finances in ruins, and convinced that he was the victim of a conspiracy by Robert Cecil, Lord Burghley's son, in January 1601 he attempted to raise London against the court. However, he had miscalculated his support, and was taken, tried and executed. The Queen was alleged to be devastated by what she had been compelled to do to her one-time favourite, and the resulting depression is supposed to have hastened her end, which came at St James's on 24 March 1603.

The succession had long been a forbidden topic, either for casual gossip or serious speculation. However, since the execution of

Mary of Scotland in 1587, the front runner (indeed the only serious contender) had been her son James VI of Scotland. A kite flown by Robert Parsons in favour of the Spanish Infanta had been taken seriously only by the more extreme Catholics, and the Queen's remote kinswoman Arbella Stuart was a non-starter. The Earl of Essex had quickly appraised this situation, and entered into a secret correspondence with James, designed to secure his own position in the new reign. His fall disconcerted the King of Scots, who did not know quite which way to turn, having been warned off Cecil by the Earl's innuendos. However, the Secretary knew about this, and after Essex's fall began his own system of communications with Scotland, which swiftly overcame the mistrust. It was therefore Mr Secretary Cecil who smoothed James's path to the throne, and who dispatched the messages on 24 March to Edinburgh to apprise James that he was now James I of England.

PART 14
THE STUARTS,
1603–1714

40

JAMES VI AND I (REIGNED 1603–1625)

James was the only child of the short-lived and stormy marriage between Mary, Queen of Scots, and Henry, Lord Darnley, the twenty-year-old son of the Earl of Lennox. Born in Edinburgh on 19 June 1566, he was eight months old when his father was killed, and thirteen months when his mother was deposed in his favour in July 1567. He had been crowned at Stirling on 29 July, and his government passed into the hands of the Earl of Morton. Morton was overthrown in 1581, when James was fourteen, and there then followed a turbulent period, during which he was kidnapped and escaped. In 1584, at the age of seventeen, he declared himself of age, and assumed the reins of government in person. In 1587 his mother, whom he had scarcely known, was executed in England, and James, having made the correct noises of indignation, began to acclimatise himself to the idea of being the heir to the English throne. This aim he pursued consistently, entering into correspondence first with the Earl of Essex and then with Sir Robert Cecil to bring it about. On 24 March 1603, the thirty-seven-year-old King of Scots became also King of England, and began to adjust his experience to deal with a totally different situation. His claim was strictly hereditary, and involved ignoring Henry VIII's last Succession Act, upon which Elizabeth's claim had been based. It was not repealed because that would have been impossible in the old queen's lifetime, and thereafter no one wanted to draw attention to it. Consequently it was quietly set aside, and James was able to claim his throne by divine right.

However, it was one thing to claim a crown by that route, and quite another to conduct a government on such assumptions. That James was inclined to do, saying that he was responsible to God alone, until it was pointed out to him that in England the prerogative was limited, not as in Scotland by the power of the nobility but by the law, and by Parliament. During the course of his reign, James was forced to come to terms with the power of Parliament, and eventually managed that institution well enough, but only at the cost of conceding his divine-right principles, something which his son was notoriously reluctant to do. At first his ideas appeared to be confirmed by the authority of the English Crown over the Church. The royal supremacy was totally unlike anything that he had experienced in Scotland, where the Kirk was ruled by its General Assembly and the King was liable to be told that he was only 'God's silly vassal'. He was therefore pleased to receive the millenary petition, while he was on his way south during April. This was a mildly puritanical document, asking for various changes in the order of the established Church, particularly the abolition of 'superstitious ceremonies'. It did not touch the authority of the bishops, except by implication. The King decided to deal with this petition himself, as became him as Supreme Head, and against the advice of his senior clergy convened a conference of divines to meet at Westminster in January 1604. This conference set up a number of commissions to look at particular reforms, but since these were all dominated by unsympathetic bishops, no significant changes resulted. The King was just not sufficiently engaged to keep the momentum going – except in one respect. The main product of the Westminster discussions was the King James Bible, a new translation in which James was deeply interested, and which was published eventually in 1611. Meanwhile Archbishop

Bancroft of Canterbury had died, and the King chose George Abbot to succeed him. Abbot was an old-fashioned Calvinist, of the kind which had been common in Elizabeth's early days, and his appointment reassured those who had been worried by Bancroft's apparent moves in the direction of Divine Right episcopacy, a tendency which seemed to threaten the royal supremacy. This was a suspicion shared by James himself, who had no time for the High Church party which was beginning to emerge. He was a staunch Calvinist, and had no desire to see his Church toying with Pelagianism.

James was also a married man with a family. He had in 1589 taken Anne, the daughter of Frederick II of Denmark, as his wife, and she had produced no fewer than six children by the time that he came to the throne of England. She had also, to his embarrassment, converted to the Church of Rome, a circumstance which gave the English Catholics extravagant hopes of his own conversion, and inhibited any possible resistance to his accession. It was the disappointment of those hopes which led in November 1605 to the Gunpowder Plot, whereby a group of Catholic extremists planned to blow up the Houses of Parliament at the time of the state opening, intending to kill the King and a large number of peers and members. At least that was alleged to be the intention; there are a number of mysterious features about this conspiracy which have cast doubts upon the whole story. It was detected in time by a search of the palace cellars, and the conspirators were rounded up, tried and eventually executed. The main consequence of the Gunpowder Plot was a strong anti-Catholic revulsion, by both the King and the people, which resulted in a tightening up of the administration of the penal laws, which many had thought would be relaxed. One of the staunchest of these Protestants was the King's eldest son, Prince Henry, who had already rejected a suggestion that he might marry a Catholic princess to ease the international tensions, and who expressed himself on this subject in unequivocal terms. Henry, who had been born in 1594, and was created Prince of Wales in June 1610, was the white hope of the English establishment. A fine upstanding youth who liked being portrayed in armour, and who was firm in his opinions, he tragically died in 1612 at the age of eighteen, leaving his expectations to his much less promising younger brother Charles, who would eventually be the ill-starred Charles I. Also in 1612 died Robert Cecil, whom James had raised to the Earldom of Salisbury and appointed Lord Treasurer. Although Cecil had failed to secure the Great Contract with Parliament which would have guaranteed the King's financial security, he had served him with distinction in other ways, and the loss of these two keys figures deprived James's government of a lot of its credibility.

James was averse to physical violence, and saw himself as a peacemaker. As such he had negotiated the Treaty of London with Spain in 1604, which had brought that long and eventually rather pointless struggle to an end. Commercial and diplomatic relations were restored, and the new Spanish ambassador Count Gondomar wasted no time in making his presence felt. Taking advantage of the King's known desire, he suggested a diplomatic marriage for the King's son with the Spanish Infanta, in an effort to bring the two sides together. James took up the suggestion and, as we have seen, proposed such a match to Henry, who had promptly rejected it. Nevertheless, building upon the same idea he married his daughter Elizabeth to the Count Palatine of the Rhine, a Protestant prince, in February 1613; and he set out on a quest to match his thirteen-year-old second son to the Infanta. Charles was biddable. But the negotiations were long and protracted, centring as they did upon Gondomar's desire to see the penal laws relaxed, and Parliament's determination to allow no such thing. Meanwhile the international situation had developed dramatically, because the Bohemians had risen in revolt against the Emperor Ferdinand III, and offered their crown to the Elector Palatine, who had been unwise enough to accept it. This had resulted in 1619 in a Spanish and Imperial assault upon Bohemia, and in the defeat of Frederick, the King of Bohemia, at the Battle of White Mountain in 1620. This defeat cost him not only his crown, but also the Palatinate, which was overrun by Spanish troops, turning him (and his wife) into fugitives who took refuge in the Low Countries. Pressure on James to intervene in his son-in-law's interest became intense, and he reacted by redoubling his efforts to finalise a Spanish match for his son, aiming to make peace in the Palatinate the diplomatic trade-off. As a result Charles set off, accompanied by James's new favourite George Villiers, Earl of Buckingham, in paper-thin disguises, to woo his intended in person. George Villiers was a courtier who had taken advantage of the fall of the Howards to ingratiate himself with the King and secure a grip on royal patronage. A homosexual relationship has been suggested, but there is no real evidence for that. James just liked him and was happy for him to accompany his son to Spain. However, the mission turned out ill. The Spanish court did not know quite what to make of this self-appointed mission, and treated them with suspicion. As a result Charles never got to see his prospective bride, and came home few months later seething with indignation. The one thing that he did gain from the visit was a profound respect for the Spanish court, and its etiquette. Being afflicted with an impediment in his speech, he much appreciated the extreme solemnity of its proceedings, which did not call for many words, and this reticence affected his own style when he became king.

The failure of Charles's mission, and his anger, helped to ease relations with Parliament, which had been pressing for war with Spain since 1618. Agitations in 1606, 1610 and 1614 had achieved little, except to turn the latter session into an 'Addled Parliament', which produced no legislation, but the rise of the Villiers family in 1616 had inflamed opinion again and led to an explosion of wrath in 1621. Ostensibly the issue was one of monopolies, a grumbling grievance which had not gone away since Elizabeth had made her deceptive 'Golden Speech' to Parliament in 1601. In 1621 the principal targets were Sir Francis Mitchell and Sir Giles Mompesson, against whom the long-forgotten process of impeachment was revived, but the real target was the Villiers' control of patronage, and the abuse of the honours system which had resulted. However, these matters would probably have raised more rhetoric than action if it had not been for the fact that the councillors in the House were divided. In particular Sir Edward Coke hated the Lord Chancellor, Francis Bacon. Bacon was a committed believer in prerogative justice, something to which Coke, as a common lawyer, was adamantly opposed. Bacon had been using the Chancery court to extend protection to insolvent debtors, and this was particularly resented in London. However, what could easily have become a political issue became a judicial one instead when an inquiry revealed ordinary charges of corruption against the Chancellor. He was also impeached, but the issue did not come to trial. Pleading ill health, the Chancellor stood down, and thus relieved the King of the necessity of having to dismiss him. The issue of ministerial responsibility, which these matters had seemed to raise, thus never came to a head. However, it had been raised, and was not destined to go away. To what extent (if at all) were the King's ministers answerable for their actions to Parliament? Was the King entitled to bestow powers of patronage, which in theory belonged to the Crown, upon a favourite, or upon a favourite's family?

The question of the debasement of honours was a vexed one. No one denied that Elizabeth had been unduly stingy. There were actually fewer peers at her death than there had been at her accession, and Mary had not been overgenerous either. There were also only about 550 knights in the whole country, and many of those were swordsmen who had been dubbed by the Earl of Essex. James had overcorrected with a vengeance, creating over 1,000 knights in the first year of his reign. At the same time peerage incomes had declined, and rich commoners were queuing up to join their ranks. Lord Burghley had been urging promotions upon the Queen for years, and shortly before his death had drawn up a list of seventeen who were, in his opinion, ripe for peerages. James soon exceeded that total, and complaints began to be raised that the status of nobleman was becoming debased. To make matters worse, there were suspicions of jobbery behind several of these promotions – of men buying peerages from a hard-up monarch, and these suspicions were reinforced by the creation of the rank of baronet in 1615, because these were openly sold, the going price being £1,095 in three instalments. It is not surprising that Parliament became exercised over these matters, especially when a parvenu baronet could be declared 'no gentleman' by the Earl Marshall's court. All ranks of the aristocracy were more familiar than they would care to admit with the process of recruitment from below, but this was too great, too sudden and too blatant. Years later the fall of royal government was blamed on this process

'Noble men were pulled down,' the Marquis of Newcastle said in 1650, 'which is the foundation of monarchy – monarchy fell soon after.'

The failure of Charles's trip to Madrid had made the 1624 parliament more cooperative, and negotiations were soon in hand to launch an expeditionary force under Count Mansfeld to Frederick's assistance. This was duly sent and paid for, but it soon became bogged down in diplomatic discussions with the French, which were aimed to provide Charles with a French bride in lieu of the Spanish one who had got away. Unfortunately Richelieu demanded English support against the Protestant stronghold of La Rochelle as the price of such a union, and this James was reluctantly forced to concede. It is questionable how much James was really in charge of affairs during the last three months of his life, but it is undoubted that more concessions were made to the French than had been envisaged in the 1624 parliament. When he died on 27 March 1625 the marriage had been secured, but the political and financial cost seemed likely to be very great, and neither Charles nor Buckingham had the relevant experience to deal with what was likely to be a crisis situation.

James had been an intellectual, and it was not for nothing that he was dubbed 'the wisest fool in Christendom'. His ideas did not fit comfortably with the political realities of England, but he did eventually acknowledge that fact. He had spent the first few years of his reign trying to persuade the English to accept a state union with Scotland, but gave up when the opposition became too strong, and settled for a union of the crowns instead. Probably the opposition in Scotland would have been even stronger, but he never tested it. Instead he imported Scottish courtiers, who caused discontents, but never of an explosive nature. He was physically ungainly, untidy in his personal habits, and his court was crude, boisterous and chaotic. It was, however, open in a way which his son's was not. After the death of Queen Anne in March 1619 he appears to have become emotionally dependent upon George Villiers, who was already his favourite, and to have been able to do nothing without his agreement and support. His relations with Parliament were constantly strained, but never irredeemably so, and he steered a careful course in religious matters, deferring on the whole to the opinions of George Abbot. He received the decisions of the Dutch Synod of Dort gladly, and showed no sympathy with the Remonstrants, who were the equivalent of the High Church party in England. However, he did allow his son to grow up as an Arminian, and that was to spell endless trouble after his death.

41

CHARLES I (REIGNED 1625–1649)

Charles succeeded in a situation of crisis. His French marriage had been secured, and was to take place within a matter of weeks, but war with Spain was also looming, and followed soon after. He was twenty-five years old, a fastidious and reticent young man, with a fine taste in art, and none of his father's robust political common sense. He was a poor communicator, partly on account of his stammer, and always refused to accept that he owed his subjects any duty of explanation for his policies. The parliament of 1625 was uncooperative. It granted two subsidies, but questioned the suspension of the penal laws, which had taken place in the previous year as a result, it was suspected, of French pressure. It was also openly contemptuous of the regime's military plans, which were to result in the disastrous attempt to repeat the 1596 triumph at Cadiz, and declined to give Charles the customary grant of the customs revenues for life. It also witnessed the first of a series of attacks upon the Arminians by John Pym, who was to become the scourge of the establishment on this subject over the next few years. Charles's decision to allow the Duke of Buckingham to defend the government's policies in person in the House of Lords also turned out to be a big mistake, because Buckingham was the scapegoat for all that was seen to be wrong with the administration. The expenses of war forced Charles back to Parliament in February 1626, and he found it in an even more hostile state of mind. This time it refused all grants, and complained that the King had gone on collecting the customs revenues without authorisation. An attempt was made to impeach the Duke of Buckingham, and Thomas Digges and John Eliot were sent to the Tower in May for managing that attempt, in a clear breach of the recognised privileges of members of the House. The session ended in a foul temper in June, with nothing achieved beyond a severe worsening of relations with the King. In September a forced loan was raised in support of the war with Spain, and William Laud, the President of St John's College, Oxford, and front man of the Arminian party in the Church was raised to the bishopric of Bath and Wells. In a conference on Church matters at York House, Buckingham spoke out warmly in support of the Arminian position, and he and the King were clearly on a collision course with Parliament.

Perhaps for that reason, Charles did not call a session in 1627, but it was an eventful year in other ways. In the summer, in spite of his marriage to Henrietta Maria, he drifted into war with France. This was largely on account of the rebellious city of La Rochelle, which was once again defying the French government. Charles, in an apparent attempt to placate opposition in England, decided to support the rebels, and launched an expedition under the command of the Duke of Buckingham to relieve the city. This may have been an attempt to rehabilitate the Duke, but if so it failed disastrously, his attack on the Isle de Rhe being defeated with heavy losses. Defeat, however, was just as expensive as victory, and Charles was forced to seek more forced loans in order to prop up his tottering finances. These provoked general opposition, and several of those assessed refused to pay. The King, exercising his prerogative power, had a number of them arrested and imprisoned, an action which the King's judges ruled to be lawful in the so-called 'Five Knights Case' in November. This judgement not only inflamed opinion against the court, it also undermined confidence in the judiciary, judges being appointed during the King's pleasure. In this case the King's special prerogative, which was recognised for cases of emergency, was invoked in a case which was not one of crisis, and the distinction between special and ordinary prerogatives became blurred, in a manner which was again hurtful to Charles's reputation. To make matters worse, Bishop Laud was appointed to the Privy Council and Archbishop Abbot was suspended for his consistent opposition to the King's Arminian policies. If 1627 was bad, 1628 was worse. Being compelled by financial necessity, Charles was forced to meet his third parliament in March, and therein the Commons, led by Eliot and Sir Thomas Wentworth, launched their expected attack against forced loans and arbitrary imprisonment. However, the Duke of Buckingham had been assiduously smoothing ruffled feathers in the House of Lords, and the bishops were by this time solidly royalist, so that Charles was able to reject a Declaratory Bill embodying the opposition's interpretation of the existing Acts. He professed himself willing to observe the law, but not to allow his subjects to define it for him. Rather than attempt a statute which was bound to fail, the Commons then resorted to the form of a petition, which became known as the Petition of Right. This included not only the well-known grievances against exactions levelled without parliamentary consent and imprisonment without lawful cause, but also the use of martial law against the civilian population and the billeting of troops without consent. Charles received the petition and assented to it, but nobody knew what legal status that conferred upon it, because it certainly was not a statute. The parliament then proceeded to pass a strongly worded remonstrance against the Arminians, and, as some compensation, to vote five subsidies – no doubt to remove any further excuse for forced loans. On 26 June the King prorogued the session, roundly condemning the remonstrance as presumptuous. In spite of the grant, relations had not significantly improved, and despite having accepted it, it is clear that Charles resented the Petition of Right bitterly.

In August the Duke of Buckingham was assassinated. This event took place at Portsmouth, where he was visiting the fleet in his capacity as Lord Admiral, and was the work of a disappointed place-seeker. The rejoicings were heartfelt and prolonged, and Charles was deeply distressed, but the removal of his favourite changed both the political and the personal landscape considerably. He had married Henrietta Maria by proxy on 1 May 1625, when she was sixteen, and relations between the married couple had at first been frosty. This was partly on account of the war, partly of her evangelical activity on behalf of the Catholic Church, and partly of his emotional involvement with Buckingham. Now that the latter was removed, and peace with France being negotiated, he began to find her a loving and supportive spouse, and their first child, Charles, was born on 29 May 1630. Politically it now became clear that the policies which the government was pursuing were not the result of 'evil counsel' but were the King's own, and this placed the opposition on an altogether different footing. When George Mountain was translated from London to Durham on 19 February 1628, and William Laud was appointed in his place, nobody could now deny that that had been the King's own doing. Charles was not being misled into Arminian paths; he was an Arminian himself, and his opponents had to come to terms with that fact.

Consequently when the second session of his third parliament convened in January 1629, there was no doubt that the resolutions passed against Arminianism were directed against the King, and he was not under any illusions about that either. At the beginning of March, amid celebrated scenes of disorder, the parliament was dissolved, and several of the leaders of the Commons, including John Eliot, were committed to prison. Charles had no intention of repeating this experience if he could possibly avoid it, and set out to govern without the participation of his obstreperous estates. Peace with France was concluded at Susa in April, and the war with Spain was in abeyance, Philip IV having quite enough to occupy himself in the Netherlands and Germany. The King was not anxious to reactivate hostilities, and peace negotiations were already in hand. They were successfully concluded in Madrid in November 1630, and the main financial burden was lifted from the English government. In the meantime, Charles had no intention of allowing attacks on his beloved Church to continue, and allowed the Court of Star Chamber to mutilate Alexander Leighton for his denunciations of the bishops. Star Chamber, which was the Council wearing other hats, had by this time taken over the discipline of the Church from the Court of High Commission, which continued to function, but at a lower level. The King was also looking for additional ways of boosting his income, and began fining those innumerable landowners worth £40 a year who had not taken up the honour of knighthood under a statute which was obviously out of date, but which ingenuity could call into service for fiscal purposes. Fines for every kind of misdemeanour were increased, and the customs went on being collected, more or less without resistance in the absence of Parliament. In 1632 Sir Thomas Wentworth, who had joined the King's side after the 1629 dissolution, and had joined the Privy Council later in the same year, was appointed Lord Deputy of Ireland, with the task of trying to pacify the Catholic discontent which was progressively eating at the fabric of government in that island.

Charles had been crowned at Westminster on 2 February 1626, but he had not yet been crowned in Scotland, and indeed had not visited that country since his infancy. He had, however, created considerable annoyance by causing an Act to be passed revoking grants of ecclesiastical property made since the Reformation. The purpose of this Act (1625) was less to withdraw the grants than to make sure that they were properly licensed, but the anger was none the less. He had also made insensitive attempts to tighten up the administration by revoking hereditary grants of office to noblemen. Consequently when he went to Edinburgh for his coronation in June 1633, he was already unpopular north of the border, and that situation was made much worse by the ritual which he employed on that occasion. The citizens of Edinburgh and the leaders of the Kirk were horrified by the High Church trappings, and made their displeasure known. If Charles had been more sensitive and flexible he could have spared himself a lot of trouble later; but he was not listening. To emphasise the point, when Archbishop Abbot died in August, the King appointed William Laud in his place, and Laud promptly shut down the Feofees for Impropriations on the grounds that they were buying up livings in the Puritan interest. By this time the High Church or Arminian party had a firm grip upon the bench of bishops, and was busily dividing the Church into two entrenched factions. To make his situation even more clear, Charles reissued his father's controversial *Book of Sports*, which was a deliberate affront to the sabbatarians; and he fined the City of London a large sum for exceeding its privileges. He did not, however, threaten to withdraw its charter, and the City Fathers submitted with a bad grace. Towards the end of the year William Prynne tempted fate by attacking the theatre as a source of immorality, and extending his attack to include the court masques and other entertainments which were favourites with the King and Queen. The *Histriomastix* was interpreted particularly as an assault upon the Queen, and Charles was understandably angry. Prynne had his ears cropped by Star Chamber early in 1634, and that added to the enemies of prerogative jurisdiction. In September of the same year Sir Robert Heath, the Chief Justice of Common Pleas, was dismissed for not being sufficiently cooperative, and replaced by the courtier Sir John Finch. The King's right to appoint and dismiss judges was thus brought under scrutiny, and another dimension added to his multifaceted unpopularity. Meanwhile the navy was costing a lot to maintain, and was becoming increasingly necessary not merely to guard the coasts, but also to deal with the threat of piracy which was being engendered by the Thirty Years' War, raging in Europe throughout the 1630s. The combatants were not always as careful as they might have been of the rights of neutrals. To enable this fleet to be serviced and kept up to standard,

Charles resurrected his ancient feudal right to ship money. This was exacted from the maritime counties and was undoubtedly lawful, but it was only one of a series of feudal dues which had been out of use for years and were now resurrected to help fill the royal coffers. Not only was there distraint of knighthood, as we have seen, but also fines for encroachments on the royal forests, those ancient hunting preserves of the king which had been delimited years ago, and much of which had long since passed under the plough. Understandably the descendants of the original encroachers were not pleased to be face with a bill for doing what they had done for years without it being questioned.

Ship money was extended to the inland counties in 1635, and new book of customs rates imposed, to take advantage of a recent recovery in the cloth trade. Like the extension of ship money this was of dubious legality without the consent of Parliament. However, the revival of the Depopulation Commissions in May was legal enough, although under statutes going well back into the previous century, when enclosure had been a real issue. These commissions were empowered to fine anyone who was farming land which had been enclosed without licence at any time over the last hundred years, and produced a large return; although whether the income generated was worth the general unpopularity of what was seen as yet another unauthorised tax may be doubted. A third writ of ship money was also issued in 1636, again including the inland counties, and it was perceived to be becoming a regular tax, which was not its original purpose. This time its lawfulness was challenged by John Hamden, a wealthy man who could well afford his assessment, but chose instead to make an issue of it. When the judges returned a 7–5 verdict in the King's favour in mid-1638, on the ground that the King was entitled to take his subjects' goods without their consent, there was universal outrage among the propertied classes. By the time that judgement was returned, the King was in serious difficulties. He felt compelled to punish the Puritan pamphleteers Burton, Bastwick and Prynne (again) in Star Chamber with further mutilations for their continued attacks on the Arminian bishops, and sent Bishop John Williams of Lincoln to the Tower for his continued opposition to Laud. At the same time the Pope sent a nuncio to Queen Henrietta Maria, who was most unwisely received at court, thus confirming the general suspicion that Arminianism was merely a stalking horse for the return of Roman Catholicism. Towards the end of 1637, with an almost incredible lack of political judgement, Charles attempted to impose a Laudian-style prayer book on the Scottish Kirk.

This provoked the National Covenant in Scotland, and resulted in agitated negotiations between the Covenanters and the King's commissioner, the Marquis of Hamilton. Charles was forced to make sweeping concessions, which involved convening both the General Assembly and the Scots parliament, and withdrawing the Prayer Book. However, these did not satisfy the Covenanters, who were by this time determined upon a showdown with their ungodly king. They raised an army and crossed into the north of England, not without the connivance of the English Puritan leadership. The result was the first so-called Bishops' War, which Charles was in no position to fight. He endeavoured unsuccessfully to raise an army, and was forced into the Treaty of Berwick, whereby he conceded virtually everything that the Scots demanded (June 1639). In the meantime Sir Thomas Wentworth was recalled from Ireland, where his strong hand had effectively held the government together, on the ground that his services were now likely to be needed in England. He became one of the King's chief councillors, and having assessed the situation quickly advised the recall of Parliament, as being the only body which might be able to cope with the breakdown of government which was by now apparent at the local level throughout the country. In October the Council was further humiliated when a Dutch fleet defeated the Spaniards in English territorial waters without the Royal Navy having the slightest chance to intervene. The Battle of the Downs marked a new low in English maritime prestige. By this time the situation of the government was desperate. The parliament which was convened in April resulted only in a chorus of grievances, and no positive suggestions for ending the crisis. It was dissolved after a month having voted no supply and achieved nothing, becoming known as the Short Parliament. The Scots were not satisfied that the concessions which they had extracted at Berwick were being properly observed, and they did not trust the King, with the result that they resorted to arms again in August, in the Second Bishops' War. This time Charles did succeed in raising an army, but it was roundly defeated by the Covenanters, resulting in the Treaty of Ripon in October 1640. This required the King to find £850 a day until a settlement was reached, and the only way in which he could hope to find that money was to recall Parliament. So fresh elections were held in a spirit of fierce antagonism, and the most recalcitrant of all assemblies convened at Westminster in November. The Commons promptly expelled all monopolists from among its members, who were not numerous, and condemned the Arminian canons which had been passed by convocation sitting at the same time. It was declared that convocation had no power to bind either clergy or the laity without parliamentary consent, an extension of the powers of Parliament which would never have been countenanced by a stronger government. At the same time impeachment proceedings were initiated against Laud and Wentworth, who had been Earl of Strafford since January. Press censorship had broken down entirely and London was flooded with opposition pamphlets, attacking every aspect of the existing regime.

During the session which continued into 1641, a whole programme of governmental reform was legislated, to which Charles was forced to agree: a Triennial Act (requiring a new parliament every three years); an Act against dissolving the existing parliament without its own consent (a clear infringement of the royal prerogative); the abolition of Star Chamber and High Commission; and an Act declaring ship money to be illegal. Above all the Earl of Strafford was condemned by Act of Attainder and executed in May, a sacrifice which caused Charles the acutest distress, but which he was powerless to resist. By the time that the second session convened in October, the opposition leaders were demanding that the appointment of Crown ministers be subject to parliamentary approval, but that was step too far even for Charles in his weakened state and he never agreed to it. By this time too, the House of Commons was becoming divided, as a substantial number of MPs thought that John Pym's leadership was driving too hard a bargain, and seeking to reduce the monarchy to a mere figurehead. As a result the Grand Remonstrance, which swept together all the remaining grievances into one denunciation, passed the Commons by only 159 votes to 148, and was never submitted to the House of Lords. On the other hand the opposition gained control of the government of the City of London at the end of the year, and more than compensated for their weakening grip on the House of Commons. Meanwhile the removal of Strafford's strong hand in Ireland had resulted in rebellion there, which threatened to sweep the English into the sea, and the question of raising an army to suppress it became urgent. If he was once in command of a large force of men, there was no knowing what the King might do, and the result in December was a demand by the opposition leaders that Parliament should control the militia – a demand which Charles again resisted. After failing to arrest five members for sedition in January 1642, the King quitted London, and gave up trying to participate in the affairs of Parliament. The country gentry were by this time as deeply divided as the Members of Parliament, and hostilities began to break out between supporters and opponents of the King. In order to force his opponents to acknowledge the reality of the situation which they had created, Charles raised his standard at Nottingham in August, thus turning the shambles which presently existed into an official civil war.

The King had reached this impasse largely because of a breakdown of communications. His court was isolated from the real world, and occupied only by favourites who flattered his self-delusions. He had no intention of converting to Rome; indeed both he and Laud detested the Catholic Church, but he never made these reservations clear, and allowed himself to be represented as a crypto-papist. He had also a very strong sense of his royal mission, and believed that the existing laws represented a just balance between the rights of the Crown and its duties. He had no difficulty in accepting that only Parliament could grant taxes, but believed that its other claims were an infringement of his prerogative. He was inflexible when he saw a principle at stake, and was ready to see principles where ordinary men saw only expediency. As a result of these failings, he was not trusted, either by the Scots or by his English subjects, and the concessions which he made were not believed in. It was felt that if his circumstances improved, he would repudiate them as having been made under duress. Consequently the opposition leaders felt compelled to drive him into such a position of weakness that he would not be able to do that, and it was over that issue that the apparently united House of Commons of early 1641 finally divided.

42

CIVIL WAR AND THE DEFEAT OF THE KING (1642–1649)

At first the auguries for a royal victory were good. The King at least knew what he was fighting for, whereas Parliament was divided. Charles was defending his executive authority, and could draw on the traditional loyalty that his office commanded. Many of those who had been highly critical of his policies, particularly his suspected Catholicism, nevertheless rallied to him when his authority was directly challenged in this fashion. At the same time most Members of Parliament could not conceive of any other kind of government, and were most reluctant to assume the executive responsibility which was now thrust upon them. Their ambitions extended no further than forcing the King to abandon what they saw as newly usurped powers, and to reduce the prerogative to its traditional limitations. In other words they were fighting for an irresistible bargaining position, rather than for total victory. They did not want such a victory, because they would not have known what to do with it. Only a minority at this early stage were sufficiently radical as to conceive of a system of government without the King, and were prepared to countenance his removal.

Having abandoned his capital, Charles was forced to see London and much of the wealthy south-east of the country pass under parliamentary control. It took some time to organise the local government in these areas, in the form of County Committees and Assessments (taxation) ordered by Ordinance of the Lords and Commons, and longer still to acclimatise the local elites to obey these Ordinances rather than royal commissions. Not all were prepared to acquiesce in such changes, and there remained a 'malignant' minority in most counties, until the system of sequestration removed them from the scene. Some joined the King; others chose to lie low at home, awaiting an opportunity to buy back their own lands when these were sold off. Meanwhile the King, who controlled most of the north and west of the country, went on using Commissions of Array to raise men, and Commissions of the Peace to govern them. His finances largely depended at this stage on voluntary contributions, which were generously provided by his backers, who included most of the wealthy men of the regions. Neither side was efficient from a military point of view, but Parliament scored a major success when the navy (largely built up by ship money) declared against the King in July 1642. The actual fighting of the first few months was inconclusive. Charles conceived the strategy of a three-pronged advance on London, and won a somewhat equivocal victory at Edgehill in October, before being turned back in a virtually bloodless encounter with the Trained Bands at Turnham Green in November. The fact was that his northern and western forces were reluctant to advance leaving such towns as Hull and Plymouth untaken behind them, so his strategy was frustrated as much by that factor as by parliamentary arms. For its part, Parliament, disappointed by the performance of it troops, decided to draw on the religious enthusiasm of its East Anglian supporters, and formed the army of the Eastern Association in December 1642. This army was professionally led, and paid for largely by the taxation of London. Nevertheless royalist successes followed in the North and West, and John Pym, the parliamentary leader, decided to invoke the assistance of the Scots. Negotiations followed because the Scots agenda was significantly different from that of the assembly in London, and it was up to the Westminster Assembly, convened in June, to decide whether the Presbyterian system which applied in Scotland could be extended to England also. Under severe pressure, it decided that it could and in September the Solemn League and Covenant was signed whereby the Scots agreed to send an army to help Parliament, and in return a Calvinist system of Church government would be established south of the border. John Pym died in December 1643, and left this poisoned chalice to his successors. Meanwhile Parliament had set up a new fiscal system to pay for its war effort, based partly on the 'weekly pay' or assessment, and partly on a selective levy on all those suspected of royalism. Both these methods, and particularly the latter, aroused considerable resentment because the judgement was a subjective one, but no effective resistance resulted.

The first benefit of the Solemn League came in January 1644, when a Covenanting army, led by the Earl of Leven, crossed the border into Northumberland. Unable to match so large and professional a force, the Marquis of Newcastle, the royalist commander in the North, was forced to retreat to York. Meanwhile the army of the Eastern Association, commanded by the Earl of Manchester and Oliver Cromwell, advanced from the South and collided with the main royalist field army commanded by Prince Rupert, the King's cousin, at Marston Moor in July. Manchester's victory on that occasion ended Charles's control of the North, leaving Leven's troops in virtual control of the Northumbria. In response to this decisive intervention, the Westminster Assembly authorised a new Directory of Worship, modelled on the Second Book of Discipline, and the Committee of Both Kingdoms was set up to ensure political cooperation between the two regimes, which had largely taken over the royal responsibilities of government. In spite of a royalist victory at Lostwithiel in August, the King's main army was defeated at Newbury in October, and futile negotiations followed between the two sides at Uxbridge. The King was not prepared to make any further concessions, and the atmosphere of the talks was soured by the fact that Archbishop Laud was executed while they were going on. The failure of these talks had a critical impact on the parliamentary leadership, because it began to seem obvious that discussions of this kind, even from a position of strength, were a waste of time. Until the King was absolutely defeated, no progress would be made, and this played into the hands of those radicals who were prepared, if necessary, to do without him. Victory became the priority, and this meant getting rid of those half-hearted commanders, like the Earl of Manchester, whose objective had always been merely to force Charles into a corner. A Self-Denying Ordinance was decreed during April 1645, whereby all existing commanders would lay down their commissions, and be reappointed if thought fit for the new task. Oliver Cromwell and Thomas Fairfax emerged as the new General Officers, and between them they set up the New Model Army, professionally officered and disciplined, which they could afford to do thanks to the financial support of London, whose trade had revived as its government became more settled. Fairfax became the New Model's commander, and at the head of his brand-new force he caught and destroyed the King's last main field army at the Battle of Naseby, near Market Harborough, on 14 June. The royalist cause no longer had the resilience to recover from such a setback, and, following a further defeat at Langport in July, Charles retreated to Oxford to face a bleak future.

In January 1645 Parliament authorised the new Directory of Worship, which had been approved by the Westminster Assembly, but for a few months its use remained optional. Then in August the use of the traditional Prayer Book was prohibited, and a parliamentary ordinance introduced the Presbyterian order for general use. However, ecclesiastical discipline had broken down by this time, and it was an ordinance more honoured in the breach than the observance. In the following March the order to set up a Presbyterian system was repeated, and the offices of bishop and archbishop were formally abolished. This meant that the enforcement of the new order became a matter for the County Committees, and in practice most congregations went their own ways, well ahead of any official endorsement of independency. In May 1546 Charles I surrendered to the Scots, perhaps thinking them to be more amenable to his programme than the English, and in June the last royalist stronghold of Oxford surrendered, bringing the First Civil War to a close. Now the time had come for the parliamentary leadership to exploit their victory, and extract the last concessions from Charles. In July they presented the Newcastle propositions to him, but he, with an obduracy which is hard to believe given his circumstances, seems to have come to the conclusion that his opponents needed him more than he needed them. He refused to concede on certain key issues and the talks broke down. By this time Parliament was seriously at odds with the army, and he may have been hoping to exploit those differences to his own advantage. Parliament was still committed to a royal system of government, however modified, but the army was beginning to come to the conclusion that power derived from the people, and that the officers of any society, including kings, derived their power by delegation – in which case Charles was dispensable. The King clearly did not understand the nature of this radicalism, otherwise he would have hastened to come to terms with Parliament while there was still time. Understanding this, and wearying of their prisoner, the Scots handed Charles over to Parliament in January 1647. He did not, however, remain long in his new custody, because Parliament, with more courage than common sense, proposed to disband the army without meeting its demands for arrears of pay. The result was a mutiny in June, and the King was seized by the soldiers. The 'Heads of Proposals' was presented to Charles by the army in August, but he, now consciously playing with fire, rejected these also, attempting to take advantage of the fact that the military grandees were now faced by a Leveller mutiny in their own ranks. In a sense this worked, because while the army was engrossed in the Putney debates on the nature of democracy, and whether the army could hold a popular mandate, he escaped from custody and took refuge on the Isle of Wight. From there in December he signed an engagement with the Scots, whereby they agreed to support the minimal position which he had by that time adopted. The result was a formal vote of 'no address' in Parliament, which indicated that they were no longer prepared to do business with him.

The Second Civil War which followed was a thing of shreds and patches, of small risings easily suppressed, except in one connection. The Scots invaded England on behalf of the King, and were defeated at the Battle of Preston in August. This defeat ended the Second Civil War, and the King was retaken by the army, which had by this time emerged as the dominant force in English politics.

Further negotiations with the grandees (Cromwell, Ireton and Fairfax) followed, and renewed threats of Leveller mutiny in the ranks. By December Cromwell had finally given up on the King, and decided that extreme measures were called for. Parliament stood in the way of such a strategy, but a new election on the existing franchise would have produced a house of royalists, so a different way had to be found. In December Colonel Pride, with a file of musketeers, descended on Westminster and excluded all those members who were not known to be sympathetic to the army's cause. This manoeuvre, known as 'Pride's purge', excluded some 140 of the 200 sitting members, leaving a rump which promptly arrogated to itself the name and powers of Parliament, and set up a court to try the King for treason against his people. This was an offence unknown to the law, as Charles immediately pointed out, standing on a constitutional propriety which no longer existed. However, by this time the soldiers were determined to have his blood, and there could only be one outcome. He was found guilty and executed on 31 January 1649. A few days later, the monarchy and the House of Lords were formally abolished, and England became a republic.

In a sense Charles had thrown away a winning hand by his obstinacy. If he had come to terms with the Scots in 1643 instead of 1648, the whole story might have been very different. He should have been able to draw on long traditions of loyalty to the monarchy, and up to a point he did that; but he was not trusted, and that was as much due to his poor communication skills as his programme. Nevertheless until the last minute he was the innovator, and until they surrendered the initiative to the army, Parliament stood for tradition, a fact reflected in the age profiles of the armies. The royalists were significantly younger than their opponents. In the event it was the King's refusal to admit that he was in any way responsible to his people for his actions, quite as much as his defence of the Church, which brought about his downfall. In January 1642 Charles had sent Henrietta Maria to the Netherlands, to take advantage of the recent marriage of their daughter Mary to the young William of Orange, and in the hope of raising some support there. She did not succeed in obtaining any money, either there or subsequently in France, but she did continue to write, encouraging his intransigence from a safe distance. Her younger children were with her, but Charles wished to keep his eldest son with him, and did so until 1645, when he sent him to take refuge in the Scilly Isles. Prince Charles then moved uneasily between that haven and the Isle of Jersey, withdrawing eventually to France in June 1647 when Jersey fell to the parliamentary fleet. He was eighteen when his father was executed, leaving him apparently without prospects. However, the abolition of the Crown of England did not apply in Scotland, and he was proclaimed in Edinburgh in February 1649. It remained to be seen what he could make of that development.

43

THE INTERREGNUM: OLIVER CROMWELL

The monarchy having been abolished, a vacuum now existed at the centre of affairs, and this was filled by the creation of a Council of State, consisting partly of Rumpers and partly of senior army officers. Such an executive was a fair reflection of the realities of the political situation, but had not a shred of constitutional standing. The same could be said of the Rump itself, which still bore the name of a parliament, but in its purged and emasculated state could hardly be said to represent anyone – certainly not the constituencies which had originally elected it. Local government, on the other hand, was much less severely disrupted than these revolutionary developments might suggest. There had indeed been a shift in all counties, as royalist activists had been removed and replaced, but these replacements had come from among the existing gentry. Minor gentlemen had come to the fore, either because they had bought up sequestered estates, or because they had been active in the parliamentary cause, but very few of the County Committees and other jurisdictional bodies were recruited from outside the 'magic circle' of the existing ruling class. Leveller ideas, such as those expressed in the Third Agreement of the People in May 1649, had little impact outside the army, and not very much inside it after the Leveller mutiny had been suppressed in the same month. Leveller propaganda was a useful bogey with which to threaten the conservative, but the Council of State, the Rump and the County Committees were all united against it, and its egalitarian programme made no progress at all. This social and administrative conservatism was one of the main reasons why, when the republic ran out of ideas in 1660, it was relatively easy to restore the traditional management structure. In May 1649 England was declared to be a free commonwealth, but it was not at all clear what that meant because the country had to be governed, and not even the most optimistic revolutionary believed that that would happen spontaneously, certainly not the members of the Council of State. The question was what form the new constitution would take, and who would be responsible for setting it up. The one thing that was not in doubt was that the country was now a republic.

Meanwhile the war was not over. In Ireland the Catholic confederates held the upper hand, and the English were hanging on by their fingertips. So it was to Ireland that the Council sent Oliver Cromwell and the New Model Army in the summer, no doubt relieved to find military employment for what otherwise looked like a political force. He landed in August 1649, and took the towns of Drogheda and Wexford by assault over the next two months, massacring the garrisons in a display of calculated frightfulness. Although these garrisons contained quite a few English royalists, the majority were native Irish Catholics whom Cromwell's men regarded as a subhuman species. Cromwell himself returned from Ireland in May 1650, but the conquest continued without him, because for the first time an English government was prepared to devote adequate resources to the reduction of the island. Extensive confiscations followed and the landholding pattern was transformed, creating long-term grievances. At home Gerrard Winstanley and his Diggers began their social experiment at Walton-on-Thames, sending shivers of apprehension down conservative spines. They need not have worried, because the Digger movement collapsed in the following year under the pressure of economic realities and their own extravagant expectations. The Diggers were a secular movement, but the absence of ecclesiastical discipline also led to the emergence and brief flourishing of strange religious sects, such as the Ranters, whose influence peaked in 1650, before the Rump pinned them back with a Blasphemy Act, passed in August. Prince Charles, having sworn to the Scottish Covenant, arrived in his northern kingdom in June, and the Covenanters rallied to him. The battle for the control of Scotland then commenced. Cromwell, who had in the meantime been created Lord General, that is Commander in Chief of all the forces of the Commonwealth, defeated the Scots at Dunbar and took Edinburgh Castle. However, that was not the end of Charles, who was crowned at Scone, the ancient coronation place of the kings of Scotland, in January 1651, and while the English were occupied with the reduction of the lowlands, led a bold (or foolhardy) expedition into England. Cromwell immediately switched his priorities and went in pursuit, catching and defeating the invaders at Worcester in September. It was after this defeat that the fugitive Charles famously hid in the oak tree at Boscobel before escaping to France in the following month. Without their king, Scottish resistance crumbled, and the fall of Dundee in September really spelled the end of Scottish independence for the time being. The country was placed under reliable agents of the English government until the union of the two former kingdoms was proclaimed in April 1654.

In foreign affairs the first thought of the Council of State was for a Protestant alliance, and negotiations commenced with the United Provinces. However, it soon transpired that commercial rivalry between the two states was too great for these to succeed. In October the Rump passed a Navigation Act which was a direct attack upon the Dutch carrying trade, and relations deteriorated still further. War broke out in May 1652, and this put the English navy, reorganised under Robert Blake, to a severe test because the Dutch were the foremost maritime power of the age. It acquitted itself well, winning victories in the Downs and the Channel before being beaten at Dungeness in November. Meanwhile the North American colonies, which had not been touched by the Civil War, except that they had received fugitives from both sides, were brought under the control of the Rump by a moderate show of naval force, and amended their constitutions accordingly. By the beginning of 1653 the Council of State had had enough of the Rump, with its non-existent mandate, but took fright when it proposed to dissolve itself and hold entirely new elections. Realising that if these were held on the existing franchise the result would be a predominantly royalist assembly, Cromwell acted to dissolve it at once, ignoring the statute which prohibited such an action without its own consent, and the Council set up instead the Instrument of Government. Before that happened, however, he experimented with a Nominated Assembly, for which the Council chose 144 members for their known loyalty to the regime, in the hope of gaining something which looked like a parliament, but which would be more biddable than the Rump had proved. This assembly, usually known from the name of one its members as Barebone's Parliament, proved too idealistic for Cromwell's taste. It launched attacks on Chancery, on lay patronage and on tithes, thereby offending most of those vested interests which were still tolerant of the unelected regime. In December Cromwell persuaded some of the more conservative members to stage a coup, and return the Assembly's powers to him. The Instrument then came into force, a written constitution under the terms of which Cromwell himself became Protector of England, Scotland and Ireland, holding roughly the executive powers formerly wielded by the King, and a parliament was to be elected to which members would also be sent from Scotland and Ireland. Since he believed in godly alliances, Cromwell was averse to the Anglo-Dutch war, and after the great naval victory at Texel in July sought means to bring it to an end. In that quest he was successful, not merely agreeing peace between the two republics at Westminster in April 1654, but forming a defensive alliance. Treaties with Sweden and Denmark rapidly followed, creating a Protestant northern bloc against the possibility of either French or Spanish aggression. Cromwell, who had grown up in the early seventeenth century, instinctively regarded Spain as being the main danger to England's interests. In December of that year he began an aggressive foreign policy with attacks on the Spanish American colonies in the Elizabethan style, which escalated into full-scale war in 1655.

The first Protectorate parliament had met in September 1654, consisting of 240 representatives from England and 30 each from Scotland and Ireland – the first United Kingdom assembly. This was elected on revised constituencies, and a substantial property qualification, and contained quite a lot of 'old parliament men'. As a result it began to attack Cromwell's policy of religious toleration, which had been established by Ordinance before it met, and to question the validity of the Instrument of Government under whose terms it was convened. Profoundly irritated by its uncooperative attitude, Cromwell dismissed it in January 1655. The real reason for Parliament's obstructiveness, it soon transpired, was discontent with the continued political role of the army, which was largely responsible for the unpopular policy of religious toleration. Cromwell felt that he owed it to his soldiers, many of whom were religious radicals, and who had fought for the toleration of their faith. The army was, however, necessary for security reasons, as Glencain's rising in Scotland and Penruddock's rebellion in Wiltshire demonstrated. Nevertheless Cromwell was sensitive to the issue and in the summer of 1655 began to plan a new militia to replace the professional troops. Unfortunately, this required the introduction of Major Generals to oversee the creation of these new units, and these officers were soon given extensive powers over local government. Ten regions were created, each with a Major General in charge, and these were deeply unpopular with those county elites who were otherwise willing to serve the

Protectorate. They were eventually abolished in June 1657 as a result of pressure from the second parliament. Meanwhile, in order to concentrate on his war with Spain, Cromwell had signed a defensive treaty with France, which resulted in the exiled Stuart court being expelled from St Germain. Charles and his followers took refuge in the Spanish Netherlands, where the welcome they were accorded was seen as an act of war. At the same time, Blake's fleet established a presence in the Mediterranean, successfully curbing the activities of the Barbary corsairs, which had been interfering in the trade of the Levant Company.

The second Protectorate parliament, which met in September 1656, proved to be no more amenable that its predecessor. It was generously supportive of the war with Spain, but fiercely critical of the Major Generals, and determined to curb the Protector's policy of religious toleration. In this last aim it made no progress, but the Major Generals were sacrificed to its wrath. Most of these were men of humble origin, hence the antagonism which they aroused, but were honest men trying to do the task which they had been allocated. They seem to have been genuinely puzzled and hurt by their own unpopularity, which shows them to have been without that sensitivity to local opinion which their positions actually required. The frustrations of having to deal with a recalcitrant parliament prompted some thought in the Council of State about the real foundation of the Protector's power, which still rested on the loyalty of his soldiers, and aroused some doubts about the republic's validity. For all practical purposes, Cromwell was king, so why not call him such? That would give him the traditional benefits of the prerogative, and might break his dependence on the army, which everyone now agreed was a handicap to the regime. The result was the Humble Petition and Advice, which was presented in May 1657, its title eloquently expressing its nature. After a struggle with his conscience, Cromwell refused the crown, but agreed to new powers for himself, and the institution of a second chamber for the parliament. He was inaugurated into his refurbished office with coronation-like splendour in June, and proceeded to nominate the members of the second chamber, who were mostly tried-and-tested Protectorate loyalists, including quite a number of senior army officers. The old House of Lords was not represented. In September 1656 a Spanish treasure fleet was intercepted, which had been the dream of English sea-dogs since the 1570s, and huge amount of booty captured. Since this was the work of the state navy, there was no call to share this loot with anyone, and the public coffers were healthily replenished. 1657 saw the agreement with France extended into an offensive alliance against Spain, and Blake won a great naval victory in the Canaries. It was to be his last service to the state, because he died in August, depriving the Commonwealth of its most successful military commander – apart from Cromwell, who had never been tested on the international stage.

The second session of the second Protectorate parliament met on 20 January 1658. It was a bitter meeting, dominated by quarrels between the two houses, and unproductive in terms of legislation. The Protector brought it to an end after less than three weeks in a fit of exasperation which did not bode well for the future. The war against Spain continued, and the French alliance was continued by a new agreement, signed in March. In June Anglo-French forces, which featured a contingent of the New Model Army, fighting in Europe for the first time, inflicted a severe defeat on the Spaniards at the Battle of the Dunes. As a result of that victory, Dunkirk was handed over to the English, who wasted no time in eliminating what had become an irritating centre of piracy. In September Oliver Cromwell died at the age of fifty-nine, and the justification for the Protectorate came to an end. The Humble Petition and Advice had given him the opportunity to name his own successor, and in accordance with the quasi-monarchical nature of his position, he nominated his elder son, Richard. Richard was a civilian, and Oliver might have done better to name his second son Henry, who was a soldier and had at least some standing with the army. Richard had none, and in May 1659 the army turned on him, forcing his resignation at the end of a fairly innocuous session of Parliament, which had failed to give him the standing which he needed to outface the soldiers. The officers, however, were running out of ideas and the rank and file began to suspect that they were being used simply to support the grandees' ambitions – whatever they might be. They could think of nothing better, having brought about the down fall of the Protectorate, than to recall the Rump, that last vestige of traditionally constituted authority. General John Lambert won some credibility by putting down a royalist rising in Cheshire in August, but inevitably the army quarrelled with the Rump, expelling it in October, and then demonstrating its own political bankruptcy by recalling it in December, simply because the officers did not know what else to do.

Into this scene of well-nigh terminal chaos came George Monck, the commander of the army in Scotland. Monck seems to have had no firm plan in mind, but recognised the urgent need to restore stability to a government which was fast disintegrating. He also had his own men under firm control, which was more than could be said for the troops in England. Having reached London, he entered into an understanding with the City Fathers, whereby they agreed to fund him while he sorted out the mess. He then took the logical step of readmitting to the parliament the survivors of those who had been expelled in Pride's purge of twelve years earlier, and urging the long-standing parliament to vote its own dissolution, which it did in March. Elections were then ordered on the traditional franchise, and excluding Scotland and Ireland, for a convention parliament to clear up the mess. At that precise moment, in April 1660, Prince Charles issued the declaration of Breda, accepting all those reforming statutes which his father had approved in 1641, and referring the political and religious settlement to a future parliament. This struck exactly the right note, and George Monck, who was by this time in command of the only viable army, declared in favour of a restoration of the monarchy. When the convention parliament met on 25 April it turned out (as expected) to be strongly royalist in its composition, and at once accepted his proposal. Charles II was proclaimed in London on 8 May, and he, having been escorted from the Netherlands by his loyal fleet, entered London on the 29th. On observing the warmth of his welcome, he is alleged to have wondered why he had been so long away. It was officially the twelfth year of his reign.

If the English republic achieved one thing, it was to ground in the minds of Englishmen of all classes a deep-rooted distrust of standing armies. Having run out of ideas, the officers of the New Model Army had eventually acknowledged defeat, and the men had settled for their arrears of pay. It was an unheroic end to what had been in many ways an enlightened experiment in government, but the lesson chiefly learned was that the laws of England could only be enforced by a civilian administration. The divine right of kings had if anything been reinforced by the experiences of the Interregnum. Democratic experiments could be forgotten, because the social hierarchy had never been displaced for all the radical politics which had gone on at the top, but there was no appetite to continue that radicalism once the Great Protector was dead. The Good Old Cause, as republicanism came to be known, was not dead, but it had been so far discredited that for the next twenty years it served mainly to keep the royal government within the bounds which Parliament decreed. There was no desire to revisit the horrendous experiences of the Civil War. Oliver Cromwell had been a virtual king, and had kept a virtual court, but that did little to preserve the continuity of courtly culture. Charles, who was a very different man from his father, had to start again from where he was.

44

CHARLES II (REIGNED 1660–1685)

Charles began as he intended to go on. In the summer of 1648, while he was still at St Germain, he took Lucy Walters as his mistress, and the future Duke of Monmouth was born sometime in 1649. However, his personal experience was not matched by political status. Although he set up his own Privy Council and styled himself Charles II after February 1649, he received no help beyond the continued hospitality of the French court. No foreign power would recognise the regicide government in England, but that did not mean that they recognised Charles II, or gave any countenance to his representatives. Disappointed by this lack of backing, he departed from France in August 1649 and went to Jersey, which was still under royalist control, where he began negotiating with the Scots. His most favoured councillors, who included George Digby, the heir to the Earl of Bristol, were all in favour of concessions in that quarter, and he duly signed the Covenant. He arrived at the Moray Firth at midsummer 1650 and was warmly welcomed to his kingdom where he had been proclaimed in the previous March. Nevertheless there were differences of opinion among his followers, the old royalists disagreeing with the 'Kirk party' of covenanters, and Charles became so offended with the latter that he considered withdrawing altogether. He might well have done so following the severe defeat inflicted upon his forces by Cromwell at Dunbar in September 1650, but instead that somewhat simplified his position. It was the covenanting army which had been defeated, which enabled him to form a new party consisting of the Old Royalists and based on Glasgow. It was this party which arranged his coronation at Scone in 1651, and enabled him to become an effective king in that part of Scotland which was not under English control. Cromwell held most of the lowlands, and as he moved to conquer Fife, Charles slipped in behind him and entered England. The New Model set off after him with about 50,000 men, and caught him at Worcester. They were numerous enough to overwhelm Charles's motley force, the whole of which was either killed or captured in the resulting battle. By incredible good luck, the Prince himself escaped and took refuge with his mother in France, where for the time being he eked out a penurious existence. At about this time he broke with Lucy Walters, and began to take other mistresses, probably fathering several bastard children for whom he was unable to provide. Perhaps for that reason he travelled extensively in Germany in 1653–54, at the same time trying to encourage rebellions in his name in Scotland, all of which turned out to be futile. Expelled from France as a result of the Anglo-French treaty of 1655, he took refuge with his small court in the Spanish Netherlands, Spain being at war with

England, and signed an agreement with the Archduke in Brussels in April 1656 whereby he was accorded a pension of 3,000 ecus (about £1,000) a month. The Franco-Spanish War was ended by the Peace of the Pyrenees in 1658, to which England was a party, but Charles's pension was continued – for the time being.

The convention parliament which had issued the invitation to Charles to return to England remained in session until December. It resurrected the House of Lords in its traditional form, continued the parliamentary excise tax and renewed the Navigation Act; but it did not make any religious settlement, and it did not make adequate financial provision for a royal government. There were protracted discussions on the former of these issues at Worcester House and at the Savoy, because Charles was in favour of conciliation, and so, generally speaking, was his Lord Chancellor Edward Hyde. However, it became obvious that political opinion on the whole was against them. On the latter issue there was confusion, because nobody knew exactly what the government cost, and Charles immediately began to show signs of extravagance which the convention parliament was reluctant to support. When it was dissolved, preparations were immediately put in hand for the election of its successor, which convened in May; and this, the so-called Cavalier Parliament was to run through fifteen sessions, until 1678. During its early sessions, this parliament was best known for its intolerant Anglicanism. Within ten days of its meeting the bishops had been restored to the House of Lords, and it was decreed that all members should take the sacrament in accordance with the established rite. In spite of the presence of about a hundred members who had sat in the Long Parliament, the Anglican reaction was in full flow. This was assisted by Venner's revolt in January 1661, which, although it posed no threat, enabled the orthodox to equate dissent with sedition in a way which had not been seen since the 1590s. Convocation amended the Prayer Book, and it was re-imposed by a new Act of Uniformity in 1662. This was the first of a series of Acts against non-conformists, misleadingly called the Clarendon Code. In fact the Earl of Clarendon (as Edward Hyde had become in 1661) did his best to water these measures down by interventions in the House of Lords, but was unsuccessful on each occasion. The real force of this reaction came from the gentry in the counties, who had decided on the basis of bitter experience that the Church and the King's government must stand together. The last time they had surrendered their ecclesiastical monopoly, the King had first lost a civil war, and then his head. Charles himself did not see it that way, and tried in December 1662 to mitigate the terms of the Uniformity Act with a Declaration of Indulgence, but the outcry in Parliament was so great that he was forced to withdraw it the following April. Charles may have hankered for the kind of absolutism which his friend Louis XIV enjoyed, but he simply did not have the resources. The Cavalier Parliament estimated that he needed £1.2 million to run the government, although how this sum was derived is not clear. This it provided by a series of grants and other measures, so that the King's income from 1660 to 1664 was just about of that order. However, the King was spending more, and by the latter date his debts stood at £1.25 million. This was likely to increase, partly because he was extravagant, partly through inadequate accounting, and partly because Parliament had underestimated his needs. Charles might prefer the racecourse at Newmarket or the brothels of Covent Garden to the dreary business of government, but that was not the sole reason for his difficulties. Taxation was simply not producing enough income, forcing the King to borrow to make ends meet. This was one reason why he married. On 22 May 1662 he wedded Catherine of Braganza, a Portuguese princess who brought a substantial dowry with her, together with the colonial ports of Tangier and Bombay. The latter was rapidly handed over to the East India Company, but the former provided a naval base in the Mediterranean which was used for a number of years until it became too expensive to maintain. His marriage inevitably involved a treaty of friendship and alliance with Portugal, which should be seen as part of the tidying-up operation at the end of the Spanish war.

In 1662 also he signed a treaty with the United Provinces, but unlike that with Portugal, this was not destined to endure. Indeed, commercial relations between the two states were as bad as they had been during the recent war, and the treaty did nothing to improve that situation. Instead the renewed Navigation Act of 1660 was a much more direct attack on the Dutch carrying trade than its 1651 predecessor had been. A state of war effectively existed from the summer of 1664, and it was formally declared on 22 February following. At first the war was popular, and Parliament cooperative. In November 1664 it granted the unprecedented sum of £2.5 million for this purpose, and the first naval encounter at Lowestoft on 3 June 1665 was a striking victory. However, thereafter incompetence and bad luck turned the situation around. Early in 1666 France and Denmark joined the United Provinces against England, the great Four Days' Battle in the Channel in June was at best drawn, and in June 1667 came the disastrous Dutch raid on the Medway, which cost England more fighting ships than all the battles joined together. Meanwhile, to the joy of Protestant zealots, London had been subjected to the twin ordeals of plague and fire. The former was not unexpected, because the disease had been endemic in the city for years, but during 1665 it escalated out of control, killing as many as 70,000 people in a year and severely disrupting the economic life of the capital. Its impact was, however, overshadowed by that of the five-day fire which raged in September 1666, destroying over 13,000 homes and goods to the value of £3.5 million. These two disasters between them reduced royal income from London by about 30 per cent, and necessitated another approach to Parliament. £1.8 million was granted on condition that an enquiry was instituted into the public accounts, an investigation to which the King felt bound to yield. Charles had begun peace negotiations with the Dutch as early as January 1667, and these had been formalised in March. However, progress was slow, and it took the Dutch raid on Chatham and the parliamentary storm which that produced before terms were finally agreed at Breda in the autumn. As the military situation dictated, this was an unfavourable peace from England's point of view, her only significant gain being the colony of New York, which was not thought to be of any significance at the time. The Medway disaster spelled the end for the Earl of Clarendon. His political enemies had been mustering against him for some time, and Charles was never noted for loyalty to his long-time servants. On 30 August 1667 he was dismissed from office, and when Parliament reassembled in October, a process of impeachment was instituted. The charges of treason were ridiculous, and the impeachment would probably have failed, but Clarendon took the hint and retired into exile in France, where he completed his great *History of the Rebellion* and died in December 1674.

After the fall of Clarendon, Charles had two options. Either he could pursue a cavalier policy, strictly enforcing religious conformity and looking for Protestant alliances abroad; or a catholic policy, relaxing the penal laws, and entering into friendship with France. His ministers were bitterly divided on these issues – which is why the term Cabal is inappropriate – and the King himself increasingly favoured the catholic option. However, for the time being he held his fire, and when the French overran the Spanish Netherlands in the autumn of 1667, he even joined the United Provinces in an anti-French league. It was the need to detach England from this alliance which caused Louis XIV to send a special envoy to London in August 1668 to propose a new treaty of friendship. Although these talks were secret, Charles was soon at loggerheads with his parliament over the issue of religious toleration, and the two sessions of 1669 produced grants of only £300,000, well short of what was needed by any standard. In May 1670 his negotiations with France bore fruit in the secret Treaty of Dover, which was signed by Charles himself and by his crypto-Catholic ministers Arlington and Clifford. By its terms, the King agreed to join Louis in an attack upon the Dutch, for the duration of which conflict he would be paid £225,000 a year – not nearly enough to support such a conflict. Charles also declared himself to be a Catholic, and accepted French money and troops to secure his position in England when he should make his position public. However, the timing of such a declaration was left entirely to his discretion, and it is highly unlikely that he had any intention of making it. In December Charles made public his commitment to the French alliance and to war with the United Provinces, but omitted any statement of his personal religious position. The prospect of renewed war with the Dutch was not unwelcome and Parliament gave the King generous financial support, so much so that by the beginning of 1672 he was almost solvent. The radical fiscal device of the Stop of the Exchequer, which was resorted to in January was probably implemented to give credibility to Charles's complaints of continuing poverty rather than because it was really needed. On 15 March 1672 he issued another declaration of Indulgence, and two days later declared war on the United Provinces in alliance with France – two aspects of the same policy.

The war did not go well. French successes in the field led to the overthrow of the republican Dutch government, and its replacement by the monarchy of William III, but that merely stiffened the people's resolve. An Anglo-French fleet was badly mauled off Southwold in the summer of 1673, and Charles's attempts to dissociate his friendship for France from the threat of popery and arbitrary government were conspicuously unsuccessful. In April he withdrew his declaration of Indulgence, but at Easter his brother James declined to communicate in the Anglican mode, and his conversion to Rome became public knowledge. He and Clifford were forced to resign under the terms of the Test Act, and the latter was replaced as Treasurer by Sir Thomas Osbourne, who shortly after was raised to the peerage as Earl of Danby. James's principal enemy in the Council, the Earl of Shaftesbury, was shortly after dismissed as Lord Chancellor, expelled from the Council, and stripped of his public offices. Charles brought his unnecessary and expensive war to an end in February 1674 by the treaty of Westminster, putting his friendship with Louis on the back burner, and showing no signs of declaring himself to be a Catholic. If anything he had reverted to a cavalier policy, but it remained to be seen whether he would reap any benefit from that. Since the spring of 1673 Parliament had been seething with anti-Catholicism, and Danby, as chief minister, tried to persuade Charles to take advantage of that. He held conferences with the bishops, designed to promote the stricter enforcement of orthodoxy, and persuaded the King to open Parliament in April 1675 with a ringing endorsement of Anglican loyalty. Nevertheless he failed to woo Charles away from his friendship with Louis XIV, and the King signed two secret agreements with the latter in August 1675 and February 1676, by which Louis agreed to pay Charles a subsidy of £112,000 a year. Danby's response was to give government support to that programme of limitations on a Catholic successor which critics had been proposing since 1673. In the absence of any legitimate offspring from Charles's marriage to Catherine, James was his heir – and James was a Catholic. By the end of 1675 Danby was closer to the Cavalier Party in the House of Commons than at any time since his coming to power. Meanwhile hostility to the King's French alliance was growing, and not only in the minds of the Country Party. As the French army swept into Flanders in the spring of 1677 there was a general demand that Charles commit himself to defending the Spanish Netherlands against France. This demand was endorsed by Danby, and as a result the King prorogued Parliament.

The adjournment changed nothing, but it did make Danby more amenable to a plan by Charles to marry his brother's Protestant daughter Mary to William III of Orange. This may have been intended to spite his brother, but it seems more likely to have been designed to curry favour at home, as news of the betrothal was greeted with rejoicings. However, most likely of all is that it was an example of Charles inveterate deceitfulness. He made as though to follow up the marriage with a full treaty of friendship, and even began military preparations against France; but he clearly had no intention of pursuing either of these initiatives. The most likely explanation is that he intended to use the marriage as a means of persuading Louis to make peace, in the hope that this would defuse parliamentary opposition to his foreign policy. If that was the intention, then it failed on both counts, and when Parliament reassembled in January 1678 it became clear that the Commons' suspicions were as strong as ever. When the session was prorogued on 15 July, many feared the imminent establishment of popery and absolutism, backed by a French army of around 30,000. There could be no better demonstration of the failure of Danby's policies.

By the time that the parliament was dissolved at the end of the year, these fears had apparently been confirmed by the discovery of the Popish Plot. This had been dreamed up by Titus Oates and Israel Tonge, who revealed it to the King on 13 August 1678. The details were vague, but they involved the assassination of the King, an Irish uprising, a sympathetic rebellion in England and an invasion from France. In spite of inconsistencies in the testimony, and obvious fabrications, the Privy Council was impressed by the circumstantial detail, and when Sir Edmund Berry Godfrey, who had taken the plotters' first testimonies, was found murdered on 12 October, all doubts apparently disappeared. Anti-Catholic hysteria gripped the country, and between the end of 1678 and 1681 about thirty-five people were tried and executed for their alleged part in this non-existent plot. The only person who was not deceived was the King, who coolly took advantage of the emotions aroused to return to his cavalier policy by issuing an anti-Catholic proclamation, and securing the passage of a new Test Act, excluding Catholics from Parliament, an Act from which he managed to get James exempted. By these devices, the opposition in Parliament was contained. However, Danby was now the prime target, and on the 21st, following a revelation that he had known of Charles's secret negotiations with Louis and had not disclosed them to the House, articles of impeachment were drawn up against him. On 30 December the King prorogued the session, and on 24 January 1679 dissolved the Cavalier Parliament.

The new parliament, which convened on 6 March 1679, was dominated by the Exclusion issue. It pursued the impeachment of Danby, but failed to secure a conviction, consigning him to the Tower instead. On 15 May the first Exclusion Bill was read, providing that on Charles's death the crown should pass not to James but to the next in line, who was not named. On its second reading, it passed by 207 votes to 128, and two weeks later the King dissolved the session. For the next two years the country was divided on this issue. The Exclusionists (who came to be called Whigs) were sympathetic to Protestant dissent, and suspicious of the oppressive policies of the bishops; while the Anti-Exclusionists (Tories) were driven principally by a desire to defend the established Church. So serious did this division appear that some feared a new civil war, but Charles was much stronger in 1680 than his father had been in 1642. The Whigs organised themselves in Parliament in 1680 and 1681, by means of Green Ribbon Clubs and printed propaganda, in a manner which anticipates the party system of more recent days. But their position appeared stronger than it was, and the fatal weakness of their programme was that they had no alternative heir to propose. Their strategy therefore remained entirely negative, and this shortly placed the initiative in the hands of the Tories, who were more numerous although less well organised. Charles remained adamantly opposed to any concessions, and in charge both of the London Trained Bands and of local government in a way which his father had not been. Surprisingly enough, he was also solvent, and not immediately dependent upon parliamentary grants. The 1681 session was called, perhaps symbolically, to Oxford, and the Whig grandees turned up with armed men behind them, but the King called their bluff. No one really wanted a return to the traumatic days of 1642, and Charles was able to dissolve the session on 28 March, having comprehensively rejected the Exclusionists' case. Shortly after he caused a proclamation to be issued, recalling the horrors of civil war, when 'religion, liberty and property were lost and gone, when the monarchy was shaken off, and could never be restored until that was revived'. So the Tories successfully smeared their opponents with the taint of republicanism, and Charles was set to enjoy the last few years of his reign in triumph.

From 1681 onward, the King harassed the Whigs, trying to ensure that they never again repeated their parliamentary ascendancy of 1679. The Earl of Shaftesbury was committed to the Tower in July on a charge of treason, and although he escaped execution he was driven into exile in November 1682. He died in Holland in January 1683. William Lord Russell and Algernon Sidney were executed in 1683 for involvement in the Rye House plot, a somewhat notional scheme to assassinate Charles on his way to Newmarket. Other executions followed. The commissions of the peace were reorganised to exclude known Whig sympathisers, and *Quo Warranto* proceedings were instituted against the City of London, which resulted in all public appointments having to have the King's approval. Many other boroughs took the hint, and surrendered their charters to the Crown, with similar results. Charles was able to take this high line for two reasons: firstly he had a lot of support in the country, particularly over the cavalier religious policies of his later years; and secondly his financial position was sound. Thanks partly to a boom in trade, and partly to improved estate management, his income in 1684/85 had risen to £1.37 million; he was also less extravagant as he got older. He died on 6 February 1685, secure in the knowledge that his brother James would succeed him.

Charles had been an intelligent, amoral king who took advantage of political circumstances as he found them, without undue sentiment or the confusions of loyalty. He was witty, lazy and profligate. John Wilmot, Earl of Rochester, was among his favourites, a man of no political significance whatsoever, but excellent with witty epigraphs. Charles's best-known mistress is Nell Gwyn, the London orange seller, but there were many others of all social ranks. He fathered about thirteen acknowledged bastards, and probably several others who were not acknowledged, providing suitably for all of them. It was not for nothing that he was known as 'the father of his people'. He had political failures as well as successes, but the greatest of the latter was his victory over the Exclusionists, which gave England her first Catholic monarch for 130 years. It remained to be seen what kind of a fist James would make of it.

45

JAMES VII AND II (REIGNED 1685–1689)

James had been born on 14 October 1633, the fourth child of Charles I and Henrietta Maria. He was scarcely out of the nursery when the Civil War erupted in 1642. He remained with his father throughout the conflict, and was created Duke of York on 27 January 1644. Although with Charles when he surrendered to the Scots in 1646, he was able to take advantage of the King's few months of liberty in 1648 to escape to France, allegedly disguised as a girl. Thereafter he remained with his mother until the court was expelled to the Netherlands in 1655, returning to England on his brother's restoration in May 1660. He was created Lord High Admiral on 2 July 1660, and married Anne Hyde, the daughter of the Earl of Clarendon in December of that year. Anne presented him with several children, but only two girls, Mary and Anne, survived. Both were to take their place on the throne in due course, and both were brought up as Protestants under their mother's influence. However, his wife died in 1671, and in September 1673 the Duke took as his second wife Mary of Modena, the daughter of an Italian nobleman and a Catholic. By that time James had been 'outed' as a Catholic himself by refusing to take communion at Easter, and he was compelled to resign as Lord Admiral on 15 June, in accordance with the terms of the Test Act. This was a loss to the government as James had been a good admiral. Thereafter he lay low, but the lightning of the Popish Plot struck close, and his former secretary Edward Coleman was executed for his alleged part in it in November 1678. There may have been more substance to these charges than to many, because Coleman was in correspondence with Rome, and his papers were made public in April 1679. When the Exclusion crisis was over, in 1684, the Duke of York was quietly restored to the Privy Council, where he remained until Charles's death brought him to the throne. As a Privy Councillor he had undoubtedly been cognisant of the purges of county commissions and town councils, which policy he continued after his accession. He was crowned on 23 April 1685 with the traditional (Anglican) rites, and the first parliament of the reign met in May. This immediately demonstrated the wisdom of the exclusion policy which had been pursued, being

Tory-dominated and voting a generous supply. The King's position was also strengthened by two rebellions which took place during the summer. The first by the Earl of Argyll in Scotland and the second by the Duke of Monmouth in the South West of England. The latter was defeated at Sedgemoor in July, and was followed by the 'Bloody Assizes', which executed large numbers of those taken after the battle. There was a considerable exodus of Whig supporters to the New World in the aftermath of these defeats. The second session of the first parliament lasted less than two weeks, and in March 1686 James began to fall out with his Tory supporters, because he issued a direction to preachers to desist from preaching anti-Catholic sermons, which were a stock part of the Tory armoury.

By 1686 James was clearly trying to infiltrate Catholics into positions of public responsibility in defiance of the Test Act, and the papacy was becoming uneasy over his aggressive tactics, fearing the reaction which in the event occurred. In June a compliant judiciary found for the King in the test case of *Godden* v. *Hales*, empowering him to dispense individuals from the provisions of the Test Act, and in July he re-established the Court of High Commission, which had been abolished in 1641. In September, High Commission suspended Henry Compton, the Bishop of London, for refusing to enforce James's directive to preachers, and the Tories began to be seriously alarmed. By September 1686 40 per cent of the officers and 67 per cent of the rank and file in the Irish army were Catholics, and the Earl of Tyrconnell was able to pursue a campaign of Catholicisation in the Irish administration. In 1687 he replaced the Protestant Earl of Clarendon as Lord Lieutenant. James seems to have believed that a significant proportion, perhaps even a majority, of Englishmen were secret

Catholics, and he attempted to tap into that vein of support, which turned out to be virtually non-existent. This intention was thinly disguised as a policy of religious toleration, and in November 1686 he set up an office to sell certificates of dispensation to wealthy dissenters. In April 1687 he issued a general Declaration of Indulgence which suspended the Test and Corporation Acts altogether. At the same time he began a legal campaign to force Magdalen College, Oxford, to elect a Catholic as its President, and dismissed the Earl of Rochester from the Lord Treasurership. 1688 was the critical year. On 27 April James issued a second Declaration of Indulgence, which Archbishop Sancroft and six of his colleagues refused to read as required. They were charged with sedition. Then on 10 June Queen Mary gave birth to a son, and the prospect of a Catholic succession loomed. Because their marriage had been infertile for a number of years, doubts were immediately cast on the authenticity of this child, who was alleged to have been smuggled into the Queen's chamber in a warming pan, but there is no real doubt that it was James's lawful offspring. In place of a short-term problem, English Protestants now faced a long-term one, and action of some kind seemed to be imperative. The on 30 June the seven bishops were acquitted of seditious libel, and a representative selection of Whig and Tory leaders wrote to William of Orange, pledging their support if he brought a force to England.

William was a grandson of Charles I and a nephew of Charles II. He therefore had a claim to the throne in his own right, and he was married to James II's daughter Mary, who had her own claim. However, the real reason why he accepted the invitation to intervene in England lay in his lifelong struggle against Louis XIV. In European terms his position had been strengthened by the revocation of the Edict of Nantes in 1685, which had greatly improved his relations with the Dutch business community, and by the formation of the League of Augsburg, a coalition of anti-French German princes in 1686. However, the financial and military power of England would make all the difference to his prospects, and England had also been alienated by the revocation, which had sent thousands of Huguenot refugees to seek asylum there. In spite of the risks involved, he therefore determined to respond to the invitation. At this stage the English navy was prepared to resist him, but was kept in port by the 'Protestant wind' which blew in early November, and on the 5th of that month he landed at Torbay. Four days later he entered Exeter, and the West Country magnates, Whig and Tory alike, rallied to him in a remarkable demonstration of Protestant solidarity. On 21 November he began slowly to advance on London, as elsewhere in the country Whig and Tory leaders declared their support for him. At this stage William's intentions are unclear, because it seemed likely that James would make a fight of it. He was with his army at Salisbury, and it appeared that the army was loyal to him. However, on 23 November he lost his nerve and ordered a retreat to London. At that point one of his leading generals, John Churchill, defected to William, and that seems to have affected the army as a whole. It stood still and did nothing while William slowly advanced on the capital. In spite of the Guildhall declaration of support by the High Tory peers, on 22 December James gave up and fled to France, having dispatched his wife and son in advance. A parliament, hastily summoned on 28 December, when it met on 22 January 1689 declared the throne to be vacant by virtue of James's abdication. After a rearguard action in the Lords in favour of a regency, the crown was offered to William and Mary jointly at the end of January, and promptly accepted. The first stage of the Glorious Revolution was thus completed. What would have happened if James had stayed to make a fight of it, as he did later in Ireland, we do not know, but probably William would have gone home, because he had no desire to fight a civil war in England. As it turned out, that was not necessary.

46

WILLIAM III (REIGNED 1689–1702) AND MARY II (REIGNED 1689–1694)

William was the only son of William, Prince of Orange, and of Mary, the sister of Charles II. Born at The Hague on 4 November 1650, he never knew his father, who had died shortly before he was born, and was consequently brought up by his mother. He was a good linguist, being fluent in English and German as well as Dutch, and became a member of the Council of State in 1667, at the age of seventeen. He was Captain General of the Dutch forces during the Second Anglo-Dutch War, and succeeded to his father's office of Stadtholder in 1672. In November 1677 he married Mary, the daughter of the Duke of York, and in spite of his being a small, stooped figure who suffered from chronic asthma, their marriage was a happy and successful one. William's priority was his struggle against Louis XIV, and for that reason he accepted an invitation to intervene in the turbulent affairs of England in November 1688, where he arrived with 250 ships and about 20,000 men on the 5th of that month. In the face of this incursion, and of the support which it received, James II fled to France and was therefore deemed to have abdicated. There was some talk in the convention parliament of recognising Mary alone as queen, but William made it clear that he was not prepared to be his wife's 'gentleman usher', and they were jointly proclaimed as King and Queen on 13 February 1689. Although there were some ominous rumblings when 400 non-jurors refused the oath of allegiance, they were crowned together on 11 April. Before that happened a Declaration of Rights was read to the King and Queen in the Banqueting Hall at Westminster, and assented to by both of them. In December it was enacted as the Bill of Rights, embodying a broadly Whig interpretation of the constitution. In March James II landed at Kinsale in Ireland and the Catholic Irish rallied to him, the Dublin parliament passing the anti-English legislation which caused it to be known as the 'patriot parliament'. However, in July Colonel Kirke relieved the confederate Siege of Londonderry, and the following month William sent an army under his Dutch general Schomberg to follow up this success in Ireland. Meanwhile the Scots were showing their Jacobite credentials; a highland army under James Graham of Claverhouse defeated a royal force at Killiecrankie in July, only to suffer defeat and dismemberment at Dunkeld in August. The convention parliament of Scotland then bowed to the inevitable and accepted William III in April 1690, asking only that their Presbyterian system of Church government be continued – which was conceded.

Meanwhile England had joined the Grand Alliance against France, and become effectively its paymaster. The first session of William's first parliament in March 1690 granted the King the excise duty for life, and the second session in October made grants of over £4.6 million in support of the war effort, which was generally approved of. In July William turned aside from his Continental preoccupations to defeat James at the Battle of the Boyne, and force him to leave Ireland. This battle was later to acquire iconic significance for the Protestant ascendancy in Ireland, and was commemorated in the foundation of the Orange Order (which still exists) in Ulster. At the time it was decisive, and when William's forces took Limerick in October 1691 the Jacobite cause in Ireland became virtually extinct. A Protestant-dominated parliament in 1692 began a vigorous campaign of anti-Catholicism, which changed the political face of the island, although it did not much affect the faith of the ordinary people. At the same time the fortunes of the Continental war were fluctuating. The French beat an Anglo-Dutch fleet off Beachy Head in June 1690, and French forces took Mons in April 1691. In May 1692 the Allied fleet was victorious at La Hogue, but the French army took Namur in June and the Battle of Steenkirk in August was drawn. This was not good enough for the English parliament, and the fourth session which met in November 1692 was fiercely critical of the conduct of the war. With an eye to England's commercial interests, it demanded a 'blue water' strategy aimed at securing command of the trade routes, which was not necessarily in William's interests, although he depended heavily on the commercial sector for his financial support. The members wanted a Triennial Bill, decreeing an interval of no more than three years between parliaments, and in return were prepared to vote a war supply of another £4 million. In a reflection of Whig dominance they also voted a 20 per cent land tax, most of the landowners being in the Tory camp. By this time William was coming to the conclusion that the Whig–Tory consensus which had brought him to the throne was breaking down, and that he would be well advised in future to rely on Whig ministers. He therefore took advantage of the resignation of the Earl of Nottingham as Secretary of State by appointing

Charles Talbot, Earl of Shrewsbury, to that post; Edward Russell as Lord High Admiral; and Charles Montague as Chancellor of the Exchequer. At the same time in the fifth session of parliament, held in November 1693, he vetoed the Triennial and Place Bills held over from the previous session, secure in the knowledge that the Whig majority in the Commons would accept that.

At the same time the King's debt was growing to an alarming extent because of the expense of the war, and the need was clear for this to become a national liability. Taking the advice of his Whig financial ministers in April 1694 he authorised the creation of a national bank to carry this debt, and against strenuous Tory opposition the Bank of England came into existence, floating on an investment which was designed to cover the debt. On the back of this, the Triennial Bill became an Act, the King withdrawing his opposition in return for backing for the bank. The Tories did not give up their attacks on Whig finance, which flared up again in the first session of the second parliament convened in November 1695. However, these attacks were somewhat blunted when the Tory alternative to the commercially based Bank of England, a Land Bank, failed after a few months. This left the Tories nowhere to go except into opposition, which became overt when some ninety Tory MPs refused the oath of allegiance to William III which was required of all elected members. This occurred in February 1696, and was apparently a delayed reaction to the death of Queen Mary which had happened in December 1694. Their argument was that their previous oath of loyalty had been directed to her as the lawful sovereign, rather than to her husband. The main result, when the second session of this second parliament met in October 1696, was that there followed a period of Whig ascendancy in the House of Commons. The financial situation was eased somewhat by the

Treaty of Ryswyck in September 1697 which ended the French war for the time being, and enabled Parliament in December to attack the standing army for which the war had provided the excuse. For good measure the members also had a go at William's Dutch favourites, although there is no indication that they were involving themselves in government. As William showed no signs of wanting to marry again, these men were particularly important to him. The King realised, as his council probably did not, that the peace of Ryswyck offered no long-term solution to the problem of what would happen to the Spanish Empire when the ailing Charles II died. In 1698 Louis XIV proposed a partition agreement with which the other main parties concurred, but unfortunately the key person in this scheme, the young Electoral Prince of Bavaria, died only a few months later. This necessitated a second partition treaty in March 1700, but that was proved redundant by the terms on which Charles left his crown when he died in November of that year. The one thing that the peace did offer to England was the recognition of William by Louis XIV, who had hitherto continued to recognise James as King of England. In the eyes of many MPs this removed the need for any further conflict, and they felt free to attack the Dutch connection in all ways possible, because it was becoming increasingly unpopular. When Charles died, he bequeathed his crown to Philip of Anjou, Louis XIV's grandson, and Louis' acceptance of that bequest blew the second partition treaty out of the water, making the renewal of Anglo-French hostilities more or less inevitable.

When William's fourth parliament met in February 1701, most of the members accepted that fact and supported the return to war. This support was increased when James II died in September and Louis recognised his thirteen-year-old son as James III, ignoring the concession which he had made at Ryswyck. By that time the succession was on everyone's mind, because although the obvious heir was Mary's younger sister Anne, beyond her the path was by no means clear. Her last surviving child, the eleven-year-old Duke of Gloucester, died in May 1700, and it seemed unavoidable, unless the young Prince James renounced his Catholicism, that the Stuart dynasty would come to an end. The Protestant alternative meant going back to James I's daughter Elizabeth who had married the Count Palatine. By 1700 that line was represented by her elderly daughter Sophia, and by Sophia's son George, the Elector of Hanover, who was aged forty. George was entirely German by language, upbringing and outlook, and his advent was not relished, but he was the only option available if the Protestant succession was to be maintained. In February 1701 Parliament therefore passed an Act of Settlement, acknowledging George's right and decreeing that henceforth no Catholic should sit on the throne of England. In the last meeting of William's parliament, in December 1701 an Abjuration Oath was therefore approved against James, who was thereafter known as the Pretender. This matter being settled, William neatly expired on 8 March 1702, from injuries received when the horse that he was riding stumbled over a molehill and threw him. Hence the Jacobite toast of later years 'to the little gentleman in black velvet'.

Born at St James's on 30 April 1662, Mary was the elder daughter of the Duke of York and his first wife, Anne Hyde. She was brought up as a Protestant, and in November 1677, at the age of fifteen, was married to William III, Prince of Orange. She made her home in the Netherlands until 1689, when with her husband she was summoned to take the throne of England. Her rule was accepted by all shades of opinion in England, and when she died on 28 December 1694 it became clear that it was her position, rather than that of her husband, which was upheld by sections of Tory opinion. Some MPs withheld their oaths of allegiance from William, although their gesture was not politically significant. Mary played little part in the regular government of England, but stood in for her husband during his numerous absences about his Continental business – that is from June to September 1690; from January to April 1691; from May to October 1691; from March to October 1692; and from May to November 1694. This together occupied rather more than half the time of the reign, but it seems that Mary took no decisions on her husband's behalf, referring everything to his judgement. Although childless, their marriage was a happy one, and William was deeply affected by her death.

47

ANNE, THE LAST OF THE STUARTS (REIGNED 1702–1714)

Anne was the second daughter of James, Duke of York, and his wife Anne. She was born at St James's on 6 February 1665, and was therefore just six years old when her mother died. Her father seems to have interfered little in her upbringing, which was Protestant, as her mother would have wished, and like that of her elder sister Mary. In 1683, at the age of eighteen, she married the Lutheran Prince George of Denmark, who seems to have been a man of great sexual energy but little character. Over the next twenty years Anne endured no fewer than eighteen pregnancies, all but one of which ended in miscarriages or infant deaths, the only exception being William, Duke of Gloucester, who survived to the age of eleven, dying in 1700. When she came to the throne in 1702 at the age of thirty-eight, Anne was childless and in poor health. Unprecedentedly, her husband remained a mere consort, not being accorded the courtesy title of king, or exercising any authority in the government of the realm. He did not even have an English title. Anne had earlier agreed not to press her claim if Mary should predecease her husband, and when that happened in 1694 she was content to allow William to rule alone for the remainder of his natural life. In return she received an allowance of £50,000 a year, and the exclusive use of a luxurious town house on the site of what is now Downing Street. Anne was crowned alone on 23 April 1702, her frailty being such that she was carried to and from the coronation in a sedan chair.

In May, England, the United Provinces and Austria declared war on France in what came to be known as the War of the Spanish Succession. This war was to be the dominant preoccupation of the reign, and the party organisation which can be seen emerging in Parliament was largely focussed on the methods used to fight it, or the financial provision which it required. The first session which convened in October was largely taken up with Tory demands for a 'blue water' strategy – fighting the war at sea, where England had an undoubted advantage – and for a bill outlawing the practice of occasional conformity whereby dissenters were evading the requirements of the Test and Corporation Acts. These demands were frustrated, but a topic which did make some progress was discussion of the desirability of merging England and Scotland into a single state, a subject which had last been raised by James I at the beginning of the previous century. It began to appear that the time might now be ripe. The same suspicion appears to have been held in Scotland, where the new parliament, faced with this threat to its existence, passed a series of anti-English measures, notably a Wine Act and as Wool Act, permitting trade in these commodities with France in spite of the war. The security fears which these acts aroused in England increased enthusiasm for a legislative union, especially as the Act for the Security of the Kingdom threatened to bar the Hanoverian succession which had recently been decreed for England, and put the union of the crowns in jeopardy. In 1705 the English parliament passed an Aliens Act in retribution, threatening to treat all Scots in England as aliens unless the Scottish parliament agreed to the Hanoverian succession. So heated had relations become that wiser heads on both sides of the border began to realise that something had to be done, and the new session of the Scots parliament, which met in June 1705, decided to appoint commissioners to negotiate for a union. The collapse of the Darien Scheme in the late 1690s, and of the Scottish Company which fostered it, had proved the relative weakness of the Scottish economy. That failure was inevitably blamed on English opposition, but the Scots merchants based in London knew better, and were converted to the need for union. In fact economic considerations were paramount in promoting the negotiations which followed the decision of the Scots parliament, and eventually prevailed. A draft treaty was drawn up in July 1706, and approved by the Scottish parliament in January 1707; it was ratified by the English parliament in March, and came into effect immediately. By its terms the Scottish parliament disappeared, and the Scots sent representatives to Westminster, as had been the case in the latter days of the Commonwealth. All economic distinctions between English and Scots were removed, giving the latter the benefit of England's preferential trade treaties, and access to all her markets.

At the same time the independence of the Scottish legal system and of the Kirk were guaranteed, so that the monarch became an Anglican in England and a Presbyterian in Scotland, a system which never seems to have caused any difficulty. So the cool heads eventually prevailed, but the animosity between the two peoples went on simmering for many years. From 1707 Queen Anne was styled 'Queen of Great Britain and Ireland', and her successors have borne that title to the present day.

Meanwhile the war was going well. In July 1704 English forces captured Gibraltar, which became thereafter the Mediterranean naval base which the Royal Navy had lacked since giving up control of Tangier; and in the following month John Churchill, Duke of Marlborough, defeated the French and the Bavarians at Blenheim on the Danube. John, who had been created Duke in December 1702, was the husband of Anne's most influential friend Sarah, who is supposed to have exercised undue political influence over the teacups at St James's. The English navy also scored a notable victory at Malaga, making 1704 a remarkably successful year for British arms – the role of Scottish regiments being particularly notable at Blenheim – a factor which gave edge to the demands for a political union. In May 1706 Marlborough was victorious again at Ramilles, and was beginning to acquire a reputation for invincibility. This situation prompted the Whig-dominated government to be intransigent in its attitude to the war, and to declare a policy of 'no peace without Spain', meaning an end to the regime of Philip V and the establishment of a more acceptable succession there. This prompted heavy criticism from the Tory Party in the House of Commons, and led to the replacement of several Tory ministers, notably Robert Harley by Henry Boyle as Secretary of State and Henry St John by Robert

Walpole as Secretary at War. These changes took place in February 1708, and were followed in May by heavy Whig gains in the general elections for the next parliament. When that parliament convened in November, there was something of a clean sweep of key office holders, members of the Whig 'junto' being appointed in their places. It was beginning to become apparent that a successful ministry needed to be able to command a majority in the House of Commons, and party discipline was appearing in the pattern of voting, something which had not been apparent before, when members had followed their own priorities, often dictated locally. In July 1708 Marlborough was once again victorious at Oudenarde, and in October died Anne's nonentity of a husband, Prince George. To what extent the Queen felt his loss is not known, but it left her even more in the hands of her personal friends, a role which Mrs Masham took over from the Duchess of Marlborough at about that time. Mrs Masham's influence was much resented, particularly her alleged role as an intermediary between the Queen and her ministers, but moves to censure her in the parliament of 1710 were aborted by indications of Anne's displeasure. As her health declined again, she had great need of her friends.

Economic hardship beset the parliament of 1709. Poor harvests had caused soaring grain prices, and the threat of famine and rural riots. In these circumstances Tory opposition to the bill for the naturalisation of foreign Protestant refugees was vehement. The argument is a familiar one to twenty-first-century eyes – they would take the jobs away from deserving natives, and swamp the employment market. Xenophobia was rife, and the economic contribution made by these immigrants was largely overlooked. Nevertheless the bill was passed, and 8,000 refugees promptly arrived from the Palatinate, giving some substance to the cries of opposition. At the same time the Tory High churchman Henry Sacheverall preached (and published) a sermon against dissent which the House of Commons judged to be seditious and Sacheverall was impeached, provoking riots in London in his support. In March 1710 he was found guilty, but given a light sentence, which seems to have appeased his supporters. By this time the balance of power was swinging back towards the Tories. In June the Whig Secretary of State, Charles Spencer, Earl of Sunderland, was replaced by the Tory Earl of Dartmouth, and in September the remaining junto lords resigned. Henry St John became a secretary of state, and the October general election returned a massive Tory majority. The resulting parliament in 1711 not surprisingly saw the enactment of the Occasional Conformity Bill, for which the Tories had been agitating for years, and the repeal of the Protestant Naturalisation Act. It also saw the beginning of a determined agitation to end the war, an agitation which was partly reflected in the dismissal of England's most successful soldier, the Duke of Marlborough, as Commander in Chief of the Allied land forces, an event which probably followed his wife's loss of influence with the Queen, and possibly the reversal suffered by British forces at Brihuega in Spain the previous December. In January 1712 the Whig Robert Walpole was expelled from the Commons and imprisoned. The Tory Henry St John was at the same time created Viscount Bolingbroke. By the time that the third session of Anne's fourth parliament met in April 1713 it was apparent that the Tories were deeply divided over the succession, a strong element favouring approaches to the pretender James in an attempt to persuade him to abandon his Catholicism. However, they remained in the ascendant, and secured the Treaty of Utrecht which ended the war with France in the same month. This treaty brought many advantages to Britain, but did not succeed in displacing Philip V as King of Spain, which had been the Whigs' declared war aim. The relief to the economy and to the Bank of England was profound. The spring of 1713 also saw the beginning of the appointment of 'Hanoverian' Tories to high office, William Bromley becoming a secretary of state, and Sir Thomas Hanmer Speaker of the House of Commons. The September elections of 1713 produced another massive Tory majority, but it was clear that the advantage now lay with those who favoured the Hanoverian succession. Such Whig colleagues as remained were of course of the same mind, and when Anne died at Kensington Palace on 4 August 1714 they acted on their principles, and to their own advantage.

By the time that Anne died, the international position of Britain had been transformed. Not only had one state been created out of two, but the military reputation of her armies and of her navy were at an all-time high. Equally important, she had become the economic driver of Europe. As a commercial and colonial power she now outranked the United Provinces, and London had replaced Amsterdam as the chief trading centre. British scientists and thinkers led the way in original speculation, thanks largely to the practical toleration which was extended to their operations. The 'republic of letters' also flourished, thanks partly to the refuge which England was prepared to grant to fugitives from more repressive regimes. How far this was due to the Stuart monarchs is a more difficult question, but Charles II certainly encouraged the formation of the Royal Society, and was genuinely interested in its speculations. Newton, Locke, Wren and Boyle all benefited from his patronage. By the time that Anne came to the throne, the initiative lay largely with professional politicians, and the monarch's attitude was less crucial. However, only the High Tories wished to operate in this country a regime as intolerant as those of France or Spain, and they were not given the chance to do so. By the beginning of the eighteenth century Britain was, politically, militarily and intellectually, a world power in a way which would have seemed impossible even half a century earlier.

Above left: 54. William Marshal, 1st Earl of Pembroke and one of the greatest of English barons. He served four kings, Henry II, Richard I, John and Henry III, for whom he acted as Regent. The 'Great Charter' was probably drawn up jointly by Stephen Langton and William Marshal. *Above right*: 55. The Articles of the Barons drafted in early June 1215, now in the British Library (Additional MS 4838). The Articles resulted from negotiations between royal agents and spokesmen from the barons, accepted by King John. The Articles served as the basis for Magna Carta.

56. Magna Carta. The 'Great Charter' of liberties King John granted to his subjects at Runnymede in late June 1215, now in the British Library (Cotton MS Augustus ii.106).

57. Edward III and St George kneel at prayer. Drawings of the lost wall paintings from St Stephen's Chapel, Westminster.

Above left: 58. The west front of Old St Paul's Cathedral as depicted in a fourteenth-century manuscript. *Above middle*: 59. Thomas, Duke of Clarence, Henry V's eldest brother. *Above right*: 60. Richard, Duke of York, father of Edward IV, Richard III and Margaret of York. *Right*: 61. Margaret Tudor, Henry VII's daughter, who was married off by her father to James IV, King of Scotland.

62. Nonsuch Palace. Built by Henry VIII from scratch between 1538 and 1547 as a palace designed to express his wealth and power.

63. Oatlands Palace in Surrey. Expanded by Henry VIII from a hunting lodge into a grand residence, it was demolished in the seventeenth century.

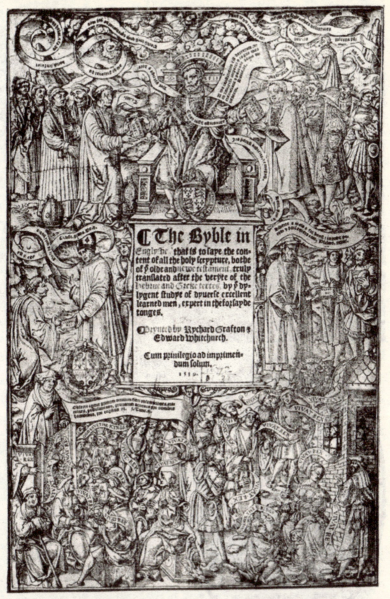

64. The title page of Henry VIII's Great Bible of 1539. On the left of the picture of Henry, Archbishop Thomas Cranmer receives the Word of God on behalf of the clergy from the king. On the right side Thomas Cromwell receives the Word on behalf of the laity.

King Henry the eyght.

Above left: 65. Henry VIII in council. *Top*: 66. The coronation procession of Edward VI in February 1547, passing Cheapside Cross on its way to Westminster Abbey. The windows and rooftops are crowded with spectators, suggesting the enthusiasm of the citizens for the new king. *Above*: 67. The reverse of the Great Seal of Philip and Mary, used for the authentiction of important documents in both their names. *Left*: 68. Queen Mary's husband, Philip, later Philip II of Spain.

Top: 69. The burning of John Hooper at Gloucester on 9 February 1555. Hooper, who was former Bishop of Gloucester, was burned on a slow fire. He was one of the first victims of Mary's 'terror'. *Above*: 70. The burning of Ridley and Latimer at Oxford on 16 October 1555. The sermon was preached by Richard Smith, who had been driven from his Regius Chair in Edward VI's time for his Catholic beliefs.

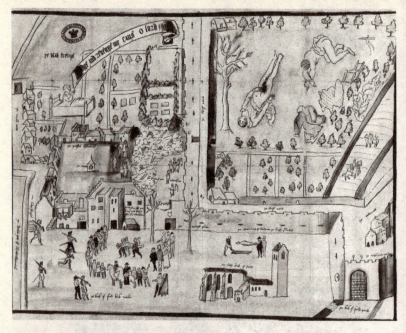

Above: 71. The murder of Lord Darnley, the husband of Mary, Queen of Scots. *Left*: 72. Princess Elizabeth, the 'Lady Elizabeth' of Henry VIII's later years.

Above: 73. George Gascoigne depicted presenting a book to Elizabeth I. She is seated in her Chamber of Presence on a throne beneath a 'cloth of estate', a formal sign of her royal status. *Top right*: 74. Elizabeth I's accession to the throne (or 'entrance'). *Above right*: 75. The Babington Plot. In 1856, the Derbyshire gentleman Anthony Babington was the central figure in a plot to liberate Mary, Queen of Scots. *Right*: 76. Francis, Duke of Alençon and later Duke of Anjou, came closer than anyone else to securing Elizabeth I's hand in marriage.

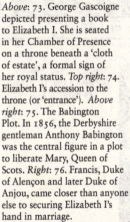

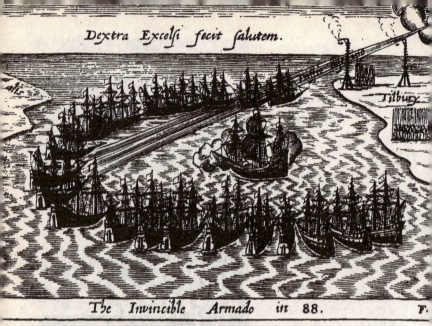

Dextra Excelsi fecit salutem.

Tilbury

The Invincible Armado in 88.

F.

FRANCISCVS DRAECK NOBILISSIMVS EQVES ANGLIÆ AN ÆT SVÆ

Above: 77. The Spanish Armada, 1588. *Left*: 78. Sir Francis Drake.

Above: 79. Robert Devereux, 2nd Earl of Essex. Pushed forward at Elizabeth I's court by his stepfather, the Earl of Leicester, he lost favour and gambled on a desperate coup attempt. *Above right*: 80. Francis Bacon. *Below right*: 81. Sir Walter Raleigh. He became the latest in a long line of Elizabeth I's favourites in the early 1580s. He fell from favour after secretly marrying one of her maids of honour. *Below*: 82. A sketch for a portrait of Elizabeth I. Here as in several surviving portraits, she is shown holding a fan of feathers, a classical attribute of power.

Above left: 83. James I and Anne of Denmark. *Centre left*: 84. James I comforts his son Prince Charles (the future Charles I) after the failure of his Spanish marriage venture in 1623 while Londoners celebrate. *Below left*: 85. Entry of Prince Charles into Madrid in 1623, part of his ill-fated trip to secure the hand of the Infanta, daughter of Philip IV of Spain. *Below*: 86. The trial of Charles I in Westminster Hall, which started on 20 January 1649.

Top: 87. Execution of Charles I in 1649 in front of the Banqueting Hall, Westminster. *Above*: 88. Cheapside, London, 1638, the procession of the Queen Mother Marie de Medici, mother of Charles's queen, Henrietta Maria. *Right*: 89. The frontispiece of *Eikon Basilike*, which was claimed to be the spiritual autobiography of Charles I. Published after the execution of the king, it proved to be immensely popular and quickly went through forty-seven editions. It provided a focus for royalists during the Interregnum.

Above left: 90. Marie de Medici arrives at St James's Palace, built originally by Henry VIII. *Above right*: 91. Oliver Cromwell from a contemporary Dutch engraving of 1651; note the decapitated head of Charles I. *Below*: 92. Proclamation of Charles II regarding the plague. *Bottom*: 93. Westminster with the abbey on the right *c.* 1650.

This is to give notice, That His Majesty hath declared his positive resolution not to *heal* any more after the end of this present *April* until *Michaelmas* next : And this is published to the end that all Persons concerned may take notice thereof, and not receive a disappointment.

London, April 22.

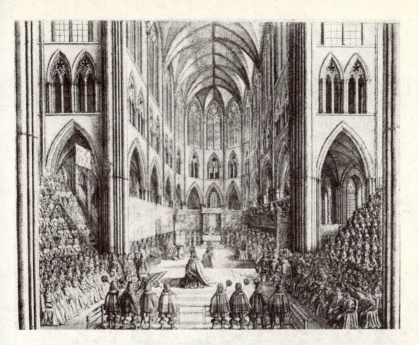

Above: 94. The coronation of Charles II in Westminster Abbey. *Centre right*: 95. The Great Fire of London of 1666 along with the plague were two major calamities to hit Charles II's reign. *Below right*: 96. Coronation procession of James II's wife, Mary of Modena.

Above left: 97. Coronation in Westminster Abbey on 23 April 1685 of James II and Mary of Modena. *Below left*: 98. Flight of James II down the Thames by rowing boat in November 1688. Contemporary engraving by Romeyn de Hooghe. *Bottom left*: 99. Coronation in Westminster Abbey on 11 April 1689 of William III and Mary II. *Below*: 100. Contemporary depiction of Queen Anne.

The Queen Addrest'd, and by new Senate to
They'll Act with more Obedience than Her o...

PART 15
THE HANOVERIANS,
1714–1901

48

GEORGE I (REIGNED 1714–1727)

George was purely German, by birth, upbringing and language. He had been born at Leinesschloss in Hanover on 7 June 1660, and had succeeded to the Electorate of that small principality on the death of his father in 1698. His only connection with England came through his mother Sophia, who was the daughter of the Elector Frederick of the Palatinate and his wife Elizabeth, the daughter of James VI and I. However, the vagaries of English politics had led in 1702 to the Act of Settlement, barring the Catholic Stuarts from the throne, and settling the succession on Sophia and her heirs. Sophia had died just weeks before Anne, so the residual beneficiary of the Act of Settlement was her son George, by then fifty-four years old. His priorities remained Hanoverian, but he was well briefed on the politics of Great Britain, not least on the lingering Jacobite threat, which was somewhat diminished by the support accorded to 'James III' by the French. In spite of the Treaty of Utrecht, the French were not popular in England. George had married in 1682, and his wife had borne him two children, but their marriage in every other respect was a disaster. By 1694 both parties had embarked upon affairs, and Sophia's lover, the Count von Konigsmark, was killed – probably murdered on George's orders. In any case, he divorced her and exiled her to Ahlden, where she was imprisoned. There was consequently no queen, and when George arrived on 18 September 1714 it was with 'a fat duchess on either arm' as one unsympathetic observer put it. Neither of these mistresses was able to fulfil the royal role, although each acquired clients and wielded some influence over patronage. More significantly the King was accompanied by his thirty-one-year-old son, also George. Prince George had married on 22 August 1705, and had been created Duke of Cambridge, in recognition of his right to the throne, in 1706. Although kept out of England by Anne for political reasons, unlike his father he spoke fluent English, and had served as a cavalry commander in the Allied army at the Battle of Oudenarde in 1708. He was well thought of in England, and was created Prince of Wales within days of his arrival, on 22 September 1714.

For a little while he acted as his father's interpreter in Council meetings, because George had so little English that his coronation service on 20 October 1714 was conducted in Latin.

Meanwhile the King had made various arrangements. As soon as word of Anne's death reached him, he appointed eighteen Lords Justice to assist the main officers of state in conducting the government until his arrival, and at the end of September rapidly made his own dispositions. He knew about the English party system and was anxious to avoid falling into the hands of the Whigs, who were his natural allies, but whom he distrusted. He was even more anxious to avoid the High Tories whom, he rightly suspected, would be antipathetic to his German priorities. Consequently he put the Treasury into commission, bringing back Lord Halifax, an old Whig, to head the commission, while making a moderate Tory, the Earl of Nottingham, Lord President of the Council. Parliament had been automatically dissolved by Anne's death and, in the autumn elections which followed, assiduous efforts were made to secure a Whig majority – efforts which were resented, but had the desired effect. No sooner had this parliament convened on 7 January 1715 than several of the Tory leaders, including Bolingbroke and the Earl of Oxford, were impeached for their intrigues with James Stuart, and fled to France. Scotland had not yet accepted George, however, and in September 1715 the standard of revolt was raised there by the Earl of Mar. James, 'the Old Pretender', did not arrive to give credibility to the revolt until the end of the year, and by that time it was too late. The Scottish insurgents failed to take Edinburgh, although the Jacobites had much support in Scotland, and an attempt to raise the north of England was defeated at Preston on 12 November. In spite of an indecisive engagement at Sheriffmuir the following day, the royal forces drove the insurgents back into the highlands, where they were finally defeated in April 1716. James withdrew to France, and Scotland finally and officially accepted the Hanoverian succession. The chief impact of 'the 1715' on English politics was to leave the Tories tainted by the Jacobite association, and the long period of Whig ascendancy began.

King George and his son were not on good terms. This may partly have been due to the King's dislike of his daughter-in-law, Caroline of Ansbach, but also partly because he was aware that the Prince of Wales attached less importance to Hanover than he did. When George departed for Germany in July 1716, he left his son as 'Guardian of the Realm' but with purely notional powers, and the fact that he took some of his English ministers with him created the conditions for a split in the government. The King was deeply suspicious of Prince George's popularity in England, which he rightly took to be an implied criticism of his European priorities, a sentiment which was increased when George I entered into an alliance with France to protect Hanover in November 1716. The Country Party (the Tories) were hostile to this alliance, and confused by the politics of the court. Prince George quarrelled openly with his father as soon as the latter was back in England, and as a result was excluded from the court at St James's. He set up his own court at Leicester House on a basis of mutual exclusion, and ordered his followers to withdraw their support from the ministry. Walpole changed sides and became a member of the 'Leicester House set'. The Tories began to recover from their electoral wipeout, and the King became paranoid, even seeking means to control the education of his grandchildren. Part of the trouble was that the court at Leicester House was both more cultured and more literate than that at St James's, and the King was well aware of the fact. However, the politics of the situation continued to be confused. Walpole changed sides over the repeal of the Occasional Conformity Act, which he now defended. However, it was repealed in spite of his best efforts, and the opposition consensus began to break up under his feet. The Duke of Argyll, a prominent member of Leicester House, returned to St James's as Steward of the Household, and an abortive Jacobite invasion in 1719 rallied the gentlemen of England to the ministry. By the summer of 1719 Prince George was sufficiently subdued and the King thought it safe to pay another visit to Hanover. When he returned in the autumn a whole range of measures, broadly intended to strengthen his position, were proposed, and ran into immediate difficulties.

However, what put an end to the courtly feud was not political success or defeat, but the rise of the South Sea Company, of which Prince George had been a governor since its formation in 1715. In 1718 the King had replaced him, but by 1719 the Company had expanded to such an extent that it was proposing to take over the National Debt, which then stood at £31 million. Awed by this apparently irresistible momentum, the Prince and his followers sued for pardon, and the King and his son were formally reconciled on 23 April – which is why the King felt it safe to go to Hanover. When he returned, the much-vaunted Company was on the brink of collapse. Rivalry with the Bank of England, and the bankruptcy of one of its constituent companies, brought about a crisis of confidence, and the whole credit structure was shaken by the panic. The royal court, including the Prince of Wales, was deeply compromised. By December 1720 Parliament was on the warpath, and was only restrained from attacking the King personally by the thought of the encouragement which that would give to the Jacobites, who had no commitment to the National Debt. Frustrated in that direction, Parliament took out its wrath on the directors of the Company, whose property was confiscated and several of whom ended up in the Tower. Only Walpole's tactical skills saved the ministry from complete collapse and the King from disastrous discredit. George was not at all grateful – he hated Walpole – but he knew that he needed him. He had checked the Country Party when it had threatened to bring down the court, and now he would check the court party if it threatened to ignore the country. The Prince, meanwhile had had a bad fright over the South Sea Company, and was behaving with markedly greater discretion. This was partly because he had taken as his political adviser Sir Spencer Compton, who was a close ally of Walpole, whose influence thus intruded into Leicester House as well. By August 1723 a sense of calm had descended upon the administration.

The King's Continental ambitions continued to be restless, and he moved backwards and forwards to Hanover, encouraged therein by Lord Carteret, one of his secretaries of state. However, good relations with Parliament were preserved thanks to Viscount Townsend and his alliance with George's mistress Ehrengard von der Schulenberg, the Duchess of Kendal, who managed by tactful pressure to maintain calm. By 1725 Walpole's management of the political machinery was well nigh complete. Never before had the resources of government been more efficiently deployed, and the King abandoned his attitude of dislike. Walpole's acceptability at court strengthened his position in Parliament, and his control of Parliament made him *persona grata* at St James's. With this consensus the Prince of Wales did not attempt to interfere. His father was now sixty-five years old and, although not in obviously failing health, his time was likely to be short. So he settled down to wait. In the event he did not have to wait very long, because George I left for a visit to Germany in June 1727. He was taken ill at Osnabruck and died on the 11th of that month. The news reached Walpole first and he hastened to Leicester House to inform the Prince of Wales that he was now the King. George I was buried in the church of his home town a few days later, with ceremonies suitable for an Elector of Hanover.

49

GEORGE II (REIGNED 1727–1760)

George II had married Caroline of Ansbach on 22 August 1705, when it was already likely that he would eventually become King of England. By the time that happened in 1727 he was forty-three years old, and the father of seven surviving children, the eldest of whom, Frederick, had been born in 1707, and the youngest, Louisa, in 1724. He was crowned jointly with his wife on 11 October 1727 at Westminster Abbey. He had spent much as his time as Prince of Wales in opposition to his father, and great hopes were entertained of him by opposition politicians at the time of his accession. However, by this time it was essential that the ministry team should be able to command a majority in the House of Commons, and that restricted the King's freedom of choice. In the short session of parliament which followed the old king's death, Robert Walpole successfully negotiated an increase in the Civil List, which had been the basis of the King's personal finances since 1698, and easily survived any challenge to his leadership. In the general election which followed, the Tories returned the smallest number of MP since 1679, at the height of the Exclusion Crisis. In May 1728 the Bank of England was persuaded to lend the government £1.75 million at 4 per cent, and Walpole's majorities in both Houses remained large and impregnable. The land tax was lowered to 3s in the pound, but Tory morale remained extremely low. In December of that year the King suddenly sent for his son Frederick, who had been maintaining a presence in Hanover since the death of his grandfather. The young man had been overspending his revenues, and acquired debts in the region of £100,000, so the King understandably wanted him where he could keep an eye on him, bearing in mind no doubt the part which he had played at a similar stage of his career. The young man was created Prince of Wales on 8 January 1729, but he was given only very limited independence, and when George II went to Hanover in May of that year, he left the Queen as regent rather than his son. Viscount Townshend travelled with George to Hanover, but his foreign policy was now too hawkish and pro-French for Walpole, who preferred a more subtle approach. This was reflected in his Treaty of Seville with Spain, signed in October, which brought an end (temporarily) to a period of tension between the countries.

When the third session of parliament began in January 1730, eighty MPs deserted the ministry in the annual vote on the employment of Hessian mercenaries, who formed a key part of the standing army, and that made the storm over the French fortification of Dunkirk a good deal more threatening than it might otherwise have been. Walpole felt reluctantly compelled to accept a backbench motion for the abolition of the salt duty, and when Parliament was prorogued in May there followed an extensive reshaping of the ministry. Viscount Townshend resigned as Secretary of State, following a thumping disagreement with Walpole over foreign policy, and the latter embarked upon a secret negotiation with Emperor Charles VI, intended to resolve Britain's European problems and hence defuse the parliamentary opposition. This resulted in the Treaty of Vienna, signed in March 1731, which temporarily pacified Spain, and which was triumphantly revealed to Parliament in April. This damped down the anxieties of the business community and enabled the session to end on a note of concord in May. When it reconvened in January 1732, the priority had switched back to revenue, and Walpole proposed a further reduction in the land tax to be made good by the re-imposition of the salt duty, which, thanks to his good management, was passed by a slender majority. Meanwhile a special committee revealed massive frauds in the collection of the customs, and the treasury proposed removing tobacco and wine from the list of customable commodities, and adding them to the excise list. Following a massive press campaign against this extension, public meetings and riots in London, and given the diminishing support in the House of Commons, a vote on the excise bill was postponed *sine die* in March 1733, and effectively abandoned. At the same time a number of excise rebel peers lost their jobs, and the government only survived censure for the way it had handled the estates of the South Sea Company directors by the votes of the bishops in the House of Lords. Walpole looked vulnerable. However, foreign policy came to the rescue, because France declared war on the Emperor in October, and Britain joined the Dutch in offering mediation, thus enabling the minister to deflect opposition calls for intervention on behalf of Austria when Parliament reconvened in January 1734. This division was most notable for the fact that seventy-seven Whig 'patriots' voted against the government. These opposition Whigs gained significantly in the general election which followed the dissolution in April and May, and numbered eighty-three when the Houses reassembled in January 1735. The King's Speech on that occasion drew attention to the wars on the Continent, and asked for increased revenue to meet contingencies, to which the Commons address responded by promising adequate supply. A government measure increasing the size of both the navy (to 30,000 men) and the army (to 25,000) was then passed against some stiff opposition in February. William Pulteney, Earl of Bath, threatened to absent himself from Parliament in 1736, being disillusioned with the failure of his opposition to make any difference to the government's ascendancy.

When Parliament reassembled in January, the attendance was disappointingly thin, particularly on the opposition benches, which meant that when the dissenting Whigs put forward a proposal to repeal the Test Acts in so far as these applied to Protestant non-conformists, it was roundly defeated. This was an occasion on which Tories found themselves uncomfortably voting with the government. At the same time Walpole decided to support relief measures for Quakers, which offended the bishops, and may have led to their revolt against the Mortmain

Bill, which passed the Commons but would have hit bequests to Anglican charities. It failed in the Lords, and Edmund Gibson, the Bishop of London and Walpole's chief ecclesiastical adviser, fell from favour in consequence. When Archbishop Wake died the following January, Gibson was passed over in the appointment of his successor. The Prince of Wales had married in April 1736, his bride being the seventeen-year-old Augusta of Saxe Gotha, and this forced an issue over money. As a bachelor he had received £24,000 from the Civil List. Now he asked for the full £100,000 which had been proposed in the Civil List of 1727. George was not prepared to concede more than £50,000, but an opposition motion for the full amount was only narrowly defeated in the Commons. The result was a full-scale quarrel between the King and his heir. Frederick was expelled from St James's and set up his rival court at Leicester House, forming thereafter a permanent focus and source of patronage to the opposition leaders in Parliament. Nevertheless they were dismayed when in the following January he declined to support their motion for a reduction in the standing army. Walpole's negotiation with Spain attracted considerable opposition, over 200 voting against it, and when it appeared to have succeeded in January 1739 a fierce debate ensued as to whether it should be included in the response to the King's Speech. After being discussed in a full house, the Anglo-Spanish Convention was mentioned in the Address, but the motion was carried by only a narrow margin. Walpole was out of step with his cabinet by this time, and by 19 October had been forced to abandon his convention in favour of war, known as the 'War of Jenkins's Ear' from the circumstances which provoked it. Meanwhile Prince Frederick's son and heir, George, had been born on 24 May 1738.

The year 1740 saw a number of ministerial changes, and Walpole hanging onto his parliamentary majority by increasingly thin margins. The Treasury Commission was remodelled, and warnings were uttered in November about the danger of a new war with France unless a better system of alliances could be put in place. Meanwhile the war with Spain languished, and Frederick II and Maria Theresa succeeded respectively to the thrones of Prussia and Austria, setting up war between them. In 1741 Walpole motivated Parliament to vote a £300,000 subsidy to the latter, and pledged support for a balance of power in Europe. In the general election in May 1741, the ministry lost vital ground, leaving its majority precarious. In July the King, without consulting his ministers, withheld Hanoverian aid from Maria Theresa, and negotiated a convention of neutrality for the Electorate in the ongoing war. As Elector, he was perfectly entitled to do that, but it caused consternation in Whitehall, lest it set a precedent for British affairs. Eventually it did not matter because Walpole succeeded in mediating a truce between the belligerents in October 1741. This proved to be his last service to the Crown, because, having narrowly survived a number of votes in a very full house on issues of confidence, he resigned on 2 February 1742. In spite of the Duke of Argyll's appeal for a broadly based government, the King could not countenance a Tory ministry, and appointed the dissenting Whig the Earl of Wilmington as First Lord of the Treasury (in effect Prime Minister) on 16 February. As a result of these changes a Commons motion to enquire into the conduct of the ministry over the last ten years was narrowly carried, a motion which died with the session on 15 July. An attempt to revive it during the next session in November was unsuccessful, so Walpole did not have to face an inquisition. The Tories remained in opposition, although they now had a different set of Whigs as their bedfellows. So disgruntled were the more extreme Tories by this situation that in April 1743 a group of them led by the Duke of Beaufort sent a secret invitation to the French to invade for the purpose of restoring the Pretender. They would rise in his support, they said, but only when a substantial force had actually landed. The French responded positively, but their preparations were wrecked by a great storm in 1744 and the whole enterprise was put on hold, for the time being.

In June, George II secured his place in history by being the last British sovereign to lead an army into battle, when he commanded the so-called 'pragmatic army' at the Battle of Dettingen against the French. This force, although paid for by Britain, was really a Hanoverian enterprise in defence of the Treaty of Breslau between Austria and Prussia, which Britain had guaranteed. Dettingen was followed up in September 1743 by the signature of the Treaty of Worms with Austria, which prompted the French to seek a new alliance with Spain, and led to the outbreak of war between the two sets of allies in March 1744. Carteret's position as Secretary of State was gravely weakened by criticisms of his foreign policy and by the refusal of Parliament to ratify the Treaty of Worms. When the Old Whigs put pressure on the King to dismiss him, he responded by resigning on 24 November. As a result of this Henry Pelham's ministry was reconstructed, several Whigs associated with Carteret being dismissed, and replaced with opposition Whigs and Tories to make a 'Broad Bottom' administration. In March 1745 Walpole's long involvement in British politics was ended by his death, and the Duke of Cumberland, Frederick's younger brother, was appointed Captain General of the army, to the Prince of Wales's great annoyance. The principal event of that year, however, was the incursion of Charles Edward, the Young Pretender, into Scotland, where he arrived on 25 July. He came without much in the way of French support, but the highlanders rallied to him and the Jacobite standard was raised at Glenfinnan on 19 August. Sweeping aside a small government force at Prestonpans, the Pretender entered Edinburgh on 21 September, and proceeding by way of Carlisle and Manchester, reached Derby on 4 December. The threat to the south of England appeared real and urgent, and the Duke of Cumberland was recalled from the Netherlands to take charge of the government forces. However, the highlanders became increasingly uneasy the further they advanced from their base, and on 6 December they began to retreat without having fought any significant battle. On 17 January 1746 they defeated a government force at Falkirk, but seemed not to know what to do next. Meanwhile the crisis had provoked mass resignations in London, as Pelham and most of his team stood down. However, the King's attempt to form an alternative ministry proved unavailing and Pelham returned to office, immediately demonstrating his strength by winning a sequence of key votes in the House of Commons. The Jacobites remained to be dealt with, although they now seemed to be a peculiarly Scottish problem, and were finally defeated by Cumberland at Culloden on 16 April. Charles Edward took refuge in flight, 'over the sea to Skye', and thence to France, leaving his luckless followers to pay the price of rebellion. Although it was not immediately apparent, the Jacobite threat was now extinguished, and only sentimental memories of 'Bonny Prince Charlie' remained.

1747 saw the Prince of Wales's party, the opposition Whigs, and the Tories move closer together, and in June Prince Frederick issued the Carlton House Declaration. This was a manifesto offering measures dear to Country hearts, and the King, seeing a confrontation looming, dissolved Parliament a year before he had to, on 18 June. The general election which followed during July proved the wisdom of his action because the ministry gained many seats at the expense of the Tories, and the danger of a major revolt disappeared. The year also saw naval victories: by Anson off Cape Finisterre in March, and by Hawke at La Rochelle in July. In other respects it was quiet year, and the same could be said for 1748, in which a deal between the Prince of Wales and the Tories was finalised and the War of the Austrian Succession was brought to an end in October by the Treaty of Aix-la-Chapelle. The only other event of note was the resignation of Philip Dormer, Lord Chesterfield, as Secretary of State. He was replaced by the Duke of Bedford, the leader of the 'Bloomsbury Gang', yet another political group which was jockeying for position. Parliament did not meet until November in 1749, when the King's Speech urged a reduction of the National Debt, and Pelham put forward a proposal to reduce the interest payable on £57 million from 4 per cent to 3.5 per cent, and then after seven years to 3 per cent. An Act embodying that programme was passed in December. Earlier in the year a new British base was established at Halifax in Nova Scotia to keep an eye on the French in Canada, and was settled by 3,000 government-sponsored emigrants. Party squabbles continued in Parliament when it reassembled in January 1750, this time between Pelham's old Whigs and the Bloomsbury Gang, but by the end of the session the East India Company had abandoned its opposition to Pelham's debt-conversion scheme, and thus guaranteed its success. The company was in urgent need of government assistance at this time, because the French had seized the initiative in India, establishing puppet rulers in the Carnatic and Deccan. This situation was partly turned back by Robert Clive's capture of Arcot in 1751, and by his victory over the French and their Indian allies at Trichinopoly in the following year.

The death of Frederick, Prince of Wales, on 20 March 1751 threw the politics of parliamentary opposition into disarray, leaving William Pitt as the leader of the Leicester House party, but without the authority to command unity. He promptly fell into a dispute with another faction led by Charles Fox, and thereby reduced their chances of successfully resisting Pelham in the House. The King promptly created Frederick's twelve-year-old son George Prince of Wales, but he was too young to have any impact on politics for several years. On a different matter entirely, an Act abolishing the old-style Julian calendar was passed on 22 May, bringing England into line with the rest of Europe. The change took effect in September 1752, when the 3rd suddenly became the 14th, giving rise to street riots in London and cries of 'give us back our eleven days'. The same act abolished the ending of the official and legal year on 24 March, bringing both into line on 31 December. In spite of the anxieties expressed, the Gregorian calendar was soon accepted and has remained in use ever since. In other respects the disarray of the opposition made 1752 a somnolent year in Parliament, and the January session was ended early in March. The following year was not significantly different, except that it saw the passage of the Clandestine Marriages Act, outlawing marriages by constraint or trickery. This might almost have been called a Child Protection Act, because it put an end to the traditional practice of marrying heirs and heiresses before they were old enough to give their consent. It came into force at once, and was surprisingly effective. During the second session, which convened in November, an attempt was made to settle the wars between the French and

English East India companies, and a conference was called at Sadras in December. In 1753 also the British Museum was founded on the basis of the library and collection of Sir Hans Sloane, who died early in the year. On 6 March 1754 the Prime Minister Henry Pelham also died and was succeeded by his brother, the Duke of Newcastle; however, the general election which followed the dissolution of Parliament on 8 April produced no great change in the balance of power. The new session convened on 31 May, but was promptly prorogued until November. Meanwhile, following the failure of the North American colonies to agree a plan for union, 1,000 regular British troops were sent to North America to counteract a perceived French threat to Virginia, a task in which they conspicuously failed in July of the following year at the Battle of Monongahela. Pitt rallied the Leicester House party against Newcastle's ministry in May 1755, but the only result was that he lost his office of Paymaster after opposing the renewal of the Hessian mercenary treaty in November. In Europe this was the year of the Lisbon earthquake, an event which aroused apocalyptic speculations in London, as well as the raising of relief funds.

By contrast with its predecessors, 1756 was an eventful year. In January, France and Austria concluded the Treaty of Versailles, and Britain and Prussia signed the Convention of Westminster, as result of which Britain declared war on France on 18 May. The East India Company's station at Calcutta fell to the Nawab of Bengal, and the British prisoners were put into the notorious 'Black Hole', news of which caused outrage in London. At the same time a British fort on Lake Ontario was captured by the French, so that it was not a good year for colonial affairs. At home Henry Fox was commissioned by George II to form a new ministry in October, but by November both he and Newcastle had resigned, and the

Duke of Devonshire was summoned to take over. He entered into partnership with William Pitt in the short-lived Devonshire–Pitt coalition. Pitt was ordered to resign in April 1757 following the court martial and execution of Admiral Byng, but was back as Secretary of State by the end of June, when he was serving in a ministry team headed by the Duke of Newcastle as First Lord of the Treasury. The politics of these years are fluid and confusing. In India Clive retook Calcutta, and became Governor of Bengal after a great victory over French and Indian forces at Plassey on 23 June. Elsewhere the Prussians suffered a number of setbacks before Frederick II won two victories – over the French at Rossbach and the Austrians at Leuthen. Meanwhile the Duke of Cumberland had been beaten by the French, and an English amphibious attack on Rochefort was frustrated. Political confusion was aggravated in England by harvest failures and food shortages which led to riots in many parts of the country. The Pittite Whigs now held a majority in the House of Commons, and in December 1758 Pitt broke his last links with Leicester House, leaving opposition firmly in the hands of the Tories. Setbacks in India were counterbalanced by success in North America, where Louisberg on Cape Breton Island, Fontenoy, Oswego and Fort Duquesne were all captured. Although British forces were repulsed from St Malo, towards the end of 1758 Cherbourg was taken and its fortifications destroyed. On balance, it had been a good year for the Allies, and a second Convention of Westminster was signed with Frederick the Great in April.

The same could be said of 1759, at least as far as Britain was concerned. A French attack on Madras was foiled by the British fleet, and soon after Musulipatam was captured; Guadeloupe was also taken; and the French Toulon fleet was routed off Lagos. A

British/German victory over the French at Minden went some way towards compensating for earlier Prussian defeats; and Edward Hawke's victory over the Brest fleet at Quiberon Bay ensured for the Royal Navy complete command of the seas. Quebec was taken in September, but its fall led to the death of General Wolfe. Parliament reassembled on 13 November in a state of high elation. Even the Tories were not disposed to complain. Success continued in 1760 with the capture of the whole of south India following Eyre Coote's victory at Wandewash in January; the failure of the French attempt to invade Ireland at Kinsale in February; and the surrender of the French forces in Canada at Montreal on 8 September. George II's reign thus ended on a high note. He was just a few days short of his seventy-seventh birthday when he died at Kensington Palace on 25 October. He had outlived both his wife and his eldest son, and was buried at his own request in Westminster Abbey in the same grave as Caroline. He had been notable mainly for his bad relations both with his father and with his eldest son, disputes which had created and led to the continuance of the Leicester House set, and shaped the politics of the period. He got on well with Walpole, but not with Pelham. However, the King's personal relations with his ministers were no longer as important as they had once been, and his likes and dislikes were only a few of the considerations which determined the make-up of a ministry. Electoral politics and construction and maintenance of parliamentary majorities were equally – if not more – important. George was, and remained, German in his sympathies. As Lord Hervey, the vice-chamberlain of his household, observed early in his reign, 'Hanover had had so completed the conquest of his affections that there was nothing English ever commended in his presence that he did not always show, or pretend to show, was surpassed by something of the same kind in Germany ...' It would be an exaggeration to say that he was popular, but when the alternative was a Catholic James Stuart, he was not lacking in support. He was succeeded by his twenty-two-year-old grandson.

50

GEORGE III (REIGNED 1760–1820)

Although German by both his parents, George III was the first Hanoverian prince to be born in England, and to think of himself as English. His first concern as King was to free himself from the Whig magnates who had dominated his father's latter days, and that meant ending the war. He was constrained to remove a reference to the 'bloody and expensive' conflict from his speech at the opening of Parliament on 18 November. Nevertheless he contrived to introduce Lord Bute into the ministry in March 1761, and was beginning to infiltrate the 'King's friends' into responsible positions, making his influence apparent. This new political grouping was predominantly Tory, but included some opposition Whigs. In August 1761 he tried to initiate peace negotiations with France, but these broke down within a month. Instead the French signed a new family compact with Spain, as a result of which Spain also declared war in December. George had married Charlotte of Mecklenburg on 8 September, and the couple were (rather belatedly) crowned at Westminster on the 22nd. At the same time the Earl of Chatham, William Pitt, resigned on the grounds of ill health, and when the Duke of Newcastle also resigned as First Lord of the Treasury in May 1762, the King was able to appoint Lord Bute in his place, thus shaping a ministry more to his liking. Meanwhile, following naval victories in the West

Indies, peace negotiations were reopened with France. These were at first kept secret, but in September the Duke of Bedford was sent to Paris with full powers to conclude an agreement, which was done. This had to be ratified by Parliament, and the King's friends were active in securing its agreement. When the debate took place on 25 November only sixty-five members voted against it and the Peace of Paris was duly signed on 10 February 1763. William Pitt opposed it in the Lords, but unavailingly. Less happily the introduction of a cider tax led to popular and parliamentary storms against Bute and he was constrained to resign after less than a year in office. Grenville took over as Prime Minister just a few days before Parliament was prorogued on 19 April.

By the latter part of 1763 a new stormy petrel had appeared on the scene in the shape of John Wilkes, a Member of Parliament who had attacked Bute and Grenville with unrestrained vigour in his newspaper the *North Briton*. Wilkes was arrested on a general warrant for seditious libel, and released on bail by the Lord Chief Justice on the grounds that he was covered by parliamentary privilege. Grenville demanded that the King should support him, and the King conceded, so that when Parliament reconvened it voted that the *North Briton* contained a false and scandalous libel that was not covered by parliamentary privilege, a decision which the Chief Justice described as 'illegal and absolutely void'. In the face of a constitutional row, Wilkes fled to France. He was expelled from the House of Commons in January 1764 for the unrelated offence of having been the author of a pornographic *Essay on Woman*, and outlawed when he failed to appear to answer the original charges against him. The ministry then won a close vote on the legality of general warrants, and overruled the Lord Chief Justice, which they were perfectly entitled to do. Grenville then outlined a plan for an extension of Stamp duties to the colonies, which he held over for a year to enable the colonial assemblies to come up with a better solution to the expense of their own defence. The Stamp Act was finally passed in March 1765, but the assemblies of Virginia and the other twelve colonies in America resolved to resist it, provoking riots in Boston, and attacks on collectors throughout North America. Meanwhile in February George III had fallen ill, and although his sickness was of short duration Grenville felt compelled to introduce a controversial Regency Bill. This failed, but the King recovered, and promptly entered into negotiations with Chatham to replace him. These failed, but the Prime Minister was sacked anyway during July and replaced by the Marquis of Rockingham, to lead a new team of the King's friends. In October 1765 a Stamp Act Congress met in New York and imposed a boycott of all British trade goods, a move which provoked the establishment in London of a committee dedicated to ending the boycott by pressure on the ministry over the Stamp Act. This led to widespread petitioning against the Act, which resulted in its repeal in March 1766, a concession resisted by Grenville and approved only reluctantly by the King. General warrants were then declared illegal in a concession to the judiciary, and the cider tax was repealed to sweeten relations with the electorate. George made a secret proposal to Lord Bute at this stage that he should form a ministry to replace Rockingham. Bute refused, but Rockingham resigned anyway during July, when the King proposed to reinstate Chatham. Having recovered from his illness, George was actively involved in the political infighting which characterised these months.

In January 1766 the Old Pretender died in Rome, and the Pope, followed by the other Catholic powers, declined to recognise

Charles Edward as Charles III, thus bringing the Jacobite threat to an end. Charles Edward was given sufficient money to support the dissolute lifestyle which he had by then embraced, and died in an alcoholic stupor in 1788. The Chatham ministry was opposed by shifting coalitions of antagonists when Parliament reconvened in the same month, but when Townsend formally announced his intention to impose indirect taxes on the American colonies, a joint opposition attack on his policies almost succeeded. Rockingham from the opposition benches then forced a reduction of the land tax (always a sensitive Country issue) from 4s to 3s in the pound, and Grenville renounced any intention to reintroduce the Stamp Bill. The opposition coalition collapsed during the summer in mutual recrimination, and there were widespread riots over the price of grain, centred on the Thames Valley, the Midlands and East Anglia, which the government was forced to use the Trained Bands to suppress. A tense and troubled year, particularly in relations with the North American colonies, where the boycott of British goods, temporarily lifted after the repeal of the Stamp Act, was re-imposed in November, following threats of other kinds of indirect taxation. John Wilkes returned from France in February 1768, and sent a letter of apology to the King, which was ignored. He then stood in the general election which was called at the end of March, and was elected for Middlesex. Wilkes surrendered himself into King's Bench to answer for his outlawry, and was imprisoned. The result was widespread rioting in London, which was only ended when the militia inflicted a number of casualties on the protesters at St George's Fields on 10 May. Lord Chief Justice Mansfield quashed Wilkes's outlawry when Parliament met on the same day as the St George's 'massacre', but then promptly returned him to prison on misdemeanour charges, which were surely created for the occasion. After the end of the session, Chatham resigned as Prime Minister, because he thought that George was trying to undermine him. The Duke of Grafton accepted the premiership, but most of Pitt's followers remained in office, giving him a bumpy ride. Disturbances against the Townshend duties erupted in Boston, Massachusetts, which led to the occupation of the town by regular soldiers, and the following May (1769) the ministry decided to repeal all the hated duties except that on tea, which was retained to establish the principle. Meanwhile the farce of Wilkes's election to the House of Commons continued. He was expelled on 3 February, and then re-elected three times before the House finally declared his election invalid. His friends then organised a nationwide petitioning campaign against the so-called 'Middlesex decision', but without success. In November 1769 the last Chathamites resigned their offices, but Grafton's attempt to draw the friends of Rockingham to support the ministry failed in December, and the Duke thought it prudent to resign early in 1770. Lord North, who was the King's personal choice, then became the seventh Prime Minister of the decade, an office which he was to retain until 1782.

When Parliament met on 9 January 1770, its first business was the repeal of the colonial duties (except that on tea), but news of this did not reach Boston in time to stop a clash between the troops and the protesters which left several of the latter dead in the so-called 'Boston Massacre' on 5 March. American politics impinged on the mother country when divisions over colonial policy prevented an opposition coalition from forming in April and May 1770, and the ministry survived to the end of the session and into the following one. In June there was a crisis in Anglo-Spanish relations caused by the expulsion of English colonists from the Falkland Islands, and war was only narrowly averted, but the issue was peacefully resolved by an agreement which was reached in the following January. A quarrel then developed between the House of Commons and the City of London over the confidentiality of parliamentary debates. The Lord Mayor and several City justices were imprisoned for contempt until the North ministry abandoned its attempts to preserve secrecy in the face of these somewhat discreditable moves, and journalists were admitted to the House for the first time – officially. The Duke of Grafton was drawn back into the ministry team in June, and John Wilkes was elected High Sheriff of London in July, in a deliberate snub to the ministry which had imprisoned him. In March 1772 Parliament passed the Royal Marriages Act, making the consent of the monarch necessary for any marriage within the royal family – an Act which was to have unforeseen consequences when applied to the heir to the throne. Trouble continued in the American colonies about taxation without representation, and food riots continued at home, fuelled by the high price of grain following a number of bad harvests. These disturbances prompted the passage of new Corn Laws in April 1773, a session which also saw the granting of a monopoly of tea sales in North America to the East India Company, which meant that when the colonists dumped the tea in Boston harbour in December, it was the company which sought compensation. The government supported this claim, and endeavoured to close Boston harbour in pursuit of it in March 1774, a move which further damaged relations with the colonies, and led to the meeting of the first Continental Congress at Philadelphia in April. As a consequence the charter of Massachusetts was revoked in May, leaving the colony unacceptably exposed to government interference. At the same time French Canadian Catholics were granted religious toleration, and the use of French forms of law – a move which was eventually to preserve their loyalty to the Crown. Parliament was dissolved on 30 September 1774, and in the general election which followed, the ministry secured a substantial majority.

The year 1775 was mainly dominated by the affairs of North America. The State of Massachusetts was declared to be in rebellion in February, and American access to all foreign trade was ended by the New England Trade and Fisheries Act. Henceforward the colonists were only permitted to trade with the mother country. Attempts at reconciliation, by Chatham in the Lords and by Burke in the Commons, were both defeated, and the Battle of Lexington on 19 April signalled the start of the American War of Independence. A general proclamation of rebellion was issued on 23 August and the American Congress's 'Olive Branch' petition was rejected in September. On the ground, the British won a pyrrhic victory at Bunker's Hill on 17 June, and American 'Patriot' forces invaded Canada and captured Montreal. In 1776 a Rockingham- and Chatham-backed move for peace was roundly defeated in both Houses, and in the second session, after failing to amend the address in reply to the speech from the throne, most of Rockingham's supporters withdrew from Parliament in protest. The American Declaration of Independence had been issued on 4 July, and it became clear that Britain was fighting to maintain her status as a colonial power. The fortunes of war fluctuated. The British evacuated Boston, but the Americans were forced to abandon Montreal; Washington's army was defeated at Brookyn Heights, and New York was captured in September 1776, but American counter-attacks led to the recovery of New Jersey between December 1776 and January 1777. An address calling for an end to hostilities was defeated in the Lords in spite of the support of both Grafton and Chatham, and a further proposal in the second session for the withdrawal of all British forces from North America similarly failed. Nevertheless the news of Saratoga, and of the defeat of Burgoyne's attack on New England from Canada, persuaded the ministry in December to set up a peace commission to look at ways of ending the conflict, and the joint forces of opposition began to make inroads into the ministry's majority. At the same time, in April 1777 Rockingham returned to Parliament in an attempt to block the payment of the King's Civil List debts, a motion which failed in the Commons by 109 votes to 137.

In February 1778 another Commons motion, this time proposed by Fox, in support of ending the war in America was defeated, but the conflict took another turn for the worse when the French allied themselves with the Americans and declared war on England on 17 June. Meanwhile the Earl of Chatham had collapsed in the House of Lords while attacking the ministry over its handling of the colonial problem, and died on 11 May. His death removed one of the administration's fiercest critics, and a formidable politician. His personal following began to disintegrate, as no one could assume his mantle of leadership. The Carlisle peace commission went to New York in June, but failed in its mission, as it reported to Parliament in December. The British won some ground in the American war, gaining control of Georgia, but the naval battle against the French fought at Ushant on 27 July was indecisive. Fox tried again to get the ministry's conduct of the American war condemned, but without success, and Spain took advantage of Britain's difficulties by declaring war on 21 June 1779. During the recess there was a move to force Lord North out of office, but it failed, and, when Parliament reassembled, Edmund Burke announced his intention to introduce measures for economic reform. These were urgently needed because there had been an outbreak of machine smashing in Nottingham during July, and the Yorkshire Association was formed to petition in support of Burke's proposals. The American war continued to be indecisive, and the Spaniards began their unsuccessful Siege of Gibraltar in June. The ministry demonstrated its devotion to religious toleration by passing a Catholic Relief Bill, and by relieving dissenting ministers and schoolteachers of the need to subscribe to the 39 Articles, both measures which would have been inconceivable fifty years earlier. When Parliament reconvened in January 1780 reform was in the air. Fox came out in favour of parliamentary changes, and a national association for that purpose was actively canvassed, although without any immediate result. Rockingam's economic reform package was defeated in detail, but the ministry was itself defeated on a motion that 'the influence of the crown has increased, is increasing and ought to be diminished' – a reflection of the King's perceived influence in the steadily changing composition of the administration. Lord North attempted to resign but George (as though to make the point for his critics) dissuaded him. A Protestant reaction against the Catholic Relief Act erupted into some of the worst riots in British history, the Gordon riots which raged from 2 to 9 June, leaving a trail of destruction through the City of London. The general election which followed the dissolution of Parliament on 1 September left the ministry with a reduced majority, and raised the hope of numerous interest groups, not least those concerned with economic reform. Eighteen Irish counties petitioned for the repeal of Poynings' Law, that early sixteenth-century Act tying the Irish parliament to its English (or

British) equivalent, and Ireland was admitted to equal trade with the colonies – for what that was worth by the end of 1780. In India the rebellion of Hyder Ali scattered the British garrisons and temporarily threatened Madras.

With the war in America now running consistently in the colonists' favour, thanks largely to French intervention, the ministry's majority in favour of continuing the conflict was getting thinner and thinner, and the news of Cornwallis's surrender at Yorktown on 19 October 1781 reduced it still further. Although a motion calling for immediate peace was defeated in December, and again in January 1782, a proposal that no further effort be made to suppress the colonists by force was carried against the ministry on 27 February. In March two votes of no confidence were survived by the slenderest of margins and the King at last allowed Lord North to resign. Rockingham formed a new ministry, but he was a sick man and died on 1 July. The King then chose Shelburne to succeed him, but that turned out to be a mistake as Fox and Portland resigned in protest, taking most of Rockingham's connection with them. When peace preliminaries were agreed with the Americans in November, Shelburne also alienated North by his abandonment of the loyalists in the colonies. In the meantime the Irish parliament had swept away Poynings' Law, and most of the rest of the constitutional settlement upon which the government of Ireland had rested for the best part of a hundred years; the Spanish had taken Minorca, but failed to secure Gibraltar; and Admiral Rodney had decisively beaten the main French fleet at the Battle of Saints in the West Indies. Peace preliminaries were agreed with France and Spain in January, but rejected by Parliament, whereupon Shelburne resigned. The King attempted to persuade William Pitt the Younger to form a ministry, but that promising young man declined, as did Lord North, leaving George with no option but to accept a Fox–North coalition, nominally headed by the Duke of Portland. Pitt's priorities were revealed soon after, when he introduced a measure for parliamentary reform, which was defeated by 293 votes to 143. The war was finally ended on 3 September by the Treaty of Versailles, which conceded full independence of the North American colonies, which thenceforth became the United States of America – a terrible blow to the King's pride which he was forced to swallow because there was clearly no alternative. In December Fox's India Bill was defeated in the Lords owing to the King's direct intervention, and the Fox–North ministry was dismissed the next day (18 December). Pitt was again invited to form a ministry, and this time he did not refuse, becoming at twenty-four the youngest man ever to hold the office of Prime Minister.

By 1783 George and Charlotte had acquired a large family: fifteen in all, starting with George, who was born on 12 August 1762, and ending with Amelia on 7 August 1783. George had been created Prince of Wales within a few days of his birth, and all but the youngest son, Alfred, survived infancy. Of the rest only the youngest daughter failed to survive her parents, which was a remarkable achievement at a time when infant mortality was still high. Of the seven sons who survived, two, George and William, succeeded their father on the throne of Great Britain, while a third, Ernest Augustus, Duke of Cumberland, became King of Hanover when Victoria succeeded William IV in 1837. George was a notable patron of both the arts and sciences, having a particular interest in music and forming a large library of books, which later became the Royal Collection of the British Museum – now the British Library. Among his scientific interests was stockbreeding, and he was a keen agriculturalist, which earned him the nickname of 'farmer George'. This is often misunderstood, as there was nothing bucolic about this cultivated man. In spite of his procreative vigour, which produced children at the rate of almost one a year, his health was uncertain, and recurrent attacks of what is thought to have been porphyria plagued him from 1764 onward. His mental stability came into question in 1788, and he finally collapsed in 1811, when the Prince of Wales took over as Prince Regent. It is very doubtful whether George III knew anything of the stirring events of the last nine years of his reign. Queen Charlotte predeceased him by two years, but it is unlikely that he was even aware of that.

The general election of 1784 gave Pitt a comfortable majority, and he began to reduce customs duties to encourage trade. At the same time, and as an aspect of the same policy, he tightened the policing of smuggling, which had become by then a significant element in the 'black economy', and was costing the government many thousands of pounds. The India Act of the same year increased the government's stake in the Subcontinent by creating a Board of Control, whereby the East India Company kept its patronage, but effective political and strategic control passed to the Governor General and the Secretary of State. The Marquis of Cornwallis became Governor General in 1786, and negotiated for himself greater powers than the act had originally envisaged. True to his stated intention, the Prime Minister introduced a measure for parliamentary reform in 1785, but it was not an issue of confidence, and its defeat did not materially affect his position. In 1786 Pitt made serious attempts to tackle the budgetary deficit by establishing a sinking fund and by reviving the imposition of excise duties on certain commodities. At the same time a new trade agreement was signed with France, and the British Empire in the Far East was expanded by the establishment of a settlement at Penang in the Malay peninsula. The loss of the colonies in North America had stirred British imperial ambitions in the East, leading to expansion of this kind, and the reorganisation of India proper. This same concern led to the impeachment of Warren Hastings for improper conduct in office there, a process which was initiated in 1787 and came to trial in 1788. On a lighter note the Marylebone Cricket Club also moved its headquarters to Lord's cricket ground in 1787. The year 1788 saw the establishment of the Triple Alliance between Britain, the Netherlands and Prussia for the preservation of European peace, a forlorn hope as it turned out as a result of events in France. George III also began to show signs of mental instability, but the Regency Bill, hastily introduced by Pitt early in 1789, was not needed because the King quickly recovered. Nevertheless a worrying new tendency had been identified. Reactions to the outbreak of the revolution in France inevitably varied. The radicals, led by Charles James Fox, welcomed the fall of the Bastille as an act of liberation, and looked forward to a constitutional development in that country similar to that in Britain, while conservatives, led by Edmund Burke, looked on the role of the Paris mob with undisguised dismay. An ominous development of these divisions took place in 1791 when Joseph Priestley's house in Birmingham was attacked by a hostile crowd because of his support for the revolutionary cause. Although Pitt announced that Britain would remain neutral in the event of war being waged against the revolutionaries, the polarisation of opinion in Britain continued and increased. In 1792 the reformers founded the London Corresponding Society and the Whig Friends of the People, while on the other side the Association movement was established, and the homes of prominent reformers in Manchester were attacked by loyalist mobs. In 1793 Pitt felt bound to renege on his undertaking of two years earlier, and in February joined the coalition against France.

By this time radicalism was being seen as seditious; two radicals in Scotland were put on trial and the *habeas corpus* procedure was suspended in May 1794. As a result the Whig Party split, but the majority remained loyal to Pitt, only a small faction following Fox into opposition, a situation which did not effectively alter the Prime Minister's control. Nevertheless twelve leading radicals who had been arrested were either acquitted or released without charge, indicating the government's unease with its own conservative policies. This situation was aggravated by widespread food riots and economic distress caused by high prices, which the Speenhamland system was introduced to ameliorate, with only moderate success. Trying to distinguish between sedition and genuine distress, the government introduced a Treasonable Practices and Seditious Meetings Act against political organisations, although it was not entirely clear which organisations were targeted, and prosecutions under it were few. Attempts to negotiate peace between Britain and France failed in 1796, and Spain entered the war on the French side. The additional expenditure required by the war effort led to a great economic crisis in the following year, when the Bank of England was forced to suspend cash payments in February 1797, and an unpaid navy mutinied twice, at Spithead in April and at the Nore in May. The French even landed at Fishguard later in the year, and Britain seemed close to military defeat. However, the invasion was not followed up, and the intruders were quickly defeated. British forces were then diverted to Ireland to deal with a rebellion led by Wolfe Tone and his United Irishmen. Tone was a republican who was relying on French intervention to establish his control in the island, but unfortunately the force defeated at Fishguard was as close as they ever got, and his rebellion was eventually put down. The United Irishmen was proscribed as an organisation in 1799. It was no doubt with great relief that London received the news of Nelson's victory at the Nile in 1798 – the navy might mutiny, but it could still do its stuff if properly led. To cope with the ever-increasing national debt, income tax was assessed and levied for the first time in 1799, adding significantly to the government's resources, but doing nothing for its popularity. The turn of the century saw a fresh attempt to resolve the Irish problem, with the passage of the Act of Union; modelled on that with Scotland in 1707, this abolished the Irish parliament, and opened the British institution to Irish members and peers. Irish merchants were admitted to all centres of British trade on equal terms, and financial distinctions were removed. The Irish parliament passed the same Act, and dissolved itself, later in the year 1800. The act was to come into force in 1801. At the same time domestic disturbances were addressed by the passage of a Combination Act, making trade unions illegal, and thus in effect driving organised labour underground in a manner which was to backfire badly in later years.

Pitt resigned in March 1801 over the issue of Catholic emancipation. He believed it to be essential to secure the future peace of Ireland, while George III believed it to be contrary to his coronation oath. He was succeeded by Henry Addington, who was the King's personal choice, thus demonstrating that the issue over the role of the Crown in the appointment of ministers was still very much alive. Faced with continued disturbances and rural distress cause by high food prices, Addington suspended the *habeas corpus* procedure again, but his ministry nevertheless remained weak, and its majority fragile. The nearest he got to parliamentary reform was a decision by the House itself that clergy of the Church of England were not eligible to sit as members, the theory being that they had their own parliament in the convocations. In 1802 the Peace of Amiens brought a brief respite in the war with France. However, it settled none of the issues between the countries and hostilities were resumed in the following year. Having struggled through nearly three years, Addington's government fell in April 1804, and was replaced by the return of Pitt, the issue of Catholic emancipation having been temporarily shelved. Meanwhile Napoleon Bonaparte had become Emperor of the French, and the revolutionary enthusiasm of the regime had been converted into a military dictatorship, which cooled the enthusiasm of the British Reform Clubs, and reduced the risk of radicalism being seen as subversive. Spain declared war on England, and this prompted the formation in 1805 of the third coalition against France, in which Britain joined forces with Austria and Prussia. As far as Britain was concerned, the war was being fought almost entirely at sea, and Nelson's victory at Trafalgar clinched her control of that element, although it cost the life of the victorious admiral, who became thereafter a national hero. At the same time a trade dispute with the United States reduced one of Britain's most profitable export markets, and seriously damaged relations with the former colonies. In January 1806 another national hero departed with the death of William Pitt at the age of forty-eight. He was succeeded by a so-called 'ministry of all the talents', which included Grenville as Prime Minister and Fox as Foreign Secretary. However, Fox died in September and thereafter the talents were not so conspicuous. Nevertheless Grenville was given an endorsement at the general election in December, and this strengthened his hand to deal with the 'Continental System' of trade embargoes imposed by Napoleon in November. He promptly retaliated with an embargo on France and her allies, which did far more damage to them than they succeeded in inflicting, largely because of the worldwide scope of British trade by this time. The 'Talents' ministry fell in March 1807, but was replaced by the Duke of Portland from the same parliamentary stable, who then received a further endorsement from the electorate. Following the Treaty of Tilsit, Britain was left to continue the war with France on her own. A power with unchallenged supremacy on the battlefield was thus left confronting a power with a similar control of the seas. It was not until 1808 that Britain challenged the French on their own ground, when Viscount Wellesley was sent to Portugal. Meanwhile at home a growing agitation was partly pacified in the abolition of the slave trade by British merchants throughout the world, a move which had serious repercussions in the sugar plantations of the West Indies.

Wellesley succeeded in denting the French reputation for invincibility when he won the Battle of Talavera in 1809, a victory which earned him the title of Duke of Wellington, and Portland resigned as Prime Minister, being replaced by Spencer Perceval. The following year Wellington began his successful defensive action at Torres Vedras, which paved the way for his subsequent advance, and at home strikes began in reaction to the effects of the government's economic policies. This situation was eased somewhat by the resumption of trade with the United States. However, in many ways the most important development of the year was in the health of the King, whose mental condition showed signs of irreversible decay by the end of 1810. He was seventy-three years old, and had already enjoyed one of the longest reigns in English history; only Henry III, who had succeeded as a minor, had reigned longer. In accordance with the terms of the Regency Act of 1789, Prince George assumed the title of Prince Regent early in 1811 and his reign effectively began at that point. The same year saw the first machine-breaking riots (Luddites) in Nottingham, which were followed up in 1812 with outbreaks in other places. This was a year of acute economic distress, during which wheat prices rose to a peak which was to be unsurpassed during the remainder of the century; war broke out with the United States, and Spencer Perceval, the Prime Minister, was assassinated in May, giving him the unenviable distinction of being the only British Prime Minister (so far) to have perished in such a fashion. The Earl of Liverpool took over the vacant office. The year 1813 saw Wellington secure decisive victories in the Iberian peninsula and advance to the frontiers of France, and in the same year the East India Company's monopoly of trade in India was ended, its governmental functions having been already taken over, this reduced its status still further. In 1814 France was finally defeated, and Napoleon exiled to Elba. The Anglo-American conflict was brought to an end by the Treaty of Ghent, and George Stephenson built his first steam locomotive. Victory over France proved to be only a temporary respite because in 1815 the Emperor returned from Elba, and swept France into a new aggressive war. This was ended by the victory of Wellington and Blucher at Waterloo in June, when Napoleon was captured and finally dispatched to St Helena in the South Atlantic, where he endured a frustrating existence until his death in 1821. The Congress of Vienna then sorted out the affairs of Europe in what was intended to be a permanent settlement, and which actually endured for about a decade.

After the war the focus of attention shifted to the domestic problems of riot and reform, the formation of radical Hampden

Clubs, and the government's failure to retain income tax in peace time. In 1817 parliamentary reform became a leading issue, and the Blanketeers marched in support; there was a rising in Derbyshire and the *habeas corpus* process was again suspended. Another Act banning seditious assemblies was passed, and the Bank of England began to resume those cash payments which it had suspended in 1797. The general election of 1818 gave the Tories a comfortable majority and reassured those who felt that the country was on the brink of collapse into radicalism or anarchy. However, the troubles continued, and in 1819 the yeomanry charged a pro-reform crowd in Manchester resulting in the so-called 'Peterloo Massacre', with reference to the great battle recently fought in the Low Countries. At the same time the government passed a group of Acts designed to suppress radicalism, which probably did more to steady the nerves of their constituents than they did for the discipline of the country. On 29 January 1820 the old king died at Windsor Castle. He was eighty-three years old, and had reigned for sixty-one of them, and, although he had not been aware of what went on around him for some considerable time, was deeply mourned by his loyal subjects, who had by then forgiven him for his interference in the political process, in accordance with his duty as he had perceived it.

51

GEORGE IV (REIGNED 1820–1830)

George IV was not at all like his father. George III had been uxorious, but he was continent, and his extravagance had been strictly in the public interest. The Prince of Wales had been a promising child, and had been given the best of contemporary educations, but he had become a wild youth, much given to sexual adventures and to haunting (secretly) the more disreputable dives that London had to offer. By the time he was twenty-one, in 1783, his finances were in total disorder and he began to press his father for more money. He was told that his Civil List allowance should be quite sufficient, and was advised to bring his spending under control, advice which he was quite incapable of heeding. In 1787 he tried again, and this time his affairs were discussed in Parliament. It was decided that the King would provide £10,000, while Parliament would clear his debts, and cover the considerable cost of finishing his new residence in London, Carlton House. A more responsible man might have got the message by this time, but George continued his extravagant lifestyle, and by 1811, when he became Prince Regent, he owed something like £500,000. After a series of affairs of a more or less sordid nature, in 1785 he contracted a morganatic marriage with a Mrs Maria Fitzherbert, already a widow twice over. Subsequent events indicate that he was genuinely fond of Maria, but his marriage was declared invalid because he had not sought his father's consent, as required by the Royal Marriage Act, and ten years later he married Caroline of Brunswick. Caroline was suitable in that she came of a German princely house, and George III was happy to consent to their union, but in other respects the marriage was a disaster. It produced one child, Charlotte, born in 1786, but then broke up in separation and recriminations. Charlotte died in 1817, and that severed the last link between them. There is no doubt that Caroline was a very unattractive woman, being profligate, lazy and vulgar, but in that she did not differ much from her husband, and the radical crowds of London took her side in every dispute with the Prince. So unpopular was George that an attempt was even made to assassinate him in 1817, and there were serious doubts about the future of the monarchy when he became king on 29 January 1820. One of his first acts as monarch was to persuade Liverpool's government to introduce a Bill of Pains and Penalties, annulling his marriage, and he successfully excluded Caroline from his coronation on 19 July 1821, when she turned up at Westminster demanding her share in the ceremony. She died just three weeks later, and her body was taken back to Brunswick for burial, an event which provoked disturbances in London. The government was strenuously trying to avoid demonstrations both against itself and against the King, so these were reckoned to be a propaganda defeat. Caroline enjoyed one further posthumous victory when in November 1821 the government abandoned any further attempt to pass the Bill of Pains and Penalties. So George's repudiated wife remained his wife, and their daughter remained legitimate – not that it mattered very much as she had died without issue.

Liverpool retained a sizeable majority in the House of Commons, and found that the anti-radical policies which he had inherited from Pitt still served their purpose in keeping the propertied electorate in an agreeable frame of mind. The economy was booming as trade picked up after the war, and Britain began to feel the advantages of being the world's first industrial power. Cash payments continued to be made by the Bank, although this was against the advice of some mercantile interests which preferred the circulation of paper money, and there was general lowering of customs duties. In 1822 the Congress of Verona began to reveal splits in the system devised at Vienna to preserve the peace of Europe as the autocracies of Russia, Prussia and Austria moved against liberal and nationalist developments in Greece and elsewhere. Britain became increasingly isolated in defending them, a circumstance which contributed to the mental collapse and suicide of Lord Castlereagh, the British Foreign Secretary, later in 1822. He was succeeded by George Canning, a man who had no scruples about pursuing an independent line, and who in 1824 was the first major statesman to recognise the independence of Argentina, Mexico and Colombia, which had recently fought and won wars of independence from Spain, whose ascendancy in South America the Congress was anxious to maintain. In the following year Britain brokered a deal between Brazil and Portugal whereby the former also gained its independence, and Britain's trade with South America doubled in five years. In 1823 the Irish Catholic Association was founded by Daniel O'Connell to campaign for Catholic emancipation, a movement which was adamantly opposed by the King, and the duties originally imposed to protect British trade were significantly reduced by William Huskisson, the President of the Board of Trade. The year 1824 saw the Combination Acts against trade unions repealed, which led to a wave of strikes and caused the government to re-impose certain restrictions in the following year. The Stockton & Darlington Railway was also opened in 1825, and a Catholic Relief Bill failed in the House of Lords, thanks partly to pressure from George IV.

Meanwhile the King had been travelling in a vain attempt to improve his public image. He went to Ireland, which had been devastated by famine, in 1821; to Scotland and to Hanover, but these gestures of royal duty were not much appreciated, especially in Ireland, where his attitude to Catholics was notorious. The religious issue was now important in Parliament, because of the failure of the Relief Bill, and Liverpool's attitude was sympathetic. The electorate too was coming round to his point of view and the general election of 1826 renewed his mandate, or could be seen as doing so. The Tory majority was preserved, because Liverpool was known to be favourable to the business interest as well as to his traditional country support, and believed that the two should be able to work together in the national interest. The Penal Laws were beginning to seem anachronistic, and the Test and Corporation Acts were repealed in 1828, putting Protestant non-conformists on the same footing as Anglicans. Meanwhile Liverpool's long term of office was over. He suffered a stroke and resigned in February 1827, to be followed by Canning, who died in August, and was succeeded in turn by Viscount Goderich. Canning's death was no doubt a great relief to the King, who could not stand him. Goderich resigned in January 1828 and was replaced by the Duke of Wellington, who then faced the unenviable task of trying to heal the split in the Tory Party which had been occasioned by the repeal of the Test and Corporation Acts, as it became obvious that traditional prejudices were not so easily overcome. Reform, however, was in the air. In 1827 the criminal code was amended by Robert Peel, the Home Secretary, to reduce the number of capital offences, particularly for theft, and the law of property was redefined. The Corn Laws were also revised to introduce a sliding scale in place of the old fixed limitations, and the Country lobby was thereby gratified. At the same time in 1828 Daniel O'Connell had won a by-election in County Clare, but as a Roman Catholic was not allowed to take his seat. This forced the issue on Catholic emancipation, which, if not granted, would lead to Irish civil disobedience on a grand scale. At the cost of splitting the Tory Party still further, and reducing the anti-reform lobby to a shambles, the Emancipation Act was passed in 1829. As a sop to the opposition, the voting qualification in Ireland was raised from 40s to £10, a move which effectively disenfranchised most of the Catholic peasantry. In the same year

Robert Peel created a new London police force (known thereafter as 'Peelers' or 'Bobbies'), the first such organisation in the country, and Oxford and Cambridge universities rowed their first boat race. In London University College was founded, the first such institution in England since the fourteenth century.

At the beginning of 1830, parliamentary reform, which had been discussed for many years, was coming to the top of the political agenda, and was bound to provide a severe test for the Tory ministry, weakened as it was by the defection of the 'ultras' over Catholic emancipation. On the international scene France, Russia and Britain guaranteed the independence of Greece in February against the crumbling Ottoman Empire. At home George IV died at Windsor on 26 June, and was buried in St George's Chapel. There can have been few royal deaths less lamented. George had scarcely appeared in public after 1823 because of his extreme unpopularity in London. He was dubbed 'the first gentleman of Europe', but he lacked both charisma and integrity, and his reign was a wasted opportunity for the monarchy to reassert itself after the sad decline of George III. He spent large sums of money, but to no effect as far as the prestige of his court was concerned. Only in his buildings did he leave a positive legacy – Carlton House, Buckingham Palace and the Brighton Pavilion all owed their subsequent form to his patronage. He presided over stirring times, which saw victory over France in the Napoleonic Wars, the legalisation of trade unions and Catholic emancipation. It was also a boom time for the British economy, as the fruits of the industrial and scientific revolutions began to translate into unrivalled trading supremacy. Unfortunately for none of this was he responsible; indeed he opposed both Catholic emancipation and democratic movements to the best of his limited ability. The Regency style was certainly created under his leadership, and he hosted the lavish entertainments with which the aristocracy amused themselves, but even that owed more to his friend Beau Brummel than it did to George himself. He was succeeded by his younger brother William, and it remained to be seen whether the monarchy could extract itself from the morass in which George IV had left it.

52

WILLIAM IV (REIGNED 1830–1837)

William was the third son of George III and Queen Charlotte, and he grew up without any thought that he might one day become king. He was born on 21 August 1765 at Buckingham House, and after receiving the same conventional education as his elder brothers, George and Frederick, in 1779 at the age of fourteen he had embarked on a career in the navy. Beginning as an ordinary seaman – or as ordinary as a royal prince was ever likely to be – he rose rapidly through the ranks until by 1787, at the age of twenty-two, he was placed in command of HMS *Andromeda*. It was this practical experience which caused him later to be known as the 'sailor king'; but after ten years in the navy, the King decided to move him on. In 1789 at the age of twenty-four, he was created Duke of Clarence and encouraged to take his seat in the House of Lords; this not being compatible with active service, he resigned from the navy and became a full-time aristocrat. Unlike his brother George, he was a man of probity, who lived within his means, but one characteristic which he did share with his brother was a taste for women whom he could not possibly marry. In George's case it had been Mrs Fitzherbert; in William's it was an actress who went by the stage name of Dorothy Jordan. For about twenty years from 1790 Dorothy was the passion of William's life, and between them they produced ten illegitimate children; however, in 1818 at the age of fifty-three, he yielded to pressure from his family to secure a suitable wife. He married the twenty-five-year-old Adelaide of Saxe Meiningen, and surprisingly their union was a happy one, resulting in three pregnancies. Sadly, none of their children lived more than three months. It was also death which paved his way to the throne. Firstly George's daughter Charlotte died in 1817 at the age of twenty-one. In spite her father's efforts, Charlotte was legitimate and would have been his heir had she lived. Secondly, Frederick, Duke of York, died in 1827 at the age of sixty-four. So William, also aged sixty-four, came to the throne on the death of his eldest brother on 26 June 1830. He wanted to assume the title of Henry IX, but was persuaded to adopt the more logical style of William IV, and as such he was crowned, along with Adelaide, on 8 September 1831.

For the next two years the political scene was dominated by the issue of constitutional reform. In the general election which followed the death of the King, the Whig supporters of reform secured a majority and Wellington resigned as Prime Minister, being succeeded by Earl Grey, who introduced the first Reform Bill early in the new year. It failed for a variety of reasons and Grey persuaded the King to allow him to go to the country on the issue, with the result that he secured a greatly increased majority. This enabled him to get a second Reform Bill passed the Commons in September only to be rejected in the Lords the following month. There then followed widespread riots, but there was nothing that the Prime Minister could do to influence the peers, where a built-in Tory majority was determined to resist all change. The

Commons returned to the charge, passing a third Reform Bill in March 1832, but difficulties persisted in the Lords and Grey resigned. Wellington, however, was unable to form a government, and Grey resumed office on the understanding that if the Lords proved obstructive again, the King would create enough Whig peers to force the bill through. This William was willing to do, partly because he was sympathetic to the reform movement, and partly to avoid the constitutional crisis which was clearly looming. Faced with this threat to their integrity, the Lords gave way and the third Reform Bill became an Act in June. It was rapidly followed by similar measures for Scotland and Ireland. This was not the revolutionary measure it is sometimes presented as being; indeed it expanded the suffrage only slightly. It did, however, remove the rotten boroughs and increase the number of urban constituencies, making the House of Commons more truly representative. Above all, it created a precedent for further change, and the general election which followed its passage produced a massive Whig majority, which pointed in the same direction. The King, whose support was much appreciated, became known as 'Reform Bill', and was so presented in caricatures of the period.

Early in 1833, the reconstituted House of Commons followed up its 1807 measure banning the slave trade by abolishing the institution itself in all British colonies and dependencies. This was the culmination of a life's work for the liberal reformer William Wilberforce, who died in the same year, and transformed the economic basis of the plantation industry. In the same year the last great trading monopoly was laid to rest when the East India Company's grip on the China trade was finally relaxed, and the beginnings of the Oxford movement revitalised theological and ecclesiastical debate within the Church of England after more than a century of somnolence. The year 1834 was dominated by labour relations, because the Grand National Consolidated Trade Union was formed as an umbrella organisation intended to coordinate workers' political activities, but collapsed after a few months in the face of particularist interests. At the same time, when the agricultural labourers at Tolpuddle in Dorset joined a union in the form of a friendly society organised by a local Methodist preacher, they were sentenced to transportation for taking an illegal oath, a scandal which caused them to be named the 'Tolpuddle Martyrs'. The early seventeenth-century Poor Law had long been anachronistic as a means of relieving poverty, and in 1834 a new administrative structure was put in place by the Poor Law Amendment Act, which professionalised and rationalised the system. Although the Whigs enjoyed an electoral majority, they were not a unified party in the modern sense, and confronted by this factionalism in the ranks Earl Grey resigned as Prime Minister in July 1834. He was briefly succeeded by Lord Melbourne, who had no better fortune and resigned in his turn in November. The King then called upon Robert Peel to form a minority government, which he did with the aid of some Whig defectors, and issued the Tamworth Manifesto, to rally Tory support and to demonstrate that they were no longer the anti-reform party. This was done in December, and had some effect in the general election which followed early in 1835, which saw some Tory gains. However, these were not sufficient to protect Peel from defeat over the Irish Church, when he was confronted by the Whig–Radical–Irish alliance which was formed at Lichfield House in March. His defeat in April saw Melbourne return as Prime Minister, and Melbourne survived for the remainder of the reign and well beyond. The resumption of Whig domination in the House of Commons saw the passage of the Municipal Corporations Act in September 1835, which was the starting point for a great deal of reform in urban local government. This was followed up in June 1836 by the formation of the London Working Men's Association, to press for further political changes, a movement which was eventually to bear fruit in 1867 with the introduction of manhood suffrage.

Apart from this, 1836 was the year of ecclesiastical reform, when the Church Commissioners were established to inaugurate a series of administrative and financial changes, which resulted in the Commissioners taking over most of the assets and liabilities of the Church of England. At the same time the Tithe Commutation Act finally abolished the ancient practice of paying tithes in kind, and relieved rural incumbents of the responsibility for disposing of large quantities of grain and livestock. Early in 1837 the civil registration of births, marriages and deaths was inaugurated, thus establishing a database from which subsequent population censuses could be compiled, and adding significantly to bureaucratic intrusion into the lives of ordinary citizens which was beginning to be resented by conservatives. England was becoming a much-governed country. Not that this was a bad thing, because it was similarly intrusive legislation which made it illegal for children under the age of nine to be employed in factories, where they had been exploited as a source of cheap labour, and restricted the hours which older children might work. At the same time in 1833 inspectors were appointed to make sure that these humanitarian laws were obeyed. The 1830s was nevertheless a boom time for the economy, and a time of peace, which relieved the financial pressures on the government, and enabled attention to be given to such matters. The role of the King in all this activity was that of a benign presence rather than an active player, although Lord

Melbourne seems to have been his personal choice as Prime Minister. He had, however, succeeded in redeeming the monarchy from the discredit in which George IV had left it. He was basically a decent, upright man, and that was appreciated by his subjects after the louche days of his predecessor. William died at Windsor on 20 June 1837, and was succeeded by his young niece, Victoria, the daughter of his brother Edward, Duke of Kent (who had died in 1820), as ruler of the United Kingdom; and by his younger brother Ernest as King of Hanover, where they operated the Salic Law.

53

VICTORIA, 'THE MOTHER OF THE EMPIRE' (REIGNED 1837–1901)

Like William, Victoria had been passed her childhood without any thought that she might one day inherit the crown. Her father Edward, Duke of Kent, was the fourth son and fifth child of George III and Queen Charlotte. Like his brothers Edward married late, and was forty-seven years old when he wedded Mary Louise Victoria, the daughter of the Duke of Saxe-Coburg-Saalfeld, in 1818. Their only child, Victoria, was born at Kensington Palace on 24 May 1819, and was consequently only few months old when her father died in January 1820. At the time of her grandfather's death on the 29th of the same month a number of lives stood between her and any prospect of inheritance. Her cousin Charlotte had died before she was born, and there seemed little prospect of her uncle George IV producing any more legitimate offspring. However, her uncles Frederick and William were still alive, and

William was married to a young wife who might well produce children who would enjoy a superior claim. Frederick then died childless in 1827, and George equally childless in 1830. William's offspring did not survive infancy, so when he came to the throne on George's death Victoria became his heir. This was a situation not lost on her mother, who began assiduously to groom her, with the aim of becoming a dominant influence when she became queen. In that she was disappointed, because the eighteen-year-old Victoria quickly demonstrated that she had a mind of her own, and if she wanted political advice she would seek it from Lord Melbourne, her Prime Minister, or from her mother's trusted brother, Prince Leopold of Belgium. She was crowned on 28 June 1838, after a delay which was by this time customary.

The political situation on her accession was unsettled, because the Whigs were increasingly dependent upon Irish votes, and consequently preoccupied with Irish issues. This enabled their Tory opponents to claim the moral high ground of representing English patriotism. The new Poor Law was also an electoral liability, and the growing conservative sentiment in the constituencies meant that many radicals who had clung on to their majorities were dumped in the general election which followed the demise of the King in 1837. Melbourne was not an energetic leader, and after 1837, although the Whigs retained a narrow majority, they were consistently out-argued in debate, not least by William Gladstone, at this stage a 'stern unbending Tory'. In May 1839 Melbourne determined to resign after his majority was cut to five on an important vote, and advised the Queen to send for Peel. This she did, only to discover that he would not assume office unless some of her Whig Ladies of the Bedchamber were removed and Tories appointed in their place. Victoria was not prepared to be dictated to, and Peel declined to serve. In order to protect his twenty-year-old sovereign from a constitutional crisis with which she would have been unable to cope, Melbourne agreed to resume office. He was promptly charged with clinging to power on the Queen's petticoats, and reshuffling his government only made the situation worse. The radicals in his own party further embarrassed him by reiterating their demand for secret ballots at elections, and by the formation of the National Chartist Convention for that purpose. By the end of 1839 the ministry was just clinging on, without any real authority. Only in the colonies was an aggressive posture retained, because the year saw the acquisition of Aden, and the outbreak of the Opium War with China which resulted in the capture of Hong Kong. War was also being waged in Afghanistan, although with mixed fortunes against the fierce frontier tribes who confronted India.

Meanwhile the Queen had fallen in love. She had originally met Albert of Saxe-Coburg and Gotha at Windsor in 1838. What she thought of him at that stage we do not know, but when their paths crossed again about a year later, an arrangement made by Baroness Lehzen, Victoria's governess, they quickly became engaged, and were married in London on 10 February 1840. Their first child was born on 21 November of that year, and Albert quickly became the dominant influence in his wife's councils, both public and private. Following the precedent established by Queen Anne, he was not offered the Crown Matrimonial, and it was not until 1857 that the lesser title of Prince Consort was bestowed on him, but his influence was very great – and beneficial. They produced ten children over the next sixteen years, beginning with Victoria and ending with Beatrice on 14 April 1857: five girls and five boys, and the girls married into princely houses all over Europe, making Victoria the 'grandmother of Europe'. From 1840 onwards the royal family was held up as an exemplar of domestic felicity, but it was a family of role reversal, in which Albert took on most of the wifely functions. Aware that his interference in the politics of Britain might not be appreciated, he also busied himself with cultural and scientific patronage, being particularly influential in the launching of the Great Exhibition of 1851. He was a wise and cultivated man, well suited to an emerging industrial power, and was to carve for himself a unique place in the affections of his adopted land. He was also, however, a severe parent, who insisted on receiving personal reports on the progress of his offspring from their tutors, and administering the whip where he thought it to be necessary. This had the most unfortunate affect on the development of his eldest son, Edward, who showed signs of an uncontrollable temper, and developed a dreadful stammer. His mother, who entertained ambitions of turning him into a replica of his 'beloved papa', became increasingly distressed. Eventually, when he was already unwell, Albert insisted in September 1861 on going down to Cambridge for a heart to heart with his unsatisfactory son, and it was on returning from that mission that he took to his bed. He died on 14 December following, and the Queen, quite unreasonably, blamed the Prince of Wales for his father's collapse. She was shattered by Albert's death and it was many months before she could even bring herself to speak to her son, who was in many ways as distressed as she was herself.

Meanwhile Britain's success abroad and uncertain politics at home continued. Upper and Lower Canada were reunited in July 1840, and the government assumed responsibility for the colonies then being established in New Zealand, taking over the sovereignty of that country. In 1841 the Convention of the Straits guaranteed the independence of what was left of the Ottoman Empire, and agreed to close the Dardanelles to warships of every nation – a clause which would have had the effect of confining the bulk of the Russian navy to the Black Sea. At the same time the election held in July overturned the Whig majority in the Commons, and Melbourne resigned as Prime Minister. Peel duly took over and formed a Tory ministry which was to last for the next five years. This time there was no 'bedchamber crisis', perhaps because of Albert's soothing influence, or perhaps because Peel had learned discretion since 1839. He had to cope at once with deep economic distress, particularly in the cotton-weaving areas, which led to an upsurge of Chartism and some violence. A second Chartist petition was presented and rejected in May 1842, which led to disturbances in many parts of the country. Peel did his best to alleviate the social problems, passing, for example, an Act to prevent women and children from being forced to work down the mines, and his budget in 1842 made significant reductions in the customs tariff. Abroad the Opium War was concluded, with the Chinese conceding greater trading rights to British companies. By this time the free trade movement was growing, and in 1843 *The Economist* was founded to promote its ideas. Nevertheless the tendency towards welfare legislation continued with a new Factory Act limiting the number of hours which women and older children might work in the textile mills which were by them dominating the economy of Lancashire, and particularly Manchester. In 1844 also the Royal Commission on the Health of Towns began its work, and the Bank Charter Act put its note-issuing function onto a modern footing by linking it to bullion reserves and securities. Peel's budget in 1845 abolished export duties entirely, and reduced the number of import duties in a significant gesture towards the free-trade lobby. However, another move in the same direction, the repeal of the protectionist Corn Laws, led to a split in the Tory Party, the conservative country interest being opposed to any such move. Peel attempted to sidestep that difficulty by persuading the Whigs to pass it, but Russell was unable to form a government, and the Prime Minister was forced to carry on for the time being. The critical Corn Law debate was held in the Commons in February 1846, when the repeal was carried with the aid of Whig votes, and the Tory Party split definitively. Peel resigned in June 1846 when he was defeated over an Irish coercion bill, and Russell succeeded at the head of a Whig government. The 'Peelites' then became a separate political group, distinct from the main Tory Party. Meanwhile state interference in social concerns continued to increase. The establishment of a pupil–teacher training scheme marked its first involvement in education; the Liverpool Sanitary Act required the appointment of the country's first medical officer of health; and the establishment of a standard gauge for the railways greatly facilitated the expansion of the rail network, which was by then advancing rapidly. The general election of 1847 confirmed Whig (or by now better called Liberal) control of the Commons, and wheat prices rose sharply, provoking the last food riots in British history. Thereafter the expansion of policing arrangements modelled on London kept such volatile situations under better control.

A combination of Britain's unique constitutional monarchy and the prosperity of a dominant economic and imperial power helped to insulate Britain from the European revolutionary movements of 1848. Even the Chartist meeting at Kennington, which had threatened violence, dispersed peacefully, and British politics was more accurately reflected in the establishment of the General Board of Health than in any concern about the powers of the Crown, which were of more symbolic than practical significance by this time. Only in Ireland were there political agitations, a circumstance which put Victoria off the Irish for a number of years. In 1849 the free trade cause was advanced further by the repeal of the Navigation Acts and the reduction of duty on West Indian sugar. In 1850 the Roman Catholic hierarchy in Britain was re-established, although the Ecclesiastical Titles Act of the following year forbade them for the time being from using titles based on British territories. 1851 was of course the year of the Great Exhibition, as Britain put her industrial supremacy on display in a successful bid to attract more business; her cultural and intellectual achievements were less well known but nevertheless real. Further signs of the times were the building of King's Cross station in London and the founding of Owen's College in Manchester. In spite of these successes the government's authority weakened towards the end of the year. Palmerston resigned as Foreign Secretary in December, and was followed by the rest of the ministry in February 1852. The Earl of Derby formed a minority Conservative government, which was defeated over Disraeli's budget in December of that year and resigned in turn. At the beginning of 1853 Lord Aberdeen succeeded in forming a replacement by bringing together Liberals and Peelites, with Gladstone taking over Disraeli's job as Chancellor of the Exchequer. His first budget in 1853 continued the move towards free trade, and announced the phasing out of income tax by 1860 – two very popular moves.

At the same time relations with Russia began to deteriorate over her expansionist policy against Turkey, the territorial integrity of which Britain had helped to guarantee, and this led to the outbreak of the so-called Crimean War in 1854. Britain and France declared war in March, and sent forces to the Crimea, whereupon followed the battles of Alma, Balaclava and Inkerman between then and November. Sebastopol was besieged, but the government faced increasing criticism of its war strategy, and when his coalition fell apart in February 1855 Aberdeen resigned. Lord Palmerston then formed a purely Liberal government, which successfully brought the siege of Sebastopol to a conclusion in September, and faced up to the implications of Florence Nightingale's nursing reforms, which highlighted one of the most unsatisfactory aspects of the Crimean War. The war was brought to an end by the Treaty of Paris in March 1856, whereby Britain and Russia agreed to respect Turkish independence, and the Black Sea was neutralised. The Russian fortifications of Sebastopol were to be demolished, so this was on the whole a successful outcome to Britain's first military involvement since Waterloo. Meanwhile further afield, the British annexed Oudh in India, giving rise to tensions with the Indian states, and provoked another Anglo-Chinese war by demanding additional trading rights which the Imperial government was not willing to concede. The Indian tensions erupted in 1857 in the form of the Indian Mutiny, during which the British garrison at Cawnpore was overrun in July and the women and children massacred, an event which led to intense anti-Indian feeling in Britain, and as result direct British rule was applied to India for the first time. Palmerston's aggressive stand was warmly welcomed, and the Liberals increased their majority in the general election which was held in that year. A government was only as strong as its party discipline, however, and when a discontented element in the Liberal majority allied with the Conservatives in February 1858, it resulted in the fall of Palmerston's apparently rock-solid ministry. On this somewhat flimsy basis the Earl of Derby formed a second minority Conservative government, which lasted a little more than a year, being brought down by the defeat of its Reform Bill in March 1859. The Conservatives in fact improved their position slightly in the general election of that year, but Palmerston again became Prime Minister. And this time succeeded in uniting the Liberals behind him, an outcome which was confirmed by Gladstone's budget of 1860, which left only a small number of items liable to duty.

The year 1860 also saw the cause of Italian unification much canvassed in Britain, where the ideas of Cavour and Garibaldi were warmly embraced by a public opinion generally favourable to nationalist movements. Ever anxious to court a little much-needed popularity, in October the government also committed itself to the same cause, and this caused diplomatic furore in several established states, although the move appears to have been prompted as much by fear of the French gaining influence there as of any ideological empathy. More difficult was the decision in 1861 to remain neutral in the American Civil War. Sympathy generally was with the North for obvious reasons, but the South supplied the cotton which kept the Lancashire mills running, and in 1862, when those supplies were cut off, the great cotton famine caused widespread economic distress in the area. There was nearly a rupture with the North when Confederate emissaries were taken off a British ship by Unionist agents, but the policy lasted the duration of the war, and led to improved relations thereafter. Gladstone meanwhile had won the support of politically aware working men by removing the paper duty, and thereby making knowledge cheaper. His reputation as a reformer was also enhanced by the Northern tours which he undertook in 1862, which were designed primarily to reassure those afflicted by the cotton famine, and to persuade them that it was not the result of government policy. As we have seen, Prince Albert died of typhoid in December 1861, and as a result the Queen became a virtual recluse, playing no part in the public life of the nation for many years. At first this was indulged sympathetically, but her gloomy appearance at the Prince of Wales's marriage in 1863 was noted unfavourably, and by 1864 her failure to appear at the state opening of Parliament was heavily criticised. In spite of his mother's disapproval, the Prince of Wales bore the lion's share of the monarch's public responsibilities, at least until she was created Empress of India in 1876. In 1862 also the first MCC cricket tour of Australia took place, establishing a sporting relationship which has lasted to the present day. The Football Association was formed in October 1863, the first organisation of its kind in the world and work was begun upon the London Metropolitan Railway – the precursor of the Underground. At the same time a row blew up between Prussia and Denmark over the border duchy of Schleswig-Holstein, a quarrel in which Britain maintained a firm neutrality, even hosting a conference in London in 1864 in a vain bid to resolve the issue. Gladstone further enhanced his reforming credentials in the same year, by making a declaration in favour of a further widening of the franchise, and the middle-class Manchester Reform Union came into existence to press the case in an orderly and peaceful fashion. The London Metropolitan Railway opened, and in the general election of July 1865 Palmerston significantly increased his majority in the Commons.

The Prime Minister, however, died in office in October and was succeeded by Lord Russell. Russell renewed his predecessor's pledge on parliamentary reform, and to emphasise the point a Reform League, consisting of middle-class radicals and trade union leaders was founded, placing the work of the Manchester Union on a national basis. However, the Liberals split over the nature of the reform to be undertaken, with the result that Russell's bill was defeated and he resigned in June 1866. This let in the Earl of Derby for a third go at forming a minority government, and since he had no commitment to reform the result was extra-parliamentary agitation in support of the great cause of the moment. As it turned out, the anxiety was misplaced, because a second Reform Bill was introduced in May 1867, and passed after numerous amendments and extensions in August. The whole provenance of this bill is confused, as are Disraeli's motives in promoting it, but eventually it ended up by giving the vote to all men over the age of twenty-one – 'manhood suffrage'. No one was yet sufficiently radical to envisage extending this privilege to women – that would have to await the twentieth century. Perhaps it was the strain of passing this measure against his conservative instincts and by calling upon Liberal votes, but Lord Derby resigned on the grounds of ill health in February 1868, and Benjamin Disraeli became Prime Minister for the first time. However, the general election in November produced a substantial Liberal majority, and Disraeli resigned without even meeting the new parliament. He could manage a parliament which was more or less hung, but not one in which his opponents enjoyed control, so William Gladstone was called upon to form his first ministry. This was to the Queen's regret, because she liked Disraeli, but the office of Prime Minister, although theoretically in the monarch's gift, was in practice disposed by other considerations – so she got Gladstone. One of his first tasks was the disestablishment of the Irish Church, a development which had been pending since the restoration of the Catholic bishops, and the reallocation of its resources to the relief of poverty and other social causes in 1869. This was followed in 1870 by the Irish Land

Act, giving protection to tenants against arbitrary eviction, and by an Elementary Education Act providing for local rate-supported board schools, although not yet making even elementary education compulsory. At the same time the civil service was reformed by providing admission (except to the Foreign Office) by competitive examination. This brought the government service into line with the universities, where the Schools and Tripos examinations had been introduced a few years earlier, and provided a more objective standard of the excellence which was now looked for.

Gladstone's second mission was to bring the Queen out of her self-imposed seclusion, an aim in which he was somewhat inhibited by the outbreaks of Fenian violence in Ireland, and the fears that these might lead to attempts on her life. He was almost completely unsuccessful for three years, but then the serious illness of the Prince of Wales in 1871 came to his rescue. Bertie's recovery caused an upsurge of popular support for the monarchy, and the Queen's decision to attend a public thanksgiving at St Paul's brought her back into the public eye. The fact that she survived an assassination attempt soon after quite restored her in the popular estimation. In 1874 Conservative success at the polls brought back Disraeli as Prime Minister, to Victoria's immense relief. She threw herself enthusiastically into his campaign to improve Britain's prestige in the world, and particularly its influence in an increasingly threatening Europe. This was a policy in which the marriages of the royal offspring played a significant part. As a gesture of solidarity with her Prime Minister, the Queen opened Parliament in person in 1876, 1877 and 1880, and she was graciously pleased to accept the title of Empress of India which was conferred on her by the Royal Titles Act of 1876. This was a development which had been under consideration for several years, and the reaction in India itself seems to have been favourable. Benjamin Disraeli was created Earl of Beaconsfield in 1876, but was defeated in the general election of 1880, and died in 1881, depriving the Queen of her main political friend. It would be fair to say that by this time Victoria's personality was fully operative again, as it had been in 1837 to 1840, before Albert's advent. She had been in a sense eclipsed by him, both in life and in death, and it had taken nearly twenty years of widowhood to escape from that influence. Apart from Disraeli, one of the main influences in this recuperation had been the highland ghillie John Brown, who had became during the 1870s her confidential servant, and emotional prop. Brown was unpopular at court because of his lowly status, and there were unsavoury rumours about their relationship; but although close it was perfectly proper, and she mourned his death in 1883 deeply. The Queen disliked Gladstone intensely, and tried unsuccessfully to find an alternative Prime Minister in 1880. She regarded herself as a true liberal, and thought that he had abandoned his principles in favour of radicalism and democracy. She particularly distrusted the 'demagogy' of his Midlothian campaign, but in the face of a large Liberal majority in the Commons, she had no choice but to accept him. The role of the monarch in the formation of ministries had diminished and was still diminishing. However, Gladstone's third ministry was defeated in 1886 over Irish Home Rule, and the Liberal Party split, which let in the Marquis of Salisbury at the head of the Conservative and Unionist Party (as it was now called), who held office until 1892.

For all her concern over the well-being of her people, Victoria did not take the support of the poor for granted, and was reluctant to gratify them by participating in the Golden Jubilee celebrations which marked the fiftieth anniversary of her accession in 1887. So although royalty gathered from all over the world, not only from Europe and India but from Japan, Persia and Siam, and were lavishly entertained, the Queen contented herself by appearing as the 'widow from Windsor', soberly clad amidst all the splendour. However, she did appear, and there was immense popular enthusiasm. At about the same time she acquired another exotic personal servant, this time an Indian called Abdul Karim, usually known as the 'munchi' or teacher, because he taught her Hindustani. Like Brown before him, he was a genuinely devoted servant, but he was also bitterly unpopular with the rest of the household, not because of his status but for racial reasons. Victoria refused to notice. Meanwhile the Conservatives had lost the general election of 1892, and that saw Gladstone back as Prime Minister at the head of a reunited Liberal Party. His fourth ministry was no more popular at Buckingham Palace than the first three had been, and when age at last forced his retirement in 1894 he was not even accorded the courtesy of being consulted over his successor. The Earl of Rosebery was the obvious choice, but he resigned following defeat in the Commons in 1895, and the Queen was happy to welcome back Lord Salisbury, whose tenure in office was to see out the remainder of the reign. He thus presided over the Diamond Jubilee celebrations of 1897, which saw a major service of thanksgiving at St George's Chapel, Windsor, where she was surrounded by three generations of her family, gathered from all over Europe. A public procession and celebrations followed on 22 June, culminating in an open-air service in Hyde Park – something which, on the occasion, the Queen appears to have enjoyed, in spite of her known dislike of large ceremonies. Gladstone died, unmourned, in May 1898, and there was almost a falling out with France over the Dreyfus Affair in 1899, because Victoria expressed her opinion of such goings on in no uncertain terms, ignoring the correctness of diplomatic practice. In spite of the fact that the outbreak of war in South Africa in October 1899 appeared to give her a new lease of life, by that time Victoria's faculties were failing. For several years she had been confined to a wheelchair for all journeys of more than a few steps, and during 1900 her health began visibly to fail. After Christmas her family again began to gather quietly, and she died at Osbourne in the presence of most of them on 22 January 1901. She was eighty-two years old, and had been Queen for nearly sixty-four years – the longest reign of any to date.

For much of her reign, and particularly during the last twenty years, she had been a symbol rather than a leader. During the years of her retirement the monarchy had withered. A frequent visitor at Balmoral and Osbourne, she was almost a stranger at Buckingham Palace, and republicanism rose to its highest level in the early 1870s – not only on the streets, but also at the highest political level: at least one member of the Liberal cabinet (although not Gladstone himself) was a closet republican. Just as the monarch had disappeared from public view, so it appeared that the monarchy might disappear also. That it did not do so was due to an astonishing process of reinvention. On the one hand, thanks largely to the efforts of Disraeli, Victoria became the 'mother of the Empire'. 'Beware of the widow at Windsor,' wrote Rudyard Kipling, 'for half of creation she owns ...' Through endless small wars and an aggressive commercial policy, British colonies and British interests were spread all over the world, and they came to focus on the person of the Queen in a way that they could never have done on her shifting ministers. And on the other hand, the monarchy adapted to the coming age of mass democracy. Having spent a century or more on the defensive against the aristocratic Georgian elite, and the wider Victorian middle class, it positively throve on mass support. Privacy had been the last resort of a queen driven out of political power, but it became the private face of the monarchy which was used as the basic tool to re-popularise it. Court ritual was not a public performance, and indeed behind closed doors it had become somewhat slapdash. Now that all changed, and the private face of the Queen became the basis of a new kind of ritual. This was worked out in the two jubilees of 1887 and 1897, in which the modest figure of Victoria, elderly and dumpy, became the focus of carefully orchestrated public performances. Out went Georgian muddle and in came thorough rehearsals and clockwork precision. The public loved it. The architect of this renaissance was Reginald Brett, Viscount Esher, who from the comparatively obscure office of Constable of Windsor Castle drove the whole operation forward. Brett was a man who shunned the limelight, but he had the confidence of the principal officers of the household, and more importantly, of the Queen herself. He was a man with a passion for organisation, who served on the committee on imperial defence which restructured the army after the debacle of the Boer War, but it is as the organiser of public spectacle that he deserves to be remembered. In effect he turned the monarchy from a failed political force into a ceremonial focus for popular adulation, giving it a new lease of life to carry it forward into the twentieth century.

PART 16
THE ANGLICISATION OF THE MONARCHY,
1901–1936

54

EDWARD VII, THE LONG-SERVING PRINCE (REIGNED 1901–1910)

Bertie, as he was always known in the family, was a survivor. As a child he survived the rigorous disapproval of his father, and as a young man the unreasonable suspicions and dislike of his mother, particularly during her years of seclusion. He emerged relaxed, good-humoured, and with a highly developed moral sense. He had excellent manners, was skilled in both French and German, and showed a natural gift for diplomacy. He was born at Buckingham Palace on 9 November 1841, the second child but eldest son of Victoria and Albert, and was created Prince of Wales and Earl of Chester about a month after his birth. He was a robust child, but the Queen's ambitions to turn him into a clone of his father were quickly disappointed. In 1847, when he was six, Albert drew up a strict regimen for his instruction, insisted on regular reports, and administered punishments in person. Bertie was never an academic child, and under this austere regime he became sulky and bad-tempered, unable to concentrate and falling behind with his lessons. When he was about eight he was placed with a tutor, one Henry Birch, to whom he took an instant dislike, becoming disobedient and impertinent. At first he shared his lessons with his younger brother Alfred, who was academically much brighter, but this arrangement fell apart after Birch resigned in 1852, when sibling hostility developed and made it impracticable. Nevertheless Bertie showed promising signs. He had an excellent memory, was very observant, and showed in many ways a sensitive nature, characteristics which should have appealed to his parents, but do not appear to have done so. He accompanied Victoria and Albert on their trips abroad, notably to Paris in 1855, which was to begin his long love affair with that city. More foreign excursions followed, all carefully chaperoned. The pretext was always study, but on one occasion he got drunk and kissed a pretty girl, an incident described by his escort as 'a squalid little debauch'. By the time that he was seventeen, everyone had given up trying to turn him into an imitation Albert, much to Victoria's chagrin. He went to Italy and met the Pope, and in October 1859 matriculated at Christ Church, Oxford.

However no normal student life awaited him, and in 1860 he went to North America, a tour which turned out to be something of a triumph because of the Prince's relaxed good humour and willingness to take things as he found them. On his return he switched universities, taking up residence at Madingley Hall, Cambridge, but his principal enthusiasm seem to have been for blood sports, and it was to Madingley that his father went in November 1861 to remonstrate with him over his lifestyle. As a result of this ill-advised visit, Albert became fatally ill, and died on 14 December following. For this the Queen blamed Bertie, and their ten-year estrangement began. In 1862 he was packed off to the Middle East on another 'study' trip, and in 1863 married (by arrangement) Princess Alexandra of Denmark, a pretty and intelligent seventeen-year-old, to whom he soon became deeply attached. Over the next few years Alexandra bore his children, and indulged his flirtations with relaxed good humour. She probably realised that they were all superficial, and did not touch her own position. Not so the Queen, who regarded her son's addiction to London club life and the racecourse at Newmarket with undisguised disapproval. The trouble, however, was largely of her own making, in that she kept him consistently underemployed, not even allowing him access to the political papers which passed between herself and the cabinet. Fortunately some politicians were more sympathetic, so that he did have a reasonable grasp of what was going on, but that was no thanks to Victoria. Because he was given no proper function, Bertie became increasingly self-indulgent, presumably on the assumption that whatever he did would be disapproved of anyway. 1870 was a bad year for the monarchy, and one observer commented, 'If more work had been found for the prince, the monarchy would never have come to such a pass,' as a result of the Queen's continued seclusion. Paradoxically the breach between them was healed by Bertie's near fatal attack of typhoid in 1871. The fear that she might lose her son, as she had lost her husband, jolted Victoria out of her paranoia, and her attendance at the thanksgiving service for his recovery was greeted with wild enthusiasm. Politically Bertie did not spring to life immediately, but the days of his rigid exclusion were over. He took on various official engagements, and represented the Queen on an extended, and very successful, tour of India in 1875–76. The Prince of Wales was a man of moderate and liberal opinions in politics, and much preferred Mr Gladstone to Mr Disraeli, a taste which directly contradicted that of his mother – as did his support for Irish Home Rule. However, unlike the Leicester House set of the 1750s, the Marlborough House set of the 1880s was not a political group, let alone one in opposition. It was more noted for its devotion to Newmarket and Cowes than to Westminster, and the Prince became a noted yachtsman and bloodstock breeder.

He also found an outlet in what might be called 'family diplomacy'. He had relatives spread around the ruling houses of Europe: the King of Denmark was his father-in-law, the King of

Greece his brother-in-law and the Kaiser his nephew. He talked to all these, and others, discreetly visited them, and reassured their governments of Britain's intentions in a way which no official representative could have done. His unique status was imperfectly understood outside the United Kingdom, and that gave him a distinct advantage in these exchanges. In 1878, for example, he was able to smooth ruffled feathers in France over Britain's acquisition of Cyprus, an achievement for which he was specifically thanked by Lord Salisbury. The latter part of Victoria's reign also saw the Prince undertaking a number of public appearances on her behalf, for instance the opening of Tower Bridge on 29 June 1886. He became president of the Society of Arts, a trustee of the British Museum and a governor of Wellington School. In other words he busied himself with good causes. Meanwhile his own children were growing up under the watchful eye of their grandmother. Eddy, the eldest, was an unsatisfactory youth, who would have been a disastrous heir to the throne. However, Eddy died on 7 January 1892, just short of his twenty-eighth birthday, leaving the normal and competent George as the heir in his place. Deeply as Bertie and Alexandra mourned the passing of their eldest child, there is no doubt that his death was a relief to the country as a whole. The Boer War was widely deplored in Europe, creating image problems for Britain, and leading to an assassination attempt against the Prince at the Gare du Nord in Paris on 4 April 1900. He shrugged the incident off, but it was a warning of what was to come. Finally, ten months short of his sixtieth birthday, and after the longest incumbency of the principality in history, Albert Edward, Prince of Wales, became king. Instead of taking the title Albert I, as his mother would have wished, he chose to reign under the more English name of Edward VII.

Lord Salisbury continued as Prime Minister, the general election giving him the requisite majority, but Edward transformed the court almost immediately. As soon as his mother's obsequies had been observed (she chose to be buried at Frogmore with Albert, rather than at Westminster), Edward introduced his own friends. The whole atmosphere, which had become gloomy and claustrophobic during Victoria's last years, was lightened and refreshed. Within a year Parliament had also revised the Civil List, giving him an income of £470,000, which, since a policy of sound investment over the years had left him with no debts, was more than adequate for his needs. Clearly his gambling had been well within his means, and he was the first sovereign to come to the throne solvent for centuries – probably since Henry VIII in 1509. There was, however, an early scare of a different kind. In the autumn of 1901 the King developed appendicitis, then a dangerous condition. Prayers were offered for his recovery all over the Empire and on 23 January 1902 he underwent a pioneering and successful operation. There was a huge collective sigh of relief. Nevertheless convalescence was slow, in accordance with the medical practice of that period, and it was 9 August 1902 before the coronation could take place. A wait of over sixty years had finally come to an end. In spite of the relaxed Edwardian style which he led and patronised, his reign was to be a troubled one politically. Most especially, Britain was threatened by the ambitions of Kaiser Wilhelm II, a ruler who enjoyed far greater power in Germany than Edward could ever wield in Britain. He had been present at Victoria's deathbed, but his relations with his uncle were never easy, and Edward made no secret of the fact that he believed Wilhelm to be slightly mad. This made family diplomacy impossible, and necessitated a search for allies where they could be found. The Anglo-Japanese naval treaty of 1902 was one of the results of this, and the Anglo-French alliance of 1904 another. The King could not directly intervene in any of these negotiations, and did not do so, but his long love affair with France nevertheless paid dividends. He loved the Mediterranean, spent months on the Riviera, and had helped to turn Biarritz into the fashionable resort which it had become by 1900. In May 1903 Edward paid a state visit to Paris, and President Loubert reciprocated in July. This exchange, as well as improving the atmosphere between the two countries, also provided an excellent screen for the two foreign ministers, Declasse and Lansdowne, to hold face-to-face discussions. The result was the so-called Entente Cordiale, which shaped Anglo-French relations down to and during the First World War. Officially Edward had played no part in this outcome, but everyone knew that his benign patronage had played a large part in bringing it about. In domestic politics the King had no longer any role, it being accepted by this time that the leader of the victorious party in a general election would automatically become the next Prime Minister. On these terms the Marquis of Salisbury was succeeded in July 1902 by Arthur Balfour, and he by Sir Henry Campbell-Bannerman in December 1905. However, when Herbert Asquith won the election of March 1908 a problem arose, because the King was in France, and was reluctant to return for the swearing-in ceremony. A new Prime Minister had to kiss hands before taking office, and that apparently meant taking the entire cabinet to Biarritz. An anguished negotiation followed, because Edward was unwilling to disrupt his holiday, and Asquith was reluctant to go so far. Eventually a compromise was agreed, whereby both parties agreed to travel to Paris, and Asquith became the only Prime Minister so far to be sworn in outside the

United Kingdom. Edward's behaviour was regarded as not a little exasperating, especially by those directly inconvenienced.

This was trivial, however, by comparison with the constitutional crisis which had developed by 1910. In 1909 the Conservative-dominated House of Lords rejected the budget presented by the Chancellor of the Exchequer, David Lloyd George, on behalf of the Liberal government. This budget was designed to prepare for both war and social reform – free school meals, old age pensions and labour exchanges – to all of which the Conservatives were opposed. The Liberals denounced the Lords' veto as unconstitutional, which it was not, and that created the difficulty. The only way around this obstruction was to persuade the King to create enough Liberal peers to force the budget through, as had been threatened by William IV in respect of the first Reform Bill in 1832. This Asquith asked the King to do, and Edward agreed on the condition that the Prime Minister went to the country to secure a new mandate. Asquith won the ensuing election, although with a reduced majority. However, the King was in poor health before the election was called, and within days of the result being declared, and long before he could do anything about creating new peers, Edward died on 6 May 1910. The constitutional crisis was therefore postponed for his son and successor George V to deal with. Edward had reigned very much as he had lived in his latter days as Prince of Wales, relaxed and good-humoured. He was disinclined to do more than was necessary, but capable of showing both wisdom and discretion when those qualities were called for. More importantly, perhaps, he shifted the monarchy back into a masculine mode after his mother's long incumbency. As a woman, Victoria had had a problem with the imagery of power, but that power was now long since gone, and Edward faced the need to readjust the imagery back into a kingly form, without seeming to claim an authority which he no longer possessed. His laid-back style and quiet manipulations provided an ideal solution. The climate and social structure of his court could best be described as 'transitional', and it would be left to his son and grandson to reinvent the monarchy in a mode more suitable for the modern world. In that process the transforming holocaust known as the First World War played a determining role, and was a crisis with which Edward would have been quite incapable of coping. He belonged to the older world in which he had grown up, and in retrospect his reign looks something like the twilight of the gods.

55

GEORGE V AND THE HOUSE OF WINDSOR (REIGNED 1910–1936)

George was the most respectable and least controversial of all the Princes of Wales. He enjoyed excellent relations with his father, and deeply mourned his passing, saying (honestly), 'I have never had a cross word with him in my life.' This was due as much to Edward's easygoing nature as it was to George's filial obedience, but it was an agreeable contrast to Edward's own relations with his parents, to say nothing of the attitudes of George II and Frederick a century and a half earlier. George was born at Marlborough House on 3 June 1865, the second son of Edward and Alexandra. From a very early age his elder brother Eddy was a problem, and it was with relief that the Prince and Princess of Wales realised that their second son was absolutely normal. From 1871 the two of them were placed under the tutelage of John Dalton, a man with whom George established an immediate bond. However, Dalton was a man of limited accomplishments, and, unlike generations of their predecessors, the boys were taught no modern languages, a circumstance which was to cause George serious embarrassment in later life. What they did learn was a lot of sporting accomplishments, such as shooting and swimming. It was altogether a different regimen from that in which their father had been brought up. Meanwhile Eddy was the heir, and George was destined for a career in the navy, as George III's son William had been. In 1877, when they were thirteen and twelve respectively, both boys were sent to HMS *Britannia* at Dartmouth, accompanied by Dalton as their resident tutor. There had been some doubt as to whether the tough naval regime would suit Eddy, but Dalton was quite clear that the move would be beneficial to him, provided that George went too. George's presence was essential, in his opinion, if Eddy were to do any work at all. They remained at *Britannia* for two years, during which time George learned the basics of cosmography and navigation, and Eddy appears to have learned nothing in particular. Thereafter their father seems to have been of the opinion that the best education would be to keep them moving, and from 1879 to 1882 they undertook a variety of trips around the world, visiting the West Indies, South America, Australia and New Zealand among other places, journeys that we know about because John Dalton accompanied them and kept a journal which he subsequently published. They returned in August 1882, and George was immediately commissioned as a sub-lieutenant, and posted to HMS *Canada*. In 1884–85 he attended the Royal Naval College at Greenwich, and passed all the regular examinations for promotion. In 1889 he received his first command, the functional and unglamorous torpedo boat 79, and in 1890 was promoted to

HMS *Thrush*, a gunboat. Neither of these were token commands, and he really was a competent naval officer. His royal status was not forgotten. He went to Canada in a semi-official capacity in 1884, and on his return his grandmother made him a Knight of the Garter.

In November 1891 he contracted typhoid, and for several weeks was seriously ill. He was still convalescent when his elder brother succumbed to pneumonia in January 1892, and he was suddenly catapulted into the direct line of succession to the throne. Later in 1892 he was created Duke of York, and took his seat in the House of Lords. His active career in the navy was over. Apart from these expectations, he also inherited from Eddy the latter's fiancée, Princess Mary of Teck. This was an arrangement made by his parents, but one to which George had no objection at all. Nor apparently did Mary. They became officially engaged on 2 May 1893, and were married in the chapel royal at St James's on 6 July. Mary was a pretty and intelligent girl, who realised quickly that she had come out of these negotiations rather well, and they became a devoted couple. Unlike most of his predecessors, George possessed all the domestic virtues, and no shadow of scandal ever clouded their relationship. Their children appeared at regular intervals, starting with David in June 1894; there then followed Albert (1895), Mary (1897), Henry (1900), George (1902) and John (1905), of whom only the last failed to survive infancy. George was an oddity in the royal family in that his tastes and lifestyle were more bourgeois than aristocratic. He was an excellent shot, collected stamps, and was interested in constitutional history. He was also very insular in his habits, and has been described as a thoroughgoing Norfolk squire. He even spent his honeymoon in the prosaic surroundings of the White Lodge at Sandringham. Like his father he was a Liberal in politics, and an admirer of William Gladstone, both of which things also distanced him from the court. Nevertheless he undertook his share of royal duties, visiting Ireland in 1897 and Germany for the Crown Prince's coming of age in April 1900. He was all set to make an extended tour of the Commonwealth when his grandmother died in January 1901, and one of the first questions his father had to answer as king was whether to allow the tour to go ahead in view of the period of mourning required. It went ahead in March, and George and Mary visited Australia, New Zealand, Canada and South Africa, a total journey of some 45,000 miles, in the course of which he is alleged to have shaken 24,855 hands – although who was counting is not recorded! He had become Duke of Cornwall and heir to the throne automatically on his grandmother's death, and on his return from the world tour his father created him Prince of Wales and Earl of Chester.

It was shortly after this that he made one of his few memorable speeches. He felt that the court and the government were too complacent about the threats facing Britain, not only from Germany, which was well understood, but from the relative decline in her industrial and economic position, and the danger of strained relations with the United States. 'The Old Country,' he claimed, 'must wake up if she intends to maintain her old position of pre-eminence.' This speech was remarkably well received both by the press and the business community, and its importance was well understood by the King, who would have been quite incapable of delivering it himself. George was reticent by nature, but in the wake of this speech his relationship with his father flourished. He saw all the state papers and was in as good a position to form a judgement on any public issue as were the officers of state themselves. He also benefited greatly from the appointment in 1901 of Arthur Bigge as his private secretary. Bigge held this position for thirty years, and the two men became close friends: 'He taught me how to be a king,' George later observed. From October 1905 to May 1906, the Prince and Princess of Wales were in India, a visit which gave him a good grasp of the problems then troubling British government in the Subcontinent, most of which he judged were self-inflicted. While they were in Burma at the end of their tour, news reached them of the landslide victory of the Liberals in the 1906 election which brought in Sir Henry Campbell-Bannerman as Prime Minister. This was good news, but the fact that his majority was boosted by fifty-three MPs belonging to the new Labour Party worried George. He saw it as evidence of the advance of popular socialism, and although he was right, his anxiety was misplaced. On his return, he wisely did not meddle with the government's social reform agenda, but concentrated his energies on imperial defence and the reform of the navy, both matters upon which he was well informed. Meanwhile he visited Berlin in 1908 in a fruitless attempt to ease tensions with Germany, and Canada again in the same year, in the course of which his suspicions of Lloyd George as Chancellor of the Exchequer began to filter into his speeches. It was Lloyd George's 'People's Budget' of 1909 which provoked the constitutional crisis already alluded to. He proposed a tax on unearned income, and this touched the Conservative peers on the raw. They rejected the measure and Prime Minister Asquith asked the King to create more Liberal peers. He obtained a new mandate for this in the general election which followed, but became more than ever dependent upon Labour Party support. The King then made it clear that the constitutional position of the House of Lords was under review, but he died on 6 May 1910, before he could do anything about it. His funeral, which took place on 22 June, was the last great gathering of European royalty before the holocaust of 1914–18 swept most of them away. It was also a celebration of Empire and a great public spectacle, in which hundreds of thousands of people lined the route – a last hurrah for Victorian splendour.

So George inherited a constitutional crisis, but he was not eventually called upon to do anything about it. An all-party conference in the autumn of 1910 resulted in deadlock, and a further general election in December reinforced the mandate for change. The result was the Parliament Act of August 1911 which removed the House of Lords' veto on any measure which had duly passed the Commons, reducing the Upper House to the delaying and deliberative function which it still has today. Unwilling to be swamped with a new Liberal intake, the Conservative majority allowed this Act to pass by the simple process of abstaining, so the royal prerogative was not called upon and the King remained an interested spectator of the drama. The passage of the Parliament Act also enabled the Government of Ireland Act to pass as well, which made certain concessions on the operations of local government, but went nowhere near meeting the nationalist demands. In 1911 George decided to visit India again. Aware of the Congress movement and its aims, he decided to hold a coronation ceremony at a great durbar in Delhi, and there on 12 December he was crowned as emperor, receiving the homage of the Indian princes. This made a great and favourable impression, but did not meet the demands of the Congress Party, which was already looking for an end to British rule altogether. In February 1912 the King and Queen returned to find the country in the grip of industrial recession and labour strikes. From these it was rescued, ironically enough, by the outbreak of war with Germany in August 1914, which stimulated the munitions industry and caused all strikes to be patriotically suspended. At first the war was popular and 'khaki fever' gripped the country; but, as it dragged on and the casualties became more and more appalling, the mood changed. There was little that the King could do about this apart from wearing military uniform in public, and remaining at his post in Buckingham Palace. What he could do, he did indefatigably, paying over 450 visits to the troops in the Low Countries, and going almost as often to hospitals, shipyards and munitions factories at home. He and Mary adopted an ostentatiously frugal lifestyle, in keeping with the hardness of the times, and his no-nonsense manner went down extremely well. In 1917, in deference to the general mood of xenophobia, and particularly the hatred of all things German, George changed his family name from Saxe-Coburg-Gotha to Windsor, which was a master stroke in the search for mere Englishness. 'I'm damned if I'll be an alien,' the King is alleged to have said. The war on the whole enhanced the prestige of the monarchy, but it left everyone emotionally and physically exhausted, and its end, although wildly celebrated, caused all the dormant domestic problems to resurface. A virtual civil war erupted in Ireland, in which George sought earnestly but ineffectually to intervene, and resulted in the formation of the Irish Free State on 6 December 1921. Nearly a decade of strikes and industrial unrest resulted in the General Strike of 1926.

There were, however, positive achievements during these years as well. As early as 1917 George issued an Order in Council liberalising the marriage rules for the royal family. His family now being English by name, it should be English in behaviour as well. So out went the protocol of royal blood, which had led to so many marriages with German princely families, and in came the commoner, opening the way for domestic unions, with mixed consequences as we shall see, but a change of historic significance. The Suffragette movement also obtained the parliamentary vote for women on the same terms as men in 1929, and the first women MPs took their seats in the House of Commons. Equally important was the constitutional accommodation of the Labour Party, the rise of which, as we have seen, had caused anxious moments at Buckingham Palace. In the general election of December 1923, 258 Conservative members were returned, 191 Labour and 159 Liberal. Stanley Baldwin's Conservative government did not resign at once, but waited until it was defeated in January 1924, whereupon the King, with strict constitutional propriety, sent for Ramsey MacDonald, as the leader of the next-largest party, to form a government. Noses were held all around Westminster, and the King allowed himself a wry comment about what his grandmother would have thought of such an eventuality. In the event MacDonald's government lasted only ten months, but it impressed everyone as a sober and serious-minded group of men, who could be well entrusted with responsibility, and in May 1929 when a further election returned Labour as the largest single party, George had no hesitation in sending for him again. The Labour Party thus became a normal part of the constitutional machinery, in a way which was to prove immensely beneficial for the political future of the country. Meanwhile, the King's health was faltering. In February 1925 he developed severe bronchitis, and the Mediterranean cruise which was supposed to restore him was a failure; then in the autumn of 1928 he became ill again, this time more seriously. He underwent two operations from which he barely recovered, and this served to focus attention on his heir.

Unfortunately relations in that direction were nowhere near as good as George's had been with his own father. It was not that David was underemployed. That had been a problem during the war, when the need to keep up appearances without exposing him to unnecessary danger had led to a series of more or less artificial staff appointments, but it was not so during the 1920s. David had followed his father in undergoing naval training, but had never experienced active service, being only sixteen when his grandfather's death had left him as heir to the throne. In July 1911 he was invested as Prince of Wales at Caernarvon Castle, a largely bogus ceremony which was invented by Lloyd George, at that time constable of the castle, and in 1912 was sent on a heavily chaperoned visit to France. In October 1912 he went up to Magdalen College, Oxford, an exposure from which he was rescued by the outbreak of war two years later, and the need to 'do his bit'. In the 1920s he interested himself in social issues, particularly in the South Wales mining areas, which he visited for the first time in 1919, and in the affairs of the Empire. He was actually travelling in East Africa when news of his father's health brought him hastily home in 1928. Unfortunately there was also a negative side to the Prince's personality, and that was what caused problems with his strait-laced father. With his good looks and superficial charm, he was altogether too like the idols of the emerging culture of the Hollywood film, and he capitalised on it. He loved the night life of London, and indulged in a series of affairs of a more or less scandalous nature. In this he resembled his grandfather, but to George he had become the embodiment of that 'modern world' which he so much deplored. In 1930 he met Wallis Simpson, and became infatuated with her, to the extent that her husband became determined to seek a divorce, and David became equally determined to take his place. The establishment was horrified, and the anxiety did untold damage to the King's fragile health. A constitutional crisis was already brewing, therefore, when George died on 20 January 1936. David, whose grief was a measure of the extent to which he was aware how much he had upset the old man, decided to take the regnal name of Edward, which was actually one of his Christian names, in deference to family feeling. It was therefore as Edward VIII that he emerged to face the realities of his new position – and the omens were not good.

PART 17
THE ABDICATION CRISIS AND DOMESTIC MONARCHY, 1936–1952

56

EDWARD VIII (AND WALLIS SIMPSON) (REIGNED JANUARY–DECEMBER 1936)

David, as he was always known until his accession, was born at White Lodge, in Richmond Park on 23 June 1894, the first child of George and Mary, at that time Duke and Duchess of York. Because she produced five more children over the next ten years, the Duchess farmed out the nursery duties to an extensive staff, and saw relatively little of them. This meant that the siblings grew close to each other, and David became inseparable from his younger brother Albert, who was born in 1895. The children were cared for by a governess, and had little contact with others of the same age. Their father had no gift with children, being gruff and off-hand, and most of the family was in Germany. After this unpromising start, things got worse, because in 1902 the two older boys were placed under the care of a tutor called Henry Hansell. The best that can be said for Hansell is that his charges liked him, and that he was good at organising football matches. He was a philistine, and possessed a self-assurance which squeezed the life out of a naturally adventurous boy such as David, who later described his regimen as 'five curiously ineffectual years'. Hansell seems to have deceived the Duke and Duchess, but in fact he was incompetent, and the boys made little progress under his tuition. They were better served by the separate tutors who taught them French and German, and in those subjects their progress was normal. David, moreover, was not another Eddy; he had a lively and enquiring mind and was described in 1908 as being 'composed and clever'. George had enjoyed his naval training and could not imagine anything more appropriate for his own sons, so in 1907 at the age of thirteen, David was subjected to the ordeal of the entrance examinations for the Royal Naval College at Osbourne. He passed well enough, and was placed about the middle of the order when he completed the course in 1909. From there he went on to Dartmouth, as his father had done, but there the similarity came to an end, because by the time that his course finished in 1910 he was the heir to the throne, and although he was gazetted as a midshipman, this was a mere formality, as he would never see active service.

On 13 July 1911 he was, as we have seen, created Prince of Wales. The ceremony, which involved a lot of ritual and was apparently modelled on that used at the creation of Henry of Monmouth in 1399, also meant that David had to learn a few set pieces in Welsh, a feature which he plainly regarded as ridiculous. Nevertheless he went through with it, fancy dress and all, and in spite of its artificiality it was surprisingly well received in Wales. The College of Arms went to considerable pains to ensure that his heraldic achievement was authentic, and Lloyd George clearly knew his audience. Off stage, however, David was having problems. He took to smoking heavily, and indulged in excessive amounts of physical exercise, being convinced, apparently, that he was running to fat. In an attempt to remedy this, when he returned from France in October 1912, he was matriculated at Magdalen College, Oxford. Academically this was a failure in spite of the best efforts of Herbert Warren, the President, who acted as his tutor, because his previous education had simply not prepared him for the demands of a university course. He enjoyed the social life, and made one or two lasting friends, but he wisely refrained from completing any course, and took no degree. In the summer of 1913 he visited Germany, where he also enjoyed himself a good deal, and his charm made a favourable impression, even on those who were vainly trying to improve his mind. But time was running out for Anglo-German relations and in the summer of 1914 David quit Oxford with some relief for a commission in the Grenadier Guards. This, it soon transpired, was little more than an excuse to put him in the fashionable khaki, and although he undertook royal duties like inspecting the troops and visiting field hospitals, finding him a proper job was another matter. In 1915 he joined the Headquarters Staff in France as an aide-de-camp to the Commander in Chief, and his well-oiled charm proved to be a great asset when dealing with the French high command. However, his reports were of little value, and his efforts to get closer to the action were repeatedly (and understandably) frustrated. In 1916 he took a break to visit Egypt and the Canal Zone, where he learned to handle large crowds with some aplomb, and enjoyed a huge success in public relations. Then it was back to France, and to more boredom. This was partly his own fault as he lacked the application to do the paperwork required of a staff officer, and was reluctant to read, which was essential for the type of work which he was supposed to be doing. He deplored the apparent endlessness of the conflict and the dreadful casualties, becoming at one point so depressed that he even contemplated suicide. However, his depression did not last, and there were compensations. He became interested in the technology of warfare, particularly tanks and aeroplanes, spent some time with the Canadian forces in northern France, and made the acquaintance of the newly arrived Americans. The latter he found refreshingly egalitarian in their attitude – his status cut no ice with them, and that he found attractive. Above all he acquired a profound admiration for the average British 'Tommy', particularly his courage and perseverance, and this respect was to turn him into the 'People's Prince' in the years after the war.

In 1918, at the age of twenty-four, David had finally grown up. This was partly thanks to the attentions of an experienced prostitute in Amiens who had, two years earlier, introduced him to the joys of sex, a discovery which led on to a series of affairs. By the end of the war the Prince of Wales was well on the way be becoming an experienced *roué*, and after the Armistice this fitted in well enough with the hedonistic atmosphere which prevailed in certain quarters as people tried to forget the appalling experiences which they had recently endured. The other, and more important, reaction to the renewal of peace was that domestic social and political conflicts, which had been suppressed in the cause of patriotic unity, resurfaced strongly. For the time being, the Prince was mainly employed on international duties, where his ease of manner gave him an immediate advantage. He toured Canada and the United States in 1919, trying successfully to reinforce those alliances which had been made during the war. The British and American governments had come to the conclusion that although they were not always in agreement, they could no longer afford to fall out, and the Prince's visit was good way of sealing that understanding without making any political commitment. In 1920 a similar visit, for a similar purpose, was made to Australia and New Zealand, and in 1921–22 to India. There the agenda was somewhat different because the Congress Party, which was strong by this time and claimed to speak for all educated Indian opinion, boycotted the entire event, and David was forced to maintain his position by an extreme formality which did not suit his style at all. He became very depressed and claimed that he was not meeting the Indians as he had expected to do, but the officials who had organised it pronounced the visit a success, which probably says it all about their attitude to 'the natives'. From India he went on to Japan, where he mixed a shrewd appraisal of the country's growing economic and military power with a bilious disapproval of the imperial family, who were not impressed by his relaxed and informal approach. When he returned in July 1922 he was fairly described as 'a great ambassador for the Empire'. It was not his fault that it was on its last legs.

At home he began to busy himself with issues of public concern, where his status and independence of party politics gave him an advantage. As we have seen, he went to South Wales in 1919, and spent four days visiting the slums of Cardiff and going down the neighbouring mines. This was to be the first of many such visits around Britain. When there was a miners' strike in South Wales in 1920, he made considerable efforts to keep himself informed of developments, and generally showed a concerned interest. He also endeavoured to be a responsible landlord on his Duchy of Cornwall estates, setting up farming cooperatives, and investing heavily in new machinery for the Cornish tin mines. This level of social concern was new, and quite distinct from the kind of charitable interests which his mother had shown. In 1926 he visited the slums of Glasgow, and warmly welcomed President Roosevelt's New Deal initiative in the United States, telling the American ambassador in 1934 that Britain could do with something of the same sort. In a sense he was feeling his way towards a new style of monarchy, but the establishment was not ready for anything so radical. His engagement with the poor, like his taste in amusements, was seen as 'advanced' and not at all respectable. He invested heavily in the Fairbridge Farm School movement in

Western Australia, and in other similar schemes elsewhere in the Commonwealth, a concern which caught the public imagination at home through its combination of philanthropy and imperial vision. He even launched an appeal through the *Times* newspaper in 1934 for £100,000 to establish more schools on the Fairbridge model on the ground that this was an imperial investment.

Then in 1930 he met Wallis Simpson. Already once divorced, she was the wife of an American shipping magnate, Ernest Simpson, and her intimacy with the Prince soon indicated that a second divorce was in the offing. She quickly took over his private life, to the impotent rage of the King and the despair of Queen Mary. By the beginning of 1936 this situation was undoubtedly affecting the King's already fragile health, and the entire political establishment was appalled by the prospect which was now in view. Early in January the Prince's chief of staff, in consultation with George's private secretary, drew up an ultimatum for the leaders of the two principal political parties, Stanley Baldwin and Ramsey MacDonald, to lay before the Prince of Wales. His private life, he was to be told, had usurped his public one, and this could not be tolerated. All the good work which he had done in the 1920s was being destroyed and, in short, unless he returned to his traditional duties and upheld traditional values, he would not be a fitting king. In the event his father's death pre-empted a response to this manifesto, but it made its relevance even more pressing, in that the unsatisfactory person described was now king. Mrs Simpson was put on hold, but she had no intention of going away, nor would Edward have allowed it. The new king swept in, as might have been expected, on a wave of innovation and modernisation, which saw the dismissal of many old and trusted servants. He revisited South Wales in the autumn, going to a number of mining villages, training centres, housing schemes, and a social centre for the unemployed. In spite of the deep economic depression, he was greeted with enthusiasm wherever he went, and made a powerful speech at Mountain Ash, pledging that his interest in the principality would never diminish. However, Mrs Simpson had not gone away. There was talk of a morganatic marriage, and of making her Duchess of Edinburgh. There was even talk of the King taking his actions to the country in a species of referendum, a course which all political parties viewed with hostility and alarm. It was a question of irresistible force meeting immovable matter, and on this occasion the political matter proved more obdurate than the royal force. The governments of the Commonwealth were consulted, and all (although in varying degree) expressed their disapproval of the King's obvious intention. Since Edward had no intention of giving up the woman he loved, or taking her as his mistress in the time-honoured fashion, there could only be one possible outcome. On 7 December 1936, without even having undergone a coronation, Edward VIII abdicated in favour of his younger brother Albert, announcing his decision through the relatively new medium of the radio broadcast. A diffident forty-year-old thus became saddled with the responsibility of rebuilding the monarchy after this desperate adventure. Characteristically he did not call himself Albert I, any more than his grandfather had done, but took the prosaic title of George VI.

Edward was created Duke of Windsor and shunted into exile within days of his abdication, and six months later married Wallis Simpson against a freezing background of family and political disapproval. Only late in 1940 did the Duke receive an official posting – as Governor General of the Bahamas – and there, safely out of the way, the Windsors sat out the war. Politically and constitutionally they had become an irrelevance. After the war they returned to France and Edward tried unsuccessfully to obtain some employment or recognition from successive British governments. He visited Britain from time to time, and outlived his brother by twenty years, but was never reconciled to his family. In marrying Wallis Simpson he had burned his boats. Eventually he was visited in Paris just days before his death by his niece, Queen Elizabeth II, when it is to be hoped that some token of forgiveness was offered. He died on 27 May 1972, and his body was flown back to England for burial. He was seventy-seven years old and had spent the last thirty-six of them in exile. He had been glamorous and flamboyant, and although that earned him some popular acclaim, it had alienated all those in power with whom he had to deal. The British monarchy was undoubtedly in need of modernisation – but he had chosen the wrong way to go about it.

57

GEORGE VI (REIGNED 1936–1952)

George V's second son was born at York Cottage on the Sandringham estate in Norfolk on 14 December 1895, and was christened Albert Frederick Arthur George. For several years he was deeply attached to his elder brother, David, and with him suffered from Henry Hansell's regime in the royal schoolroom. He appears to have been a fragile, diffident child, and early developed the stammer which remained with him until after his accession. Nevertheless he followed David into the navy, enrolling at Osbourne in 1907 at the age of twelve, and then on to Dartmouth in 1909. He was not apparently as naturally gifted as his brother, preferring cricket to his studies, but he was more serious in his intentions, and these were unaffected by his father's accession to the throne in 1910. He was gazetted as a midshipman on HMS *Collingwood* at the outbreak of war, and stayed in the navy, being promoted second lieutenant in 1916. He served throughout the war, and was present at the Battle of Jutland in the same year, a circumstance which caused his parents acute anxiety, but did his self-confidence no harm at all. While David fretted as a staff officer in France, Bertie was in the thick of the action. He transferred to the Royal Naval Air Service, and qualified as a pilot in 1918. At the end of the war he was serving with the Royal Air Force, of which he was one of the original officers. The King had celebrated his twenty-first birthday by creating him a Knight of the Garter, then at the age of twenty-four he gave up his uniform and spent a year as a mature student at Trinity College, Cambridge, without apparently benefiting very much from the experience. In 1920 he was created Duke of York, and took his seat in the House of Lords. He went about his share of the royal duties diligently and without fuss, and was not at all resentful of David's much higher profile. Nor did he undertake the same overseas tours as David, possibly because his stammer made it difficult for him to deliver speeches. His principal interest was in education, and he was responsible for creating the Duke of York's camps. In 1923 he married, his bride being the twenty-three-year-old Elizabeth Bowes Lyon, the daughter of the 14th Earl of Strathmore – a marriage only made possible by the Order in Council of 1917, which had altered the rules. In spite of her aristocratic lineage, Elizabeth was a commoner in royal terms. Their first child, Elizabeth, was born in April 1926 and the second, Margaret, in August 1930. From the first the Duke and Duchess of York presented to the world a face of harmony and domestic comfort, very much at odds with David's louche lifestyle and restless search for gratification.

When Edward VIII, as David had become on the death of their father, was embroiled in the crisis which led to his abdication, Albert did his best to make him see the course of duty. However, it was all very well for him to take the high moral ground; he was happily married and could afford to be sceptical about his brother's matrimonial intentions. In any event his intervention was fruitless, and on 7 December 1936 he found himself king, a position for which he appeared to have no natural talent, and only the most rudimentary training. He and Elizabeth were crowned on 12 May 1937, and the service was broadcast by the BBC, in a groundbreaking exercise in technology for which the King had to give his consent. It was a precedent for what was to come, as George VI strove valiantly under the guidance of Lionel Logue, and with eventual success, to overcome that stammer which had so long afflicted him, and was thus able to use this new means of communicating with his people. Stanley Baldwin continued as Prime Minister until he gave way to Neville Chamberlain in May 1937, by which time relations with the National Socialist regime in Germany were close to breaking point. The Nazis (as they were called) had come to power as a direct result of the short-sighted Versailles settlement which had ended the First World War and penalised Germany severely. Ignoring the restrictions imposed by that treaty, the Nazis revitalised the German economy by a policy of rearmament, and began to adopt an aggressive stance, both towards their neighbours and towards dissident minorities within the country. The particular sufferers were the communists and the Jews, against whom a patriotic xenophobia was worked up, which resulted in several atrocities. Confronted with this implicit challenge, not merely to Britain but to the international order, Chamberlain was faced with a dilemma, which may be summed up as follows: rearmament or appeasement? The Prime Minister decided on the latter option, and even following the German Anschluss or takeover of Austria in 1938 endeavoured to negotiate with Adolf Hitler, the Nazi Chancellor. He returned from Munich, famously, with the 'scrap of paper' which he claimed guaranteed peace with honour, and upon which the King congratulated him. However, Hitler's territorial ambitions were very far from being satisfied. Britain had signed a treaty with Poland, guaranteeing that country's integrity, and in August 1939 the Germans ignored this by invading. Chamberlain was forced to issue an ultimatum to Hitler, and when that was disregarded, to declare war. For the second time in a generation Britain found itself at war with Germany, only this time there was an ideological agenda which had been missing in 1914, because the Nazis were racial supremacists of a sort which had not been known in the earlier conflict. As in the wars against Napoleon in the early nineteenth century, Britain was also up against a European power with hegemonic pretensions.

Of this unfolding tragedy the King was a virtual spectator, supporting his government as protocol demanded. In May 1939 he and the Queen visited the United States and Canada, in a goodwill tour which was to have momentous consequences, as the US entered the war on the Allied side in 1941. As the conflict developed, and more and more of the world became sucked into it, George VI did not don khaki as his father had done, but rather he and the Queen became the leaders of what came to be known as the 'home front'. As the eighteen-year-old Elizabeth enrolled in the ATS and learned to strip car engines, her parents sat it out at Buckingham Palace. This was against much political advice, but it was a sound decision, because as the air raids on London intensified in 1940, their position assumed many of the characteristics of the front line. The King and Queen visited those parts of East London which had suffered most severely in the 'Blitz', and Buckingham Palace suffered several direct hits. No one was injured, least of all the royal family, but the Queen famously remarked that now she 'felt able to look the people of the East End in the face'. Once the Blitz was over, and their exposed position became less evident, the royal family became the symbols of national pride and defiance. Winston Churchill, who succeeded Neville Chamberlain as Prime Minister on 10 May 1940, headed a coalition government dedicated to winning the war, and became a great war leader, but it was the King who symbolised the spirit of the nation. Politically he had virtually no input, beyond issuing the formal invitation to Churchill to take office, but that did not matter. Indeed it was an advantage because industrial and other social issues, although suppressed by the war effort, did not go away, and as the war drew to an end and various blueprints for a post-war society began to be posted, he was not disposed to take sides. VE (Victory in Europe) Day in 1945 was the royal family's finest hour, when they appeared on the balcony at Buckingham Palace (which had been designed for such a purpose) and were wildly cheered by the immense throngs which had gathered in the Mall. Outside Europe the war continued, and British lives continued to be lost, but the victory over Japan, which followed, was largely an American affair, and the celebrations in Britain were comparatively low-key.

In July 1945 the coalition government resigned, and Churchill went to the country to secure a new mandate of the traditional kind. The result was an overwhelming victory for the Labour Party, which had the more convincing agenda for social reform. There was a strong disinclination to make the same mistakes as had been made after the First World War, when the returning 'heroes' from the trenches had found, as often as not, unemployment and economic distress. Clement Attlee became Prime Minister on 26 July 1945, and the King accepted his new government without a flicker of disapproval. The regular consultations which had been a feature of royal participation in government since the previous century continued amicably, and if George had any doubts about the radical agenda with which Attlee presented him, he kept discreetly quiet about them. The next five years were hard. Rationing continued after the war, and the food shortages were worse than at the height of the conflict. These were the years of austerity, during which the government introduced its socialist programme. The National Health Service was founded, the railways and the coal mines were nationalised, and the electricity and gas supplies brought under central control. The Welfare State was founded, and the sceptical noises emanating from the Conservative opposition in the Commons appeared, for the time being, misplaced. Meanwhile, the royal family had to find a new role for itself, because although the country was no less embattled than it had been during the war, its enemies were now intangible, and a patriotic rallying cry was no longer appropriate. Instead it became the 'first family', setting standards and examples of domestic harmony and felicity. For this innovative and effective approach the Queen was probably more responsible than the King, although she allowed him to take the credit. The royal broadcast became a feature of every family's Christmas, and the royal family was looked up to for its behaviour, its probity and its integrity. It was a difficult and, as it turned out, unstable position to adopt, but it served the needs of post-war Britain admirably.

Nowhere was this better exemplified than in the marriage of their elder daughter Elizabeth to Philip Mountbatten in November 1947. Philip was a great grandson of Alice, a younger daughter of Queen Victoria, who had married the Grand Duke of Hesse. His mother, another Alice, had married Prince Andrew of Greece, so Philip had royal blood in his veins, and was a distant kinsman of Elizabeth, although not close enough to cause any anxiety. At the time of his wedding he was a serving naval officer, and after the honeymoon took her off with him to his posting in Malta, a time which she later described as being the happiest days of her life. Their wedding came like a shaft of sunlight into the grey austerity of London, with its lavish exchange of gifts and its reception for over 2,500 guests. The ceremony, as the Archbishop pointed out, was the same as that enjoyed by any cottager getting married in the Dales: 'the same prayers are offered, the same blessings given'. However, the setting was totally different, and the glamour of the occasion caught the public imagination. The BBC and the press had a field day, and this pointed to the secret of the family monarchy. The royals were news, and the press appetite for stories was insatiable. Buckingham Palace had learned this lesson long before, and a press office had been established as early as 1920. This interest had backfired to some extent during the abdication crisis, but it powered ahead in the 1950s, fuelled by such newsworthy events as the birth of Prince Charles on 14 November 1948 and his sister Anne on 15 August 1950. The heir to the throne was ensuring the succession, and all was right with the world! Philip had been created Duke of Edinburgh in time for his marriage, and the family monarchy had effectively transferred itself to the Duke and Duchess well before she acceded to the throne. This was just as well because her sister Margaret was not cast in the same respectable mould, and at twenty was showing no signs of settling down in a similarly comfortable fashion. In her case it was a question of keeping the media at bay, which was another reason why the royal press office kept the focus firmly upon Elizabeth.

Meanwhile, the King's health was giving cause for anxiety. He had been operated upon for a duodenal ulcer as early as 1917, and had suffered from stomach problems throughout the First World War. However, this was something different. He was a heavy smoker, and developed lung cancer, a condition imperfectly diagnosed at the time. When Philip and Elizabeth flew off for a tour of the Dominions in January 1952 he was well enough to go to the airport to see them off, but he became worse and on 6 February 1952 he died in his sleep at Sandringham, at the age of fifty-six, and his heir and her husband had to be summoned home from Kenya in haste. George's reign had lasted sixteen years, and had been dominated by the war, but other momentous events had taken place, not least the granting of independence to India and Pakistan and Burma in 1948. Other former colonies, such as Australia, Canada and New Zealand had long since achieved Dominion status, and it was only logical that the same should follow for the teeming multitudes of the Subcontinent. However, the other transformations had come about peacefully, whereas India was torn with religious strife. It was only after trying to contain this situation for several years that the British government eventually arranged a partition, and created two Dominions instead of one. It was not quite the triumph that the Congress Party had looked for, and it left a long legacy of tension, but it is difficult to see what else could have been done. The continuation of British rule was not an option, given the strength of opinion in India, and the dwindling of Britain's imperial motivation and resources. Burma opted out of the Commonwealth altogether, but India and Pakistan remained as republics within it. The other momentous event which the reign also saw was the creation of the welfare state, with its aspiration for cradle-to-grave care in the public domain. This was an ideal which has been chipped away, but still remains fundamental to British society. The family monarchy which George VI and Elizabeth created has withered away, but the social revolution of the 1950s has endured to the present day.

58

HAPPY AND GLORIOUS?
ELIZABETH II (SUCCEEDED 1952)

Although she was her father's heir from the time of his accession to the moment of his death, Elizabeth was never created Princess of Wales. It was apparently the King's opinion that on marriage such a princess would convey her title to her husband, and thus confuse the succession to the throne. It may be for that reason that only males have held the status, because Victoria did not, in spite of being William IV's heir throughout his reign, and Henry VIII's daughter Mary had not held it either, although she was dispatched to carry out the duties at Ludlow in 1525. It may also be that, in view of the traditionally fraught relations between the princes and their fathers, George VI was taking no chances – but it does not seem very likely. Elizabeth was born at 17 Bruton Street, London, on 21 April 1926, the oldest child of the then Duke and Duchess of York, and there was little expectation that she would one day succeed to the throne. She was brought up, as was normal for an aristocratic daughter, by a nurse, and later educated at home. She was taught the usual range of subjects, and made good progress, but there was no thought of training her for a career, other than marriage and motherhood. She was ten when her uncle David's abdication transformed her father's position and her own prospects, but for the time being she merely played her part in that projection of the royal family which her mother seems to have invented and in which the contemporary press was a willing accomplice. She was thirteen on the outbreak of war, and still tied to the schoolroom, so it was not until 1944, when she was eighteen, that Elizabeth was able to 'do her bit' in any independent sense. In that year she enrolled in the Auxiliary Territorial Service, not in a staff job but as a normal officer, and in the process of training got her hands seriously dirty. It was all a long way from David's role in the First World War, and marked an important stage in the democratisation of the monarchy. In 1947 she met and married Philip Mountbatten, who in spite of being a Greek prince had been educated in Britain and was serving as an officer in the navy at the time. Tens of thousands of people lined the processional route to Westminster Abbey, and millions more listened to the broadcast commentary. It was just the kind of glamorous event that austerity Britain needed, and popular identification with the royal couple was obvious. It was an extension of the family monarchy, which was completed on 14 November 1948 by the birth of Prince Charles. 'The representative monarchy,' *The Times* declared, 'has made every one of its subjects feel friend and neighbour to the royal family.' Times had changed indeed since the death of Queen Victoria. In 1949 Philip and Elizabeth moved out of Buckingham Palace into the newly refurbished Clarence House, where a nursery was established for Charles and his sibling Anne, who was born on 15 August 1950. Philip was still a serving officer, and spent much of his time abroad, while Elizabeth found that her father's declining health was placing more and more of the formal royal duties on her shoulders. Consequently, although she did her best to find 'family time', it became increasingly difficult, and Charles did not react well to this situation. He became close to his grandparents, and particularly to his grandmother, with whom he established a bond which lasted for more than fifty years.

The times were changing. In 1951 George inaugurated the Festival of Britain, partly to celebrate the centenary of the Great Exhibition and partly to shake the country out of its post-war economic lethargy. In this latter aim it was partly at least successful and the general election of October returned a Conservative government whose priorities were more business-orientated. At the same time British colonies and dependencies, particularly in Africa, were agitating for and securing their independence, because Britain no longer had the will, or the means, to preserve its imperial ascendancy. It was with an eye on that situation that Philip and Elizabeth set off on their ill-fated tour in January 1952, only to be recalled by the news of George's death on 6 February. This created an upsurge of popular emotion ('he saw us through the war'), and few monarchs can have come to the throne with a greater fund of goodwill than Elizabeth II. There was a sense of new beginnings – a new Elizabethan Age – and the young Queen, with a young family, was the principal beneficiary. On 29 May 1953 she issued a proclamation simultaneously in London and the other Commonwealth capitals, assuming a different title for each. In the United Kingdom her style was 'Elizabeth II, by the Grace of God of the United Kingdom of Great Britain and Northern Ireland, and of her other realms and territories, Queen, Head of the Commonwealth, Defender of the Faith', which was adjusted appropriately for the other Dominions. This provoked protests in Scotland on the ground that the previous Elizabeth had been Queen of England, not Great Britain, and that she should be styled Elizabeth I, which was strictly accurate. Elsewhere her titles seem to have caused no problems. Elizabeth was crowned at Westminster on 2 June 1953, to scenes of tumultuous enthusiasm, and (a great innovation) the cameras of the newly developed BBC television channel were allowed into the Abbey. The Prime Minister, Winston Churchill, was opposed to this intrusion, but the palace press office got it right. Many people went out and bought television sets in order to watch the ceremony. Prince Charles was too young to be anything other than a spectator at these events, but his early education was in the hands of an experienced primary teacher, and he was progressing satisfactorily. Meanwhile Philip had given up his naval career in order to become a full-time consort, and it was probably on his initiative that Charles was sent to school. This was an unprecedented move for a royal prince, let alone the heir to the throne, and was undertaken for the specific purpose of giving him a more 'normal' childhood than he could otherwise have enjoyed. He spent a year at Hill House in West London, before moving on to Cheam School in Berkshire, a boarding establishment specifically for the sons of the aristocracy. Cheam was undoubtedly Philip's choice, because it had been there that his own introduction to English education had taken place. It was at Cheam that Charles made new friends and generally learned to look after himself at an age when his predecessors had all been closeted with private tutors. In 1958, at the age of ten, he was created Prince of Wales, an elevation upon which his school friends hastened to congratulate him, much to his embarrassment, and a fortnight later was given a wildly enthusiastic reception when the royal yacht called at Anglesey. Wales had a prince again, and perhaps this one would be less disappointing than the last.

Meanwhile the Queen had settled down to a busy schedule of official engagements, punctuated by the arrival of Andrew in February 1960 and Edward in March 1964. In spite of her professionalism, and the sympathy created by these additions to the royal family, the 1960s were a decade of social revolution, and the abandonment of deference in public and private affairs. Questions began to be asked about the functioning and resources of the monarchy, and even about the need to have such an institution at all. Ostensibly Elizabeth paid no attention to these murmurings, continuing with her punishing round of official engagements, but she was perfectly well aware of them and in 1969 sanctioned the making of a BBC documentary, simply entitled *The Royal Family*, which went some way towards satisfying the public curiosity. In the meantime Charles had progressed from Cheam, where he was Head Boy in 1962, to Gordonstoun, that 'alternative Eton' near Elgin in Morayshire, which specialised in physical activities and self-reliance. This was undoubtedly Philip's choice, and probably reflects an anxiety that his son was becoming too intellectual, and needed a dose of the 'real world' to restore the balance – to say nothing of an ability to deal with the media, which was showing an intrusive interest in his progress. While there he gained the silver standard in the Duke of Edinburgh's Award scheme, a project set up several years earlier to encourage city youngsters to take an interest in the outdoors without undergoing the discipline required by the uniformed movements such as the Scouts and Guides. It was a similar consideration which caused the Duke to intermit his son's stay at Gordonstoun with a two-term visit to Timbertops, which is an offshoot of Geelong Grammar School in Victoria,

Australia. At Timbertops he learned to play polo, to muster cattle on horseback, and generally grew up a great deal. He also came to love the country and its people, a feeling which was reciprocated, and guaranteed him a warm reception on his subsequent visits. Then it was back to Gordonstoun, where in July 1967 he became the first royal prince to sit public examinations, taking A-Levels in French and History. His results were good enough to send him to Trinity College, Cambridge, in October of that year, where he opted to read for the joint honours degree in Archaeology and Anthropology. This whole exposure to the public arena in education was altogether unprecedented, because although both his uncles and his grandfather had spent time at Oxford, none had enrolled on an honours degree course, and again his father's influence appears to have been critical. Philip was well aware that standards had changed, and the criteria for judging royal performances had moved on since the 1910s. Elizabeth must have concurred in these judgements, although her role is obscure. Within the royal marriage, the normal roles were reversed, as had been the case with Albert and Victoria, although by this time no one was surprised to see Philip performing the domestic functions. By 1969 Charles was living in two different worlds. On the one hand he was an undergraduate, attending lectures and making friends, and on the other hand he was a public figure, a member of the Council, Knight of the Garter, and the Queen's representative on selected occasions. In 1968 he successfully completed Part I of his Tripos examinations at Cambridge, and on 1 July 1969 was inducted as Prince of Wales, having intermitted his Cambridge studies with a term at Aberystwyth to learn Welsh. His induction was a modest ceremony by comparison with that of 1911, but on this occasion the Prince spoke in fluent Welsh, and the crowds cheered him to the echo. If the Welsh nationalists had been thinking of causing trouble, they thought again, in the face of this demonstration of approval. In February 1970 he took his seat in the House of Lords, and three weeks later flew off for a highly successful tour of Australia, New Zealand, Hong Kong and Japan. He was hardly back in the UK when he had to return to Cambridge to sit his finals. In view of the amount of disruption which his studies had suffered, a place in the lower half of the second class was little short of a triumph, and was greeted with plaudits all round. The Prince of Wales, BA (with a half blue for polo) was the first of his kind!

In 1971 the House of Commons undertook a kind of 'stocktaking' of the monarchy, which resulted in an increase in the Civil List allocation to the Queen from £475,000 to £980,000, with proportionate increases for other members of the royal family. It was, however, suggested that some of the younger royals might consider earning a living in the normal way, a suggestion taken up, with very mixed reactions, when Prince Edward later sought a career in the theatre and media. The year 1972 saw a protracted visit to South East Asia and the Indian Ocean, which Elizabeth found oppressive on account of the heat, and a state visit to France. In the course of the latter she paid a visit to her terminally ill uncle, Edward, in Paris. This was a diplomatic rather than a personal visit, but it afforded some consolation to the Duke, who died ten days later. The news was received with little grief at Buckingham Palace. More traumatic in some ways was Princess Anne's desire to marry Captain Mark Philips in 1973. Philips was a commoner of middle-class background, and the Princess should have abandoned her royal status by marrying him; however, a way was found round this difficulty and the couple were united on 14 November. The ceremony won universal popular acclaim, and that went some way towards alleviating the Queen's anxieties, because it proved that the younger royals were playing their part in the democratisation of the monarchy in a way which Elizabeth could never have done herself. Anne and Mark subsequently divorced, and Anne remarried Timothy Lawrence, to whom she remains married, but that has not affected her royal status either. Meanwhile negotiations were going on for Britain to join the European Common Market, and she finally adhered to the treaty in January 1974. This was a move which deprived the country of certain aspects of its territorial sovereignty, but did not greatly affect the position of the monarchy, which had long since been more ornamental than effective in constitutional terms. The Queen celebrated her Silver Jubilee in 1977, and that provided the pretext for an upsurge of popular loyalty, manifest in street parties and other junketings. Superficially it seemed that nothing had changed since 1953. In the same year Prince Andrew spent two terms at Lakefield College in Alberta, Canada, in imitation of his brother's stay at Timbertops, and in 1978 followed him into the navy, where he learned to fly helicopters, and became a front-line pilot during the Falklands war which followed in 1982.

Meanwhile, Prince Charles had married Lady Diana Spencer on 29 July 1981. This 'fairytale wedding' was the victim of excessive media attention from the first, and when Prince William was born on 21 June 1982 at St Mary's Hospital, Paddington, with Charles in attendance, the press went wild. This was the first time that any child so close to the throne had been born in a public hospital, and the first time that the father had been present. The Prince of Wales was hailed as 'a thoroughly modern dad', and when he repeated the process on the birth of Prince Harry, in 1984, similar praises followed. In spite of these prompt tokens of affection, the marriage was not a happy one, and by 1990 had descended into a slanging match, with the Princess on the whole taking the initiative. The media sided with her, with an eye on viewing and circulation figures, and gave the Prince a rough ride which was not altogether deserved. In 1992 they separated, and in 1996 divorced – an unprecedented experience for one so close to the throne. 1992 was notoriously the Queen's 'annus horribilis', as her children's marriages collapsed around her. Anne headed for the divorce court in the same year, and also Prince Andrew, who had wedded Sarah Ferguson in 1986, both in circumstances of some acrimony. The model of the royal family as an example of stability and social duty was well and truly dead, to be replaced with the kind of dysfunctional unit which was so painfully familiar to many of Elizabeth's subjects. Towards the end of the year Windsor Castle caught fire, causing her further distress, and leading to an unseemly row about who was the pay the cost of refurbishment, because the castle was not insured and the bill was estimated at £40 million. Nor was that all, because questions had begun to be asked (again) about the tax exemption enjoyed by the Queen's personal wealth and it was in 1992 that she finally agreed that such exemption was inappropriate, and that her income should be taxed along with the rest of her people – another stage in reducing the mystique of the monarchy, but probably a necessary one in the light of the other adjustments which were being made to the image of the royal family. Then in 1997 Princess Diana was killed in a road accident in Paris. She had become a gadfly to the establishment, and an appalling nuisance to her ex-husband, so conspiracy theories flooded the press with speculation – all more or less unfounded. There was an extraordinary outburst of national grief, which caught the Queen and the intellectual establishment seriously off balance. Elizabeth and her son responded in a restrained fashion, which was no doubt in keeping with their feelings, but was promptly labelled as 'heartless' and 'out of touch'. It was only later that her advisers got the message, and persuaded her to make some of the gestures which were looked for. The royal image suffered severely from this strange episode, and it is not surprising that the Queen's Golden Jubilee, which was celebrated in 2002, should have been a comparatively low-key affair.

The festivities of that year were in any case marred by the death in February of the Queen's younger sister, Margaret. Margaret, whose lifestyle had earlier attracted unfavourable comment, had married Anthony Armstrong Jones in May 1960 after an on-off courtship which had lasted several years. That marriage lasted seventeen years, until rumours of affairs on both sides, particularly her relationship with Roddy Llewelyn, had forced them apart in 1977. She suffered a stroke in 2001, which left her partially paralysed, and died in the following year. Elizabeth had never been close to her sister, but mourned her death, as one would expect of a sibling. The death of her mother, which occurred later in the same year, was altogether more traumatic. The Queen Mother, as she had been since 1952, had been a great influence on her daughter, especially for the call of duty in her everyday life. Also, with her taste for gin and horseracing, the 'Queen Mum' had become in many ways the most popular member of the royal family. She was not touched by the scandals which so damaged the younger royals, and as she became older seemed in many ways the most normal of them all. In August 2000 she passed her one hundredth birthday, and longevity alone guaranteed her a place in the popular affection. The event was celebrated with great and genuine rejoicings. And her death at the age of 102, although not unexpected, was a cause of universal grief. The whole family had suffered a serious loss, not least the Prince of Wales, who had been close to her since his childhood. So Elizabeth soldiers on, and Charles remains in waiting, now the longest-serving of all the Princes of Wales. There has been talk of the Queen abdicating in favour of her son since at least 1976, but she has shown no inclination to do so. In the 1990s such thoughts were obviously discouraged by the unfavourable media attention which the Prince was then attracting. However, his image, although remaining eccentric, has since then improved, and even his second marriage to Camilla Parker Bowles in 2005 has now been accepted both by the Queen and the country. So Charles still waits his turn, and as his father passes ninety and his mother eighty-five, it looks as though his wait will go on for a few more years. If Elizabeth lives as long as her mother, he will be a very old man by the time that he comes to the throne.

EPILOGUE: THE NEXT KING OF GREAT BRITAIN, CHARLES III

The granting of devolution to Scotland, Northern Ireland and Wales, although it has affected the role of the UK government in those countries, has not so far much altered the position of the Crown. This may change if the Scottish National Party has its way, and Scotland becomes fully independent, but that has not happened yet. So Charles can look forward, as he has been doing for many years, to inheriting the position in Great Britain and Northern Ireland that his mother currently occupies. He will be the head of a democratic state, and of a Commonwealth of Nations, in which he is the only hereditary element, because inherited peerage no longer carries a place in the House of Lords, and money is unquestionably more important than status in opening the corridors of power. He will have little influence in the struggles of party politics, and his aides and officials will need to be constantly vigilant to protect what privacy remains to him from the intrusions of computer hackers. However, as the Head of State he may be in a better position to fend off that intrusive media attention from which he has suffered as heir. Particularly as he gets older his private life will no longer have the same fascination as that of a younger man. Already his second marriage has settled down into that semi-morganatic state in which Camilla shares his title of Cornwall, but not that of Wales. Presumably she will in due course be recognised as consort, but not as queen, a situation which Charles appears to be willing to accept.

While he was still at Gordonstoun, and particularly after his return from Timbertops, he acquired a number of those tastes and attitudes which were to be characteristic of him thereafter. Under the influence of the art teacher Robert Waddell he became interested in classical music, painting and literature, and a friend wrote to his uncle, Louis Mountbatten, 'This is a young man who reminds me very much of you; he is immensely interested in humanity, and in the details of human suffering.' These concerns were put on hold while he was an undergraduate, on the ground that he had quite enough to do in undertaking his public duties and completing his studies. However, they began to surface again while he was still a serving naval officer. Even during those years, from 1970 to 1976, he was ultimately responsible for the management of the Duchy of Cornwall, and was Chancellor of the University of Wales, as well as serving on various other bodies involved with educational and conservation issues. In 1972 the idea of the Prince's Trust was first mooted because there was much public concern about 'disenchanted youth' during the social revolution of the 1960s and early 1970s, and Charles was anxious to help. It did not happen at once because of his naval commitments, but with the assistance of a professional probation officer, a scheme began to be put in place that would give the Prince's enthusiastic ideas some practicable shape. As soon as Charles left the service the Trust was officially launched with the assistance of the £7,500 which the Prince received from the navy as severance pay. This has remained very important to him ever since, and has become a 'flagship enterprise' of his sense of social responsibility. Although there have been sceptical voices raised from the beginning, during the economic recession of the 1980s, its strategy was more than justified. Since its inception it has helped nearly 600,000 young people with practical support from financial assistance to training and mentoring. The Prince's Trust is a very personal initiative, which the Queen would be constitutionally unable to take, but for which Charles's status and open-mindedness qualify him perfectly. Under its cover he has also worked to defuse ethnic tensions, negotiating with community leaders, and reinterpreting his own role as he has gone along. In spite of this, and perhaps because if it, he has been subject to intense and often hostile media scrutiny, using a technology of intrusion never before available. One wonders how Bertie or the Prince Regent would have fared under a similar spotlight!

Much of this interest was stimulated by his private life, and particularly by his ill-fated marriage to Diana. In the controversies surrounding this acrimonious break-up, the Prince was made to appear cold and distant, as though that were sufficient justification for her behaviour – a 'Princess in search of love' as the tabloid newspapers put it. However, he enjoyed, and still enjoys, the warmest of relationships with his two sons, from skiing holidays during their schooldays to his present support for their military careers, and to William's recent marriage. The Prince is an intensely busy man. As his private secretary David Checketts observed when there was speculation over his future after leaving the navy in 1976, the real question was not what was he going to do, but how he was going to find the time to honour all the commitments which he already had. The situation has not grown any easier over the years. Even during his moments of relaxation, he paints in watercolours, and his efforts are sold in aid of the Prince's Charitable Foundation. He also designed and developed the organic gardens at Highgrove, his country residence in Gloucestershire, and developed the Duchy Originals line of produce. He is an untiring advocate of environmental causes, setting carbon emission targets for his household (which have been met), converting all his cars to run on biodeisel, and setting up the May Day network of companies committed to tackling climate change. His Rainforest Project, established in October 2007, has brought together fifteen of the world's largest companies, together with experts on economics and the environment to address the devastating effects of deforestation. And he has been notoriously a thorn in the side of modern architects, seeing conservation of the built environment as a proper extension of his other environmental concerns. His restless energy, which is barred from domestic politics, has also found an outlet in numerous trips abroad, particularly those slightly tricky assignment when being 'not quite the monarch' was the most appropriate status, like the Fijian independence celebrations of 1970, or his more recent trip to Uganda in 2007 where he went with the Duchess of Cornwall to visit several charity-backed aid projects. He and the Duchess also visited Turkey in the same year, and were able to act on behalf of the United Kingdom government in a way which no minister could have done. Altogether he carried out 600 engagements in 2007–08, 77 of which were overseas, while the Duchess notched up 201, of which 50 were overseas. He also attended with the Queen a Commonwealth Heads of Government Conference, marking a first for their joint participation, and was able to talk informally, as Elizabeth could not, with several Commonwealth leaders.

He has a comprehensive philosophy of life, which may be summed up as 'making a difference', in which he has used his status and his wealth to promote causes – some fashionable and some unfashionable – with which he has an engagement. In this he is completely different from all his predecessors, with the possible exception of David, who certainly engaged with the social problems of the 1920s, although not to such good effect. In spite of his undoubted talents, it is hard to imagine the pleasure-loving Bertie putting himself out in this kind of way, and one would have to go back to Frederick in the 1740s to find an equally energetic prince. Frederick's activity was all directed to the Leicester House set and the promotion of oppositional politics, an outlet denied to Charles in the late twentieth century. In fact the Prince of Wales's lack of a constitutional function has been a blessing, in that he has been constrained to direct his formidable energies into social and commercial activities which most of his predecessors would have considered beneath them. He is in fact a very good example of the positive effects which democratisation has had upon the monarchy. So what kind of king will he make when (or if) he gets the chance? He will have to hand over the direction of most of his cherished projects to others, and withdraw into a more detached position. This may not suit his style at all, but then he has had plenty of experience of discharging the formal duties of the monarch as well, and has shown no sign of flinching from them. His relaxed attitude and communications skills may well lead him to seem more accessible than his somewhat hidebound mother, and this may well go down well with the generations which he will have to serve. He also has the benefit of a formal academic training, which will appeal to the educated middle class. At the same time he will need careful marketing, because neither his attitudes nor his social engagement (nor his intelligence) will disappear, and each may seem partisan in terms of the politics of the future. He will need to address uncongenial Prime Ministers with studious courtesy, and not to react with anger or frustration if his favoured projects cease to have popular appeal. However, that same sense of duty which has carried his mother through so many crises and periods of distress is manifest in him also. In view of his somewhat controversial image, it has been suggested that Charles may give up his chance to be king, and allow the throne to pass directly to his popular son William, who would not carry the baggage of so many years as heir. This would require an alteration to the law, and is very unlikely to happen. It may be that he will serve a token span, and then abdicate in William's favour, but that is not likely to happen either. If he turns out to be as long-lived as his parents, we may be in for several years of King Charles III, before he makes way for William V.

When Prince William married Catherine Middleton in 2011 he became Duke of Cambridge. The rules of succession have recently been altered so that if William and Catherine's first child had been female, she would have followed William on the throne irrespective of whether or not a son was subsequently born. This change had been agreed by the other countries of the Commonwealth, for whom the monarch is also head of state. Their first child, however, was a boy: George Alexander Louis, born in July 2013. This relegated William's younger brother, Harry, to fourth place in the order. At the moment, the heir to the throne remains Charles, who is now the longest-serving Prince of Wales and a grandfather.

GENEALOGICAL TABLES

101. The Wessex Line.

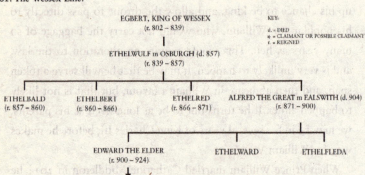

EGBERT, KING OF WESSEX
(r. 802 – 839)

KEY:
d. = DIED
q = CLAIMANT OR POSSIBLE CLAIMANT
r. = REIGNED

ETHELWULF m OSBURGH (d. 857)
(r. 839 – 857)

ETHELBALD
(r. 857 – 860)

ETHELBERT
(r. 860 – 866)

ETHELRED
(r. 866 – 871)

ALFRED THE GREAT m EALSWITH (d. 904)
(r. 871 – 900)

EDWARD THE ELDER
(r. 900 – 924)

ETHELWARD

ETHELFLEDA

102. The English Line.

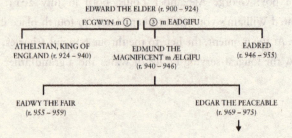

KEY:
d. = DIED
q = CLAIMANT OR POSSIBLE CLAIMANT
r. = REIGNED

EDWARD THE ELDER (r. 900 – 924)

ECGWYN m ① ③ m EADGIFU

ATHELSTAN, KING OF
ENGLAND (r. 924 – 940)

EDMUND THE
MAGNIFICENT m ÆLGIFU
(r. 940 – 946)

EADRED
(r. 946 – 955)

EADWY THE FAIR
(r. 955 – 959)

EDGAR THE PEACEABLE
(r. 969 – 975)

103. The English Line.

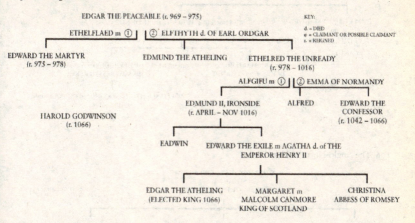

EDGAR THE PEACEABLE (r. 969 – 975)

ETHELFLAED m ① | ② ELFTHYTH d. OF EARL ORDGAR

EDWARD THE MARTYR
(r. 975 – 978)

EDMUND THE ATHELING

ETHELRED THE UNREADY
(r. 978 – 1016)

ALFGIFU m ① | ② EMMA OF NORMANDY

EDMUND II, IRONSIDE
(r. APRIL – NOV 1016)

ALFRED

EDWARD THE
CONFESSOR
(r. 1042 – 1066)

HAROLD GODWINSON
(r. 1066)

EADWIN

EDWARD THE EXILE m AGATHA d. of THE
EMPEROR HENRY II

EDGAR THE ATHELING
(ELECTED KING 1066)

MARGARET m
MALCOLM CANMORE
KING OF SCOTLAND

CHRISTINA
ABBESS OF ROMSEY

104. The Danish Line.

HAROLD BLUETOOTH (d. 988)
KING OF DENMARK

SVEIN FORKBEARD (r. 988 – 1014)
KING OF DENMARK

CANUTE (r. 1016 – 1035) KING OF ENGLAND

AELGIFU OF NORTHAMPTON ① | ② m EMMA OF NORMANDY

HAROLD HAREFOOT
(r. 1035 – 1040)

HARTHACANUTE (r. 1040 – 1042)

105. The Norman Line.

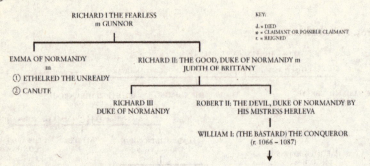

KEY:

d. = DIED
❀ = CLAIMANT OR POSSIBLE CLAIMANT
r. = REIGNED

RICHARD I THE FEARLESS
m GUNNOR

EMMA OF NORMANDY
m
① ETHELRED THE UNREADY
② CANUTE

RICHARD II: THE GOOD, DUKE OF NORMANDY m
JUDITH OF BRITTANY

RICHARD III
DUKE OF NORMANDY

ROBERT II: THE DEVIL, DUKE OF NORMANDY BY
HIS MISTRESS HERLEVA

WILLIAM I: (THE BASTARD) THE CONQUEROR
(r. 1066 – 1087)

106. The Anglo-Norman Line.

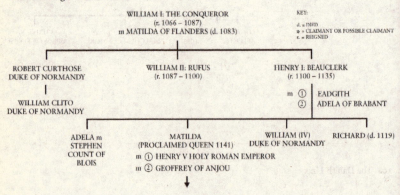

KEY:

d. = DIED
❀ = CLAIMANT OR POSSIBLE CLAIMANT
r. = REIGNED

WILLIAM I: THE CONQUEROR
(r. 1066 – 1087)
m MATILDA OF FLANDERS (d. 1083)

ROBERT CURTHOSE
DUKE OF NORMANDY

WILLIAM II: RUFUS
(r. 1087 – 1100)

HENRY I: BEAUCLERK
(r. 1100 – 1135)

WILLIAM CLITO
DUKE OF NORMANDY

m ① EADGITH
② ADELA OF BRABANT

ADELA m
STEPHEN
COUNT OF
BLOIS

MATILDA
(PROCLAIMED QUEEN 1141)
m ① HENRY V HOLY ROMAN EMPEROR
m ② GEOFFREY OF ANJOU

WILLIAM (IV)
DUKE OF NORMANDY

RICHARD (d. 1119)

107. The Blois Line.

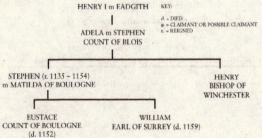

HENRY I m EADGITH

KEY:

d. = DIED
❀ = CLAIMANT OR POSSIBLE CLAIMANT
r. = REIGNED

ADELA m STEPHEN
COUNT OF BLOIS

STEPHEN (r. 1135 – 1154)
m MATILDA OF BOULOGNE

HENRY
BISHOP OF
WINCHESTER

EUSTACE
COUNT OF BOULOGNE
(d. 1152)

WILLIAM
EARL OF SURREY (d. 1159)

Genealogical Tables

108. The Plantagenet Line.

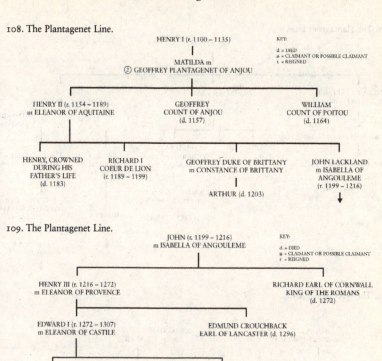

HENRY I (r. 1100 – 1135)

MATILDA m
② GEOFFREY PLANTAGENET OF ANJOU

KEY:
d. = DIED
∗ = CLAIMANT OR POSSIBLE CLAIMANT
r. = REIGNED

HENRY II (r. 1154 – 1189)
m ELEANOR OF AQUITAINE

GEOFFREY
COUNT OF ANJOU
(d. 1157)

WILLIAM
COUNT OF POITOU
(d. 1164)

HENRY, CROWNED
DURING HIS
FATHER'S LIFE
(d. 1183)

RICHARD I
COEUR DE LION
(r. 1189 – 1199)

GEOFFREY DUKE OF BRITTANY
m CONSTANCE OF BRITTANY

JOHN LACKLAND
m ISABELLA OF
ANGOULEME
(r. 1199 – 1216)

ARTHUR (d. 1203)

109. The Plantagenet Line.

JOHN (r. 1199 – 1216)
m ISABELLA OF ANGOULEME

KEY:
d. = DIED
∗ = CLAIMANT OR POSSIBLE CLAIMANT
r. = REIGNED

HENRY III (r. 1216 – 1272)
m ELEANOR OF PROVENCE

RICHARD EARL OF CORNWALL
KING OF THE ROMANS
(d. 1272)

EDWARD I (r. 1272 – 1307)
m ELEANOR OF CASTILE

EDMUND CROUCHBACK
EARL OF LANCASTER (d. 1296)

ALPHONSO EARL
OF CHESTER (d. 1284)

EDWARD II (r. 1307 – 1327)
m ISABELLA OF FRANCE

110. The Plantagenet Line.

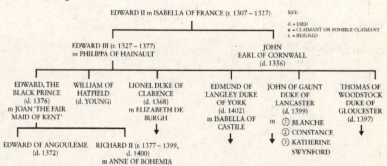

EDWARD II m ISABELLA OF FRANCE (r. 1307 – 1327)

KEY:
d. = DIED
∗ = CLAIMANT OR POSSIBLE CLAIMANT
r. = REIGNED

EDWARD III (r. 1327 – 1377)
m PHILIPPA OF HAINAULT

JOHN
EARL OF CORNWALL
(d. 1336)

EDWARD, THE
BLACK PRINCE
(d. 1376)
m JOAN 'THE FAIR
MAID OF KENT'

WILLIAM OF
HATFIELD
(d. YOUNG)

LIONEL DUKE OF
CLARENCE
(d. 1368)
m ELIZABETH DE
BURGH

EDMUND OF
LANGLEY DUKE
OF YORK
(d. 1402)
m ISABELLA OF
CASTILE

JOHN OF GAUNT
DUKE OF
LANCASTER
(d. 1399)
m ① BLANCHE
② CONSTANCE
③ KATHERINE
SWYNFORD

THOMAS OF
WOODSTOCK
DUKE OF
GLOUCESTER
(d. 1397)

EDWARD OF ANGOULEME
(d. 1372)

RICHARD II (r. 1377 – 1399,
d. 1400)
m ANNE OF BOHEMIA

111. The Plantagenet Line.

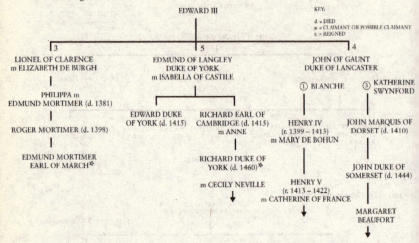

112. The Wars of the Roses.

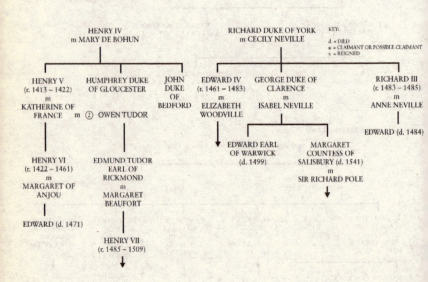

113. The Wars of the Roses.

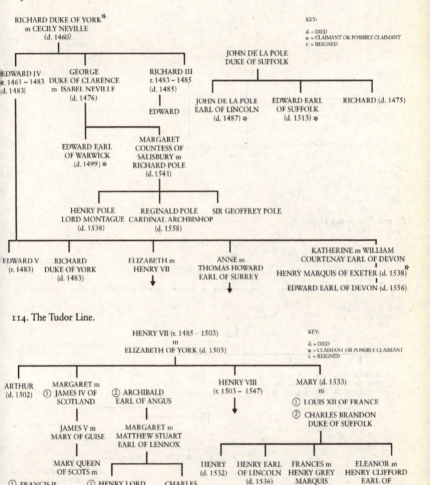

KEY:
d. = DIED
✷ = CLAIMANT OR POSSIBLE CLAIMANT
r. = REIGNED

RICHARD DUKE OF YORK ✷
m CECILY NEVILLE
(d. 1460)

EDWARD IV
r. 1461 – 1483
(d. 1483)

GEORGE
DUKE OF CLARENCE
m ISABEL NEVILLE
(d. 1476)

RICHARD III
r. 1483 – 1485
(d. 1485)

JOHN DE LA POLE
DUKE OF SUFFOLK

EDWARD

JOHN DE LA POLE
EARL OF LINCOLN
(d. 1487) ✷

EDWARD EARL
OF SUFFOLK
(d. 1513) ✷

RICHARD (d. 1475)

EDWARD EARL
OF WARWICK
(d. 1499) ✷

MARGARET
COUNTESS OF
SALISBURY m
RICHARD POLE
(d. 1541)

HENRY POLE
LORD MONTAGUE
(d. 1538)

REGINALD POLE
CARDINAL ARCHBISHOP
(d. 1558)

SIR GEOFFREY POLE

EDWARD V
(r. 1483)

RICHARD
DUKE OF YORK
(d. 1483)

ELIZABETH m
HENRY VII

ANNE m
THOMAS HOWARD
EARL OF SURREY

KATHERINE m WILLIAM
COURTENAY EARL OF DEVON
HENRY MARQUIS OF EXETER (d. 1538) ✷
EDWARD EARL OF DEVON (d. 1556)

114. The Tudor Line.

HENRY VII (r. 1485 – 1503)
m
ELIZABETH OF YORK (d. 1503)

KEY:
d. = DIED
✷ = CLAIMANT OR POSSIBLE CLAIMANT
r. = REIGNED

ARTHUR
(d. 1502)

MARGARET m
① JAMES IV OF
SCOTLAND
② ARCHIBALD
EARL OF ANGUS

HENRY VIII
(r. 1503 – 1547)

MARY (d. 1533)
m
① LOUIS XII OF FRANCE
② CHARLES BRANDON
DUKE OF SUFFOLK

JAMES V m
MARY OF GUISE

MARGARET m
MATTHEW STUART
EARL OF LENNOX

MARY QUEEN
OF SCOTS m

HENRY
(d. 1532)

HENRY EARL
OF LINCOLN
(d. 1536)

FRANCES m
HENRY GREY
MARQUIS
OF DORSET

ELEANOR m
HENRY CLIFFORD
EARL OF
CUMBERLAND

① FRANCIS II
KING OF
FRANCE
③ JAMES HEPBURN
EARL OF BOTHWELL

② HENRY LORD
DARNLEY

CHARLES
EARL OF
LENNOX m
ELIZABETH
CAVENDISH

JANE (r. 1533) ✷
(LADY JANE GREY)
'9 DAYS QUEEN'

KATHERINE ✷ MARY

MARGARET m
HENRY STANLEY
EARL OF DERBY

JAMES VI AND I
(r. 1603 – 1625)

ARABELLA
STUART ✷
(d. 1615)

The Kings & Queens of England

115. The Tudor Line.

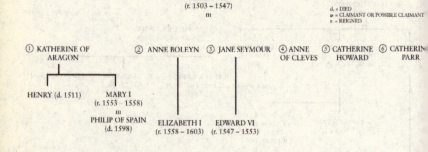

HENRY VIII
(r. 1503 – 1547)
m

KEY:

d. = DIED
✳ = CLAIMANT OR POSSIBLE CLAIMANT
r. = REIGNED

① KATHERINE OF ARAGON   ② ANNE BOLEYN   ③ JANE SEYMOUR   ④ ANNE OF CLEVES   ⑤ CATHERINE HOWARD   ⑥ CATHERINE PARR

HENRY (d. 1511)   MARY I (r. 1553 – 1558) m PHILIP OF SPAIN (d. 1598)

ELIZABETH I (r. 1558 – 1603)   EDWARD VI (r. 1547 – 1553)

116. The Stuart Line.

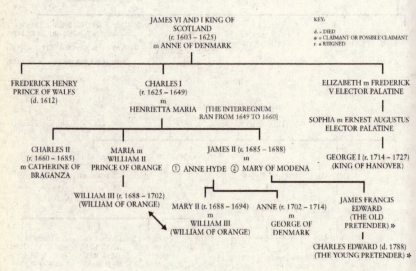

JAMES VI AND I KING OF SCOTLAND
(r. 1603 – 1625)
m ANNE OF DENMARK

KEY:

d. = DIED
✳ = CLAIMANT OR POSSIBLE CLAIMANT
r. = REIGNED

FREDERICK HENRY PRINCE OF WALES (d. 1612)

CHARLES I (r. 1625 – 1649) m HENRIETTA MARIA   [THE INTERREGNUM RAN FROM 1649 TO 1660]

ELIZABETH m FREDERICK V ELECTOR PALATINE

SOPHIA m ERNEST AUGUSTUS ELECTOR PALATINE

CHARLES II (r. 1660 – 1685) m CATHERINE OF BRAGANZA

MARIA m WILLIAM II PRINCE OF ORANGE

JAMES II (r. 1685 – 1688) m ① ANNE HYDE ② MARY OF MODENA

GEORGE I (r. 1714 – 1727) (KING OF HANOVER)

WILLIAM III (r. 1688 – 1702) (WILLIAM OF ORANGE)

MARY II (r. 1688 – 1694) m WILLIAM III (WILLIAM OF ORANGE)

ANNE (r. 1702 – 1714) m GEORGE OF DENMARK

JAMES FRANCIS EDWARD (THE OLD PRETENDER) ✳

CHARLES EDWARD (d. 1788) (THE YOUNG PRETENDER) ✳

Genealogical Tables

117. The Hanoverian Line.

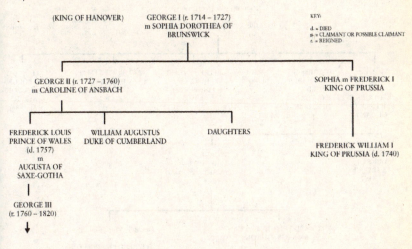

(KING OF HANOVER) GEORGE I (r. 1714 – 1727)
m SOPHIA DOROTHEA OF
BRUNSWICK

KEY:
d. = DIED
♔ = CLAIMANT OR POSSIBLE CLAIMANT
r. = REIGNED

GEORGE II (r. 1727 – 1760)
m CAROLINE OF ANSBACH

SOPHIA m FREDERICK I
KING OF PRUSSIA

FREDERICK LOUIS
PRINCE OF WALES
(d. 1757)
m
AUGUSTA OF
SAXE-GOTHA

WILLIAM AUGUSTUS
DUKE OF CUMBERLAND

DAUGHTERS

FREDERICK WILLIAM I
KING OF PRUSSIA (d. 1740)

GEORGE III
(r. 1760 – 1820)

118. The Hanoverian Line.

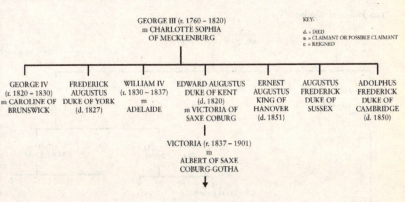

GEORGE III (r. 1760 – 1820)
m CHARLOTTE SOPHIA
OF MECKLENBURG

KEY:
d. = DIED
♔ = CLAIMANT OR POSSIBLE CLAIMANT
r. = REIGNED

GEORGE IV
(r. 1820 – 1830)
m CAROLINE OF
BRUNSWICK

FREDERICK
AUGUSTUS
DUKE OF YORK
(d. 1827)

WILLIAM IV
(r. 1830 – 1837)
m
ADELAIDE

EDWARD AUGUSTUS
DUKE OF KENT
(d. 1820)
m VICTORIA OF
SAXE COBURG

ERNEST
AUGUSTUS
KING OF
HANOVER
(d. 1851)

AUGUSTUS
FREDERICK
DUKE OF
SUSSEX

ADOLPHUS
FREDERICK
DUKE OF
CAMBRIDGE
(d. 1850)

VICTORIA (r. 1837 – 1901)
m
ALBERT OF SAXE
COBURG-GOTHA

119. House of Saxe-Coburg.

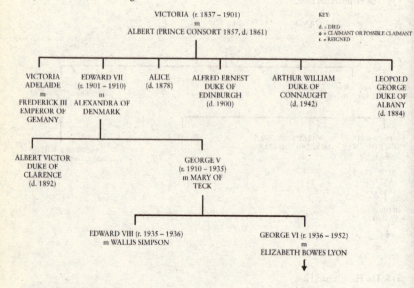

VICTORIA (r. 1837 – 1901)
m
ALBERT (PRINCE CONSORT 1857, d. 1861)

KEY:
d. = DIED
✻ = CLAIMANT OR POSSIBLE CLAIMANT
r. = REIGNED

VICTORIA ADELAIDE
m
FREDERICK III EMPEROR OF GEMANY

EDWARD VII (r. 1901 – 1910)
m
ALEXANDRA OF DENMARK

ALICE (d. 1878)

ALFRED ERNEST DUKE OF EDINBURGH (d. 1900)

ARTHUR WILLIAM DUKE OF CONNAUGHT (d. 1942)

LEOPOLD GEORGE DUKE OF ALBANY (d. 1884)

ALBERT VICTOR DUKE OF CLARENCE (d. 1892)

GEORGE V (r. 1910 – 1935) m MARY OF TECK

EDWARD VIII (r. 1935 – 1936) m WALLIS SIMPSON

GEORGE VI (r. 1936 – 1952) m ELIZABETH BOWES LYON

120. House of Windsor.

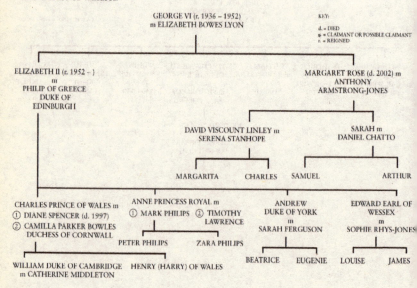

GEORGE VI (r. 1936 – 1952)
m ELIZABETH BOWES LYON

KEY:
d. = DIED
✻ = CLAIMANT OR POSSIBLE CLAIMANT
r. = REIGNED

ELIZABETH II (r. 1952 –)
m
PHILIP OF GREECE DUKE OF EDINBURGH

MARGARET ROSE (d. 2002) m ANTHONY ARMSTRONG-JONES

DAVID VISCOUNT LINLEY m SERENA STANHOPE

SARAH m DANIEL CHATTO

MARGARITA   CHARLES   SAMUEL   ARTHUR

CHARLES PRINCE OF WALES m
① DIANE SPENCER (d. 1997)
② CAMILLA PARKER BOWLES DUCHESS OF CORNWALL

ANNE PRINCESS ROYAL m
① MARK PHILIPS ② TIMOTHY LAWRENCE

ANDREW DUKE OF YORK m SARAH FERGUSON

EDWARD EARL OF WESSEX m SOPHIE RHYS-JONES

PETER PHILIPS   ZARA PHILIPS

WILLIAM DUKE OF CAMBRIDGE m CATHERINE MIDDLETON   HENRY (HARRY) OF WALES

BEATRICE   EUGENIE   LOUISE   JAMES

BIBLIOGRAPHY

Allmand, C., *Henry V* (1992). An up-to-date, scholarly account of the reign.

Anglo-Saxon Chronicle, ed. S. Tucker, D. Whitelock and D. C. Douglas (1965). The standard source for the pre-Conquest period.

Ashley, M., *Charles I and Oliver Cromwell* (1987). A conflict of ideals.

Ashton, R., *The English Civil War: Conservatism and Revolution* (1989). An attempt to make sense of the contradictions of the period.

Barlow, F., *Edward the Confessor* (1970). Still the standard biography.

Barlow, F., *The Feudal Kingdom of England* (1987). A scholarly general account.

Barlow, F., *William Rufus* (1983). The standard account of this controversial king.

Barlow, F., *Kings and Lords in the Conquest of England* (1991). How William I carved up the country among his followers.

Bassett, S., *The Origins of the Anglo-Saxon Kingdoms* (1989). How did the original war lords become kings?

Baumgartner, F., *Henry II* (1996). An appraisal of the effectiveness of his rule.

Beattie, J. M., *The English Court in the Reign of George I* (1967). The effect of the German connection on English factions and parties.

Beddard, R. (ed.), *The Revolution of 1688* (1991). A collection of essays of varying quality.

Bogdanor, V., *The Monarchy and the Constitution* (1995). How did we get to where we are?

Brooke, C. N. L., *The Saxon and Norman Kings* (1963). A straightforward scholarly account.

Brooke, J., *Horace Walpole: Memoirs of King George II* (3 vols, 1985). An insider's view of the reign.

Brooks, E. C., *The Life of St Ethelbert, King and Martyr* (1995). How does a king become a saint?

Bruce, M. L., *The Usurper King: Henry of Bolingbroke, 1366–1399* (1998). A semi-popular account, stopping short of the reign itself.

Burke's Guide to the Royal Family (1972).

Burnet, G., *History of My Own Times* (6 vols, 1823). An edition by M. J. Routh of Burnet's original publication of 1724.

Cannadine, D., and S. Price, *Rituals of Royalty: Power and Constraint in Traditional Societies* (1987). Widely based analysis of the role of monarchy in politics.

Carpenter, D. A., *The Reign of Henry III* (1996). A modern scholarly appreciation of this long and varied reign.

Chaney, W. A., *The Cult of Kingship in Anglo-Saxon England* (1970). How the church took over the rites of rule from their pagan origins.

Cheshire, Paul, *Kings and Queens: An Essential A–Z Guide* (2001).

Chrimes, S. B., *Henry VII* (1972). A bit out of date, but still the best general account.

Coss, P. R. and S. D. Lloyd (eds), *Thirteenth-Century England* (1986). A standard narrative account.

Coward, B., *Oliver Cromwell* (1991). A good biography from a master of seventeenth-century synthesis.

Delderfield, E., *Kings and Queens of England and Great Britain* (1998).

Elton, G. R., *The Tudor Constitution* (1982). Covers the role of the monarch in some detail.

Figgis, J. N., *The Divine Right of Kings* (1914/1965). The classic account of this controversial doctrine.

Fraser, A., *The Laws of the Kings and Queens of England* (1993). A piece of popular constitutional theory.

Fraser, A., *King Charles II* (1993). An imaginative and scholarly biography.

Gillingham, J., *The Angevin Empire* (2001). Sets the English monarchy in its Continental context.

Green, J., *The Government of England under Henry I* (1986). With particular emphasis on his role as a lawgiver.

Green, J., 'William Rufus, Henry I and the Royal demesne', *History*, 64, 1979. A specialist piece on resources.

Gregg, E., *Queen Anne* (1980). A full life including her parental misfortunes.

Gregg, P., *King Charles I* (2000). A sensitive and sympathetic study.

Griffiths, R. A., *The Reign of Henry VI* (1981). By far the fullest account of this turbulent period.

Gwyn, P., *The King's Cardinal* (1991). An exhaustive study of the life of Cardinal Wolsey.

Haigh, C., *Elizabeth I* (1988). Incisive, but controversial.

Harvey, J., *The Plantagenets* (1959). An old-fashioned narrative account, but good for basic information.

Hibbert, C., *George IV: Regent and King* (1973). George was simply not suited to a position of responsibility.

Hibbert, C., *Queen Victoria* (2000). A personal history of a long reign.

Higham, N. J., and D. Hill (eds), *Edward the Elder, 899–924* (2001). A popular collection of essays on Alfred's little-known son.

Hobhouse, H., *Prince Albert: His Life and Work* (1983). How a German princeling won the heart of his adopted country.

Hollister, C. W., *The Military Organisation of Norman England* (1965). The relationship between the King, his vassals and his sub-vassals is explored.

Hollister, C. W., 'The Rise of Administrative Kingship: Henry I', *American Historical Review*, 83, 1978. The robe takes over from the sword.

Holmes, G., *British Politics in the Age of Anne* (1987). The growth of the party system.

Holmes, R., *The English Civil War* (2000). Mainly to do with the battles.

Holt, J. C., *Magna Carta* (1992). What can happen if a king falls out with his barons. The best account of the provenance of the Great Charter.

Horowitz, H., *Parliament, Policy and Politics in the Reign of William III* (1977). The confused conflict before the development of party discipline.

Hutton, R., *George I: Elector and King* (1978). The effect of his German priorities upon the politics of his reign.

Houts, E. Van, *William of Jumieges: Gesta Normanorum Ducum* (1996). A prime source.

Ives, E. W., *Lady Jane Grey* (2009). Defending her right to the throne.

Jolliffe, J. E. A., *Angevin Kingship* (1963). The best of the older accounts; plenty of information.

Jones, M. K., and D. Underwood, *The King's Mother* (1992). The life and times of Margaret Beaufort. The standard account.

Jones, J. R., *The Revolution of 1688* (1972). A somewhat Whiggish account, but thorough.

Kenyon, J. P., *The Stuarts* (1958). An old-fashioned narrative account.

Kenyon, J. P., *The Stuart Constitution* (1986). Strong on the theory of royal power, and its opponents.

Keynes, S., 'A Tale of Two Kings: Alfred the Great and Ethelred the Unready', *Transactions of the Royal Historical Society*, 5th series, 36, 1986. A contrast in effectiveness.

Kirby, D. P., *The Earliest English Kings* (1991). The heptarchy and before.

Kishlansky, Mark, *A Monarchy Transformed, 1603–1714* (1996). A long overview; scholarly but idiosyncratic.

Lander, J. R., *Crown and Nobility, 1450–1509* (1976). The gradual replacement of the nobility by royal commissions in local government.

Laslett, P., *The World We Have Lost* (1971). A lament for departed cultures.

Laslett, P., *The World We Have Lost Further Explored* (1983). More of the same.

Lockyer, R., *The Early Stuarts: A Political History of England, 1603–1641* (1989). History straight down the middle, without biases. One of the best accounts of the origins of the war.

Loach, J., *Edward VI* (1999). A posthumous work, edited by Penry Williams and George Bernard; original and interesting.

Loades, D., *Politics and the Nation* (1999). A systematic analysis.

Loades, D., *Henry VIII* (2011). The latest full-scale biography.

Loades, D., *Mary Tudor: A Life* (1989). The standard biography.

Loades, D., *Elizabeth I* (2003). Emphasises her feminine side.

Loades, D., *Princes of Wales: Royal Heirs in Waiting* (2008). Including quite a few who never made it!

Longford, E., *Victoria RI* (1964). A panegyric.

Longford, P., *A Polite and Commercial People: England 1727–1783* (1989). Social analysis of the pre-industrial revolution world.

Loyn, H. R., *Anglo-Saxon England and the Norman Conquest* (1991). The continuities and discontinuities.

MacCaffrey, W., *Elizabeth I* (1993). The most complete one-volume study of this fascinating queen. The culmination of thirty years of research.

Magnus, P., *King Edward VII* (1964). Mainly a sympathetic study of the Prince of Wales. Strong on the Entente Cordiale.

Manning, S. B., *The English People and the English Revolution* (1976). A socio-political history of the great revolt.

Miller, J., *Charles II* (1991). A balanced and scholarly appraisal, particularly strong on the Exclusion Crisis.

Miller, J., *James II: A Study in Kingship* (1989). A king who misjudged his power and circumstances.

Morrill, J., *Charles I* (1988). A king undone by his own shortcomings.

Morris, J., *The Age of Arthur: A history of the British Isles from 350 to 650 AD* (1973). Trying to distinguish the fact from the fiction.

Myers, A. R., *The Household of Edward IV* (1959). Based on the Household books. Excellent.

Nicholson, H., *King George V: His Life and Reign* (1952). A journalist's approach; full of good stories.

Oresko, R., G. C. Gibbs and H. M. Scott (eds), *Royal and Republican Sovereignty in Early Modern Europe* (1997). A wide-ranging collection of essays, not for the most part about Britain.

Ormrod, W. M., *England in the Thirteenth Century* (1991). A general history, with a strong line on the royal family.

Oxford Dictionary of National Biography (2004).

Painter, S., *The Reign of John* (1949). Still useful, although its interpretation is now out of date.

Peck, L. L., '"For a king not to be bountiful were a fault": perspectives on court patronage', *Journal of British Studies*, 25, 1960.

Pimlott, B., *The Queen: Elizabeth II and the Monarchy* (2001). A careful study, prepared in advance of the Golden Jubilee celebrations.

Plumb, J. H., *The Growth of Political Stability in England. 1675–1725* (1967). The classic analysis of politics leading up to, and after, the Glorious Revolution.

Powick, F. W., *The Thirteenth Century* (1962). A general history, treating the monarchy somewhat mechanically.

Prestwich, M., *Plantagenet England* (2005). The best and most up-to-date treatment of the subject.

Richardson, H. G., and G. O. Sayles, *The Governance of Medieval England* (1963). Still the best general account of medieval administration.

Robertson, R. J., *The Lives of the Kings of England from Edmund to Henry I* (1925). Old-fashioned narrative. Many of its interpretations now superseded, but basically useful.

Ross, C., *Edward IV* (1974). The best account of this reign, benefiting from many years of research.

Ross, C., *Richard III* (1981). A judicious appraisal of this controversial monarch. Inclined to be sympathetic.

Rumble, A. R. (ed.), *The Reign of Cnut* (1994). One of the very few things on this neglected ruler.

Salway, P., *Roman Britain* (1981). A socio-economic analysis, not particularly strong on the politics.

Sawyer, P. and I. N. Woods (eds), *Early Medieval Kingship* (1977). Essays addressing the European question as a whole.

Sawyer, P., 'The last Scandinavian rulers of York', *Northern History*, 3, 1995. An examination of the end of the Norse Kingdom.

Scarisbrick, J. J., *Henry VIII* (1968/1989). An excellent study of the reign. Particularly strong of the theology of the divorce, 1527–34.

Sharpe, K., *The Personal Rule of Charles I* (1992). A sympathetic look at these much-maligned years. Points out the legal correctness of many of the King's actions.

Smith, Robert and John S. Moore (eds), *The Monarchy: Fifteen Hundred Years of British Tradition* (1998). A theoretical exposition of the development of the British monarchy, particularly strong on the early section.

Smythe, A. P., *King Alfred the Great* (1995). Another look at this much worked-over king. Disposes of the story of the cakes!

Stacey, R. C., *Politics, Policy and Finance under Henry III* (1987). Largely a study of his minority, and the various powers which operated then.

Stenton, F. M., *Anglo-Saxon England* (1971). The basic work, from which all others derived, but many of its views are unfashionable now.

Stone, L., *The Crisis of the Aristocracy, 1558–1641* (1965). An exhaustive study of the aristocracy in all its aspects, particularly the end of noble violence.

Warren, W. L., *King John* (1978). The standard account, except where superseded by Holt.

Warren, W. L., *Henry II* (1973). A straightforward narrative account, now somewhat out of date, particularly on the legal aspects of the reign.

Warren, W. L., *The Governance of Norman and Angevin England, 1086–1272* (1987). An update of his earlier work, in a more general format; particularly good on Henry I.

Western, J. R., *Monarchy and Revolution* (1972). A general examination of this theme in the early modern and modern worlds.

Wheeler Bennett, J. W., *King George VI: His Life and Reign* (1958). The approved biography, with all its strengths and weaknesses.

Williamson, D., *Kings and Queens of Britain* (1991).

Willson, D. H., *King James VI and I* (1962). Long the standard account; now somewhat outdated.

Woolfe, B., *Henry VI* (1981). A good piece of work, somewhat overshadowed by Griffiths. Good on estate management (or lack of it).

Wormald, J., 'James VI and I: Two Kings or One?', *History*, 68, 1983. Compares his performances north and south of the border.

LIST OF ILLUSTRATIONS

INDEX

Index

Index